(Ray & Cox) Beyond the Basics—1

BEYOND THE BASICS

A TEXT FOR ADVANCED
LEGAL WRITING

By

Mary Barnard Ray
University of Wisconsin

Barbara J. Cox
Professor of Law
California Western School of Law

WEST GROUP

Bancroft-Whitney • Banks-Baldwin • Clark Boardman Callaghan
Lawyers Cooperative Publishing • WESTLAW® • West Publishing

ST. PAUL, MINN., 1991

COPYRIGHT © 1991 By WEST PUBLISHING CO.
610 Opperman Drive
P.O. Box 64526
St. Paul, MN 55164–0526

Library of Congress Cataloging-in-Publication Data

Ray, Mary Barnard.
    Beyond the basics : a text for advanced legal writing / by Mary
Barnard Ray and Barbara J. Cox.
      p.   cm.
    Includes index.
    ISBN 0–314–85410–X
    1. Legal composition. I. Cox, Barbara J., 1956–   . II. Title.
KF250.R38 1991
808'.06634—dc20   91–10236
                                                    CIP

ISBN 0–314–85410–X

    (Ray & Cox) Beyond the Basics
    4th Reprint–1999

*Mary Barnard Ray dedicates this work
to Kathryn, Mark, and Dennis.*

*Barbara J. Cox dedicates this work
to her family in Lexington, Madison, and San Diego.*

*

Preface

This book is our attempt to convey to the students of legal writing beyond our classrooms a realization of the breadth, depth, and sheer quantity of knowledge about writing that is available for the learning. We want to help students see the quality that is possible, to invite them to set their horizons beyond adequacy to excellence. In this process, we hope to help the profession as a whole as it moves beyond the status quo to a higher quality of writing.

We hope to expand students' horizons by extending their experience to more forms of legal writing than the office memorandum and appellate brief. These new forms range from jury instructions to letters of retainer. We also hope to expand their view to include a knowledge of writing gleaned from other fields, such as communication science and theory of persuasion. Finally, we hope to expand their repertoire of solutions for more common legal writing situations, such as structuring a memo along any of several large-scale organizational plans.

Yet, with all these dreams, we have tried to keep our feet firmly on the ground by recognizing the real time limitations legal writing instructors face. For that reason, the book includes enough topics to allow the teacher to choose which documents and writing techniques to emphasize, to omit others, and still to have enough material to fill a course. There are enough examples, exercises, and assignments to allow the teacher to assign different ones in different semesters. There are also enough discussable points to provide for lively classes. We want to enable teachers to introduce an advanced legal writing course without facing an impossible workload in the first years or burnout in later years.

There is no way to avoid the fact that both writing and teaching writing are work, but they need not be a grinding chore. We hope that, as you use this book, you as a student or teacher will allow yourself to experiment. Although this approach means you will make more mistakes, it also means you will learn more. We hope it means you can laugh more as well. In keeping with this goal, we hope you develop with your fellow students and teachers a sense of mutual effort, learning, and exploration. Share with each other how a text can be improved, but focus more on the improvement than the initial flaws. Focus on future possibilities more than past failures. Humor, hard work, and hopefulness are the elements of the process upon which you can most rely.

For over a decade, we have enjoyed teaching the course on which this book is based. We hope this book provides you with not just the content of that course, but also some of its intellectual excitement and sense of perennial discovery.

MARY BARNARD RAY
BARBARA J. COX

Acknowledgements

We have to acknowledge the mutual determination that led us to persist in writing this book. When one person's energy lagged, the other was there cajoling, encouraging, prodding, and plodding. For that alternating drive and support, we thank each other.

Thanks also to the many people who provided personal support.

Mary Barnard Ray especially thanks:

Kathryn Barnard Ray, for tolerating innumerable commercial hamburgers;

Mark Wilson Ray, for wearing a torn coat to school, uncomplaining, through the fall of 1990;

Dennis J. Ray, for support ranging from sweeping the floor to soothing the mind; and

Kathryn Soukup, for quality child care and a good deal of parent care, too.

Barbara Cox especially thanks:

HP;

Mollie Martinek, for unwavering support;

Peg Habetler, for sustaining her spirit;

Connie Anderson and Julie Eckenwalder, for sharing their home and helping her through the final seven weeks of writing;

Jean and Lyn Cox, Louise Cox, Anne Howard, and Margaret Hanrahan, for always being there; and

all her friends and family, whose help and support made it possible for her to survive this project.

Thanks for technical support go to:

Kim Karcher and Mary Ann Polewski, for their careful review of later drafts, when fresh insights were essential;

Lynda Hicks, Sandra Murray, and Mary Ellen Norvell, for typing the final drafts;

Dave Ward, Ruth Saaf-Falter, Billie Bortz, for duplication;

Terre Gosdick, for proofreading;

Donna Park, for keeping us connected across the 2200 miles between San Diego and Madison;

Frank Daniels and Mary Lou Mitchell, for graphics;

California Western School of Law, for research grant support;

the aides who have helped over the years with research, footnote checks, photocopying, running to libraries, and countless other necessary tasks: Deanna Bushendorf, Eleonora DiLiscia, Frank Halm, Patrick McKlosky, Tracy Thompson and Debra Van Wormer;

the research assistants who worked through the final tedious stages: Renee Guolee, Tracy Macuga, Nancy King, and Julieanne Mizer;

the practitioners whose experience provided us with reality checks for our content throughout the writing process: Constance L. Anderson, R. Oak Dowling, Ralph Adam Fine, Lisa Kane, James Polewski, Philip Shaver, and James Spohn;

the scholars whose reviews provided checks of our theory: Maureen Arrigo, Michal Belknap, Janet Bowermaster, Susan Channick, Christine Hickman, Penn Lerblance, and Glenn Smith;

Bill Ebbott for advice in research planning;

Nori M. Cross, who with Mary Ray designed and taught the first section of Wisconsin's advanced legal writing course; and

the many students who have taken Advanced Legal Writing at the University of Wisconsin in the past twelve years, providing us with the experience and enthusiasm that inspired us to take on the challenge of writing this book.

Finally, we want to thank Mary Ann Polewski for all the creative energies she has invested over the years in helping develop the course upon which this book is based. Her files, her memories, and her eye for detail made the course and this book possible.

Summary of Contents

Table of Contents

BEYOND THE BASICS

A TEXT FOR ADVANCED
LEGAL WRITING

*

Chapter 1

INTRODUCTION

Like childhood, learning about writing is a process with a beginning, but no clear ending. Or perhaps writing is more like parenthood. You begin the process with feverish enthusiasm, endure through the burgeoning pendency of anticipation, labor long and hard, and finally gaze with wonder at the product. Yet, at that moment, you realize your work has just begun. As you work through this text, we know you will labor hard and advance far in your work, but we also know that you will not finish learning all there is to know about writing.

To help you learn advanced legal writing, this book incorporates information from many areas, such as communication science, psychology, classical rhetoric, and cognitive learning. It blends the academic and the pragmatic, moving between abstract theories and concrete applications and referring to both academic studies and practitioners' observations. It includes techniques for all aspects of writing, such as large-scale organization, sentence structure, word usage, and punctuation. It provides opportunities for practice, reflection, and second attempts. We offer this book to you in the spirit of wonder, humor, sweat, and challenge that occupies us when we ourselves write.

THE NATURE OF WRITING

Writing is probably the most complex mental task any human being undertakes,[1] taxing human capabilities close to their limits, to the extent that "[e]ven slight adjustments in the air we breathe can make our handwriting falter."[2] It does not come naturally.[3]

Even when the writer knows clearly what he or she wants to communicate, successful writing still involves (1) transmitting a message from the writer's brain to the hand; (2) funneling that message through the sequential, relatively limited dimension of words on pa-

---

[1]. "The act of writing must tie together diffusely located parts of the brain, making writing perhaps the most difficult neurological task a human can undertake." Robert Ochsner, *Physical Eloquence and the Biology of Writing* 56 (1990).

[2]. *Id.* at 58.

[3]. H.D. Giles and John M. Wiemann, "Language, Social Comparison, and Power" in *Handbook of Communication Science* 372 (C. Berger and S. Chaffee, eds. 1987) (emphasis deleted).

1

per;[4] (3) getting the message transmitted from that sequence of words on paper to the reader's brain via the reader's eye; and (4) reconstructing that message (completed by the reader) to fit within the reader's previous knowledge and experience.[5] At any point in this process, the communication can be sabotaged. For example, it can be interrupted by the writer's word choice or even by breakdowns in any of the systems involved, such as spelling or delivery of the mail.[6] As if that were not enough, choosing what to say is also complex.

> What is written without effort is in general read without pleasure.[7]

> Do not expect yourself to get it exactly right the first time; reconcile yourself to a process of trial and error.

> The main rule of a writer is never to pity your manuscript. . . . I say that the wastepaper basket is the writer's best friend.[8]

> Yet for all the work, writing is also play, an ability developed gradually through practice.

> You must feel free to take risks . . . discovering how many different ways you can view the same experience, trusting in your ability to continually reenvision your thoughts.[9]

Just as athletes and artists begin developing their ability through playing for the joy of it, you can play with writing, learning as you play. You can work hard at writing without losing your sense of fun.

> The most solid advice for a writer is this, I think: Try to learn to breathe deeply, really to taste food when you eat, and when you sleep, really to sleep. Try as much as possible to be wholly alive, with all your might, and when you laugh, laugh like hell, and when you get angry, get good and angry. Try to be alive. You will be dead soon enough.[10]

This playful practice allows you not only to develop many mental skills, but also to develop and coordinate neurological habits involving the eye, ear, and hand, which a neuropsychologist has described as three "neurological melodies."[11] You synthesize these physical skills so they work together smoothly; you "subsume all three melodies into one system."[12] Then your mind is free to think, taking the basics of

4. Howard S. Babb, "Prolegomena to the Analysis of Prose Style" in *Essays in Stylistic Analysis* 41 (H. Babb ed. 1972).

5. William M. Schutte and Erwin R. Steinberg, *Communication in Business and Industry* 26 (1983).

6. Carl Bereiter and Marlene Scardamalia, *The Psychology of Written Composition* 156 (1987).

7. William Seward, *Anecdotes of Distinguished Persons: Chiefly of the Present and Two Preceding Centuries* 309 (4th ed. 1989) (quoting Samuel Johnson).

8. William Kerrigan, *Writing to the Point: Six Basic Steps* 135 (1974).

9. Lil Brannon, Melinda Knight, and Vara Neverow–Turk, *Writers Writing* 3–4 (1982).

10. William Saroyan, "Preface to the First Edition" in *The Daring Young Man on the Flying Trapeze and Other Stories* 216–218 (1934).

11. "The physiology of writing can be divided into three neurological melodies: kinesthetic, visual, and auditory. Melody results when neurons coalesce into a patterned behavior, that is, when they have 'learned' something as an engram and can repeat it." Ochsner, *supra* note 1, at 55.

12. *Id.* at 57.

writing for granted. Just as children master and then synthesize the complex melodies needed for walking, talking, and solving problems through their play, you can master and synthesize the complex melodies of writing through playing with words, structures, and ideas.

THE NATURE OF THE BOOK

The first half of the book presents many advanced techniques, which you will master as you work through those chapters. The second half, beginning with the chapter on argument, does not introduce new techniques so much as it introduces various uses of those techniques, broadening your understanding as you broaden your experience.

The book is structured around different kinds of legal documents so you can address each topic individually. This organization allows the book to serve as a useful reference. Each chapter contains several elements: (1) an explanation of the priorities for that kind of legal writing; (2) the relevant strategies and concerns; (3) a series of specific how-to points to help you through the task; (4) examples, both good and bad; (5) exercises for discussion and practice; (6) larger writing assignments; and (7) a bibliography of sources you may find useful if doing further research on the topic. When good and bad examples are compared, the good example is in bold face. We have minimized the research required in the exercises and assignments, so you can focus your time on the writing itself.

The order of the chapters arises from the writing concepts that come into focus as we address each legal writing task. In Chapter 3 on statutes, you begin grappling with the centrality of accuracy and clarity in legal writing. Chapter 4 on jury instructions adds understandability, and the contracts chapter addresses the need for consistency and thoroughness. Chapter 6 on issues introduces ways to focus and shade meaning through word choice. The two chapters on statements of fact address the structure of paragraphs and sentences, focusing on clarity in objective statements and on emphasis in persuasive statements.

The discussion and argument chapters focus on large-scale concerns, such as the organization of the whole document. Chapter 11 applies thoroughness concerns to pleadings; Chapter 12 on orders, notices, and motions again addresses clarity and avoiding legalese. Then Chapter 13 on interrogatories helps you develop skills in thinking through a strategy and implementing it precisely, adding in a concern for writing to lay readers. General correspondence moves you further into the world of strategies for lay readers, basing writing decisions on knowledge of people, rather than solely on the law. Opinion letters leads you to blend knowledge of people and the law into a document that is deeply concerned with both. Wills and trusts takes this concern and adds to it the rigorous drafting demands discussed in earlier chapters. The final chapter on research papers shows you how to present rigorous scholarship in a form that allows something of your personal professional style to emerge.

In summary, by focusing on different aspects of writing and then combining and recombining those concerns in different ways, this book helps you synthesize your skill and knowledge into the unified ability to be a flexible, sophisticated, and broadly skilled writer.

Woven through this book are four general principles:

(1) consider and respect your reader,

(2) know what you mean to say,

(3) adapt the basic techniques you have learned to address the particular circumstances at hand, and

(4) work step by step rather than attempting to do too much at once.

These principles will guide you as you experiment to improve your writing, helping you evaluate the success of your attempts and synthesize the many bits of information you will learn.

Additionally, three common priorities are woven throughout legal writing: accuracy, readability, and appeal. Although the relative importance of these three aspects of writing varies from one legal writing task to another, they remain in all circumstances the general goals of excellent writing. As a reference for you, we have devised the following list of general priorities of legal writing, each illustrated with ways the priority exemplifies itself in various aspects of writing.

GENERAL PRIORITIES FOR LEGAL WRITING

First priority, to be met in all events: be accurate.

"The writer should so write that the reader not only may, but must, understand." Quintilian

Examples

1. Regarding organization, organize to reveal the logical structure of the content to

    (a) state your main points directly and

    (b) include any supporting information needed.

2. Regarding sentence structure, use structure to reveal the relative importance of the content of the sentences. To do this

    (a) put the main point in the subject, verb, and object;

    (b) put supporting information in supporting phrases in the sentence;

    (c) omit information that is not needed to support this main point; and

    (d) when needed, use transitions that signal the logical relation of this sentence to the previous sentence.

3. Regarding word choice, use words that communicate the correct content. These words will be

    (a) unambiguous and

    (b) sufficiently specific.

4. Regarding mechanics, make sure you remove any small errors, which can inconvenience or irritate your reader. For example,

    (a) use correct grammar and punctuation,

    (b) use correct citation form, and

    (c) use correct spelling.

Second priority, to be met most of the time: Be readable.

"One can only continue to expect to be read if, as far as possible, one omits everything that is unimportant." Albert Einstein

Examples

1. Regarding organization,

    (a) omit information that adds neither needed content nor interest,

    (b) prefer a straightforward organization, and

    (c) organize to minimize repetition.

2. Regarding sentence structure,

    (a) omit unnecessary prepositional phrases, passive voice, or other cumbersome phrases and

    (b) keep the subject and verb close together.

3. Regarding word choice,

    (a) use words the reader understands and

    (b) if unfamiliar words are needed, incorporate definitions.

4. Regarding mechanics,

    (a) use tabulation or enumeration for long lists and

    (b) keep headings and other visual structures in parallel form.

Third priority, to be met whenever time allows, or when the circumstances require it: be appealing.

"The difference between the almost right word and the right word is . . . the difference between the lightning bug and the lightning." Mark Twain

Examples

1. Regarding organization, organize so the main points are in positions of emphasis.

2. Regarding sentence structure, use rhetorical devices (imagery, repetition, etc.) to underscore key points where appropriate.

3. Regarding word choice,

    (a) use words that create the appropriate level of formality,

    (b) use concrete words rather than abstract when possible, and

    (c) use interesting, apt words for points to be remembered.

4. Regarding mechanics, when possible choose the auxiliary verb (could, can, would, etc.) or person (one, he or she, they, you) that suggests the relationship you want your reader to have with the content.

Another theme of this book is the need for each writer to discover and develop his or her own process for writing. For example, although common wisdom applies in drafting, persuasive writing, and correspondence, each writer will still develop habits of organizing and phrasing that will work together to establish that writer's style. This process does not reduce the thinking aspect of writing, but rather enables you to communicate your thoughts more effectively. We will help you make decisions, rather than reduce the need to make those decisions. The goal of this book is to empower you to write excellent documents consistently; you, the writer, rather than the document itself, are the book's central concern.

Accordingly, the second chapter will deal with the process of writing, one of the most personalized aspects of writing this book covers.

Bibliography

Babb, Howard S., *Essays in Stylistic Analysis*. New York: Harcourt Brace Javanovich, Inc., 1972.

Bereiter, Carl and Marlene Scardamalia, *The Psychology of Written Composition*. Hilldale, NJ: Lawrence Erlbaum Associates, 1987.

Berger, Charles R. and Steven H. Chaffee, Eds., *Handbook of Communication Science*. Newbury Park, CA: Sage Publications, 1987.

Booth, Wayne C., *Modern Dogma and the Rhetoric of Assent*. South Bend, IN: University of Notre Dame Press, 1974.

Brannon, Lil, Melinda Knight, and Vara Neverow–Turk, *Writers Writing*. Montclair, NJ: Boynton/Cook Publishers, Inc. 1982.

Flowers, Frank C., *Practical Linguistics for Composition*. New York: Odyssey Press, 1968.

Gregg, L.W. and E.R. Steinberg, Eds., *Cognitive Processes in Writing*. Hillsdale, NJ: Lawrence Erlbaum Associates, 1980.

Kerrigan, William J., *Writing to the Point: Six Basic Steps*. New York: Harcourt Brace Javanovich, Inc., 1974.

Oscher, Robert S., *Physical Eloquence and the Biology of Writing*. New York: State University of New York Press, 1990.

Pearsall, Thomas E. and Donald H. Cunningham, *How To Write for the World of Work.* New York: CBS College Publishing, 2d ed. 1982.

Saroyan, William, *The Daring Young Men on the Flying Trapeze and Other Stories.* New York: Modern Age Books, 1934.

Schutte, William M. and Erwin R. Steinberg, Chapter 2 of *Communication in Business and Industry.* New York: Holt, Rinehart, Winston, 1983.

Sebeok, Thomas A., Ed., *Style in Language.* Cambridge, MA: MIT Press, 1960.

Seward, William, *Anecdotes of Distinguished Persons: Chiefly of the Present and Two Preceding Centuries.* London: Jun and Davies, 4th ed. 1989.

Shannon, Claude E. and Warren Weaver, *The Mathematical Theory of Communication.* Urbana: University of Illinois Press, 1949.

Simons, Herbert W., *Persuasion: Understanding, Practice, and Analysis.* New York: Random House, 2d ed. 1986.

Singer, Isaac Bashevis, *Writing to the Point: Six Basic Steps.* New York: Harcourt Brace Javanovich, Inc., 1974.

Chapter 2

PROCESS

Generally, the concern of your employer, client, or judge will be the product: its content, quality, timeliness, professional appearance, and so forth. The process by which this writing is produced is your concern. This does not make the process unimportant; it makes it individual.

Even though the process of writing is secondary to the product, that process is integral to your overall success as a legal writer. Process is critical to such important concerns as avoiding burn-out, taking too long to finish a task, and coping with challenges such as meeting multiple deadlines, handling a new task, or writing for a difficult reader. Process improves the product. Perhaps most important, a comfortable process helps you enjoy your work, thereby improving the quality of your professional life. However you use your law degree, you will likely spend much of your workday writing. You want to become comfortable with the task that will occupy so many hours of your career.

UNDERSTANDING YOUR PROCESS

Many writing texts address the topic of process,[1] and many of these advocate following the particular general process described in this book. We have found over the years, however, that the variety of workable personal processes defies specific prescription.[2] As a result, this chapter helps you explore, evaluate, and improve your own process of writing. It also discusses some successful processes and summarizes their common qualities. To understand your process, (1) describe your current writing habits and (2) evaluate how those habits work and whether you need to alter them.

Describing Your Current Writing Habits

The first step in understanding your writing process is seeing what your current writing habits are. This requires a sense of humor and

---

1. *See, e.g.,* Linda Flower, *Problem–Solving Strategies for Writing* (1981); Elizabeth Tebeaux, *Design of Business Communication: The Process and the Product* (1990); Lil Brannon, Melinda Knight, and Vara Nevero–Turk, *Writers Writing* (1982).

2. In each advanced legal writing class we have taught, we have spent time both in class and in conference discussing writing process with students. This chapter is based largely on that experience.

nonjudgmentalness, because you need to look at what you do, rather than what you intend to do but never accomplish. For example, consider the following description.

1. Dump all my research note cards on the kitchen table.

2. Stare at the pile, then shuffle through the cards hoping for an inspiration.

3. Get a soda.

4. Sit staring at the pile while I finish my soda.

5. Stack the cards into one neat pile and then read through them, pulling out cards that seem like major points. Feel confused after pulling out about three cards.

6. Get up and walk around the room.

7. Stand staring at the cards and shuffle through them again.

8. Go scrub the bathroom.

9. . . . .

A useful account of your current process also requires specificity. For example, rather than noting only that you outline, look at what you write on the paper. Do you start outlining with a roman numeral "I"? Do you write down a few key terms? Do you write out an opening sentence? To prime your pump, read the following three samples of ways students in our advanced legal writing seminars have described their processes.

Sample 1

1. Procrastinate.

2. Arrange all research according to the order the research will be used in the paper.

3. Reread or skim research notes.

4. Attempt to jot down outline for paper.

5. Write out introduction, briefly outlining points to be covered in the paper.

6. Begin arguments.

7. Delete everything and begin again.

8. Repeat # 5, # 6, and maybe # 7.

9. Rework outline, working on making first argument more detailed.

10. Reread specific case language and holdings while writing out the argument.

11. Repeat # 9 and # 10 for other arguments.

12. Break for coffee. (This is the official break because inevitably I would have gotten up earlier.)

13. Reread draft and make corrections.

14. Write conclusion.

15. Print out hard copy.

16. Work on structural changes.

17. Make corrections.

18. If paper isn't due, or is past due, wait a day.

19. Reread and make corrections.

20. Print final copy.

Sample 2

When I am sitting down to start a big research project or a paper, the first thing I do is get a large cup of coffee! If I have a memo, I usually will highlight the important parts and place numbers next to things I must do. This way, if there is more than one question, I won't forget it.

When I'm ready to start my research, I will usually go to the library and do all my research before I write anything. I usually start with statutes, then case law. As I do the research, I get a list of cases. Then I will go through the list and find all the cases on point.

When I have a group of cases that I like, I Shepardize those cases, making new lists of cases. I continue this process until I have the best cases that are the most recent I can find. Now I'm ready to write.

I was never good at outlining, so when I started work, I used to write out memos long-hand. Now I am comfortable with a dicta-phone and just try to speak through the entire memo. Once I get it back, I can make more serious corrections and rewording.

How I write a specific memo will depend on what I find. In general, I put the strongest cases first. Then I will say how the other side may counter this. I then will summarize with how we can still win in light of all the cases.

When I wrote my law review article, I collected all the re-search I wanted. I had everything photocopied and organized in a file by topic. I read through each one once, highlighting the articles. Then I wrote out key phrases on index cards and used that to organize my paper. That way I could rearrange the piles and visually see how it would develop. After that, like a memo, I sat down and wrote. I saved later rewrites until I could see the whole project.

Sample 3

I start by reading through my notes several times. Next, I write several versions of the problem I want to solve or the conclusions I want to reach, until I find a satisfactory version. After this, I make a list of topics. I usually rearrange the topics several times. I move to my word processor and pull out the provisions of notes according to each topic. Under each topic, I start arranging things into paragraphs. Under each topic, I do several versions until the text flows coherently.

This is not a time to be judgmental. Whatever form your process takes, you will find that some elements of the process work well for you and that some need to be improved.

EXERCISE

Before reading the rest of the chapter, write out what you do when you sit down to write a project. Be as honest and specific as possible.

Evaluating and Improving Your Process

Now that you have described your writing habits, or process, on paper, you can begin to evaluate the significance of those habits and determine how your conceptual processes work. Study your process to identify the individual parts that seem ineffective, inefficient, or uncomfortable for you. If you have trouble determining which parts these are, consider at which points you make more mistakes, perhaps even watching for such small things as spelling errors. An increase in the number of these errors can indicate that you, the writer, are under greater stress.[3]

At those points, try substituting a new approach, rather than starting from scratch with a completely new process. This small-scale approach is useful because your writing process is a collection of habits you have built up over time, and these habits, like any others, will not be easy to change. By changing only the parts of the process that do not work, you can avoid unnecessary effort, saving more energy for making changes where they matter most.

As you begin modifying parts of your process to improve it, view the changes you make in the spirit of trial and error, proceeding in stages, gradually moving toward your goal of a streamlined, effective writing process. Give yourself the freedom to experiment. "[A] good plan needs to be detailed enough to test, but *cheap enough to throw away.*" [4]

As you evaluate your current process, you may find the following questions helpful. Ask yourself how you learn,[5] which may be revealed by what you remember most readily. For example, when you review a law class, do you find you first remember the fact situations of particular cases? Do you first think of the major headings listed in the table of contents? Or does your memory come as a checklist, listing key legal terms arising in that area of law? The way you remember information is likely to influence how you write; it is particularly likely to influence the central task for all writers: organization.

---

3. *See* Mina P. Shaunessey, *Errors and Expectations* (1977).

4. Flower, *supra* note 1, at 61.

5. *See* David A. Kolb, *Learning Style Inventory: Self–Scoring Test and Interpre-* tation Booklet (1976). Information about this inventory and the theory behind it is available in David A. Kolb, *The Learning Style Inventory Technical Manual* (1976).

If you remember specifics first, you might find it helpful to start organizing by writing out a preliminary draft, a draft in which you simply dump words on paper, or write out everything you think you might need to include, with no concern for organization or eloquence. When you are finished, you can read over this dump draft, listing its valid points, grouping related points together, determining headings for those groupings, and building up from the details to the broad categories that organize your paper.

In contrast, if you remember general points first, you may find it more useful to start organizing by listing the broad issues that arise in the relevant area of law. For each area, list all possible subissues, eliminating any that would not apply to the situation at hand. Continue listing and evaluating them until you have divided the major issues into their individual subissues; then apply the law to each subissue, determining how to resolve it.

Alternatively, if you find yourself naturally writing out a checklist, proceed with that list until you have written out all the possibilities. Then group the listed items, experimenting with different groupings until you arrive at a grouping that reveals the larger issues. You can then outline your points based on those groupings and subissues, filling in support, additional subpoints, and any other points you missed as you wrote out the outline. Start with what you do naturally and well, and use that as the basis from which to move into areas of organization you find more difficult.

Another question to ask yourself is which tasks involved in writing you are most likely to avoid. Those are likely to be the parts of the writing process you most need to modify. For example, do you work steadily on a writing project until you are ready to write the first draft, but then find yourself too sleepy to work? Do you feel compelled to play video games or clean house before you begin organizing? Do you find it difficult to stop researching, even though you find the same cases and statutes turning up again and again in your research?

If you find the first draft difficult, try reducing your expectations for that draft. Perhaps dictate the draft so you can compose more quickly and with less self-criticism. If you are writing on a computer, cover the screen so you see only the line you are writing. Or write without stopping to include citations. Somehow reduce the tasks you ask yourself to accomplish on that draft so the writing will become manageable.

If you find organizing overwhelming, forego the idea of a traditional outline, at least at this stage of writing. Perhaps you can write a dump draft first. Perhaps you can list points you want to make without labelling them, so you are not yet determining their order or level of generality in the outline. Later you can organize the listed points in relationship to each other in a separate step.

If you find it hard to stop researching, consider whether you are hesitating to take a position because the question could go either way.

If so, flip a coin to determine your answer, and write or outline to support that answer for a time. Then write or outline a rough answer on the opposite position. This will provide a more concrete basis for comparison, which may make the decision easier. If you are afraid to stop researching for some other reason, either address the reason honestly and move on, or sidestep it. Whatever the problem that makes you hesitate, identifying the problem alone will be taking a large step toward the problem's solution.

In summary, when you face a writing task that seems to be too much for you, (1) try to reduce your expectations to a more attainable level, (2) try a different approach to accomplishing the task, or (3) identify the problem specifically so you can more readily choose possible solutions. Each of these techniques allows you to break the challenging task into smaller, more manageable components.

A final question to ask is whether you dwell on any stage. Spending a long time on one stage may signal an area of your writing process that is inefficient, uncomfortable, or distracting for you, which you need to improve. For example, do you tend to rewrite the opening passage again and again, working to get it perfect, until you find yourself left without enough time to do a good job writing the rest of the paper? Or do you find yourself revising the completed draft beyond the deadline when the paper is due?

If you keep rewriting the first passage, consider whether you are expecting too much of the draft.

> In all my writing I have always revised very heavily. I used to hope that as I got better, I would have to revise less, but the opposite seems to be happening . . .[6]

Try to accept that the draft will need much revising later; focus now on getting the complete draft written. Your rewriting will be more effective later in your process, when you have already clarified some of the larger-scale questions of the paper.

If you find yourself revising to the point of diminishing returns, as when you miss a deadline, then consider whether you need to clarify in your mind what is needed in this revision. Are you revising for eloquence when what the document needs to function is clarity? Are you revising for conciseness when accuracy is the critical issue? Are you revising for perfection, when what you need is adequacy and timeliness? Focusing your revisions on specific qualities can help you make more effective use of the limited revision time you have. To determine your priorities, review the list at the end of Chapter 1. Allot your time so you complete essential tasks before optional ones.

Now that you have described your writing habits, determined what parts of your process could most use improvement, and considered some

---

6. Brannon, Knight, and Neverow-Turk, *supra* note 1, at 13 (quoting professional writer Kathryn Lance).

alternative ways to accomplish those parts of the process, consider your process generally and see how the changes you have in mind fit together.

As you study your process, you may repeat steps, as if you are circling in on your goal rather than marching in a straight line. This is natural, even typical of many writing processes. As you compare your process to others, you will also notice that many different processes still manage to get the job done. One approach to the process of writing is not superior to another, although one may be superior for you, given your own ways of thinking, your strengths, and your weaknesses.

Improving your writing process not only means finding ways to smooth the spots that slow you down. It also means adding new dimensions to your process so you can make improvements in your product that were not possible before. One way to do this is to develop expertise using writing techniques that compensate for any negatives inherent in your current style.

In general, each technique is an asset that brings with it the potential for liability. For example, if you are outstanding at writing concisely, you may find that your letters sound unfriendly because they are so terse. If you are strong in using dramatic short sentences to underscore a point, your fact statement may sound choppy because you overuse the technique. You can compensate for these possible problems by adding an extra step to your process. For example, if you are habitually concise, you can make sure you check all correspondence for tone. If you use short sentences, you can stop to scan your text for too many periods coming too close together.

Often a change in process helps you improve your handling of large- or small-scale writing concerns, especially if you are strong in one of those areas. For example, if you have an excellent eye for detail, so that your citation forms are impeccable, your grammar perfect, and your wording precise, then study large-scale organization techniques to develop similar strengths in that area. If you are quick with broad concepts and can readily develop an overall organization for a document, you may need to develop a detailed checklist for revision to make sure you do not overlook the small but necessary details that will make your presentation of the larger ideas effective. One helpful source of ideas for revising your process is your fellow students or colleagues. With this in mind, we encourage you to discuss your writing problems and solutions.

EXERCISE

Identify the part of your writing process with which you feel most comfortable and explain to the class how you approach that task. Then identify the part with which you feel least comfortable and ask other students how they handle that task.

OTHER CIRCUMSTANCES AFFECTING PROCESS

Although you have developed your basic process for writing, you will adapt that process over time as your abilities and knowledge change. Indeed, as you work through this text you will probably make significant changes in your process. Additionally, you will adjust your process as the circumstances under which your writing changes. The following section discusses some of the more common circumstances and suggests how you may need to adjust your process accordingly.

Working With Other Writers

One challenge is collaborating with other authors on a joint project. Although criticism of writing-by-committee has been common, educators have recently come to see collaborative writing as an effective, if not always efficient, method for learning about writing. Whatever the evaluation of collaborative writing, attorneys often find themselves working together because a project is too large or too critical for one person to handle. Even when one writer is solely responsible for the document, he or she often submits work to colleagues for extensive commenting.

For these reasons, develop a second general writing process to use when working with other writers. This process will still be influenced by the individual writer, but it will also be influenced by the priorities and style of the working group and of the supervisory staff. Because of this, you may need to make significant changes in your writing process when working with other writers. For example, you may prefer to work late the night before the deadline polishing your writing, but your co-writer may pale at the thought of this last-minute push. You will need to negotiate your processes, compromising and deferring to the plan that promises the best outcome.

Similarly, adjust your writing process when working with a reviewer. For example, you may prefer to leave polishing concerns such as spelling and citation form until the last stages of writing, but these small errors may distract your reviewer. If he or she spends much energy noting criticisms in that area, less energy will be devoted to comments on the things of concern to you. To avoid this frustration, adjust your process to address concerns you know are important to your reviewer. Additionally, submit some specific questions with your text to increase the reviewer's response on those topics. For example, attach a note asking the reviewer to consider whether the organization seems logical, whether the scope is sufficiently broad, or whether a particular image is effective. These questions can make the process more pleasant for you because you get the feedback you need, and for the reviewer because he or she has a focus and can complete the review more readily.

If your reviewer prefers to give feedback in meetings, take notes and summarize at the end of the conference to make sure that your understanding of his or her advice is correct. Although you do not want to suggest a lack of trust by taking detailed notes, you do want the points to be clear enough to avoid misunderstanding and to give you a general direction for revision.

Reviewing Another's Writing

Another challenge is editing the work of another writer.

Being an editor/critic is very difficult. It takes understanding, decisiveness, a lot of courage, and a lot of tact. It takes someone whom the writer can respect but need not fear; someone who can flatter you without fawning, encourage you with full awareness of the forces he [or she] sets in motion, and squelch you where you need to be squelched, but without rancor; someone who can tell you that you are being pedantic and get away with it.

Handholding, fostering, pruning, snipping, squelching, and encouraging have always been the true functions of the editor.[7]

When you review another's writing, whether as a colleague or a supervisor, remembering a few simple rules can help you be effective without causing resentment. First, focus on the task of preparing this document to do the job that is needed. Look first to accuracy, and then to the other qualities needed for this document. Avoid commenting on aspects of the writing that displease you but do not reduce the effectiveness of the document. For example, unless the writer has asked you to comment on wordiness, let wordiness on a contract pass as long as it does not make the contract less clear or in some other way reduce its effectiveness. In this way, you can distinguish between changes you need to make in the document and matters of personal style.[8]

Second, when you suggest any significant changes for which the reason is not immediately apparent, explain the reason for the change in positive terms. This may take only a few words, such as **"to avoid ambiguity"** or **"for conciseness."** These phrases are much more palatable to the writer than the negative versions: "this was ambiguous" or "wordy." When explaining a problem in the writing, speak in terms of the reader or the document, rather than in terms of the writer or your own opinion. For example, write **"The reader may not understand whether this means** . . . ." rather than "You're unclear here" or "I can't understand your meaning here." Although this explanation may take a few more words, the reduction in possible resentment will be worth the time invested.

If you and a colleague work together regularly, coordinate your efforts so you build on each other's strengths. For example, a writer who has a gift for being concise can readily suggest ways to improve your document in those areas. On the other hand, you may be excellent at being thorough and clear, and you can suggest changes in your colleague's writing to add those qualities. Similarly, you may find

---

7. Ernst Jacobi, *Writing at Work: Dos, Don'ts, and How Tos* 69 (1979).

8. R. Tortoriello, Stephen J. Blatt, and Sue DeWine, *Communication in the Organization: An Applied Approach* 104 (1978).

it much more efficient for both of you to proofread each other's work rather than to proofread your own writing. Although this cooperation cannot be forced if colleagues are not willing, it is worth trying when possible. Sharing the revising load can improve the quality of everyone's writing while reducing the fatigue each writer feels, and it can build that pleasant sense of camaraderie and mutual empathy that is a comfort to any writer.

Working With Different Technologies

Another aspect of the writing situation that substantially affects your writing process is the technology you are using to produce your text. Two common technologies legal writers use are the dictaphone and the computer.

The Dictaphone

The dictaphone has been around long enough for the guidance in its use to be developed and refined.[9] Effective dictation of anything longer than a paragraph or more polished than a preliminary draft requires some outlining. This may be as simple as a list of the three points to make in a letter or as complex as a detailed outline for a brief. If it is foreign to your process to begin with an outline, then you may find using a dictaphone difficult.

At the technical level, remembering some basic steps in dictating can greatly improve the quality of the typing you receive. First, begin your dictation by giving the typist instructions. If you will be using a typing pool, identify yourself and spell your name if needed. Then give the general instructions for the dictation, including

(1) what format to use (letter, memo, etc.);

(2) what quality of paper to use (state whether this is a working draft or a final one);

(3) how many copies to send you;

(4) whether to store the document on the computer and how to label it for retrieval, if you have an opinion about how that should be done;

(5) approximately how long the document is, so the typist knows how much time to allow for the project; and

(6) whether the job is urgent. If you want an urgent request to be met, make sure you make the request as rarely as possible. It may not hurt to take on an apologetic tone, too, when requesting urgent attention.

---

9. *See* Richard Hatch, *Business Communication: Theory and Technique* (1977); Tortoriello, Blatt, and DeWine, *supra* note 9, and Elizabeth Tebeaux, *Design of Business Communications: The Process and The Product* (1990).

When dictating the document, remember to do the following.

    (1) Speak more slowly and distinctly than you do in normal conversation. It is especially important to enunciate the endings to words.[10]

    (2) Use two distinct tones for your voice, one when stating words to be typed and another when talking to the typist, as when you dictate punctuation, spell out a name, or indicate the start of a new paragraph.

    (3) Add punctuation orally when you dictate.[11]

    (4) Spell out names and any technical terms that may not be familiar to the typist.

    (5) Practice and experiment with your dictating equipment so you are comfortable with it when dictating.

    (6) Use the stop button freely, stopping after every few words to allow yourself to think about how you want to phrase the next part of the sentence.[12]

    (7) When you will not be able to revise the document extensively after it is typed, use more obvious signals of your organization, such as enumeration of points ("first," "second," or "additionally") and transitional phrases ("if . . . then," "therefore," etc.) to help you keep track of your organization as you dictate.

With practice, dictation will become more comfortable, and you will need to begin watching for the newfound errors that can appear because of the technology. In particular, be on guard for wordiness. Because generating words on a dictaphone is relatively easy and because you do not see the text mounting up before you, your motivation for conciseness can become dulled. To avoid this, periodically edit your dictated texts specifically for wordiness, and watch for wordy phrases that creep into your dictating vocabulary.

A second problem to watch for is using inappropriately informal language. Spoken English is generally less formal than written English, so that phrases and words that sound acceptable as you dictate

---

10. One supervising attorney came to us perplexed with the ungrammatical letters of one of his new attorneys. He knew the writer was able, but the grammatical errors were nevertheless forcing him to consider firing the new attorney. After some investigation, we discovered that the attorney had a slight Southern drawl and weak proofreading skills. As a result, the typist was not hearing the endings of his words and he was not catching the errors when reviewing the documents. With a few practice dictations and a proofreading checklist, the attorney was able to eliminate the problems that threatened his job.

11. Although saying "Dear Mr. Smith, colon, Here is a draft of the contract you requested, period" may seem awkward at first, you will become accustomed to it in time. One doctor who does a great deal of dictating confessed to us that she had been known to say in conversation at a party, "Otherwise, comma"!

12. Analysis of dictation tapes has shown that writers who can dictate well-composed letters use the stop and revise buttons more frequently than less skillful users of the equipment. Jeanne Halpern, "Effects of Dictation/Word Processing Systems on Teaching Writing" in *Business Communications: Academic and Professional Perspectives* 1–8 (J. Ferrill and S. Moskey, Eds.1982).

them look inappropriate on the typed page. As with wordiness, periodically edit your dictation and eliminate bad habits that appear.

The Computer

Even though you may have already adjusted to the use of word processors, computer-assisted research, and even spelling checkers, you will probably find yourself adapting your writing process to the use of computers more in the future. For example, grammar checkers, readability checkers, and other analysis software are now common. These programs can be an asset, a liability, or both, depending on how you use them. In general, these various software packages automate some aspect of writing that the writer before accomplished only through careful reading. Thus spelling checkers take over some of the work of proofreading and readability checkers take over some of the work of revising for readability.

They do not complete all the work, however, and if trusted too much, these programs can become a liability. For example, spelling checkers catch strings of letters that are non-words, but they generally do not catch the substitution of one word for another, such as "the" for "they." You must proofread for these errors. But because such mistakes occur less frequently in texts than general spelling errors, you may be lulled into less careful reading, and you may miss the few errors that do occur. As a result, the use of spelling checkers changes the nature of proofreading, but does not replace it.

Similarly, using word processors changes revision, but does not make it unnecessary. Word processors make it easier to generate text, and this has several implications for the writer. First, if you generate the words more quickly, you have less time to reflect on the content and sound of those words. This can be an advantage if you find you tend to revise too much too soon; you may find it much easier to write a dump draft on a computer than with pen and paper. It can be a disadvantage, though, if you neglect revising for clarity. You may generate junk without realizing it. The quicker production of words can lead to wordiness too, so when using word processors edit for redundancy and wordiness.

Second, computers show the writer one screen of words at a time. This is neater than a desk and an overflowing waste can, but it may not make for neater organization. Because the computer limits your vision to a paragraph or two, you may improve your transitions between paragraphs and sentences but neglect organization between larger parts. You may drift off topic. To prevent this, print out your text periodically. Look at it as the reader will, seeing if the major points are consistently and readily apparent.

Third, computers produce a neater copy, and laser printers allow for more pleasing graphics. This allows you to prepare a document that looks polished and interesting. This appearance can fool you; the paper may look more organized and finished than it is. As you enjoy the benefits of computer-assisted writing, protect the quality of your own thought. No eloquence can compensate for gibberish; no other aspect of writing is as impressive as valid thought clearly expressed.

CONCLUSION

In this chapter, you have studied your writing process and begun adapting it to suit your personal style and the writing situations you face. You will continue adapting as you work through this book. You will adjust your writing process to meet the shifting priorities of each legal writing task, just as you adjust to co-writers and technologies. As you adjust, some elements will remain consistent. These consistencies will indicate how you work as a writer. Build on these strengths, just as you build on physical abilities, such as eye-hand coordination, as you learn different sports.

Bibliography

Brannon, Lil, Melinda Knight, and Vara Nevero–Turk, *Writers Writing.* Montclair, NJ: Boynton/Cook Publishers, Inc., 1982.

Ferrill, June and Stephen Moskey, Eds., *Business Communication: Academic and Professional Perspective.* Houston: The Aetna Institute for Corporate Education, 1982.

Flower, Linda, *Problem–Solving Strategies for Writing.* New York: Harcourt Brace Jovanovich, Inc., 1981.

Hatch, Richard, *Business Communication: Theory and Technique.* Chicago: Science Research Associates, Inc., 1977.

Jacobi, Ernst, *Writing at Work: Dos, Don'ts, and How Tos.* Rochelle Park, NJ: Hayden Book Co., 1979.

Kolb, David A., *Learning Style Inventory: Self–Scoring Test and Interpretation Booklet.* Boston: McBer and Company, 1976.

Sebeok, Thomas A., Ed., *Style in Language.* Cambridge, MA: M.I.T. Press, 1960.

Shaunessey, Mina, *Errors and Expectations.* Oxford: Oxford University Press, 1977.

Tebeaux, Elizabeth, *Design of Business Communication: The Process and the Product.* New York: Macmillan Publishing Company, 1990.

Tortoriello, R., Stephen J. Blatt, and Sue DeWine, *Communication in the Organization: An Applied Approach.* New York: McGraw–Hill Book Company, 1978.

Chapter 3

STATUTES OR RULES

Drafting statutes is a useful task with which to begin improving your writing because it requires you to address many issues that occur in other legal writing tasks, and yet it allows you to focus on a smaller unit of text. Statutes may be long, but they are often crafted phrase by phrase, or sentence by sentence, in contrast to jury instructions and contracts, which require you to draft larger documents. Nevertheless, to write even one phrase or sentence in a statute well, you need to address many considerations.

Although most attorneys do not draft statutes, many are involved in reviewing proposed legislation, drafting or reviewing administrative rules, or developing personnel rules. These rules function as statutes because they describe, prohibit, or regulate conduct. Their drafting is controlled by the same considerations controlling statute drafting. Drafting statutes or rules requires focusing on accuracy and clarity. Although other concerns also arise, the primary ones are accurately stating the content of the statute and making it clear, so those who must use the statute will be able to understand whether and how it applies to them. When drafting, continuously return to focus on accuracy and clarity.

Drafting statutes is challenging; you must draft language that is both comprehensive and specific, handling those problems the statute is intended to resolve and anticipating problems as yet unknown. Either you must fit the statute into an already developed body of law, which requires amending and incorporating by reference, or you must create a new body of law, which requires developing substantive and administrative provisions and handling the numerous details that arise.

Resolving concerns of accuracy and clarity requires taking several steps: (1) interviewing the clients to determine what they intend and researching the existing law, rules, or policies to see how to fit the new language within the old; (2) learning how legislative intent and canons of statutory construction will control judicial interpretation of statutes; (3) choosing and organizing the possible clauses for inclusion in the statute; and (4) drafting the statute. After drafting, revise to ensure that your language is accurate and clear. Each step is needed to draft a statute that meets your clients' objectives and avoids future problems.

INTERVIEWING YOUR CLIENTS AND RESEARCHING THE LAW

Whenever you begin drafting a statute, as with any drafting project, meet with your clients and determine their intent. Your clients have specific information you must glean before proceeding because your role is to draft language effectuating their intent. Determining that intent can be difficult. When drafting legislation, you will usually work with several sponsors or a committee, and each person may have significantly different purposes for seeking the new statute or amendment. Your clients frequently have only the vaguest sense of what they want. They may know their purpose but may depend on the drafter to suggest possible approaches, including how to accommodate current law. Thus, an initial meeting may not provide you with much assistance, and you may have to complete your research before meeting with your clients again to clarify their desires. Question your clients together to determine what consensus or compromises have been reached and what they as a group believe is the purpose for drafting the statute. This may be a lengthy meeting, and perseverance may be required on your part to enable your clients to state their purpose.

While you must hold discussions and conferences with your clients, try to keep them from joining you in the drafting process. It is preferable, and quicker, to have in-depth conferences with your clients throughout the drafting process than to have them actually participate in drafting. For example, as part of this ongoing process, you may refer to the standard clauses listed in a later section and question your clients about each clause you should include.

Determine your clients' priorities and discuss the possible options for resolving various questions. Among the information you must obtain is whether their intention is to permit, regulate, or prohibit conduct. This fact is significant because it affects decisions such as whether to include sanctions and what types of sanctions to include. For example, if your clients want a statute prohibiting the dumping of toxic materials, determine whether violations of the statute will result in civil sanctions, such as liability for damage caused, or criminal sanctions, including fines. Next determine whether an administrative department and procedures exist to implement the statute or whether those will need to be established, along with developing the offices, personnel policies, and duties of those who will implement the statute. Also determine whether you need to include a grant of power to promulgate administrative regulations interpreting the statute. When these questions are resolved in as much detail as possible, you can understand your clients' intent and be efficient when drafting language.

Also consider how this new statute fits within the existing statutory scheme. If the statute will be regulating an area never before regulated, less research needs to be completed than if you are amending or adding to an area already regulated. But you must consider how this addition may alter other areas of the statutory scheme, and you may want to research how other jurisdictions have handled this problem. Thus, if you are adding a new rule to your company's personnel policies regulating parental leave, which had never been regulated before, you may want to contact other corporations to see how they have handled the issue and to review their policies for possible use. You may also consider how the parental leave policy affects other policies concerning disability leave, sick leave, and insurance coverage.

If the statute amends or adds to an already regulated area, then you must consider how to fit this change into the existing scheme. Your research should include (1) analyzing the existing statute, (2) studying court decisions interpreting the statute, (3) studying the administrative practices under the old statute, (4) considering the regulatory experience of other states with similar statutes, and (5) considering what other areas in the statutes will be affected and how to change or amend them to fit the altered situation.[1]

The steps of researching and working with your clients may take the bulk of your time. Cooper relates the experience of Professor Harry Jones in drafting an amendment to a state statute on which the committee members had reached "complete agreement."[2] Jones' time sheet for the project, which resulted in a four and one-half page proposal, was research time (58 hours), conference time (18 hours), and writing time (4 hours). Much of the conference time resulted after he completed his research, which unearthed policy questions about which the committee members completely disagreed. While your drafting may take you longer than it took Professor Jones, it will entail a relatively small portion of the total time expended. In part, this is because drafting is made more efficient by the time spent gaining an understanding of what your clients want and researching the area in which the statute will operate.

LEGISLATIVE HISTORY AND CANONS OF CONSTRUCTION

After you interview your clients and research the law, take the time to understand the role that legislative history and canons of statutory construction play in interpreting the statute you draft.[3] By keeping in mind that the courts will use legislative history and canons of statutory construction to help them interpret your statute, you can draft your language to say to these courts exactly what your clients want. After you understand how the statute will be read, you will be able to (1) make your language as accurate and unambiguous as possible; (2) organize the draft to increase its clarity, both large-scale

---

1. Frank Cooper, *Writing in Law Practice* 304 (1953).

2. *Id.* Cooper also notes "that only four hours were taken to write a four-page statute indicates that the committee was not permitted to participate in the actual drafting. Had this been the case, the 'actual writing time' would surely have been at least forty hours." *Id.*

3. These considerations are not as important when drafting personnel rules, but they are important when drafting administrative rules because they undergo the same interpretation process as statutes.

and small-scale; (3) choose the words that precisely convey the intended meaning; and (4) use punctuation that clarifies, not confuses.

Understanding the way the courts interpret statutes is essential to effective drafting. Even with the care you take in drafting, you may find your statute in court, with a judge given the responsibility of interpreting that statute's language. That is the court's role: to determine the legislature's intent in passing the statute and to determine whether the legislature intended the statute to cover the situation facing the court. The court begins by reading the statute to determine whether, under its plain meaning, the statute controls the factual situation facing the court. If the court cannot make this decision after considering the statute's plain meaning, it will then turn to the legislative history of the statute. Legislative history is best documented at the federal level, where the resources are available to compile this information throughout the drafting and political process. In contrast, most states do not have these resources and thus provide very little information on legislative history. Perhaps because of this, many state courts do not consider legislative history to be a valid step for interpreting statutes and use it only to support or detract from what the canons of statutory construction say.

If the court cannot determine the legislative intent from the plain meaning of the statute or from the existing legislative history, then the court may turn to standard canons of statutory construction to interpret the statute's meaning. The problem with using statutory canons is that different ones lead to contradictory interpretations. For example, "a statute cannot go beyond its text" is countered with "to effectuate its purpose a statute may be implemented beyond its text." [4] Consider these other examples as well.

> Titles do not control meaning; preambles do not expand scope; section headings do not change language.

or

> The title may be consulted as a guide when there is doubt or obscurity in the body; preambles may be consulted to determine rationale, and thus the true construction of terms; section headings may be looked upon as part of the statute itself.

and

> Words are to be interpreted according to the proper grammatical effect of their arrangement within the statute.

or

> Rules of grammar will be disregarded where strict adherence would defeat purpose. [5]

4. K. Llewellyn, *Remarks on the Theory of Appellate Decision and The Rules or Canons About How Statutes Are To Be Construed,* 3 Vand.L.Rev. 395, 401–406 (1950).

5. *Id.* at 403–04.

Because of these contradictions, some commentators believe that these canons may be irrelevant when drafting statutes. Although courts use the canons to resolve inconsistencies or to supply omissions, the drafter "who tries to write a healthy instrument does not and should not pay attention to the principles that the court will apply if [the drafter] fails. [The drafter] simply does his [or her] best, leaving it to the courts to accomplish what [the drafter] did not." [6]

Nevertheless, we agree with others who believe drafters should consider these canons when drafting.[7] Therefore, become acquainted with some of the basic canons of construction that most courts use when interpreting statutes. Your knowledge of these canons will help you anticipate how courts would approach interpreting your statute and allow you to clarify your language or organization so interpretation may be unnecessary.

Drafters can use these canons to clarify statutory language.[8] For example, Professor Pratt discusses the canon of "last antecedent," which "provides that a qualifying phrase modifies the immediately preceding word or phrase and not words or phrases that are more remote." She illustrates this canon using the following statutory excerpt.

(3) "Conditions of ordinary visibility" means daylight and, where applicable, nighttime in nonprecipitating weather.[9]

A court using the last antecedent canon would interpret the phrase "nonprecipitating weather" as referring to nighttime alone and not to daylight, although the legislature probably intended it to refer to both options.[10] If you were aware of the canon of last antecedent when drafting a similar statute, then you would be able to anticipate this problem and revise the definition. Thus, you can use your knowledge of canons to avoid ambiguities or errors that would force a court to interpret the statute. You may also want to spend some time researching which statutory canons of construction are used frequently by the courts in your jurisdiction. Read cases where the courts used these canons and anticipate the occasions when their use may be required. This knowledge will enable you to alter your drafting to avoid those problems.

In addition to these canons, both the federal statutes and some state statutes have interpretation acts intended to control the reading of all statutes, including future ones. Technically, as drafter, you can ignore these acts because no past legislature can tie the hands of future legislatures.[11] Nevertheless, you should research whether your statutes include interpretation acts and then, if you use definitions from that

---

6. Reed Dickerson, *The Fundamentals of Legal Drafting* § 3.9, at 47 (1986).

7. Pratt, *Legal Writing: A Systematic Approach* 14 (Supplemental chapter on Understanding Statutes 1990).

8. *Id.* at 15.

9. *Id.* quoting the Colorado Ski Safety and Liability Act, Colo.Rev.Stat. § 33–44–103(3) (1984).

10. *Id.*

11. Dickerson, *supra* note 6, at § 13.7, at 289.

act, clarify that you are incorporating the definition in the statute you are drafting. One way to do this is to say "In addition to the definitions in sections 1–5 of Title 1, the following definitions apply to this title." [12]

In summary, understanding the roles of legislative history, canons of statutory construction, and interpretation acts in judicial interpretation of statutes can help you clarify the statutory language you draft. Having this broader knowledge will help you in the next step, choosing the clauses to include and determining their organization.

CHOOSING AND ORGANIZING STANDARD CLAUSES

When choosing what clauses to include, consider the purpose of the statute you are drafting, because the clauses you will need to include will depend on the purpose and comprehensiveness of the statute. Comprehensive statutes may include most or all of the following standard clauses.

Official Title (or long title)
Enacting Clause
Short Title
Purpose Section (in lieu of preamble)
Definition Section
Substantive Provisions
Administrative Sections
Miscellaneous Clauses
> Exceptions
> Severability Clauses
> Saving Clauses
> Effective Dates

If you are simply amending a statute to add a particular provision, you will not be concerned with all the clauses that would be included if this were a comprehensive statute addressing a new topic.

Next you must decide how to organize the clauses you have selected. The organization will depend on the comprehensiveness of the statute and the needs of the intended and predominant readers. For example, if the statute's focus is to prescribe conduct for the layperson, place the clauses that do so as close to the beginning of the statute as possible; put clauses addressing administrative concerns later in the statute. If the focus is to describe administrative procedure, then place the sections addressing those concerns earlier in the statute and the prescriptive clauses later. Thus, audience is a consideration when determining how to organize a given statute.

---

12. *Id.* Sections 1–5 of Title 1 are part of the federal counterpart to state interpretation acts. 1 U.S.C. §§ 1–5 (1988). Section 4, for example, states "The word 'vehicle' includes every description of carriage or other artificial contrivance used, or capable of being used, as a means of transportation on land." 1 U.S.C. § 4 (1988). Thus if you knew of the existence of this section, and incorporated it into your statute, you would not need to define "vehicle" again and would not invite the possible inconsistencies that may result from having two definitions.

The following subsections discuss the specific drafting concerns for some of the standard clauses found in most comprehensive statutes.

Official Title

All statutes begin with an official, or long, title which precedes the enacting clause and states what the statute covers. The official title states the content of the statute, often in detail.

> To amend the Alaska Native Claims Settlement Act to provide Alaska Natives with certain options for continued ownership of lands and corporate shares pursuant to the Act, and for other purposes.[13]

No standards are prescribed for the titles of federal statutes, and drafting the official title is left to the drafter.[14] Most states, however, do expressly regulate the titles of their statutes, with the regulation most frequently being located in the state's constitution.[15] Additionally, some states have legislative drafting rules that control titles.[16]

Given these restrictions on the official titles of statutes, wait to draft this clause until after you have drafted the statute. This will ensure that the title includes all the subjects that are covered in the bill and the statute will not fall prey to challenges due to conflicts between the title and the subject matter.[17] Additionally, when drafting, remember the political attractiveness of statutes whose titles include such terms as "Reform Act" or "Public Protection Act." Your clients may want you to include these terms in the title of your statute to make it easier to pass.

Enacting Clause and Short Title

The enacting clause is the technical beginning of the statute.[18] The form of federal statutes' enacting clauses is fixed by statute.[19]

> Be it enacted by the Senate and House of Representatives of the United States of America in Congress assembled:

Immediately following the enacting clause is the short title. The short title allows for easy reference to the statute and helps both the legislature and the public understand the act by stating its subject

---

13. P.L. 100–241, 101 Stat. 1788 (1988).

14. Dickerson, *supra* note 6, at § 13.6, at 282.

15. For example, article 4, section 17 of the Minnesota Constitution states: "No law shall embrace more than one subject, which shall be expressed in its title." All states except North Carolina and the New England states have a one-subject provision in their constitutions. Nutting, *Legislation: Cases and Materials* 686 (1978).

16. For example, Minnesota's joint legislative rules state that "the title of each bill shall clearly state its subject and briefly state its purpose" and "that when a bill amends or repeals an existing act, the title shall refer to the chapter, section, or subdivision." Eskridge and Frickey, *Cases and Materials on Legislation* 834 (1988).

17. *See* for example, the cases cited in Read, *Materials on Legislation* 152–157 (1982).

18. Some states require the enacting clause to be the first section of the act. Singer, 1A *Sutherland Statutory Construction* § 20.06, at 86 (4th ed. 1985). In those states without such a requirement, consider placing the enacting clause after the official title. *Id.*

19. 1 U.S.C. § 101 (1988).

matter. As noted earlier, the long title cannot allow for this easy reference because of the constitutional requirement that everything included in the act be noted in the long title. For example, the long title, the enacting clause, and the short title may look as follows.

[Long Title]

AN ACT to revise and consolidate the statutes relating to the organization and jurisdiction of the courts of this state; the powers and duties of such courts, and of the judges and other officers thereof; the forms and attributes of civil claims and actions; the time within which civil actions and proceedings may be brought in said courts; pleading, evidence, practice and procedure in civil actions and proceedings in said courts; to provide remedies and penalties for the violation of certain provisions of this act; and to repeal all acts and parts of acts inconsistent with, or contravening any of the provisions of this act.

[Enacting Clause]

The People of the State of Michigan Enact: . . . .

[Short Title]

Sec. 101. This act shall be known and may be cited as the "revised judicature act of 1961." RJA may be used as an abbreviation for the revised adjudicature act.[20]

Thus, the short title provides a name that is easy to use and allows for easy reference to the bill, especially when using the short title to cite the act in subsequent legislation.

Purpose Clause

Whether you need to include a purpose clause depends on several factors. First, do not include this clause solely to compensate for mistakes or imprecision in drafting. Instead, focus on the statutory language you are drafting and make it clear. Consider including a purpose clause, however, when the statute you are drafting is regulating a new area, because its scope or purpose are unknown.[21] Second, include a purpose clause if it helps the reader interpret the statute in light of any uncertainty in the statute that you cannot remove by clarifying the specific provisions.[22] Third, when the legislature wants to permit discretion in the statute's application, include a purpose clause to provide guidelines to administrators implementing the statute.[23]

Because clauses preceding the enacting clause are not considered part of the statute, many draftpersons choose to include a purpose clause within the statute, rather than a preamble, which precedes the

20. Read, *supra* note 17, at 175.

21. Singer, *supra* note 18, at § 20.05, at 85.

22. Dickerson, *supra* note 6, at § 13.5, at 285.

23. *Id.*

enacting clause.[24] If you include a purpose clause, eliminate the legalese so often found in older statutes.

> Whereas, there are pending before the Legislature of the State of Minnesota, certain bills, which, if enacted into law, would materially decrease the amount of income for said School District for the ensuing years, and . . .
>
> Whereas, the said School Board wish in fairness to all of their employees who come under the provisions of said Teachers Tenure Act to make no adjustments in salaries which are unwarranted by the final circumstances which will be determined on the basis of whether or not the aforementioned bills become laws;
>
> Now, therefore, be it resolved. . . .[25]

The intent of this clause is to clarify the scope or meaning of the statute. Make its language as clear as possible.

Definition Section

Using a definition section allows you to clarify terms and to indicate that a defined term will have the same meaning throughout the statute. Definitions of words must be clear because your audience will not be able to conform their behavior in the way the legislature intends unless they understand the words.

But insert written definitions sparingly. If you simply use a word in its ordinary meaning, do not define it. To determine whether a definition is needed, consider whether you are adding something or subtracting something from its ordinary meaning or connotation. If you are, define it. Then the courts will follow that definition, even if it is challenged. For example, in *Commonwealth v. Massini,* the defendant was convicted of violating § 941 of the Pennsylvania Penal Code for shooting and killing his neighbor's cat.[26] Section 941 made it a misdemeanor to "wilfully and maliciously kill . . . any domestic animal of another person" and defined "domestic animal" as any equine animal, bovine animal, sheep, goat or pig.[27] The trial court submitted the question of whether the cat was a domestic animal to the jury, thus ignoring the statutory definition of domestic animal, which clearly excluded cat.

On appeal, the court stated the following:

> When the legislature defines the words it uses in a statute, neither the jury nor the court may define them otherwise. . . . The legislature may create its own dictionary, and its definitions may be different from ordinary usage. When it does define the words

---

24. Singer, *supra* note 18, at § 20.05, at 85. The majority of American jurisdictions follow the rule that, because the preamble precedes the enacting clause, it was not enacted by the legislature and thus is an extrinsic aid to interpretation. Read, *supra* note 17, at 158.

25. Read, *supra* note 17, at 162, quoting from *Downing v. Independent School Dist. No. 9,* 207 Minn. 292, 291 N.W. 613 (1940).

26. 200 Pa.Super. 257, 188 A.2d 816 (1963).

27. *Id.* at 258, 188 A.2d at 817.

used in a statute, the courts need not refer to the technical meaning and deviation of those words as given in dictionaries, but must accept the statutory definitions.[28]

The appellate court noted that the legislature's definition, which omitted "cat," was not simply an oversight but was based on common law.[29] The legislature could make it a violation of § 941 to kill a cat but that "decision must be theirs and not ours." [30] When the legislature defines its language, those definitions are binding on the courts interpreting the statutes, unless the definitions are arbitrary or uncertain.[31] Therefore, define your terms carefully.

Using a definition section also allows you to increase the readability of the statute by defining classes within the statute. The statute can then refer to the classes by name throughout the rest of the statute, thus shortening each provision and keeping definitional terms out of the substantive provisions. For example, if you are drafting a statute concerning the powers of cities and those powers vary depending on size, you might want to use the following definitions.

> **Class I cities have populations of 20,000 or less. Class II cities have populations of more than 20,000 and less than 100,000. Class III cities have populations of 100,000 or more and less than 500,000. Class IV cities have populations of 500,000 or more.**

Then throughout the statute, when referring to each type of city, simply refer to the class.

> **All Class II cities must have a city manager elected by the residents of the city.**

rather than

> All cities having populations of more than 20,000 and less than 100,000 must have a city manager elected by the residents of the city.

When deciding what definitions to include, review the definitions already stated in the interpretation act for your state's statutes. Although the legislature can amend the interpretation act, you should incorporate its definitions into your definition section unless you have been told to amend the interpretation act's definitions. Add additional definitions only as needed to clarify the meaning of the statute and to aid in its interpretation. Conversely, if you do not want terms to have the definition accorded them in the interpretation act, you can state that within your statute. The following sentence is a way to do this.

> No legislative enactment shall control the meaning or interpretation of any word or phrase used in this statute, unless the

---

28. *Id.* at 259, 188 A.2d at 817.

29. *Id.* at 261, 188 A.2d at 818. Cats could not be subject to larceny at common law because they had no intrinsic value. Thus the legislature had seemingly incor-

porated the common law into its definition of domestic animal.

30. *Id.*

31. Singer, *supra* note 18, at § 20.08, at 88.

enactment specifically refers to this chapter or is specifically referred to in this chapter.

When defining terms, be sure to explain your intended meaning clearly and then use the defined term consistently throughout the statute. If you use legal terms of art given meaning through judicial usage, be sure to define those terms whenever your intended meaning is different from the traditional usage. For example, you would define terms such as "negligence" or "strict liability" if you do not want a court to impute a common law meaning to those terms.

Place the definition section after the introductory sections (the enacting clause, the short title, and the purpose clause). But place it before the substantive and administrative sections, so the reader will understand the terms that are used throughout the remainder of the statute. This placement is contrary to the practice of putting this section at the end of the statute.[32] Putting the definition section at the end would result in confusion and misunderstanding because the reader would have to infer how terms are used while reading the statute.

Substantive and Administrative Clauses

These two sets of clauses comprise the heart of most statutes, especially those that are comprehensive rather than amendments to existing legislation, and thus you will always include them. The substantive clauses set forth the rights and duties of those affected by the statute, as well as defenses and exceptions to the statute. The administrative clauses identify the agencies responsible for creating or enforcing the regulations that implement the substantive clauses of the statute.

Each section should contain only one point, with subsections used for subpoints. Using this organization will increase clarity and the reader will be able to understand the point of each section easily. Then use clear headings and titles to help the reader work through the statute.

When drafting substantive clauses, focus on presenting a logical organization. Consider your audience, and then organize the statute so it proceeds from a logical beginning point to its completion. Start with those sections that regulate or proscribe conduct and then move to enforcement and sanctions. When drafting the clauses controlling conduct, balance the need for generality against the need for specificity. "[I]f the standards of conduct are too general the act may be invalidated for uncertainty and if they are too exact they may violate constitutional requirements of equality and due process." [33] When drafting the sanction clauses, consider the different types of sanctions available (criminal, civil, or administrative) and determine how your clients' policy considerations comport with their choice of sanctions.

32. *Id.* at § 20.09, at 92–93.   33. *Id.* at § 20.16, at 101.

When drafting administrative clauses, continue making only one point per section. This is particularly important with these clauses because they tend to be revised frequently to change salaries, the number and duties of the officers, and even the administrative structure itself. Limiting the subject matter for each section allows for easy amendment.[34] The usual organization of these sections is to start by creating the department, selecting the officers, and stating the length of their terms. Then move on to listing the powers and duties of the department.[35] When stating the powers and duties, move from the general to the specific so the reader will be able to understand the breadth of the department's powers and duties from the beginning.[36]

Miscellaneous Clauses

Having drafted most of the statute, now determine if any clauses need to be added to fit the new statute into the existing statutory framework and into the affairs of the people whose conduct will be affected by it. To do this, you may add clauses that amend or repeal other statutes, incorporate provisions from other statutes, permit exceptions, or address severability if some part of the statute is declared unconstitutional. You may also add clauses to preserve rights, remedies, and privileges currently in effect that would be destroyed by the statute's enactment. Finally, you may declare when the statute will take effect.

Amending Other Statutes

When drafting amendments to prior legislation, two options are available. You can use the strike-and-insert method, where you note specific words that are deleted and others that are inserted.[37] This method works well if you need only a few changes in other statutes to make them consistent. If, however, your statute requires major changes in other statutes, amend those statutes by drafting clauses that substitute new sections (with the necessary changes) for the old sections.

Incorporating Provisions

When drafting clauses that incorporate language or concepts from other statutes by reference, be careful not to destroy the clarity you worked so hard to attain. For example, extensive references to other statutory sections make it difficult to understand what the current statute means. Consider the following example, which is virtually incomprehensible.

34. *Id.* at § 20.15, at 96–97.

35. *Id.* at 97.

36. Singer provides a detailed sample of administrative provisions covering the officers, powers and duties, organization, salaries, and personnel matters. *Id.* at § 20.15, at 97–101.

37. Some states prohibit the strike-and-insert method of amending and require that amended sections be set out in their entirety. Eskridge and Frickey, *supra* note 16, at 836.

Section 202(p) of the Social Security Act (1956)

(P) In any case in which there is a failure—

(1) To file proof of support under subparagraph (D) of subsection (c)(1), clause (i) or (ii) of subparagraph (E) of subsection (f)(1), or subparagraph (B) of subsection (h)(1), or under clause (B) of subsection (f)(1) of this section as in effect prior to the Social Security Amendments of 1950 within the period prescribed by each subparagraph or clause. . . .[38]

As this example shows, care must be taken so cross-references do not get out of hand. For example, the following provision is much easier to understand.

Section 212(a) of the Revenue Act of 1918

That in the case of an individual the term "net income" means the gross income as defined in Section 213, less the deductions allowed by Section 214.

While this cross-reference is less complicated than the one above, it shows how you can incorporate by reference without losing the ability to present information so the reader can understand it.

Exceptions

When drafting clauses that limit the general terms of the statute, use exceptions, and include them in a separate "Exceptions" section. Do not use a proviso, which is a clause added to a section establishing a general rule and which begins "provided, however. . . ." The proviso structure is problematic because it often leaves the reader unclear whether the limitation is general to the entire act or specific to the section in which it is included.

Severability Clause

When drafting severability clauses, your purpose is to allow for enforcement of those sections of the statute that remain constitutional, despite the unconstitutionality of a particular section.[39] Some courts try to sustain the constitutionality of statutes whenever possible. These clauses clarify what is to happen if the courts find part of the statute unconstitutional. Other courts presume the inseverability of the statute as a whole; then the severability clause is necessary to show that the legislature intends to rebut that presumption. Additionally, the clause can indicate that, although some applications of the statute may be invalid, the legislature intends for the statute to apply to those situations where it remains valid. The following example shows the legislative intent to allow severability.

If any provision of this Act is invalid, then all valid provisions that are severable from the invalid provision remain in effect. If a provision of this Act is invalid in one or more of its applications,

38. James Peacock, *Notes on Legislative Drafting* 28 (1961).

39. Singer, *supra* note 18, at § 20.27, at 112.

then the provision remains in effect for all applications that are severable from the invalid applications.

Savings Clause

A savings clause indicates that the statute applies prospectively and preserves the rights and duties existing at the time the statute takes effect. This clause softens the effect of a new law or the amendment or repeal of an old law by not disrupting transactions already in progress under the old law.

> This Act does not affect rights and duties that matured, penalties that were incurred, and proceedings that were begun before its effective date.

Effective Date

If you want to set the statute's effective date, include a clause stating when the statute takes effect. Otherwise the statute will take effect according to the standard law of your jurisdiction. For example, federal acts take effect when they are signed by the President, unless stated otherwise.[40] In over forty states, the effective dates of state statutes are regulated by their constitutions.[41]

Most comprehensive statutes include these standard clauses, and reviewing them will help you decide which clauses to include in the statute you are drafting. This review allows you to be more thorough when you start to draft because you can focus on drafting, not on choosing which clauses to include.

DRAFTING CONSIDERATIONS FOR STATUTES

Having determined the clients' intent, completed your research, and determined which clauses must be included in the statute, rule, or policy you are drafting, you now begin drafting. The work you have done in the preceding steps should have enabled you to choose and organize the content. Therefore, now that you are starting to draft, accuracy and clarity are your main focus.

Be Accurate

Accuracy is especially important when drafting statutes. The reader is trying to determine what behavior is permitted, required, or prohibited by the statute. Your task is to ensure that the statute tells the reader accurately whether he or she can do, must do, or cannot do some action that is controlled by the statute. Accuracy is also important because concerns about constitutional due process attach to statutes, with the Supreme Court noting that statutes can be unconstitutional when they are vague, ambiguous, or unclear.[42] Four ways to increase accuracy in statutes are to (1) use words that communicate

---

40. Nutting, *supra* note 16, at 725.

41. For example, *see* Ind. Const. art. IV, § 28; Ore. Const. art. IV, § 28.

42. *See, e.g., Kolender v. Lawson*, 461 U.S. 352 (1983); *City of Mesquite v. Aladdin's Castle, Inc.*, 455 U.S. 283 (1982).

your meaning; (2) organize sections of the chapter logically, putting all related sections together when possible; (3) use sentence structure to reflect the logical structure of the content; and (4) use correct punctuation so the intended meaning of the sentence is conveyed.

Use Words That Communicate Your Meaning

Making statutory language clear is often difficult because language you may consider clear might present different meanings to others. For example, if you review your state's statutes, you would probably find examples like the following.

A person more than twenty-one years old . . .

Does this mean twenty-two and over or twenty-one and one day? Clarify the meaning by revising.

A person who is twenty-one years old or older . . .

After the Administrator appoints an Assistant, he or she shall supervise . . .

Who is supervising, the Administrator or the Assistant? Clarify the meaning by revising.

After the Administrator appoints an Assistant, the Assistant shall supervise . . .

The better versions in these examples use language that states the meaning more clearly. This choice of clearer wording is preferable to simply adding words. The difficulty caused by adding words is that many drafters try to clarify by including extensive lists. But this creates long sentences, and the solution becomes more of a problem than the original. The following rules provide guidance for resolving this problem. But the first step is to state your points clearly.

Organize Sections of a Chapter Logically

Disorganization of a chapter's sections reduces its accuracy by making it difficult for readers to know whether they have found every applicable section of the statute. If the readers do not have all the relevant sections, they may make decisions based on incomplete understandings or inaccurate readings. For an example of how disorganization reduces accuracy, consider the following organization of Wisconsin Statutes Chapter 80 on Laying Highways.

Sec.
80.01.   Creation, Alteration and Validation of Highways.
80.02.   Town Highways; Petition to Lay, Alter or Discontinue.
80.02.5 Highways Abutted by State Park Lands; Discontinuance or Relocation.
80.03.   Restrictions on Condemning for Town Highways.
80.04.   When Supervisor Disqualified; Vacancies.
80.05.   Notice of Meeting; Service and Publication.
80.06.   Proceedings After Notice.
80.07.   Order; Survey; Award; Recording; Presumptions.

The organization of this chapter defies understanding, and its accuracy is questionable because of the number of sections that are related but spread throughout the chapter. For example, sections .01, .02, .03, .33, .38, .39, and .40 are all concerned with creating highways. Sections .08 and .64 both address highway width. Sections .09, .10, .30, and .65 all address highway damage. Readers concerned with any of these issues must read through the entire chapter, or at least through the entire table of contents, carefully enough to make sure they have found every section relating to the relevant issue. Many readers will not spend the time to read so carefully; they will not attain an accurate understanding of the law because they will miss sections related to the topics with which they are concerned.

Statutory disorganization sometimes results from the constant process of amending statutes. To minimize this problem when drafting amendments, pay particular attention to selecting the appropriate location in the chapter for the amendment. If you are creating a new section or new chapter, try to place the section or structure the chapter so all related sections are in one place. This increases the chances that the statute will accurately indicate to the reader what actions can or must be taken.

Use Sentence Structure to Reflect the Content's Logical Structure

Consider the content of the language you are drafting and then use sentence structure to increase the accuracy of your statutes. When the sentence structure corresponds to the logical structure of the content, the reader will be able to understand the statute more easily and its accuracy will be increased.

To do this, first decide what is the main point and what is supporting or explanatory information. Put the main idea in the main clause and then put dependent ideas in dependent clauses. For example, the following provision places the point of the section in the main clause and adds supporting information in a dependent clause.

> Benefits shall be paid to each unemployed and eligible employe from his [or her] employer's account, under the conditions and in the amounts stated in . . . this chapter.[43]

This structure indicates to the reader quickly and directly the main point and the elaboration.

Alternatively, you can use an introductory phrase if it introduces the main idea of the sentence. This structure can serve as a transition between two points by showing the reader how the first leads into the second, or the structure can indicate preliminary information necessary for understanding the main point contained in the main clause.

> Except as provided in par. (b), no employer or agent of an employer may directly or indirectly solicit, require or administer a polygraph, voice stress analysis, psychological stress evaluator or any other similar test purporting to test the honesty of any employe or prospective employe.[44]

Thus, the reader immediately understands the limitation on this section by reading the introductory phrase.

For example, consider how changes in sentence structure would clarify the meaning of the following statute.

43. Wis.Stat. § 108.025. **44.** Wis.Stat. § 111.37(1)(a).

If an inmate is placed in temporary lockup by a security supervisor, the security director, superintendent, or the person in charge of the institution on that day shall review this action on the next working day.

The problem with this sentence structure is that the introductory phrase does not have any clear ending; the comma following the introductory phrase is lost in the list of individuals separated by commas. As a result, there is some ambiguity about who is placing the inmate in temporary lockup. An easy way to clarify this using sentence structure is to use the "if . . . then" format for this sentence, placing "if" at the beginning of the introductory phrase and placing "then" before the main clause. This sentence structure introduces the situation in which the rule comes into play and then states the rule: **"If an inmate is placed in temporary lockup by a security supervisor, *then* the security director, superintendent. . . ."**

The sentence structure in the following example obscures the meaning of the statute and makes it difficult to understand.

> No person, firm or corporation shall engage in the business of manufacturing or bottling or distributing at wholesale or selling at wholesale to retail establishments for the purpose of resale any soda water beverages without a license from the department.[45]

In this sentence structure, the main idea is split by a long list. Rewriting the statute to put the entire main clause together would clarify the sentence.

> **A person, firm or corporation must have a license from the department to manufacture or bottle soda water beverages, to distribute soda water beverages at wholesale, or to sell soda water beverages at wholesale to retail establishments for the purpose of resale.**

This redrafting puts the main subject and verb together and puts the dependent list in a dependent clause that clarifies the restriction stated in the statute.[46] In the past, many statute drafters have followed the pattern of stating (1) what group of people, things, or events the statute addresses and then (2) what the statute says about that group. We do not encourage that approach. Although this two-part organization seems logical when stated, in practice it frequently creates sentences that are actually quite unclear. This happens because of a conflict between the structure of English and the nature of the law. English puts the subject of the sentence first when using natural order, so putting the group at the beginning leads to making the group the subject. But the group the statute addresses usually takes many words to define: "Any public restaurant that is open on Sundays and has as part of its frequent clientele groups of diners that include persons

---

45. Wis.Stat. § 97.34.

46. Additionally, the original is stated negatively, which makes it even more difficult to read. Whenever possible, state your points in the affirmative, as will be discussed in detail in the jury instructions chapter.

under the age of eighteen or who employs people who are under the age of eighteen . . . ." This means that the subject consists of many words, which pushes the verb farther and farther away. By the time the readers reach the verb ("must provide"), they are too overwhelmed with detail to absorb the main point of the sentence. Thus any logic which might have been present is lost in the grammatically cumbersome sentence which this order created. To avoid this problem, we have chosen an approach that creates a clearer subject and verb, moving the detail to the end of the sentence where the reader can more readily understand it.

Use Correct Punctuation

Punctuation plays a major role in clarifying the meaning of sentences. Ambiguous punctuation in sentences can make the meaning of a statute unclear. For example, section 1951(b)(2) of the Hobbs Act states:

(b) As used in this section—

. . .

(2) The term "extortion" means the obtaining of property from another, with his consent, induced by the wrongful use of actual or threatened force, violence or fear, or under color of official right.[47]

Because the punctuation is unclear, in a prosecution for extortion, the question remains open whether the government has to prove that the property was induced by the public official or simply that it was obtained under color of official right.[48] The defendant would argue that the punctuation of the clause gives it the following meaning: "with his consent, induced (1) by wrongful use of actual or threatened force, violence, or fear, or (2) under color of official right." In contrast, the government would argue that the punctuation of the statute gives it a different meaning: "with his consent, (1) induced by wrongful use . . . or (2) under color of official right." The meaning of the statute could determine whether a conviction is obtained. By punctuating to divide separate points into separate clauses, the meaning of the statute would be clear.

Additionally, incorrectly punctuated sentences are unclear because they are hard to read. As this example shows, the punctuation of the statute obscures its meaning and needs to be revised.

Owners of lands who do not maintain and keep in repair lawful partition fences shall not be entitled to recover any damages whatever for trespasses by the animals of owners of any adjoining lands with whom partition fences might have been maintained if such lands had been enclosed; but the construction of such a fence

---

47. 18 U.S.C. § 1951 (1988).　　　　　**48.** Eskridge and Frickey, *supra* note 16, at 695–96.

shall not relieve the owner of swine from liability for any damage they commit upon the enclosed premises of an adjoining owner.[49]

One problem is that, in one long sentence, the statute regulates two entirely different actions. Remember to limit a sentence to one thought. Simply dividing this sentence into its two separate parts would help to clarify its meaning significantly.

> **Owners of lands who do not maintain and keep in repair lawful partition fences shall not be entitled to recover any damages whatever for trespasses by the animals of owners of any adjoining lands with whom partition fences might have been maintained if such lands had been enclosed. The construction of a partition fence, however, shall not relieve the owner of swine from liability for any damage they commit upon the enclosed premises of an adjoining owner.**

Because each separate point now is contained in a separate sentence, the reader can more accurately understand the statute and conform his or her behavior to its demands.

Be Clear

Clarity is also important when drafting statutes because it helps your reader better understand the meaning of the statute. Three ways to increase clarity are (1) use words the reader understands, (2) prefer straight-forward organization, and (3) omit information that does not add needed content.

Use Words the Reader Understands

When drafting statutes, you are trying to communicate with a reader who is turning to the statutes to determine what actions are allowed, required, or prohibited. The reader can glean this information more readily when you use words your reader understands and when the words you use are unambiguous.

Use words that will be understood readily by lay readers, because they are among the people who will be reading your statutes. Additionally, these words are more likely to be clear under the plain meaning doctrine, so courts will interpret your language correctly. This is not the place to consult your thesaurus. For example, the following federal regulation on voting by members of the armed forces would be much clearer if more familiar words were used.

> (b) It is recommended, in order to minimize the possibility of physical adhesion of State balloting material, that the gummed flap of the State envelope supplied for the return of the ballot be separated by a wax paper or other appropriate protective insert from the remaining balloting material, and, because such inserts may not prove completely effective, that there also be included in State voting instructions a procedure to be followed by absentee

---

49. Wis.Stat. § 90.04.

> voters in instances of such adhesion of the balloting material, such as a notation of the facts on the back of any such envelope, duly signed by the voter and witnessing officer.

The unfamiliar wording raises unnecessary questions in the reader's mind. In line two, does "physical adhesion" mean the same thing as "sticking"? Does "such adhesion" in line ten mean the same thing? Using "sticking" throughout would make the statute clear because it would be more readable. In line four, is "appropriate" protective insert needed to differentiate an "appropriate" protective insert from an "inappropriate" protective insert? If not, why introduce that possibility by using the modifier "appropriate"? In summary, changing the language to make it less stilted would help clarify this almost incomprehensible statute.

Additionally, do not vary your word choice by using several different words to refer to the same thing. This variation confuses the reader, who is not sure whether the words are intended to refer to the same things or to different things. For example, review Wis.Stat. § 90.10.

> In case any person shall neglect to repair or rebuild any partition fence which by law he ought to maintain, the aggrieved party may complain to two or more fence viewers of the town, who, after giving notice as provided in s. 90.07, shall examine the same. If they determine such fence is insufficient, they shall signify the same to the delinquent party and direct him to repair or rebuild the same with such time as they shall deem reasonable. If such fence shall not be repaired or rebuilt within the time so fixed, the complainant may repair or rebuild the same and recover the expense thereof as hereinafter provided.

The drafter uses "any person" in the first line and "delinquent party" in the sixth line when referring to the person who does not repair or rebuild the partition fence. The drafter also uses "aggrieved party" in the second line and "complainant" in the ninth line to refer to the party who is affected by the person not maintaining the partition fence. This variation causes confusion for the reader, who must sort out who is whom.

Even more confusing than using different words for the same meaning is using the same word for different meanings. Having once deciphered the meaning of the word, the reader must then redefine the word when it is used later to convey a different meaning. In the example above, the drafter uses "same" several times and its meaning changes from use to use: the first, third, and fourth times "same" is used, it means fence; the second time "same" is used it refers to the insufficiency of the fence. By substituting different words for each meaning of "same," we can clarify the statute. If we make the changes noted here and eliminate the legalese, the statute is easier to read.

> **In case any person shall neglect to repair or rebuild any partition fence which by law he ought to maintain, the ag-**

grieved party may complain to two or more fence viewers of the town, who after giving notice as provided in § 90.07, shall examine the fence. If they determine that the fence is insufficient, they shall signify its insufficiency to the person and direct him to repair or rebuild the fence within a reasonable time. If the fence is not repaired or rebuilt within the time they fix, the aggrieved party may repair or rebuild the fence and recover the expense of doing so as provided below.[50]

Making small changes in wording adds up to a substantially clearer statute.

Prefer Straight–Forward Organization

Good organization can significantly affect whether the statute is understandable. This organization should be not only logical, as discussed earlier, but also as simple and straight-forward as possible. For example, the statute above on voting for armed forces personnel was confusing because its organization was not clear to the reader; logically distinct ideas were combined. Rewriting could clarify the content.

(b) It is further recommended

(1) that the gummed flap of the return envelope for the ballot be separated from the balloting material by waxed paper or other protective insert to minimize the possibility that the balloting material will stick together; and

(2) that the voting instructions include a procedure to be followed by the voter if the balloting material does stick together, such as noting the facts on the back of the envelope, and having it signed by the voter and the witness.

The following statute also is poorly organized because it tries to do too much in one sentence. This problem is typical in statutes where drafters try to include all the information necessary for one statutory section in one sentence.

Whenever any highway has been divided into 2 roadways by an intervening unpaved or otherwise clearly indicated dividing space or by a physical barrier so constructed as to substantially impede crossing by vehicular traffic, the operator of a vehicle shall drive only to the right of such space or barrier and no operator of a vehicle shall drive over, across, or within any such space or barrier except through an opening or at a crossover or intersection established by the authority in charge of the maintenance of the highway, except that the operator of a vehicle when making a left turn to or from a private driveway, alley or highway may drive across a paved dividing space or physical barrier not so constructed as to impede crossing by vehicular traffic, unless such crossing is

---

50. Another revision that needs to be made is to make this statute gender-neutral. Thus, you would change the statute either to make the subject plural (with pronouns also plural) or include "he or she."

prohibited by signs erected by the authority in charge of the maintenance of the highway.[51]

This statute section covers three points. The first five lines indicate that the driver is to drive only on the right side of a divided highway. The next five lines prohibit drivers from crossing the median except through an authorized opening. The next six lines explain an exception for left turns. The statute would be clearer and its meaning more understandable if it were divided into at least three sentences, each indicating separate points.

> **Whenever any highway has been divided into 2 roadways by an intervening unpaved or otherwise clearly indicated dividing space or by a physical barrier so constructed as to substantially impede crossing by vehicular traffic, the operator of a vehicle shall drive only to the right of such space or barrier. No operator of a vehicle shall drive over, across, or within any such space or barrier except through an opening or at a crossover or intersection established by the authority in charge of the maintenance of the highway. The operator of a vehicle making a left turn to or from a private driveway, alley or highway, however, may drive across a paved dividing space or a physical barrier not so constructed as to impede crossing by vehicular traffic, unless such crossing is prohibited by signs erected by the authority in charge of the maintenance of the highway.**

Preferring straight-forward organization, primarily by dividing statute sections into their separate components, will increase clarity and thereby help the reader understand the statute's meaning.

Omit Unneeded Information and Passive Voice

Statutory sections should be as lean as possible so unnecessary words do not confuse the reader and unnecessary passive voice does not hide the actor. Do this by (1) using affirmatives rather than negatives; (2) using possessives when possible to delete prepositional phrases; and (3) using active voice, instead of passive voice.

Using affirmatives rather than negatives eliminates the negative words that do not add content to the statute. Review the following statute.

> Owners of lands who do not maintain and keep in repair lawful partition fences shall not be entitled to recover any damages whatever for trespasses by the animals of owners of any adjoining lands with whom partition fences might have been maintained if such lands had been enclosed. The construction of a partition fence, however, shall not relieve the owner of swine from liability for any damage they commit upon the enclosed premises of an adjoining owner.[52]

---

51. Wis.Stat. § 346.15.   **52.** Wis.Stat. § 90.04.

The use of negatives forces the reader to take more time to discern the meaning of the statute. Negatives not only result in unnecessary words, but also include unneeded logical steps that the reader must sort out. Eliminating negatives whenever possible will reduce the confusion.

> **Owners of lands who maintain and keep in repair lawful partition fences shall be entitled to recover damages for trespasses by animal of owners of any adjoining lands. The construction of a partition fence, however, shall not relieve the owner of swine from liability for any damage they commit upon the enclosed premises of an adjoining owner.**

Redrafting this section would require care. There is a tendency to change the second sentence to make it parallel to the first and say "Owners of swine who construct . . . are not relieved . . . ." But this causes ambiguity and a chuckle as well, because it becomes unclear whether the owners or the swine are constructing the fence. Whenever you revise your language to follow one of these suggestions, be sure the revision does not cause confusion in some other way.

Another way to remove unneeded content is to remove unneeded prepositional phrases. For example, using possessives to clarify the link between words allows you to delete prepositional phrases. In section 90.04 above, consider the phrase "the animals of owners of any adjoining lands." It is possible to revise that phrase to "the animals of adjoining landowners" or "adjoining landowner's animals." Similarly, you can use single words to indicate possession, instead of using prepositional phrases. This same section begins with "Owners of lands." It is more direct and clear if you revise this to say "Landowners."

In the push to eliminate unneeded language, however, do not give conciseness unfettered freedom. Some prepositional phrases are necessary to prevent a string of nouns that becomes dense and difficult to read. For example, if you eliminated prepositional phrases in the statute above, you could create "swine farmer's lawful partition fence construction." You could solve this problem by writing "swine farmer's construction of lawful partition fences."

Eliminating unnecessary prepositional phrases makes it easier for the reader to understand the connection between the words of the statute. For example, note the number of prepositional phrases in the following section of the armed forces balloting statute.

> It is recommended, *in* order to minimize the possibility *of* physical adhesion *of* State balloting material, that the gummed flap *of* the State envelope supplied *for* the return *of* the ballot be separated *by* a wax paper or other appropriate protective insert *from* the remaining balloting material. . . .

This statute could be revised to eliminate many of the prepositional phrases.

> to minimize the possibility of State balloting material
> sticking, the State envelope's gummed flap should be separat-
> ed by a waxed paper insert . . . .

This revision directly states the point, omits unneeded words, and thus
clarifies the needed content.

Another way to clarify this statute, and others, is to minimize the
use of the passive voice, especially because it often leaves the actor
unidentified.[53] A statute's purpose is to indicate behavior that is
permitted, regulated, or prohibited. This purpose will be clearer if you
include the actor in the statute. For example, in the armed forces
statute, the passive voice is used repeatedly. This usage makes it
unclear who is supposed to do what. The statute starts with "It is
recommended." By whom? It goes on to say that the gummed flap
should "be separated." By whom? And that a procedure "be included." By whom? Using the active voice would clarify the actors and
would help the reader understand what he or she was told to do.

CONCLUSION

Taking the steps indicated in this chapter will help you draft
statutes that provide meaningful assistance to those reading them. By
interviewing your client, researching the law, learning about legislative
history and canons of construction, and selecting needed clauses, you
ensure that the statute thoroughly covers its intended situations and
will be understandable when applied to new ones. By focusing on
accuracy and clarity when drafting and by using the suggestions for
revision listed above, you increase the likelihood that the statute will
convey its intended meaning and will be understood by those using it.

EXERCISES

1. Rewrite the examples in light of the section about using words to
communicate your meaning.

    a. The guard shall issue security badges to the employees who
work in Building D and Building E

    b. No one may park his car near a fire hydrant.

2. Change the punctuation in the following statute to make it more
accurate and easier to read.

> In case any person shall neglect to repair or rebuild any
> partition fence which by law he ought to maintain the aggrieved
> party may complain to two or more fence viewers of the town, who,
> after giving notices as provided in § 90.07, shall examine the same,
> and if they shall determine such fence is insufficient they shall
> signify the same to the delinquent party and direct him to repair or
> rebuild the same within such time as they shall deem reasonable.

---

53. The passive voice occurs when the actor is eliminated from the sentence, such as saying "The ball was kicked" or "The ball was kicked by John" rather than "John kicked the ball."

If such fence shall not be repaired or rebuilt within the time so fixed, the complainant may repair or rebuild the same and recover the expense thereof as hereinafter provided.[54]

3. Review Wis.Stat. § 346.15, concerning divided highways in the section: prefer straight-forward organization. Reorganize it to eliminate some of its prepositional phrases and clarify its meaning.

4. Revise the section on armed forces voting to eliminate the passive voice.

5. Revise the following statute, including its title, so that it is more accurate and readable.

346.47 When vehicles using alley or non-highway access to stop. (1) The operator of a vehicle emerging from an alley or about to cross or enter a highway from any point of access other than another highway shall stop such vehicle immediately prior to moving on to the sidewalk or on to the sidewalk area extending across the path of such vehicle and shall yield the right of way to any pedestrian and upon crossing or entering the roadway shall yield the right of way to all vehicles approaching on such roadway.

ASSIGNMENT 1

You are a new associate at the law firm of Sazama and Osburg in Pleasantview, Illinois. The firm represents the city in all legal matters. Ms. Sazama said that the firm is in the process of revising several city ordinances. One of these ordinances is 8–5–6. Ms. Sazama asked you to rewrite 8–5–6.

ORDINANCES of the CITY of PLEASANTVIEW, ILLINOIS

8–5–6 USE OF THE PUBLIC SEWERS:

(A) Sanitary Sewers: No person(s) shall discharge or cause to be discharged any unpolluted waters such as storm water, ground water, roof runoff, sub-surface drainage, or noncontact cooling water to any sanitary sewer.

(B) Storm Sewers: Storm water and all other unpolluted water shall be discharged to such sewers as are specifically designated as storm sewers, or to a natural outlet approved by the Approving Authority and other regulatory agencies. Unpolluted industrial cooling water or process waters may be discharged, on approval of the Approving Authority and/or other regulatory agencies, to a storm sewer, or natural outlet.

(C) Prohibitions and Limitations: Except as hereinafter provided, no person shall discharge or cause to be discharged any of the following described waters or wastes to any public sewer:

54. Wis.Stat. § 90.10.

1. Any gasoline, benzene, naphtha, fuel oil, or other flammable or explosive liquid, solid, or gas.

2. Any waters or wastes containing toxic or poisonous solids, liquids, or gases in sufficient quantity, either singly or by interaction with other wastes, that could injure or interfere with any waste treatment or sludge disposal process, constitute a hazard to humans or animals, or create a public nuisance in the receiving waters of the wastewater treatment facility.

3. Any waters or wastes having a pH lower than 5.5, or in excess of 9.0, or having any corrosive property capable of causing damage of hazard to structures, equipment, and personnel of the wastewater collection and treatment facility.

4. Solid or viscous substances in quantities or of such size capable of causing obstruction to the flow in public sewers or other interference with the proper operation of the wastewater collection and treatment facilities, such as, but not limited to, ashes, cinders, sand, mud, straw, shavings, metal, glass, rags, feathers, tar, plastics, wood, unground garbage, whole blood, paunch manure, hair and fleshings, entrails, and paper dishes, cups, milk containers, etc., either whole or ground by garbage grinders.

5. The following described substances, materials, waters, or waste shall be limited in discharges to sanitary sewer systems to concentrations or quantities which will not harm either the sanitary sewers, wastewater treatment process, or equipment, will not have an adverse effect on the receiving stream, or will not otherwise endanger lives, limbs, public property, or constitute a nuisance. The Approving Authority may set limitations more stringent than those established below if such more stringent limitations are necessary to meet the above objectives. The Approving Authority will give consideration to the quantity of subject waste in relation to flows and velocities in the sewers, materials of construction of the sanitary sewers, the wastewater treatment facility and other pertinent factors. No person shall discharge any of the following waste materials into any City sewer:

a. Any liquid or vapor having a temperature higher than one hundred forty degrees (140 degrees) (60 degrees Celsius).

b. Any wastewater containing more than twenty five (25) mg./l. of petroleum oil, nonbiodegradable cutting oils, or products of mineral origin; wastewater containing more than one hundred (100) mg./l. of nonpetroleum based oils such as animal or vegetable oil or fats. The method for determining grease and oil content shall be as stated in the current edition of Standard Methods.

ASSIGNMENT 2

On November 14, 1986, Central County Sheriff's Deputy Beth Radke stopped a 1974 Ford Mustang, which was travelling on Highway 69, because both tail lights were not working. As Deputy Radke approached the car, she noted that there was a lot of movement by the people in it.

Radke got the driver's license from the driver, Mark Friske, 22. As she was telling him about his defective tail lights, she detected a strong odor of beer coming from inside the car.

Radke radioed for a back-up, and Deputy Arthur Gordee arrived shortly. They searched the car and found seven open but empty beer cans, eleven unopened beer cans, and two large wet spots that smelled strongly of beer on the carpet under the front seat. They determined that Friske's father was the owner of the car. Deputy Radke gave Mark Friske a citation for violating Wis.Stat. § 346.935(3)

The following statute does not seem to cover this fact situation because the open beer cans were empty. It is possible that Friske emptied the cans on to the carpet when he was stopped by Radke. Revise the statute to resolve this problem.

346.935 Intoxicants in motor vehicles. (1) No person may drink alcohol beverages in any motor vehicle when the vehicle is upon a highway. **(2)** No person may possess on his or her person, in a privately owned motor vehicle upon a public highway, any bottle or receptacle containing alcohol beverages if the bottle or receptacle has been opened, the seal has been broken or the contents of the bottle or receptacle have been partially removed. **(3)** The owner of a privately owned motor vehicle, or the driver of the vehicle, shall not keep, or allow to be kept in the motor vehicle when it is upon a highway any bottle or receptacle containing alcohol beverages if the bottle or receptacle has been opened, the seal has been broken or the contents of the bottle or receptacle have been partially removed. This subsection does not apply if the bottle or receptacle is kept in the trunk of the vehicle or, if the vehicle has no trunk, in some other area of the vehicle not normally occupied by the driver or passengers. A utility compartment or glove compartment is considered to be within the area normally occupied by the driver and passengers.

Bibliography

American Bar Association, *Guide To Legislative Research and Drafting* (1978).

Biskind, Elliot L., *Legal Writing Simplified.* New York: Clark Boardman Co., 1971.

Cohen, Julius, *Materials and Problems on Legislation.* Indianapolis: Bobbs–Merrill Co., 1967.

Cooper, Frank E., *Writing in Law Practice.* Indianapolis: Bobbs–Merrill Co., 1963.

Dickerson, Reed, *The Fundamentals of Legal Drafting.* Boston: Little, Brown and Company, 1986.

Dickerson, Reed, *Materials on Legal Drafting.* St. Paul: West Publishing Company, 1981.

Dickerson, Reed, *Legislative Drafting.* Boston: Little, Brown and Company, 2nd ed. 1977.

Dickerson, Reed, *Plain English Statutes and Readability—Part 1,* 64 Mich.Bar J. 567 (June 1985).

Dickerson, Reed, *Readability Formulas and Specifications For A "Plain English" Statute—Part 2,* 64 Mich.Bar J. 714 (July 1985).

Dickerson, Reed, *How To Write A Law,* 31 Notre Dame Law. 14 (1955).

Eskridge, William N. and Philip P. Frickey, *Cases and Materials on Legislation.* St. Paul: West Publishing Company, 1988.

Kuzara, Christine M., *Plain English in Legislative Drafting,* 62 Mich. Bar J. 980 (November 1983).

Legislative Council of California, *Legislative Drafting Manual* (1975).

Llewellyn, Karl N., *Remarks on the Theory of Appellate Decision and the Rule or Canons About How Statutes Are To Be Construed,* 3 Vand.L.Rev. 395 (1950).

Nutting, Charles Bernard, *Legislation: Cases and Materials.* St. Paul: West Publishing Company, 1978.

Peacock, James Craig, *Notes on Legislative Drafting.* Washington D.C.: REC Foundation, Inc., 1961.

Pratt, Diana V., *Legal Writing: A Systematic Approach* (Supplemental Chapter on Understanding Statutes). St. Paul: West Publishing Company, 1990.

Read, Horace Emerson, *Materials on Legislation.* Mineola, N.Y.: The Foundation Press, Inc., 1982.

Singer, Norman J., *Sutherland Statutory Construction.* Chicago: Callaghan & Company, Sands 4th ed. 1985.

Statsky, William P., *Legislative Analysis and Drafting.* Boston: Little, Brown and Company, 2nd ed. 1977.

White, James Boyd, *The Legal Imagination.* Boston: Little, Brown and Company, 1973.

Chapter 4

JURY INSTRUCTIONS

While drafting statutes entails creating law, drafting jury instructions entails explaining existing law to nonlawyers. It may require less research time than statutes, but substantially more drafting time. Drafting effective instructions requires accuracy and clarity, but it also requires more because the purpose of jury instructions differs substantially from that of statutes.

Jury instructions are generally viewed as important, even the most critical part of the trial.[1] They are statements explaining the law to nonlawyers. Jury instructions appear at the crossroads in a trial, when the focus is shifting from the witness box to the jury box, and when the jury is turning from listening to deciding. Furthermore, the instructions are situated between many tasks and participants: between advocating and informing, between two communicators (the judge and the attorney), between readers who see the instructions (the judges) and those who only hear them (the jury, in some states [2]) and between lay readers (the jury) and technical readers (the appellate courts).

The intersection of all these aspects makes drafting instructions complex.[3] Perhaps this is why a successful set of instructions, one approved by reviewing courts and understandable for the jury, is rare. "When I read instructions to the jury, I hope that I will see a light go on in the juror's eyes, but I never do."[4] Rather than despairing about the complexity of the situation, however, work your way through the various considerations involved, making informed choices and improving the status quo until you reach your goal.

1. John Kennelly, *Closing Arguments: Instructions are the Key,* 6 Trial Law.Guide 53 (1962); M.M. Cramer, *A View From the Jury Box,* 6 Litigation 3 (1979).

2. Some states send a copy of jury instructions in with the jury, but some expect the jurors to follow the instructions based only on the judge's oral presentation of those instructions.

3. Dean E. Hewes and Sally Planalp, "The Individual's Place in Communication Science" in *Handbook of Communication Science* 147 (C. Berger and S. Chaffee, eds. 1987).

4. Personal communication from an Oregon trial judge, quoted in Laurence J. Severance and Elizabeth F. Loftus, *Improving the Ability of Jurors to Comprehend and Apply Criminal Jury Instructions* 17 L. & Soc'y 153, 154–55 (1982).

The first section of this chapter delineates the general considerations involved in choosing and revising instructions. The second section covers specific techniques you can use to implement the decisions you made in light of those considerations. The final section summarizes these techniques in a checklist to give you an overview of the process as a whole.

GENERAL CONSIDERATIONS WHEN CHOOSING AND REVISING INSTRUCTIONS

Jury instructions have changed substantially in the past sixty years.[5] Throughout your legal career, you may see additional dramatic improvements [6] as the legal system becomes more aware of how jurors process information. Commentators have discussed the problems with jury instructions currently in use.[7] Linguists have tested instructions, have found disturbingly low levels of understanding within juries, and have attributed these problems to writing structures.[8] Others have complained that the length of instructions makes it impossible for the jury to comprehend its task.[9] Still others have complained about the judges' presentation of the instructions [10] and the time at which instructions are presented in the trial.[11] As the following judge's description illustrates, it is not a pretty scene.

> Probably the most discouraging part of the trial is the time when the judge tries to cram into twelve non-legal minds all the law applicable to the case at hand. The blank expressions on the faces of citizen jurors [are] pitiful. They [are matched] only by the bleak look of the judge [while plodding] through the legal terminology that [the judge] knows is making little if any impression on [the] listeners. Yet, the law continues to go under the assumption that this type of material is clearly understood and applied to trials that are of the utmost importance to the participants.[12]

These considerations fall into two broad areas: (1) those judges address when reviewing submitted instructions or preparing their own instructions, and (2) those litigators address as they prepare instructions for the judge's review.

5. In the 1930s, Judge William J. Palmer began working on jury instructions in California. In 1955, the state of Illinois began its study of jury instructions and eventually developed the first patterned (or model) jury instructions.

6. Montana has added a communications specialist to their jury instructions drafting committee, and the Oregon, Connecticut, Florida, and California judiciaries have held conferences, run pilot projects, and done other work toward improving jury instructions.

7. For a particularly helpful review of the history and development of jury instructions, *see,* Harvey Perlman, *Pattern Jury Instructions: The Application of So-*

cial Science Research, 65 Neb.L.Rev. 520 (1986).

8. One of the first systematic studies in this area is described in Robert and Veda Charrow, *Making Legal Language Understandable: A Psycholinguistic Study of Jury Instructions,* 79 Col.L.Rev. 1306 (1979).

9. Perlman, *supra* note 7, at 537.

10. William Schwarzer, *Communicating with Juries: Problems and Remedies,* 69 Cal.L.Rev. 731, 756 (1981).

11. *Id.* at 755.

12. Raymond Buchanan, *The Florida Judge–Jury Communications Project,* 8 Bridge.L.Rev. 297, 298 (1987).

Considerations of the Judiciary

The trial judge is responsible for jury instructions. He or she decides what instructions to give the jury, reads the instructions as coming from the judge rather than the attorneys, and is finally responsible for making sure the jury receives all the instructions they need to reach a verdict and to avoid appealable error. The last two tasks can be at odds. For example, to avoid appealable error, a judge may think the unchanged model jury instruction is safer, simply because the judge then can rely on the understanding of specialists in instructions.[13] In contrast, a judge may believe that a previously established instruction in a particular case may not be clear to the jury without modification. Judges work to balance these two forces.

In general, concerns for clarity and the ability to stand up under appeal are better served by revising instructions. Even the drafters of model jury instructions agree: "Model instructions can be most useful as servants. There is danger in letting them become masters."[14] In light of all this, receiving revised instructions from the attorney is an improvement appreciated by many courts.

> [E]ven technically correct instructions should be reviewed with an eye to their comprehensibility. The test should not be simply whether the instruction was substantially correct, but whether it enabled the jury to reach a fair and informed verdict. An egregious departure from this standard should concern appellate courts as much as a traditional legal error in the instructions.[15]

Appellate courts generally do not strike down revised instructions if the content remains correct,[16] and indeed judges have praised instructions that have been adapted to specific situations.

> At its best [the jury instruction] is a simple, rugged communication from a trial judge to a jury of ordinary people, entitled to be appraised in terms of its net effect. Instructions are to be viewed in this common-sense perspective, and not through the remote and distorting knothole of a distant appellate fence.[17]

The judiciary is also considering greater use of special verdicts or instructive interrogatories (where the jury answers specific questions but also renders a general verdict).[18] By guiding the jury to answer a series of specific questions, the special verdict shows the jury precisely what they need to determine to deliver a verdict. These specific

---

13. *See* Graham Douthwaite, *Jury Instructions, Pattern and Otherwise,* 29 Def. L.J. 335 (1980).

14. *Id.* at 347.

15. Schwarzer, *supra* note 10, at 758. This article might be a useful supporting source if you are arguing to the court for a revision of a model instruction.

16. Edward Devitt and Charles Blackmar, *Federal Jury Practice and Instructions* 241 (3d ed. 1977).

17. *Time, Inc. v. Hill,* 385 U.S. 374, 481 (1967) (Fortas, J. dissenting).

18. Robert Berdon, *Instructive Interrogatories: Helping the Civil Jury to Understand,* 55 Conn.B.J. 179 (1981); and Robert Berdon, *Instructive Interrogatories: One Method to Aid the Jury,* 8 Bridge.L.Rev. 385 (1987).

findings in turn establish a clearer record for any appellate questions that may arise. So, for example, rather than asking the jury to find for the consumer (plaintiff) or the manufacturer (defendant) on the issue of breach of a duty in a products liability case, the judge might ask a jury to decide the following questions

1. Did the manufacturer exercise ordinary care in the design, construction, and manufacture of its product so that the product was safe for its intended use?

2. In exercising ordinary care, did the manufacturer make all reasonable and adequate tests and inspections of its product to guard against any defective condition that would render it unsafe?

3. Did the manufacturer exercise ordinary care in warning consumers of dangers which it knew or should have known are associated with use of its product? [19]

This series of questions would avoid allowing the jury to find for the plaintiff out of sympathy for his or her plight without first determining whether the defendant was at fault.

If you become a judge yourself, you will have an opportunity to address some of these considerations directly. But if you are a practicing attorney, you will work within the limits set by the preferences of your judge and by the regulations of your jurisdiction.

Considerations of the Litigator

As a litigator, you will routinely submit your jury instructions to the judge, who then chooses which instructions to submit to the jury. Although attorneys sometimes leave the choice of instructions to the judge when they think the standard ones are sufficient, instructions are too important to omit from your advocacy. When you submit instructions, you are both advocating for your client and acting as a servant of the court. You advocate when you choose instructions that show the jury (1) how they can find in favor of your client, (2) why damaging information is not critical to the outcome of the case, and (3) why favorable facts are critical. You want to revise the instructions you have chosen to communicate the applicable law clearly so the jury will see how it supports your position.

The first consideration in your jury instructions is that they are written to be given to the jury by a neutral party, the judge. This means you need to exercise some caution in preparing instructions. For example, when dealing with an unsettled area of law, prepare instructions early in the process; do not wait until the trial is in progress to address the critical issues these instructions can raise. Also prepare alternative requests, so you have some recourse if the court does not use your primary instruction. [20] Similarly, in your instructions

---

19. Based on Wis.Civ.J.I. 3240–3242.   20. Devitt and Blackmar, *supra* note 16, at 244.

use clear-but-neutral descriptions the judge would use, avoiding any biased words and any statements implying that your client should win. Finally, do not omit an instruction just because you would prefer that it were not needed. Instead, prepare your own version so the judge has an alternative to consider when reading the instruction the opposition prepared on that point.

Another consideration is whether to request a general or special verdict. Instructive interrogatories are generally useful when the jury's sympathy is likely to run against your client, but the law runs in your favor. The instructive interrogatory limits the jury's focus to more specific questions so the jury may find that their sympathies are not relevant to answering some or all of the interrogatories. In contrast, a general verdict allows the jury broader discretion in the factors it considers relevant when deliberating. For example, an attorney representing a corporation in a strict liability case might request an instructive interrogatory that asks for findings on the specific elements of the charge rather than asking for an overall verdict about whether the plaintiff should receive compensation. The plaintiff's attorney might request a general verdict that allows the jury more scope to act on its sympathy for the person injured.

How you approach developing your jury instructions depends on your jurisdiction. When your state has model jury instructions, as do most states, you begin by choosing those. Then, as allowable, you adapt them to fit your situation and to increase understandability. If your jurisdiction allows the jury to have a copy of the instructions, revise those instructions to make their organization visually clear. If the jury does not receive a copy, revise them so they are easy for the judge to read clearly to the jury. This increases the chance that the judge will communicate, through inflection and pause, the organization you have given to the instructions. In turn, the jury will hear the organization more clearly and find the content easier to absorb. To communicate this organization to the judge, introduce listed items with visual clues, such as tabulation and parenthetical numbers. To communicate the organization to the jury, use verbal clues, such as introductory phrases before lists.

Your approach also depends on how your state uses model instructions. Although some states require you to use these model instructions with few modifications,[21] most encourage modifying the model instructions to fit the case at bar: "It must be emphasized that in very few cases will it be possible to use these instructions verbatim." [22]

There is good reason for this modification. Model instructions are necessarily written to fit any possible situation. By applying to every general situation, they apply to no particular one. The introduction to

21. Douthwaite, *supra* note 13, at 348–349 (footnotes omitted).

22. This is the opening sentence in the preface written by Professor John E. Con-way, editor of the 1978 supplement of the Wisconsin Civil Model Jury Instructions.

the Wisconsin Model Civil Jury Instructions makes the limitations of model instructions explicit.

We forcefully disclaim that:

1. It is free from error, completely accurate, or a model of perfection in form, statement, or expression.

2. It is presented as a standard of instructions pattern to be blindly and unquestionably followed.

. . .

4. It will remove all need for the trial judge's industry and ingenuity in the preparation of instructions.

. . .

5. It will lessen the duties of the trial attorneys with respect to the preparation and submission of timely written instructions.

. . .

8. It forestalls any constructive suggestions for its improvement.

9. It is as clear, concise, and correct as it can or ought to be.[23]

Furthermore, using an unmodified jury instruction, which covers many situations rather than one particular situation, contradicts the basic rules of effective public speaking, going back to Aristotle. Effective speakers know that listeners remember concrete images, so they use anecdotes and images to clarify their points. The model instructions do not allow for this because specifics arise from the facts of individual cases. Therefore, if the jury is to be expected to understand and apply the law to a particular situation, the instructions must be modified to explain the law clearly, concretely, and specifically.

Precisely because accurately modified instructions are clearer, some attorneys request the vaguer, pattern instructions when the sympathy runs in favor of their client but the law does not. The reasoning behind this was bluntly stated by Jamison Wilcox, although he did not particularly favor it.

> Simply put, when instructions are ineffective, the rules of law are ineffective in exercising their appropriate influence over the jury. Jurors then act more on their feelings and prejudices, and less on the law, than they do when effectively instructed.[24]

Nevertheless, leaving instructions vague on purpose is risky for two reasons. First, people's "feelings and prejudices" often are not predictable; you might be lighting the fuse of a loose cannon. Second, "[A]n instruction which will win a lawsuit but will not stand up on appeal is worse than no instruction at all." [25] The better choice is to adapt the

---

23. A.W. Parnell, Chairman Jury Instructions Committee, Introduction to the 1960 Edition of the Wisconsin Model Jury Instructions.

24. Jamison Wilcox, *The Craft of Drafting Plain–Language Jury Instructions: A* *Study of a Sample Pattern Instruction on Obscenity,* 59 Temp.L.Q. 1159, 1183 (1986).

25. Devitt and Blackmar, *supra* note 16, at 245.

model instructions to your case, taking pains to maintain accuracy and still clarify how the law supports the result your client wants.

In summary, the task of drafting jury instructions raises many questions for judges and litigators alike, questions that sometimes conflict, sometimes coordinate, but always interact. When writing jury instructions, you will make many complex decisions. To help you make these decisions comfortably and competently, you need a clear sense of what makes jury instructions readable and how to achieve it.

TECHNIQUES FOR CHOOSING AND REVISING INSTRUCTIONS

Because people untrained in the law must understand jury instructions, you need to focus on understandability when writing them. The jury's task is complex,[26] so unclear passages and missignals in the instructions are very likely to cause confusion. For this reason, all your revisions will make those instructions more understandable.

To attain understandability, instructions need to be readable, clear, and unambiguous. Jury instructions can meet this goal, although they often do not. For an example of their common failings, read the following instruction aloud at a normal rate of speech.

If you find that, by reason of public improvements already made or planned to be made in the immediate future, special benefits have accrued to the remaining property of the plaintiff, so as to affect its market value, you should offset the fair market value of such special benefits against the severance damages, if any, found by you, or against the value of the land taken, but in no event should you allow special benefits in excess of the damages.

A special benefit, as used in the foregoing instruction, is a benefit that in fact enhances the value of the land not taken either because the public project improves the physical condition of the remaining land, or because the public project, by its proximity to the remaining land, immediately increases the market value of the land for an existing use or for a different and more profitable use.

The burden of proof is on the defendant condemnor to establish by the greater weight of the credible evidence that there was in fact a direct and immediate special benefit accruing to the remaining land by reason of the taking for the public improvement. The condemnor must show that the claimed special benefits are direct, immediate, and certain, as to both time and place, rather than remote or speculative.[27]

It is hard to imagine a juror understanding and correctly applying the law after listening to that instruction read once.

While it is easy to see the problem from this example, it is harder to know exactly what, in terms of rewriting, will solve the problem.

26. Hewes and Planalp, *supra* note 3, at 161.

27. Wis.Civ.J.I. 8115.

The rest of this section focuses on showing you how to improve both the instructions you draft yourself and those you find in pattern instruction books. If you are drafting an instruction rather than revising a model, begin by writing a rough draft including all needed content. For example, if you are writing an instruction on a novel theory of law or a specific municipal ordinance, include all the elements necessary to establish whether the theory is met by the facts. Then revise, just as you would revise model instructions.

For example, the following revision avoids many of the problems plaguing the instruction above. Read this version aloud.

> **Sometimes the expansion of a park will increase a lot's market value, even though that expansion took some of the lot's land. This can happen if any of following three things occur:**
>
> (1) **if the expansion improved the physical condition of the lot,**
>
> (2) **if the lot is more valuable because it is close to the park's expansion, or**
>
> (3) **if an owner can now put the lot to a different and more profitable use.**
>
> **If you find that the market value of Mr. Oliveras's lot has or will increase because of the park's expansion, then you should subtract that increase from the damages you determined. If you find that this increase in market value is greater than the damages you determined, then you should decide that the damages are zero.**
>
> **But even if the increase in market value is greater than the damages you determined, you should not subtract anything from the value of the land actually taken from Mr. Oliveras's lot for the park's expansion.**
>
> **The city has the burden of proving whether Mr. Oliveras's lot increased in value because of the expansion of the park. To prove this to you, the city must have convinced you by the greater weight of the credible evidence that this increase exists. The city must also have convinced you that this increase in the value of the lot is direct, immediate, and certain. It is not enough if the benefit is remote or speculative.**

To avoid some of the problems in the original, this revision uses several writing techniques to make the content clearer. It personalizes the instructions, so the jury can understand more readily how the law applies to this situation. It substitutes plain English for unfamiliar words whenever possible. It also uses more understandable sentence structure. It keeps the subject and verb close together; it also uses clearer signals of structure and avoids long introductory phrases that would put confusing details before the main point. Taken together, these individual techniques work substantial changes in the instruction's overall readability. The following subsections explain each technique, taking you through a plan of attack for clarifying jury instructions.

Regarding when to prepare jury instructions, the authorities are in agreement: frame jury instructions as soon as possible, at least while preparing for trial.[28] This helps you focus on the points you need to make to win your case. It also helps you work out the wording of those points, so throughout the trial you can point toward the conclusion you want the jury to reach. You have much to gain and nothing to lose by starting early.

Choosing Instructions

When choosing instructions, you need to request all necessary instructions to avoid waiving them, but nevertheless you must be selective. A general guide is do not tell the jury things they do not need to know.[29] In your initial proposal for instructions, for example, do not include instructions for the jury to disregard the opposition's objections. Request those only after significant objections are made. When selecting instructions, keep the list as short as possible.[30] This is important because the jury, if overwhelmed, may give up and decide the case on their own.

The important points must not be lost in a mass of jury instructions. In general, keep the instructions to thirty minutes reading time (the length of the average sermon), shorter if possible.[31] You do need to prepare legally sufficient instructions, but this may not require a quantity of instructions.[32] Occasionally, you may need to choose from several applicable model instructions, perhaps even between those for civil and criminal cases. For example, in a criminal case, you may need an instruction to address the idea of "falsis in uno," the idea a jury may find a witness's testimony to be false generally if it has been shown to be false on a particular point. Perhaps your state has a model instruction on this point in its civil instructions, but not its criminal instructions. Rather than creating a new criminal instruction, consider adapting the civil model instruction to fit the circum-

28. A.H. Reid, *The Law of Instructions to Juries in Civil and Criminal Cases* 483 (3d ed. 1960). "Some courts request that the parties submit their instructions at the outset of the trial; others after all the evidence is in. Generally, approval of jury instructions occurs before closing arguments, so that the parties know better how to structure their last appeal to the jurors." Mark A. Dombroff, *Burdens, Inferences and Presumptions: A Tactical Perspective*, 8 Trial Dipl.J. 36 (1985).

29. Anthony Partridge, *When Judges Throw Gibberish at Jurors*, 8 Update of L.Rel.Ed. 7 (1974).

30. Reid, *supra* note 28, at 484.

31. Berdon, *Instructive Interrogatories, supra* note 18, at 390. "Few cases, if properly prepared, should require instruction taking more than twenty to thirty minutes to read." William Schwarzer, *supra* note 10, at 747. Also see Judge Learned Hand's comments supporting a trial judge's rejection of 366 requests for instructions in *United States v. Cohen*, 145 F.2d 82, 93 (2d Cir.1944).

32. Reid, *supra* note 30, at 484–85 n. 1.

stance. You may need to draw from both civil and criminal model instructions in quasi-criminal actions, such as some violations of municipal ordinances.

When choosing specific jury instructions, you should include instructions that:

(1) explain law critical to your theory or theories;

(2) explain your theories for damages, if applicable;

(3) include a special verdict if advantageous to your client;

(4) make your case hold up on appeal;

(5) forestall misunderstanding if you are quite sure something at trial will be likely to be misunderstood or misinterpreted by the jury;

(6) you believe the judge will want to submit and you want to revise to fit clearly with your client's position; and

(7) are needed to present a clear charge to the jury.

You will take the first four steps by determining what arguments you will make and what evidence you will present. They are an adaptation of the research and thought you invest as you write the research memo, the brief, or both. When choosing instructions, look to your jurisdiction's model instructions on your critical theories. The commentary accompanying these instructions may provide helpful guidelines and may also tell you what instructions are legally essential.[33]

As you move to step five, consider what aspects of the law or the case are likely to be confusing to a jury, and select instructions that forestall confusion. For example, assume you are representing the defendant in a negligence case in which the plaintiff slipped on a patch of ice in the defendant's driveway. Assume the defendant had scraped the ice off as best he could; there were patches of ice but also enough clear spots so the plaintiff could have avoided the ice. Finally, assume there were only two witnesses at the trial, the defendant and the plaintiff. In this case, along with the legally necessary instructions for negligence, you might include an instruction on comparative negligence. Because your opponent will raise this issue, you should include your version of this instruction so the judge can consider an instruction that is more favorably worded for your client.

---

33. For example, Schwarzer, *supra* note 10, at 748–49, states the following:

Case law suggests that, depending on the context, instructions on the following subjects may be mandatory regardless of whether they are requested:

1. Each essential element of the offense charged that is in issue and particularly the requisite intent;

2. The burden of proof and probably the presumption of innocence;

3. The need for caution in accepting uncorroborated testimony of an accomplice or an informer, at least where it may be suspect;

4. In a multiple conspiracy case, the restriction against using evidence from one conspiracy to prove another; and

5. The limitation on the use of a confession as evidence when voluntariness is in question.

Then, under the last two steps, include instructions you know the judge will want to include, either because this judge always includes them or because they are common in your jurisdiction. These may be the instructions you revise least, because it is hard to overcome the traditional wording. But try to revise them when the instruction's language does not communicate accurately to the jury.

When submitting the instructions, follow the format requested by the judge. If you have no sense of what format the judge prefers, put each instruction on a separate sheet of paper so the judge can re-order the instructions, insert others, or delete instructions easily. With each instruction, include relevant citations supporting the proposed instruction, which may come from statutes, appellate cases, dictionaries, law review articles, or other sources. This chapter's bibliography is a good starting point for finding this support. When you have each instruction typed, make its layout easy to read, using tabulation and double spacing as needed. This will help the judge, but it will also help your case by getting a clearer reading of your instructions to the jury.

Revising Instructions

When you have selected the instructions, your next task is to revise those instructions for understandability. "Jury instructions . . . are on average more successful as each additional drop of abstruseness or complexity is wrung out of them."[34] One way to approach this task without feeling overwhelmed is to divide the revision into the following ten steps.

1.   Delete any irrelevant information.
2.   Personalize the instructions.
3.   Substitute common spoken English wherever possible.
4.   Define any critical, uncommon words.
5.   Find all the lists in your instructions, structure each of them clearly, and move each list to the end of the sentence.
6.   Make sure all signal words are clear.
7.   Use verbs instead of nouns stating action.
8.   Put modifying phrases next to the words they modify.
9.   Delete unneeded negatives.
10. Divide or simplify any remaining complicated sentences.

Learning to use each of these techniques will give you the ability to improve the understandability of your instructions.

Delete Any Irrelevant Information

When using model instructions from your jurisdiction, delete any information irrelevant to your case.[35] For example, if your case involved a limousine, you would instruct as follows.

---

34. Wilcox, *supra* note 24, at 1177.

35. "Make things as simple as possible—but no simpler." Richard Hatch,

Any driver hired by a limousine service . . . .

rather than keeping all of the language in the original model instruction.

Any driver hired by a company that provides taxicabs, commercial vans, limousines, private trolleys, chartered buses, or other motorized vehicles for public transportation . . . .

This technique alone will make the instruction more focused on the case in question, and thus clearer. It also should reduce jurors' misunderstanding.[36]

Personalize the Instructions

Next, if allowed in your jurisdiction, personalize the instruction by adding the names of the persons, places, and things involved. This helps the jury by presenting a more concrete picture of the facts they must determine. For example, use the following instruction.

You must decide whether Mr. Oliveras should receive severance damages. If you decide that he should receive these damages, you must also decide how much money he should receive. When deciding these two questions, you should consider all the credible evidence relating to two things: (1) Mr. Oliveras's claim that his lot's market value was reduced when the state changed the highway's grade and (2) any other facts shown during the trial that affect the market value of his lot.

rather than the original, more abstract model.

In making your determination of severance damages, if any, you will consider all the credible evidence bearing upon the claimed diminution in market value of the land remaining as a result of the change of grade of the highway, as well as all other facts and circumstances shown, by the credible evidence in the case, to affect the market value of the remaining land.[37]

Personalizing the jury instructions helps the jury comprehend and use new information. Messages directed to persons inexperienced in the topic at hand are more effective when "links between actions and goals are stated explicitly." [38] Similarly, explanations of the law are more effective when linked explicitly to the specific facts of the case.

As you personalize, avoid phrasing that assumes guilt or innocence. For example, write

To determine whether the defendant failed to yield the right of way, you must answer the following questions. . . . .

Business Communication: Theory and Technique 77 (1977), quoting Albert Einstein.

36. As the number of relevant dimensions or variables in a problem increases, the complexity of the problem increases and also the chance for error. Lyle E.

Bourne, Jr., *Human Conceptual Behavior* 52 (1966).

37. Wis.Civ.J.I. 8110.

38. Hewes and Planalp, *supra* note 3, at 160.

If your answer to all of the questions is "yes," then you should find that the defendant did fail to yield the right of way. If, however, your answer to any one of the questions is "no," then you should find that the defendant did not fail to yield the right of way.[39]

rather than

You should find that the defendant failed to yield the right of way if . . . .

To keep jury instructions neutral, avoid using "you should find" at the beginning of a sentence; some judges are concerned that the phrase steers the jury toward a certain outcome.[40] The judge must be able to accept your instruction as a neutral statement of law.

Substitute Common Spoken English Wherever Possible

Substitute common language, or plain English, for legalese whenever you can. For example, write

You should also be aware that, during the course of a trial, the lawyers will often refer to and read from depositions. Depositions are *written copies* of testimony taken *after the lawsuit began but before this trial began.*[41]

rather than

You should also be aware that, during the course of a trial, the lawyers will often refer to and read from depositions. Depositions are *transcripts* of testimony taken *during the pendency* of a lawsuit.

Generally choose words used in everyday speech.[42] After you choose the clearest word, use that same word for the same idea throughout the instructions. This should help the reader understand how points are related. For example, write

The statutes further provide that when two *cars* approach an intersection . . . . If you find that the Smith *car* and the Jones *car* both . . . .

rather than

The statutes further provide that when two *vehicles* approach or enter an intersection . . . . If you find that the *automobiles* in question . . . .[43]

You may need to keep a legal term when it states the standard. For example, keep such words as "reasonable doubt" or "evidence that is clear, satisfactory, and convincing."

If you are working with a judge who is skittish about varying the wording of model instructions, try retaining key words from the origi-

---

39. Adapted from Wis.Civ.J.I. 1157.

40. *See Bursten v. United States,* 395 F.2d 976 (5th Cir.1968) and *Gibson v. Erie–Lackawanna R. Co.* 378 F.2d 476 (6th Cir. 1967) as cited in Devitt and Blackmar, *supra* note 16, at 243.

41. Wis.Civ.J.I. 50.

42. "The use of legal terminology in instructions should be avoided." Devitt and Blackmar, *supra* note 16, at 243.

43. Wis Civ.J.I. 1157.

nal instruction and focusing instead on inserting clearer structure and signal words. Often readers will not see the structural changes as critical as word changes, yet those structural changes can greatly increase the clarity of the content.

Define Any Critical, Uncommon Words

After you have identified terms that are necessary but perhaps unfamiliar, you can add definitions. Because the instructions will be read, you will probably not choose parentheses to mark your definition. You may, however, use a separate sentence, as in this example:

Beyond a reasonable doubt means. . . .

Or you might be able to use an added clause, if this does not make the sentence too complex, as in:

beyond a reasonable doubt, or. . . .

These approaches allow you to maintain your focus on the main point while explaining your term.

Find All Lists in Your Instructions, Structure Each of Them Clearly, and Move Each List to the End of the Sentence

To structure lists clearly, begin by explaining the structure and purpose of the list in an introductory phrase. For example, you may begin with the following.

In order to find the defendant guilty, you must find that all three of the following are true:

This introduction tells the jury when it must use the information, (to find the defendant guilty), how many items are on the list (three), and how the list is structured (they must find all items, not any one). With this overview in mind, each juror has a better chance of remembering the information so he or she can apply it.

Then end the sentence after the list. A list presents the reader with enough information for one sentence. For example, write the following version.

> **In some situations, the law allows a jury to infer that a defendant was negligent in making an item based solely on the evidence of the accident caused by that item. In this case, if you find both of the following to be true, you may infer that Ms. Henderson was negligent when she wove the plant hangar that broke:**
>
> **(1) Ms. Henderson had exclusive control of the production of the macrame plant hangar that broke when the plant was placed in it and**
>
> **(2) the hangar would not have broken when a plant was placed in it if Ms. Henderson had exercised the ordinary care a macrame weaver should exercise.**

rather than the original

If you find that defendant had exclusive control of the production of the items involved in the accident and if you further find that the accident claimed is of a type or kind that ordinarily would not have occurred had the defendant exercised ordinary care, then you may infer from the accident itself and the surrounding circumstances that there was negligence on the part of the defendant.

Finally, look at the items in the list and make sure they are all needed, logically parallel, and written in parallel form.

If you find that Ms. Jamison exercised due care, then you must find in her favor. To find that Ms. Jamison did exercise due care, you must find all of the following:

(1) she noticed the warning sign on the sidewalk,

(2) she stepped carefully around the blockade,

(3) she at no time walked within the area marked as dangerous,

(4) she . . . .

Because lists are essential to many instructions, taking time to structure and word each list carefully helps you ensure the instruction's clarity.

Use Signal Words as Needed to Clarify Structure

Clear signals of sentence organization operate like the glowing flashlight covers used by parking lot attendants at a stadium to direct you to your parking spot. One waves you left, another right, through the lot to the next available space. Similarly, signals guide the reader or listener through an instruction, past explanations, through conditions, and ultimately to the main point.[44] Examples of such signals are "if" and "then," "only if," "all of the following," and "after." Although punctuation and visual aids serve as signals in other writing, they offer little help with the oral challenge of jury instructions.

You will probably find you use more verbal signals in jury instructions than in other writing. For example, the following instruction makes effective use of a series of signals.

_If_ you choose to, you _may_ take notes about the evidence during this trial. _But_ it is your choice. _If_ you do take notes, _then_ you _must_ be careful that taking those notes does not distract you from carefully listening to and observing the witnesses.

---

44. Indeed, their power is so strong that it sometimes overrides content. In an experiment in 1984, students were instructed to cut in front in a line at the copying machine; the variable was whether they offered no reason, said "because I am in a rush," or added the redundant "because I have to make some copies." The number of persons allowing the student to cut in front was higher when the student added a "because" phrase, but was equally high with either of the two "because" phrases. Herbert W. Simons, *Persuasion: Understanding, Practice, and Analysis* 55 (2d ed. 1986).

Compare it with the following.

> You are not required to but you may take notes of the evidence during this trial. In taking notes, you must be careful that it does not distract you from carefully listening to and observing the witnesses.[45]

You also might write the following

> **A hospital employee has the duty to provide a patient with *whatever* services, care, and attention that patient reasonably requires under the circumstances.**

or this

> ***If* a patient in a hospital has a reasonable need for any required services, care, or attention, *then in that case* a hospital employee has the duty to provide them.**

rather than

> A hospital employee has the duty to provide *such* services, care, and attention *as* a patient reasonably required under the circumstances.[46]

These clear signals are particularly helpful when the law differs from what the jury might expect; the signals help increase the chance that the jury will see the distinction being made.[47] In some jurisdictions, the jury does not receive written copies of instructions. If this is so in your jurisdiction, then you need to be especially sure that you use clear verbal signals. Your listeners must be able to hear the organization of the instructions, because they will not have the text as a reference while deliberating.

Use Verbs Instead of Nouns Stating Action

Using verbs rather than nouns makes it easier for the jury to see what you mean.[48] Verbs communicate an action, something that the listener can imagine. This vision creates a more concrete image, so the point is more easily remembered. Use verbs to state actions important to the meaning of the sentence. If you cannot use a verb, state the meaning as the object of some form of "to be," a linking verb. Avoid nominalization, or making the verb into a noun. For example, write

> **If the employee *failed* to perform this duty, the hospital *is negligent.***

45. Based on Wis.Civ.J.I. 61, with one sentence not relevant to the point omitted.

46. Wis.Civ.J.I. 1385.

47. "Messages targeted to naive readers might be designed to emphasize how the new information is different from what they might expect." Hewes and Planalp, *supra* note 3, at 160.

48. Rulon Wells, "Nominal and Verbal Style" in *Style in Language* 213–220 (T. Sebeok ed. 1960).

rather than

A failure to perform this duty is negligence.

Nouns that state actions are less effective because they are harder to understand. It takes a reader or listener longer to process these nominalizations than verbs, suggesting that the reader has to work harder mentally to understand the word's meaning.[49] Out of consideration, you can do this work for your jury.

Put Modifying Phrases Next to the Words They Modify

The human mind can keep only a limited number of things in active thought at one time.[50] Group your information. Because modifying phrases are commonly used to group information, your handling of these phrases is important.

Modifying phrases are groups of words that work together to add information about another word. For example, "of the participants" is a modifying phrase in "one of the participants," and "with evidence that is clear and convincing" is a modifier in "must convince you beyond a reasonable doubt with evidence that is clear and convincing." The latter example illustrates the problem; "with evidence . . ." modifies "convince," but that is not easy for the reader or listener to understand because other words intervene. Although you cannot always place a modifying phrase next to the word it modifies, do so whenever possible. For example, the first instruction that follows is much easier to understand than the second.

in other previous use of the premises. . . .

rather than

in the previous use of the premises by others. . . .

Similarly, the following sentence is easier to understand if the modifiers are untangled.

An owner of an automobile when granting permission to another for use of the automobile may restrict or limit the length of time or the kind of use to which the automobile is to be put by the one borrowing it.

When granting permission for another to use an automobile, the owner of that automobile may place restrictions on the automobile's use. The owner may limit the length of time the one borrowing it may use it. The owner may also restrict the purposes for which the automobile may be used.

If you have trouble placing modifiers next to the word modified, consider whether you are trying to put too much information in one sentence. If so, divide the sentence, as discussed in a later section.

49. Charrow and Charrow, *supra* note 8, at 1321–1322.

50. Research suggests that adults may remember as few as five or as many as seven groups of information. Carl Bereiter and Marlene Scardamalia, *The Psychology of Written Composition* 93–176 (1987).

Delete Unneeded Negatives

Use negatives only when needed. Because negative statements take longer for the reader or listener to process,[51] they decrease the understandability of the content. You will need to use some negatives in your instructions, but you can minimize their use. For example, instead of writing "if you determine that the defendant could not have failed to be able to see," write **"if you determine that the defendant must have been able to see."** Subtler forms of the negative are particularly difficult to understand,[52] so especially minimize the use of words listeners will not recognize as negative, such as "unless" or "failure," and negative prefixes, such as "un-." By doing what you can to reduce negatives, you reduce the burden on the jury.

Finally, use only one negative at a time. For example, write

> **An "implied warranty" is a warranty that arises legally from either the parties' acts or circumstances of the transaction. It requires no intent or particular language or action by the seller to create it.**

> . . . . *The warranty, however, does not apply to any use. If the user of the product put it to some use other than that for which it was sold, the warranty will not apply. If the user did not use it according to the directions, the warranty will not apply.*

rather than

> An "implied warranty" is a warranty that arises by operation of law from the acts of the parties or circumstances of the transaction. It requires no intent or particular language or action by the seller to create it.

> . . . . There is no breach of warranty if the product sold is put to a use for which the product was not intended or used not in accordance with the directions given as to its use.

Divide or Simplify Any Remaining Complicated Sentences

Finally, make sure you do not have too much action in one sentence. Divide important points to explain the law one step at a time. For example, in the earlier revision of an instruction with many negatives, the instruction was divided into several shorter sentences.

> **The warranty, however, does not apply to any use. If the user of the product put it to some use other than for which it was sold, the warranty will not apply. If the user did not use it according to the directions, the warranty will not apply.**

51. Charrow and Charrow, *supra* note   **52.** *Id.* at 1325.
8, at 1324–1325, 1337.

rather than

> There is no breach of warranty if the product sold is put to a use for which the product was not intended or used not in accordance with the directions given as to its use.

Your goal here is not simply to make sentences shorter, but to make sure they do not include more concepts than the jury can manage at once. Because a person can process only a limited amount of information in one reading of a sentence, you must limit the number of ideas in each sentence. If you include too many, you force the reader or listener to forget some of the information,[53] no matter how carefully you have placed your modifying phrases.

Finally, shorter sentences help the judge, who has to read these sentences aloud; he or she needs to reach the period before reaching the end of a breath. This step is last because it allows you to check for long sentences after your other revisions are made, so long sentences have no opportunity to insinuate their way back into your instructions. Reading the text for long sentences also allows you to move away from looking at individual words and move back to looking at the overall effect of the instructions. This review is your opportunity to see if you have synthesized the ten techniques into a workable whole. It also allows you to appreciate the cumulative benefits of many small improvements, an awareness that will be useful when you work with longer units of text, such as arguments and research reports.

CONCLUSION

The following two checklists summarize the techniques discussed in the chapter.

When choosing jury instructions, follow these steps.

1. Include instructions that explain law critical to your theory or theories.

2. Include instructions that explain your theories for damages, if applicable.

3. Determine whether a special verdict would be advantageous to your client and, if so, draft this.

4. Include instructions needed to make your case hold up on appeal.

5. If you are quite sure that something at trial will be likely to be misunderstood or misinterpreted by the jury, choose instructions to forestall misunderstanding. Examples of this would be when the defendant does not testify or when the opposition will emphasize some fact that you argue is irrelevant. If the problem only might arise, wait and submit the instruction later if needed.

---

53. George Gopen, *Let the Buyer In Or-dinary Business Beware: Suggestions for*   *Revising the Prose of the Uniform Commercial Code,* 54 U.Chi.L.Rev. 1178 (1987).

6. Include any general instructions that you believe the judge will want to submit and that you want to revise to fit clearly with your client's position.

7. Include any other instructions needed to present a clear charge to the jury.

When revising the instructions you have chosen, follow these steps.

1. Delete any irrelevant information.

2. Personalize the instructions.

3. Substitute common spoken English wherever possible.

4. Define any critical, uncommon words.

5. Find all lists, structure them clearly, and move each list to the end of a sentence.

6. Make sure all signal words are clear.

7. Use verbs instead of nouns when stating actions.

8. Put modifying phrases next to the words they modify.

9. Delete unneeded negatives.

10. Divide or simplify any remaining complicated sentences.

EXERCISE

Modify the following jury instructions to make them more understandable and applicable to the situation described below. (These instructions are adapted from several states' model instructions.)

The Situation

You are defending Dan Zimmerman against a charge of theft of an automobile, among other charges. Dan Zimmerman is an eighteen-year-old who earns money by mowing lawns for several people. John Hartwig, an adult neighbor, often allows Dan to borrow his pick-up truck to transport Dan's lawnmower to these jobs. On one occasion, John let Dan borrow it for another reason. Before using the truck, Dan always asked to use it, and Dan did not have a key to the truck. While John was on vacation for two weeks, however, he gave Dan keys to his truck so Dan could use it if needed to transport his lawnmower to a job. In return, Dan agreed to mow John's lawn.

While John was on vacation, Dan drove the pick-up truck around town several evenings. On one evening, Dan tried drag racing in the truck on a city street, lost control, ran into a street light, demolished the truck, and broke three ribs.

The Instructions

3112   Owner's Permission for Use of Automobile

A person who obtains the consent or permission of the owner of a motor vehicle for the use of that motor vehicle has the right to use it as long as he makes no substantial deviation from the initial permission granted. Permission may be granted expressly, or permission may be implied from all the circumstances surrounding the relationship between the persons involved, including the purpose for which the car is to be used under such permission.

An owner of an automobile when granting permission to another for use of the automobile may restrict or limit the length of time or the kind of use to which the automobile is to be put by the one borrowing it.

(A person who has borrowed a car with permission of the owner may allow another person to drive it unless expressly prohibited by the owner from so doing, and so long as such driving is within the scope of the permission granted by the owner. Any express prohibition by the owner against another person driving must be recognized by the jury as binding the borrower.)

The scope or extent of the permission must be determined from the understanding, either express or implied, between the owner and the borrower as to the purpose of the borrowing and as to the limitations, if any, placed upon the permission given by the owner. This understanding is to be determined from all the facts and circumstances surrounding the giving of permission.

It is for you, the jury, to determine whether under the facts of this case the owner restricted the permission given by limiting the time or purpose of such use, and if there were restrictions on such permission, whether the borrower made a substantial deviation from the permission given by retaining and using the vehicle beyond the time limitation set or for a purpose other than the one for which permission was granted.

As used in these instructions, a "substantial deviation" means a gross deviation from the terms of permission, thereby definitely exceeding the scope of the use of the car that was in contemplation by the parties at the time it was loaned.

It is for you to determine whether the borrower was granted initial permission to use the car, and if so, what if any limitations were placed upon such use, and whether or not the borrower made any substantial deviation from the permission granted.

324.02.1 Stealing: Without Consent

((As to Count _____, if) (If you do not find the defendant guilty of felony stealing as submitted in Instruction No. _____, you must consider whether he is guilty of misdemeanor stealing.)

(As to Count _____, if) (If you find and believe from the evidence beyond a reasonable doubt;

First, (on) (on or about) [date], in the (City) (County) of _____, State of Wisconsin, the defendant (took) (obtained) (used) (retained Possession) (transferred) (concealed) [Describe property or services], property (owned by) (in the possession of) (in the charge of) (operated by) [name of victim], and

Second, the defendant did so without the consent of [name of victim], and

Third, the defendant did so for the purpose of [Insert one of the following. Omit brackets and number.]

> [1] (withholding it from the owner permanently) (,) (or) (using or disposing of it in such a way that made recovery by the owner unlikely,)

> [2] restoring it only upon payment of reward or other thing of value,

> [3] depriving the owner of such services, and

Fourth, [Insert one of the following. Omit brackets and number.]

> [1] the (property) (services) so (taken) (obtained) (used) (retained) (concealed) (transferred) (has) (have) a (combined) value of at least one hundred fifty dollars,

> [2] the property was physically taken from the person of [name of victim],

> [3] the property (taken) (obtained) (used) (retained) (concealed) (transferred) was [Insert any type of property from the list in Section 570.030.2(3).],

then you will find the defendant guilty (under Count _____) of (felony) (misdemeanor) stealing.

However, unless you find and believe from the evidence beyond a reasonable doubt each and all of these propositions, you must find the defendant not guilty of offense.

If you do find the defendant guilty (under Count _____) of (felony) (misdemeanor) stealing, you will assess and declare one of the following punishments:

. . .

101.2

If in these instructions any rule, direction, or idea is repeated or stated in varying ways, no emphasis thereon is intended by me and none must be inferred by you.

102.5

As to any questions to which an objection was sustained, you must not speculate as to what the answer might have been or as to the reason for the objection.

ASSIGNMENT 1

You are a new associate at the law firm of Sazama and Osberg in Pleasantview, Wisconsin. The firm represents the city in all legal matters.

On October 11, 1989, two employees of the waste water treatment plant went to the sewer access hole outside Henry's Fine Laundry Service to set up equipment to test the water the Laundry Service was discharging into the public sewers. While they were at the access hole, one of the employees discovered that water was backing up in the sewer. He investigated and discovered a sixteen ounce measuring cup and several rags lodged in the pipe leading from the laundry service to the sewer.

The treatment plant supervisor sent the attached report to the firm. On behalf of the city, the firm asked the police department to issue a citation against Henry's Fine Laundry Service for violating section 8–5–6(c)(4) of the city ordinances (attached).

The case will go to trial in March. Ms. Sazama has asked you to put together the jury instructions the city will submit to the judge at the final pre-trial conference.

You must write the instruction that explains the elements of city ordinance 8–5–6(c)(4) to the jury. The burden of proof is "reasonable certainty" established by evidence that is "clear, satisfactory, and convincing."

Also, you must review the following five criminal jury instructions: 100, 460, 480, 2050, and 2055. Revise the instructions to make them more accurate and readable. Put the six instructions in the order in which you want them read to the jury.

———

CITY OF PLEASANTVIEW, WI

WASTE WATER TREATMENT PLANT

WWTP　　　　　　　　　　　　**CITY HALL**

West 8th St.—10th Ave. West　　　　　　Box 200
Pleasantview, WI　　　　　　　　　　Pleasantview, WI
　　　　　　　　　　　　　　　　　October 12, 1989

SUBJECT: Henry's Fine Laundry Service, Inc.

On the morning of Oct. 11, 1989, Thomas Burkhalter and I, Richard Vincent, were directed to perform industrial sampling equipment set-up at three industries. They were Henry's Fine Laundry Service, Anderson Rubber Mills, and Greasy Joe's French Fry Co.

Our first sampling set-up site was to be the laundry service. We arrived at the site at about 8:15 a.m. The weir had not been placed in the sampling equipment van; therefore Thomas had to return to the waste water treatment plant to pick up the weir. This period of time allowed me to set up the sampler and flow meter in the above-ground sampling equipment box and to read the laundry's water meters.

Thomas returned to the site at 8:35 a.m. with the weir. We then resumed standard set-up and calibration procedures. I entered the access hole after checking the air quality and found about nine inches of water backed up in the access hole. There seemed to be some obstruction at the point where the water normally flows out of the access hole to the main sewer line.

When these articles were removed, the water flowed away freely and there was no further flooding during the time that I was in the sampling access hole.

The articles were placed on the ground near the access hole and observed by Thomas and a laundry service employee. The articles were then placed in a sampler cover and placed in the sampling van. The collection of articles was brought back to the waste water treatment plant at 10:30 a.m. They were placed in a plastic bag and refrigerated. They were later transported by Superintendent Ellefson to the Pleasantview Police Department.

> Richard Vincent
> WWTP Operator
>
> Thomas Burkhalter
> WWTP Operator

ORDINANCES of the CITY of PLEASANTVIEW WISCONSIN

8-5-6 USE OF THE PUBLIC SEWERS:

(A) Sanitary Sewers: No person(s) shall discharge or cause to be discharged any unpolluted waters such as storm water, ground water, roof run-off, sub-surface drainage, or noncontact cooling water to any sanitary sewer.

(B) Storm Sewers: Storm water and all other unpolluted water shall be discharged to such sewers as are specifically designated as storm sewers, or to a natural outlet approved by the Approving Authority and other regulatory agencies. Unpolluted industrial cooling water or process waters may be discharged, on approval of the Approving Authority and/or other regulatory agencies, to a storm sewer, or natural outlet.

(C) Prohibitions and Limitations: Except as hereinafter provided, no person shall discharge or cause to be discharged any of the following described waters or wastes to any public sewer:

    1. Any gasoline, benzene, naphtha, fuel oil, or other flammable or explosive liquid, solid, or gas.

    2. Any waters or wastes containing toxic or poisonous solids, liquids, or gases in sufficient quantity, either singly or by interaction with other wastes, that could injure or interfere with any waste treatment or sludge disposal process, constitute a hazard to humans or animals, or create a public nuisance in the receiving waters of the wastewater treatment facility.

    3. Any waters or wastes having a pH lower than 5.5, or in excess of 9.0, or having any corrosive property capable of causing damage of hazard to structures, equipment, and personnel of the wastewater collection and treatment facility.

4. Solid or viscous substances in quantities or of such size capable of causing obstruction to the flow in public sewers or other interference with the proper operation of the wastewater collection and treatment facilities, such as, but not limited to, ashes, cinders, sand, mud, straw, shavings, metal, glass, rags, feathers, tar, plastics, wood, unground garbage, whole blood, paunch manure, hair and fleshings, entrails, and paper dishes, cups, milk containers, etc., either whole or ground by garbage grinders.

5. The following described substances, materials, waters, or waste shall be limited in discharges to sanitary sewer systems to concentrations or quantities which will not harm either the sanitary sewers, wastewater treatment process, or equipment, will not have an adverse effect on the receiving stream, or will not otherwise endanger lives, limbs, public property, or constitute a nuisance. The Approving Authority may set limitations more stringent than those established below if such more stringent limitations are necessary to meet the above objectives. The Approving Authority will give consideration to the quantity of subject waste in relation to flows and velocities in the sewers, materials of construction of the sanitary sewers, the wastewater treatment facility and other pertinent factors. No person shall discharge any of the following waste materials into any City sewer:

a. Any liquid or vapor having a temperature higher than one hundred forty degrees (140 degrees) (60 degrees Celsius).

b. Any wastewater containing more than twenty-five (25) mg./1. of petroleum oil, nonbiodegradable cutting oils, or products of mineral origin; wastewater containing more than one hundred (100) mg./1. of nonpetroleum based oils such as animal or vegetable oil or fats. The method for determining grease and oil content shall be as stated in the current edition of Standard Methods.

WIS JI–CRIMINAL

100 OPENING INSTRUCTIONS

Members of the Jury:

The court will now instruct you upon the principles of law which you are to follow in considering the evidence and in reaching your verdict.

In applying these instructions, keep in mind the following:

First, you should consider all instructions.

Second, you should consider the instructions as a whole and apply them to the evidence.

Third, the fact that the instructions are given in a particular order does not mean one is more important than the other.

Take the law as it is given in the judge's instructions and apply that law to the facts in the case which are properly proven by the evidence. Consider only the evidence received during this trial and the law as given to you by these instructions and from these alone, guided by your soundest reason and best judgment, reach your verdict.

If any member of the jury has an impression of my opinion as to whether the defendant is guilty or not guilty, disregard such impression entirely and decide the issues of fact solely as you view the evidence. You, the jury, are the sole judges of the facts, and the court is the judge of the law only.

460 CLOSING INSTRUCTION

Now, members of the jury, the duties of counsel and the Court have been performed. The case has been argued by counsel. The Court has instructed you regarding the rules of law which should govern you in your deliberations. The time has now come when the great burden of reaching a just, fair, and conscientious decision of this case is to be thrown wholly upon you, the jurors, selected for this important duty. You will not be swayed by sympathy, prejudice, or passion. You will be very careful and deliberate in weighing the evidence. I charge you to keep your duty steadfastly in mind, and as upright citizens, to render a just and true verdict. [Give instructions on the verdicts submitted.]

480 VERDICTS SUBMITTED FOR ONE DEFENDANT: SINGLE COUNT

The following two forms of verdict will be submitted to you for your consideration concerning the charges against the defendant (*name of defendant*).

One reading: "We, the jury, find the defendant, (*name of defendant*), guilty of (*name offense charged*), as charged in the (information) (complaint)."

And the other reading: "We, the jury, find the defendant, (*name of defendant*), not guilty."

It is for you to determine which one of the forms of verdict submitted you will bring in as your verdict.

2050 BURDEN OF PROOF: FORFEITURE ACTIONS

In determining the guilt or innocence of the defendant, you should scrutinize the evidence with the utmost care and caution. You should act with all the judgment, reason, prudence, and discrimination you possess. The burden of proving the defendant guilty of every element of the offense charged is upon the (City) (County) of _____. Such burden is to satisfy or convince you to a reasonable certainty by evidence that is clear, satisfactory, and convincing that the defendant is guilty as charged in the (complaint) (information).

If after a fair consideration of all the evidence bearing on the question, you become so satisfied or convinced that the defendant is guilty, then you should find him guilty but if not so satisfied or convinced, you should find the defendant not guilty.

2055 FIVE–SIXTHS VERDICT: FORFEITURE ACTIONS

The law provides that a verdict in a civil case like this one agreed to by five-sixths or more of the jury shall be the verdict of the jury. Any verdict returned by the jury shall be agreed to by at least ten of the jurors. I ask you to try to be unanimous if you can. At the foot of the verdict, you will find a place provided where dissenting jurors, if there be any, will sign their names. Either the blank lines or the space below them may be used for that purpose.

ASSIGNMENT 2

Write a jury instruction for Wis.Stat. § 346.935(3), which describes the offense of keeping open intoxicants in a motor vehicle. The burden of proof is "reasonable certainty" provided by evidence that is "clear, satisfactory, and convincing." Assume you are the assistant district attorney for Central County and tailor your instruction to fit the following facts. Then revise the following model instructions 160, 200, 300, and 327, assuming Mark Friske is the defendant. [These instructions were selected for their variety; in reality, they might not all be used at the trial.]

On November 14, 1986, Central County Sheriff's Deputy Beth Radke stopped a 1974 Ford Mustang, which was travelling on Highway 69, because both tail lights were not working. As Deputy Radke approached the car, she noted that there was a great deal of movement by the people in it.

Radke got the driver's license from the driver, Mark Friske, 22. As she was telling him about his defective tail lights, she detected a strong odor of beer coming from inside the car.

Radke radioed for a back-up, and Deputy Arthur Gordee arrived shortly. They searched the car and found seven open beer cans, eleven unopened beer cans, and two large wet spots that smelled strongly of beer on the carpet under the front seat. They determined that Friske's father was the owner of the car. The passengers in the car were David Granstrom, 22, and Steven Granstrom, 21. Deputy Radke gave Mark Friske a citation for violating Wis.Stat. § 346.935(3)

346.935 Intoxicants in motor vehicles. (1) No person may drink alcohol beverages in any motor vehicle when the vehicle is upon a highway. (2) No person may possess on his or her person, in a privately owned motor vehicle upon a public highway, any bottle or receptacle containing alcohol beverages if the bottle or receptacle has been opened, the seal has been broken or the contents of the bottle or receptacle have been partially removed. (3) The owner of a privately owned motor vehicle, or the driver of the vehicle, shall not keep, or allow to be kept in the motor vehicle when it is upon a highway any bottle or receptacle containing alcohol beverages if the bottle or receptacle has been opened, the seal has been broken or the contents of the bottle or receptacle have been partially removed. This subsection does not apply if the bottle or receptacle is kept in the trunk of the vehicle or, if the vehicle has no trunk, in some other area of the vehicle not normally occupied by the driver or passengers. A utility compartment or glove compartment is considered to be within the area normally occupied by the driver and passengers.

WI JI–CRIMINAL

160 ARGUMENTS OF COUNSEL

Consider carefully the closing arguments of the attorneys but their arguments and conclusions and opinions are not evidence. Draw your own conclusions and your own inferences from the evidence, and decide upon your verdict according to the evidence, under the instructions given you by the court.

200 EXPERT TESTIMONY: GENERAL

The general rule is that a witness may testify only to facts known by him. A witness, however, who has special knowledge, experience, skill, training, or education in a particular profession or occupation is permitted to give an opinion as an expert in the field. In determining the weight to be given to the opinion of an expert, you should consider the qualifications and credibility of the expert, whether the opinion is based upon established facts or agreed facts in the case, and the reasons given for the opinion. Such evidence is received for the purpose of aiding you in arriving at a conclusion, if it does aid you. You are not bound by the opinion of any expert. You should consider carefully the opinion evidence with all the other evidence in the case, giving to it just such weight as you decide it is entitled to receive.

300 CREDIBILITY OF WITNESSES

It is the duty of the jury to scrutinize and weigh the testimony of witnesses and to determine the effect of the evidence as a whole. You are the sole judges of the credibility of the several witnesses and of the weight and credit to be given to their testimony.

In determining the weight and credit you should give to the testimony of each witness, you should consider his interest or lack of interest in the result of this trial, his conduct, appearance and demeanor on the witness stand, his bias or prejudice, if any has been shown, the clearness or lack of clearness of his recollections, his opportunity for observing and knowing the matters and things testified to by him, and the reasonableness of his testimony.

You should also take into consideration the apparent intelligence of each witness, the possible motives for falsifying, and all other facts and circumstances appearing on the trial which tend either to support or to discredit his testimony, and then give to the testimony of each witness such weight and credit as you believe it fairly entitled to receive.

[GIVE THE FOLLOWING PARAGRAPH ONLY WHEN THE DEFEN-
DANT TESTIFIES.]   (Assume Friske will testify.)

[Under the law a defendant is a competent witness in his own
behalf, and you should not discredit his testimony merely because he is
charged with a crime.   His testimony should be weighed as the testimony of any other witness; considerations of interest, appearance, manner
and other matters bearing upon credibility apply to the defendant in
common with all witnesses.]

327   IMPEACHMENT OF DEFENDANT AS A WITNESS: PRIOR CONVICTION

Evidence has been received to the effect that the defendant
_____ has heretofore been convicted of a crime.   This evidence was so
received solely because it bears upon the credibility of the defendant as
a witness.   The fact of conviction is one that you may take into
consideration in weighing his testimony and determining his credibility.   It must not be used for any other purpose, and, particularly, you
should bear in mind that conviction of the defendant of a crime at some
previous time is no proof that he is guilty of the offense with which he
is now charged.

Bibliography

Berdon, Robert I., *Instructive Interrogatories: One Method To Aid the Jury,* 8 Bridge.L.Rev. 385 (1984).

Bereiter, Carl and Marlene Scardamalia, Part II of *The Psychology of Written Composition.*   Hillsdale, NJ: Lawrence Erlbaum Associates, 1987.

Berger, Charles R. and Steven H. Chaffee, *Handbook of Communication Science.*   Newbury Park, CA: Sage Publications, 1987.

Bourne, Lyle E., Jr., *Human Conceptual Behavior.*   Boston: Allyn and Bacon, 1966.

Buchanan, Raymond W., *The Florida Judge–Jury Communications Project,* 8 Bridge.L.Rev. 297 (1984).

Charrow, Robert P. and Veda R., *Making Legal Language Understandable: A Psycholinguistic Study of Jury Instructions,* 79 Colum.L.Rev. 1306 (1979).

Devitt, Edward J. and Charles Blackmar, *Federal Jury Practice and Instructions.*   St. Paul: West Publishing Co., 1977.

Dombroff, Mark A., *Burdens, Inferences and Presumptions: A Tactical Perspective,* 6 Trial Dip.J. 36 (1985).

Douthwaite, Graham, *Jury Instructions, Pattern and Otherwise,* 29 Def. L.J. 335 (1980).

Gopen, George, *Let the Buyer in Ordinary Course of Business Beware: Suggestions for Revising the Price of the Uniform Commercial Code,* 54 Univ.Chi.L.Rev. 1178 (1987).

Hatch, Richard, *Business Communication: Theory and Technique.* Chicago: Science Research Associates, Inc., 1977.

Mellinkoff, David. *Legal Writing: Sense and Nonsense.* St. Paul: West Publishing Co., 1982.

Mellinkoff, David. *The Language of the Law.* Boston: Little Brown and Company, 1990.

Partridge, Anthony, *When Judges Throw Gibberish at Jurors,* 8 Update on L.Rel.Ed. (1984).

Perlman, Harvey S., *Pattern Jury Instructions: The Application of Social Science Research,* 65 Neb.L.R. 520 (1986).

Reid, Judge A.H., *The Law of Instructions to Juries in Civil and Criminal Cases.* Indianapolis: Bobbs–Merrill, 1960.

Schwarzer, William W., *Communicating with Juries: Problems and Remedies,* 69 Cal.L.Rev. 731 (1981).

Sebeok, Thomas, A. Ed., *Style in Language.* Cambridge, MA: M.I.T. Press, 1960.

Severence, Lawrence J. and Elizabeth F. Loftus, *Improving the Ability of Jurors to Comprehend and Apply Criminal Jury Instructions* 17 L.Soc'y 153 (1982).

Simons, Herbert W., *Persuasion: Understanding, Practice, and Analysis.* New York: Random House, 2d. ed. 1986.

Wilcox, Jamison, *The Craft of Drafting Plain–Language Jury Instructions: A Study of a Sample Pattern Instruction on Obscenity,* 59 Temp.L.Q. 1159 (1986).

Wisconsin Civil Model Jury Instructions, 1978 Supplement, 1960 edition.

Chapter 5

CONTRACTS

If writing legal documents were sporting events, then writing contracts would be a long distance, high hurdles, relay race. It would be long distance because the drafter must express the parties' expectations and duties toward one another over the long term, given numerous unexpected contingencies. It would be the high hurdles because lurking everywhere are problems that can cause the drafter to land on the wrong foot, lose his or her stride, and crash into a barrier. Finally, it would be a relay race because the parties and the drafter must work in synchronized motions to ensure that the result is one everyone on the team desires. To succeed, the drafter must produce a contract signifying the mutual understanding of the parties, and thus the drafter must work with the parties to complete this team event.

A contract is private legislation between the parties. It delineates the obligations of all parties to the contract and provides for contingencies that may arise during the contractual term, especially if it is a long-term contract. The parties want this private legislation to shape their agreement; the contract cannot fulfill its purpose if the parties must consult an outside source, especially one as time-consuming and expensive as a court, to mediate their differences.

Careful drafting can prevent problems that otherwise might have to be settled in court. Avoiding problems, however, requires an unrelenting willingness to take care while drafting. If the parties disagree about even so much as one word, they can find themselves facing expensive and lengthy litigation, as happened in a case resulting from a misunderstanding between the parties about what was meant by "chicken" in a purchase contract.[1] The contract was dated May 2, 1957; the court's decision was delivered in 1960. Three years were spent and a full trial was held, only to have the plaintiff's case dismissed. If the parties had included a definition section in their contract and had taken the time to come to an agreement on the meaning of "chicken," they could have avoided the expense and aggravation of being embroiled in a lawsuit for three years.

1. *Frigaliment Importing Co. v. B.N.S. International Sales Corp.*, 190 F.Supp. 116 (S.D.N.Y.1960).

Careful drafting of the contract can help the parties ascertain what they actually want from the agreement and whether they will be able to achieve their objectives. For example, if the parties above had tried to clarify what each meant by "chicken," they might have discovered they were unable to come to an agreement. But once they determined that they could not achieve a mutual understanding of the term, they could have gone their separate ways. They could have contracted with others to provide the goods or services desired, rather than discovering their disagreement during the course of the contract and then having to litigate.

Careful choice of other terms, such as articles, prepositions, and conjunctions, also could have avoided the litigation that has occurred hundreds of times.[2] For example, the meaning of "about" had been litigated in more than 150 cases by 1930.[3] Courts have used at least thirteen methods to interpret the meaning of words in various contexts, including literal interpretation, etymology, technical meaning, dictionary meaning, context, and interpretation based on intent or fact.[4] The varying interpretations that can be accorded to even one word illustrate how important each word is to the meaning of the contract.

This chapter focuses on teaching you to write a contract using writing techniques that will help you ensure the contract conveys your client's meaning. First, it discusses the general writing concerns you must address when drafting a contract. Then it explains the steps you need to complete before starting to draft and the steps needed during the drafting process. Finally, it provides exercises to help you practice incorporating these concerns and steps when drafting a contract.

This chapter also includes a checklist of some of the clauses you should consider including in your contract. By using a checklist, you will be able to draft contracts across a wide range of specific situations and be assured that you have included the clauses needed in each situation. This chapter, however, cannot cover all the points presented in the myriad books and articles addressing contract drafting. Some of these sources provide examples of selected contract provisions; some address the special concerns for drafting specific types of contracts, such as works-in-progress or entertainment contracts.[5]

WRITING TECHNIQUES FOR CONTRACTS

While statutes and jury instructions focus on word choice and sentence structure, contracts add larger scale concerns. Two primary concerns vital to effective contract drafting are thoroughness and consistency. Both concerns foster the same result: the contract, as a

2. Note, *Avoiding Inadvertent Syntactic Ambiguity in Legal Draftsmanship,* 20 Drake L.Rev. 137, 138 (1970).

3. *Id.* at 138, n. 11.

4. *Id.*

5. We have listed sources in the bibliography at the end of the chapter to provide you with further information about particular drafting problems. This chapter does not include examples of particular contract provisions; look to a form book for that assistance. But always remember to revise the clauses you find in the form books so that they apply to your client's particular situation.

written document, accurately presents the relationship the parties will have over the life of the contract.[6] Thus, the contract will thoroughly cover all the details that comprise the parties' expectations of their agreement and will state that agreement consistently throughout.

Thoroughness results from spending time thinking through the purposes of the contract. To achieve thoroughness, ask yourself questions such as these.

1. What needs to be included to state the parties' working relationship if all goes well?

2. What are the concerns of each party and what is needed in the contract to meet those concerns?

3. What are the possible problems that could arise?

4. What needs to be included to resolve any of these problems?

5. What changes or events in the future may affect the performance of the contract?

6. What remedies are needed in the event of breach or default?

7. What miscellaneous clauses need to be included to make the agreement function?

Asking yourself these questions will help you envision everything you need to include, allowing you to enhance the thoroughness of the contract.

Consistency results from ensuring that each provision corresponds to the total agreement between the parties and meshes with the other provisions in the contract. Address consistency concerns when rewriting and revising. In these stages, ask yourself questions such as the following.

1. Is each term, heading, and provision used consistently throughout the contract?

2. Are all sections organized consistently throughout the contract?

3. Are both parties' duties handled consistently?

4. Are the results of breach or default consistent throughout the contract and for each party?

5. Are remedies for breach or default consistent throughout the contract?

6. Are all numbers and dates consistent throughout the contract?

Asking yourself these questions will allow you to revise the contract so it will be internally consistent. You must review each clause of the contract to ensure that it is congruent with the other clauses.

---

6. But this agreement will remain flexible over time. "A deal is a living thing, a contract is static. And the purpose of a contract is to support the living, evolving deal, not to supplant it." Mark H. McCormack, *The Terrible Truth About Lawyers: How Lawyers Really Work and How to Deal With Them Successfully* 17 (1987).

This congruency can be difficult to achieve, especially when you start with provisions from other contracts or from form books. It is not necessarily a problem to adapt provisions from other contracts you have drafted. Oftentimes these provisions have been effective in the past, and you will have revised them often enough to be an accurate statement of what the parties want to accomplish. Be particularly careful, however, about using provisions from form books because they are often incomplete, unedited, and drawn from litigated cases.[7] They did not do what they were intended to do, which was to keep the parties out of court, and by using them, you may lead your client into court. Never include a provision you do not understand just because you found it in a form book or other sample contract. If, as is likely, your client asks you about that particular provision, you will have the embarrassing job of telling him or her that you do not know its meaning or purpose.

Form provisions are also of limited usefulness because they were not written with your parties in mind. The agreement you are drafting is unlike the agreement between any other parties and even unlike other contracts previously drafted for the same parties. The factual situations and legal parameters are always changing and, because of this, a provision that effectively stated one aspect of the parties' agreement five years ago, or even five months ago, will no longer effectively do so. Most likely things have changed, which is why the parties want a new contract.

In summary, while previously drafted provisions may provide a solid starting point for drafting, you must alter each provision so it explicitly addresses the needs of the parties in this given situation at this particular time with an eye toward the future. There are no shortcuts for effective contract drafting.

STEPS FOR DRAFTING THE CONTRACT

The process for drafting a contract resembles the process for all writing projects. For example, there are five stages of the writing process: prewriting, writing, rewriting, revising, and polishing.[8] Similarly, after developing a plan of organization, there are five steps in drafting a legal instrument: preparing a first draft, revising, making across-the-board checks, checking with others, and applying the polish.[9] While these two plans label their terms and divide the steps differently, both plans essentially tell the writer to work step-by-step.

As the following list illustrates, you cannot draft a thorough and consistent contract in one step. Keeping your client out of court and accurately conveying the parties' agreement requires serious thought throughout the writing process.

7. Harry J. Haynsworth IV, *How to Draft Clear and Concise Legal Documents,* 31 Prac.Law. 41, 44 (1985).

8. Mary Barnard Ray and Jill J. Ramsfield, *Legal Writing: Getting It Right and Getting It Written* 247 (1987).

9. Reed Dickerson, *The Fundamentals of Legal Drafting* 51–69 (1986).

When drafting a contract, follow these steps.

1. Research the parties' relationship and the law.

2. Think through what is needed in the contract.

3. Write either a draft or outline, concentrating on setting out the entire agreement between the parties.

4. Rewrite, concentrating on logical and clear organization of major elements.

5. Revise, concentrating on thoroughness and consistency.

6. Obtain editing assistance from someone else.

7. Polish for clarity.

We have arranged these steps in the order we find most useful. You should feel free, however, to adapt any drafting process to your own particular situation. For example, if you have drafted numerous contracts, you may find it easier to think through what to include in the contract before doing the research; this may make your research more focused. Or, if you find it difficult to think through the contract, you may find drafting or outlining the contract will better prepare you to think through what else to include.

Drafting contracts, like all writing at an advanced level, requires working through many steps before completing the project. But do not worry that completing these steps will take more time than is available given the demands of a busy practice. As you become more proficient at drafting contracts, you will still do each step of the process, but you will discover that each step takes less time to complete and sometimes may combine with other steps.

Research the Parties' Relationship and the Law

This step consists of two parts: learning what your client wants and learning the law. You will begin to determine what the client wants at your initial meeting. But it may take several meetings with your client, and perhaps with the other parties to the contract or their representatives, to discover the essential element of a contract: a mutual understanding between the parties. Part of identifying this understanding will be learning whether there were any previous negotiations or contracts between the parties and, if so, what the terms were.[10] Another part is finding out whether the parties completed a previous contract successfully or had problems implementing it. Learning this information will help you determine the parties' current understanding.

You may also want to do background research about the parties and their business or industry. Becoming familiar with the nature of the business involved is important because a court construing the contract will consider common trade practices for that business.[11]

---

10. Frank E. Cooper, *Writing in Law Practice* 272 (1963).

11. *Id.*

Oftentimes, your client will be able to give you this information during your initial meetings, or you can use such tools as Standard & Poor's or Dun & Bradstreet reports.[12] Also become familiar with your client's day-to-day business; otherwise, you may include requirements in the contract that your client simply cannot meet.

Your client may ask you to draft a contract focusing on what he or she wants from the agreement without considering the other party's desires or goals, because your client wants to obtain the most favorable terms possible.[13] Although you can attempt to do this, realistically your client's needs must mesh with the other party's needs. Part of your job may be to remind your client that trying for absolute control or diminishing the other side's needs will not result in a satisfactory working relationship.[14] Help your client understand that part of achieving a favorable contract includes drafting a contract all the parties can accept. Otherwise, the more lopsided the contract, the greater the incentive for the disadvantaged side to try to disrupt or terminate the contract.[15] "The ultimate purpose of any contract is not to get a stranglehold on the other party but to formalize the understanding that is of real and proportionate benefit to both sides over time."[16] Determine what your client must have in the contract; what is his or her bottom line. Then determine what your client can give up and try to draft the agreement accordingly.

You can, however, try to make the contract more favorable for your client. If you draft the contract yourself, a "mildly coercive" effect favoring your client will result because the other side must then show why this contract does not state the agreement.[17] Also, by drafting the agreement, you can set the tone between the parties from the start and can have some initial control over the parties' agreement. But be careful in setting the tone. It must not sound too positive for your client or too negative for the other party. You can destroy a deal even though the negotiations were successful, simply because of the way the contract sounds.

After researching the particular situation between the parties, you next determine what is the applicable law controlling the contract. Particular provisions relating to the substantive law may be required to protect your client's legal expectations or to prevent your client from being forced to litigate.

To determine if any statutes will affect the contract, become familiar with the statutes of the state or states where the contract will

---

12. Michael L. Goldblatt, *Well-drafted Contracts Keep Client and You Out of Court. Here's How!,* 7 Prev.L.Rep. 14, 14 (June 1988).

13. Steven L. Kirshenbaum, *Drafting Commercial Agreements* 10 (1988).

14. David Crump, *The Five Elements of a Contract: Avoiding Ambiguity in Them,* 43 Tex.Bar J. 370, 372 (April 1980).

15. McCormack, *supra* note 6, at 144.

16. *Id.* at 176.

17. David W. Maxey, *Fundamentals of Draftsmanship—A Guide in Preparing Agreements,* 19 L.Notes 87, 89 (Summer 1983).

be performed. For example, South Carolina requires the words "This agreement is subject to arbitration" appear on the contract's first page for an arbitration clause to be enforced.[18] If you did not meet the requirements of this particular statute, an arbitration clause contained in a South Carolina contract would be rendered useless.

When drafting, consider relevant common law or statutory canons of construction because the courts use them to interpret the meaning of contracts.[19] You should be aware, however, as when writing statutes, that you can find a canon of construction that contradicts any other canon; therefore, a court can use canons to support any decision it chooses.[20] Besides the canons included below, you can find others in the applicable state statutes, in cases, or in reference books.[21]

Check both the common law and the statutory canons that the courts in your jurisdiction use most frequently so you can draft your contracts to meet the demands of those canons. Examples of common law canons are "the expression of one thing implies the exclusion of all others" and "an interpretation should always be made such that the instrument may stand rather than fall."[22] Examples of statutory canons include "the language of a contract is to govern its interpretation if the language is clear and explicit, and does not involve an absurdity"[23] and "the whole of a contract is to be taken together, so as to give effect to every part, if reasonably practicable, each clause helping to interpret the other."[24]

Also become familiar with the following canon, because most courts will use it to interpret a contract: "in cases of uncertainty not removed by the preceding rules, the language of a contract should be interpreted most strongly against the party who caused the uncertainty to exist."[25] This canon usually means the court will construe the contract against the party who drafted it. Therefore, as drafter, you are responsible for any uncertainty caused by your contract, and that uncertainty will be imputed to your client.

When drafting, include all the provisions necessary to state the entire agreement between the parties, keeping in mind the parol

---

18. Haynsworth, *supra* note 7, at 50–51.

19. Alan R. Perry, et al., *Introduction to Drafting California Legal Instruments* 45 (1983).

20. Most of these canons of construction are also used for interpreting statutes. *Cf.* Karl N. Llewellyn, *Remarks on the Theory of Appellate Decision and the Rules or Canons about How Statutes Are to be Construed,* 3 Vand.L.Rev. 395, 401–406 (1950). Examples of canons that support both sides are provided in Chapter 3, Statutes or Rules.

21. *See,* Hollis Hurd, *Writing for Lawyers* 103–05 (1982).

22. Perry, *supra* note 19, at 46. These common law canons are usually expressed in Latin. For example, the first canon above is commonly referred to as "expressio unius est exclusio alterius." These canons are not actually Latin phrases, but rather are English dressed up in Latin words. Hurd, *supra* note 21, at 105. Although they may be incomprehensible to classical scholars, courts know them and use them frequently when a contract needs to be interpreted.

23. Cal.Civ.Code sec. 1638.

24. Cal.Civ.Code sec. 1641.

25. Cal.Civ.Code sec. 1654.

evidence rule you learned in contracts.[26] Your client may need your help to understand that discussions or promises the parties do not include in the contract will be unenforceable in court. Generally, the court will consider the contract to be the final, binding agreement of the parties. Thus you must include all provisions that the parties intend to control their agreement.

Think Through What Is Needed in the Contract

At this point, you have determined what the parties want and what the law requires. Nevertheless, do not rush into writing. Before drafting, you must have a clear picture in mind of what you hope to accomplish through the contract. Just as the best teachers determine their objectives before teaching a class and litigators consider the remedy they want before drafting a complaint, you as the contract drafter must consider the contract's objectives before starting to draft.

To determine whether you understand the intent of the parties, think through the contract and decide its intended objective. This usually should happen before you set pen to paper, fingers to computer, or thumb to dictation machine.[27] Focus on fully understanding the needs of the parties, the scope of the contract, and the length of the agreement. Stating the parties' entire agreement will be quite complex, and you must analyze that complexity to state the agreement clearly. You will recover this thinking time later.

Write a Draft or an Outline, Concentrating on Setting Out the Entire Agreement Between the Parties

At this stage, what you write or how you write is less important than that you write. "Good writing does not depend on whether you start in the right place; it depends on whether you do all you need to before you stop."[28] Work with a broad brush to outline what the parties are to do for themselves and for each other, what the focus of their agreement is, what the subject matter of the contract is, and how long the contract will continue.

Many authorities assert that using an outline is the best way to start writing; they especially encourage this for drafting contracts, which often have the same type of organization and headings as an outline. Others believe that writing a draft is the best first step. They either draft the actual language of particular provisions or draft language covering what upon revision will turn into several provisions and

26. When the parties have stated their agreement in writing, evidence of any oral agreement that might alter the written document in any way (vary, add, subtract) will not be accepted in court. There are some exceptions, such as for fraud. Paul H. Till and Albert F. Gargiulo, *Contracts: The Move to Plain Language* 11 (1979).

27. Some people find it easier to think through an agreement by writing a rough

draft. We are not intending to discourage that "write-to-think" style. Instead, we are simply warning that the process of thinking through the needs of the parties must occur at some point during the drafting process before revision.

28. Ray and Ramsfield, *supra* note 8, at 81.

then organize the provisions later. As drafter, you will learn which method works best for you.

At this point in the drafting process, try to include all the major sections and portray accurately what you believe are the parties' intentions for each major section. Do not worry yet about the sentence structure, word choice, or even the large-scale organization. What is important is getting the gist of the agreement down on paper; it is unimportant at this point whether the language is stellar. The remaining steps will provide the revisions and polishing needed.

While keeping your client's objectives in mind, try to consider all foreseeable contingencies and address those that do not seem too remote.[29] By considering all the problems that can arise and doing your best to resolve them, you will help your client stay out of court.

Using a checklist, such as the one following, is the easiest way to ensure you have included all the required provisions. You may obtain other checklists by asking senior members of your firm for their contract checklists or by using formbooks or other books about drafting contracts.[30] Over time, you will want to develop your own checklist, drawing from the ones you have used and complete with your own sample provisions.

CHECKLIST OF COMMON CONTRACT PROVISIONS

The following checklist includes provisions you must consider including in all but the simplest of contracts. While this list is not exhaustive, it does present those provisions regularly found in most contracts.

Initial Clauses

> Definitions
>
> Each parties' duties or obligations
>
> Statement of consideration
>
> Purpose or goals
>
> Duration of the contract
>
> Payment to whom, by when, and any conditions for payment

Liability, Damages, and Remedies Clauses

> Liability and responsibility between parties
>
> Limitation of liability because of acts of God
>
> Default or breach
>
> Termination and right to terminate

---

29. Ludwig Mandel, *The Preparation of Commercial Agreements* 14 (1979).

30. *See,* Cooper, *supra* note 10, at 274.

        Notice for breach or termination

        Damages and liquidated damages

        Remedies

        Mediation or arbitration before litigation

Assignability

        Delegation

        Assignability

        Permitting or prohibiting a change of parties

Timing

        Time for performance

        Time of the essence

        Extensions, option to renegotiate or flexibility

        Time and manner of giving notice

        Automatic renewal

Miscellaneous Clauses

        Assumption of good faith

        Representations, warranties, or conditions

        Headings not part of contract

        Incorporation of other documents

        Severability of terms

        Merger clauses incorporating oral representations

        Choice of governing law and governing forum

Ending Clauses

        Acknowledgement clause

        Testimonium clause

        Signatures

        Dates

At this stage of the drafting process, keep each section on a separate sheet of paper so you can rearrange the sections without difficulty.[31] While this method is perhaps less important in this day of word processors and easy reorganization of sections, separating the sections still gives you a sense of whether the major provisions have been included and allows for easy comparisons to your checklist.

When drafting provisions, limit each provision to one subject only. Doing this applies the same concept as having only one subject in each paragraph. Each provision should include a topic sentence and the

---

31. Dickerson, *supra* note 9, at 62.

necessary supporting statements. For example, the following provision from an insurance contract includes all information on personal property, regardless of who owns the personal property.

> We cover personal property owned or used by any insured while it is anywhere in the world. At your request, we will cover personal property owned by others while the property is on the part of the residence premises occupied by any insured. In addition, we will cover, at your request, personal property owned by a guest or a residence employee while the property is in any residence occupied by any insured.

Focusing the subject matter of each provision on one point will help you increase the readability and clarity of the contract. Including unrelated matters in each provision can only be confusing. For example, the provision above is already complex and would have become confusing if the drafter had included the insurance company's liability for injuries to guests or residence employees. If you believe the contract needs to address related matters, state those matters in separate provisions and then include cross-references to those related provisions. For example, at the end of the above provision, the drafter could add: "(Liability for injuries to guests and residence employees is covered in section D below.)"

In summary, at this stage you are concentrating on drafting the important provisions for the contract and working on the content of the provisions. Focus on being thorough and including everything needed to state the parties' agreement. To help achieve this, use the questions on thoroughness and a checklist. Once you have most of the provisions drafted, your next step will involve the overall organization of the contract.

Rewrite, Concentrating on Logical and Clear Organization of Major Elements

When you begin to fix the organization of the contract, do so with the reader in mind, focusing on the sequence that is most functional for the contract's purpose. The best organization is often apparent from the internal logic of the contract itself. For example, in a real estate broker's agreement, the agreement could follow the transaction through its major components. The major sections would be organized as follows:

(1) the parties,

(2) the period of agreement,

(3) the owner's obligations,

(4) the broker's obligations,

(5) the price at which the property will be offered,

(6) the broker's commission,

(7) the submission of the listing to a multiple listing service,

(8) the authorization for the "for sale" sign, and

(9) the parties' signatures.

Above all, organize to exemplify thoroughness and consistency. For example, the broker's agreement above is both thorough and consistent because (1) it opens with the parties, (2) it moves to both parties' obligations, (3) it then states the offering price and the broker's commission so both parties know what money is involved, and (4) it ends with the niceties of the deal by including the multiple listing service and "for sale" sign provisions. All the needed provisions are included and the contract consistently addresses both parties' needs.

You will facilitate thoroughness and consistency by grouping related provisions under general headings, which helps the reader understand the relationships of the various aspects of the contract. Be careful when drafting headings not to depend on the headings to convey meaning, because that meaning can sometimes contradict, limit, or expand the language stated in the particular provision. For example, in the broker's agreement, if a heading stated "Owner's obligations after the expiration of this agreement" but the provisions following the heading included references to the owner's obligations during the agreement, then the owner could argue that any obligations to be performed during the agreement were not binding because the heading only referred to obligations after the agreement expired. To avoid this problem, carefully draft your headings to portray accurately what is in each section or provision. Also consider inserting the following provision:

> The table of contents and the headings to the various sections of this Agreement are inserted only for reference. They are not intended, nor shall they be construed, to modify or define this Agreement.

To make your organization clear and help readers locate particular provisions, include a table of contents at the beginning of the contract if the contract is long (over five pages single-spaced). Many readers also find it useful if you number your paragraphs so it is easy to locate a desired provision. Then you can use cross-references, such as "see paragraph 14," to lead the reader to the correct provision. This is clearer than "see company's liability," which could refer to several different provisions. Double-check when polishing to ensure that these cross-references correlate to the referenced provision.

This step of drafting ensures that your organization enhances the contract, rather than detracts from it. Your organization should show that the contract is more than a collection of individual provisions, but that those provisions are logically interrelated. You can unify the organization by having the provisions present the parties' agreement in logical sequence, grouping provisions under general headings, and using cross-references.

Revise, Checking Thoroughness and Consistency

The next step, revising, ensures that the wording also enhances the contract. As part of revision, complete two checks during this step. The first check, for thoroughness, is to see that you have included everything in the contract that is needed. The second check, for consistency, is to see that you have used each word or idea consistently throughout the contract. To make these checks, select an aspect of the contract and revise with only that aspect in mind. For example, when doing checks for thoroughness, use your checklist to ensure each provision is included or excluded for good reason. Using your background research and the questions on thoroughness, determine whether you have included each step needed to present the parties' agreement.

When doing checks for consistency, read through the contract to verify that you have used all terms consistently throughout the contract. Contracts are not the place for elegant variation. Using the same words throughout the contract may diminish it as great prose, but it will increase the chances of avoiding litigation. Then identify any terms that could have more than one meaning in the context of the contract and revise their usage, giving each term only one meaning.

Define any term that has a specific meaning for the contract that is different from its general use or is a technical word you cannot eliminate from the contract's language. Put these defined terms in the first section of the contract and consider putting all defined words in bold or in capitals throughout the contract so the reader knows when to refer to the definition section. If you object to a separate definition section because it forces the reader to move back and forth between the body of the contract and the definition section, define the terms in context.[32] To include a definition in context, you could use any of the following methods:

> Adjusted gross income, which is your total gross income minus deductions . . .

> Adjusted gross income (total gross income minus deductions) . . .

> . . . adjusted gross income. Adjusted gross income is your total gross income minus deductions.

Use definitions only when needed. There is a significant movement toward using plain English in contracts. Using plain English throughout the contract means choosing everyday terms and eliminating unnecessary technical words, terms of art, or legal jargon. While this movement originally centered around consumer contracts, the movement has now expanded into contracts in general. Revise your language so it presents the parties' understanding as directly and clearly as possible.

32. Carl Felsenfeld and Alan Siegel, *Writing Contracts in Plain English* 98 (1981).

Obtain Editing Assistance From Someone Else

After you have completed these checks, the next step is to ask someone to review the contract. Preferably the person who reviews your draft will be someone who also drafts contracts and perhaps has had some previous contact with your client, so he or she will be better able to focus on what the contract should say. Because readers give their best editorial critique on the initial review of a document,[33] you will make the best use of your colleagues' time if you seek the first review after having completed the content, organization, and revision steps. This will allow them to critique the contract with most of its substance in place.

When requesting the review, ask the reviewer to focus on determining whether the contract accurately, thoroughly, and consistently states the parties' needs and responsibilities. While this person may provide some general editing assistance to make the language more readable or legally accurate, his or her primary purpose is to determine whether you have stated the parties' objectives. You need to remind the reviewer of this purpose or the reviewer may spend his or her time editing minor points.[34]

To help the reviewer focus, consider providing a list of questions to clarify what you want the reviewer to do. By using these questions, the reviewer will be able to respond to your concerns more quickly and will not get off track. For example, you might ask the reviewer the following questions:

Thoroughness

1. Are all routine duties covered?

2. Are all contingencies adequately covered?

3. Are any provisions so specific that they do not allow adequate flexibility?

Clarity

4. Will the organization be clear to the users of the contract?

5. Will the parties be able to read, understand, and accurately interpret the contract?

6. Is the contract clear within the context of the parties' standard practices (construction industry, shipping, retail, insurance, etc.)

7. Will the contract be clear to a court that does not understand the standard practices?

Consistency

8. Are any terms used in ways that contradict standard usage and thus invite misunderstanding?

---

33. Dickerson, *supra* note 9, at 67.

34. For more help in how to work with reviewers, see the section on this in the process chapter.

9.   Are all necessary cross-references included?

10. Are the provisions internally consistent with one another?

Also consider reviewing this draft of the contract with the client.[35] Have your client read the contract and then explain to you his or her understanding of the agreement. As you listen, you can determine whether you have actually stated what your client wants from the agreement or need to make changes and corrections.

Whether you review the contract with your client before or after polishing is a decision you make given your situation and your particular client. It may be wise, however, to obtain this review before polishing because, if major changes or corrections need to be made, it will save time to make those changes before polishing.

Polish for Clarity

Polishing, the final step, means focusing on the details. Doing this ensures the material presented is of high quality, which increases the likelihood the contract will achieve its purpose. Try to spend at least one revision polishing the language. As illustrated at the beginning of the chapter, words as seemingly innocent as prepositions or even articles have been the focus of numerous cases. Carefully read each provision to make sure each word accurately indicates what you believe are the parties' objectives.

The time you spend polishing will depend on the complexity of the contract and the needs and resources of your client. This step requires concentrating on writing rather than substance. For example, read the contract for subjects and verbs too far apart, misspellings, awkward sentence structure, and problems peculiar to your own writing, such as dangling modifiers, overuse of passive voice, or improper use of semicolons.[36] Correct any errors in your grammar, punctuation, usage, and word choice. Your reader will be focused on detail.[37] You must be too.

CONCLUSION

After polishing the language, put the contract aside for one day and then review the contract one more time for overall impression. In this final review, read through the entire contract quickly in one sitting. Look for contradictions between sections of the contract because, when polishing, you can often become too focused on the details and forget to look at the contract as an integrated document. By working step-by-step, you will be able to reach your goal. The contract will be thorough and consistent and will accurately state the parties' agreement.

35. Larry A. Christiansen, *Drafting Contracts* 32 (1986).

36. Ray and Ramsfield, *supra* note 8, at 153.

37. *Id.*

EXERCISES

1. As an in-class exercise related to the first out-of-class assignment below, spend time brainstorming about the possible contract provisions you will include in the contract. Work together to develop a list that will both thoroughly and consistently frame the agreement between you and the professor for the duration of the semester.

2. Review these sample excusable delay or "Act of God" clauses from numerous contracts. Discuss which clause or clauses state their restrictions most clearly and how those clauses could be improved. Discuss which clause or clauses are the most problematic, why they are problematic, and how they could be improved. In your discussion, consider the numbers and headings and whether they are helpful. Then draft your own excusable delay clause.

Example A

4. EXCUSABLE DELAYS

The Company will notify the Customer promptly of any material delay and will specify the revised delivery date as soon as practicable. The Company shall not be liable for any delay in delivery or performance, or for any failure to manufacture, deliver or perform due to (i) any cause beyond its reasonable control, or (ii) any act of God, act of the Customer, act of civil or military authority, governmental priority, strike or other labor disturbance, flood, epidemic, war, riot, delay in transportation or car shortage, or (iii) inability on account of any cause beyond the reasonable control of the Company to obtain necessary materials, components, services or facilities. In the event of any such delay, the date of delivery or of performance shall be extended for a period equal to the time lost by reason of the delay.

Example B

The Company is not responsible for failure to fulfill its obligations under this Agreement due to causes beyond its control or, except as agreed herein, to provide any services hereunder for features or model conversions located outside the United States and Puerto Rico.

Example C

9. FORCE MAJEURE

The Company shall not be responsible for failure of performance of the Agreement due to causes beyond its control including, but not limited to, work stoppages, fires, civil disobedience, riots, rebellions, acts of God, and similar occurrences.

Example D

6. FORCE MAJEURE

Buyer may cancel, without liability, any unshipped portion of this order if Buyer is unable to accept or utilize in its ordinary business said goods due to causes beyond its control, including but not limited to fire, storm, flood, earthquake, explosion, accident, acts of the public enemy, sabotage, riots, war, strikes, lockouts, labor disputes, labor shortages, civil disorders, work stoppages, transportation embargoes or delays, failure or shortage of materials, supplies or machinery, Acts of God, or acts of regulations or priorities of the federal, state or local governments or branches or agencies thereof.

Example E

Neither Seller nor Buyer shall be liable for delay or default in performance hereunder to the extent such delay or default is due directly or indirectly to acts of God or any governmental agency, war, labor disturbance, or any like or different cause beyond the control of the party whose performance is thereby delayed or prevented.

Example F

The duty to perform under order on the part of the Company and the price thereof is subject to approval of its Credit Department, and is also contingent upon strikes, accidents, fires, the inability to procure materials from the usual sources of supply, the requirements of the United States Government (through the use of priorities or preference or in any other manner) that the Company diverts either the material or the finished product to the direct or indirect benefit of the Government, or upon any like or unlike cause beyond the control of the Company.

Example G

10. *Excusable Delays.* Seller will not be liable for damages or delays in delivery due to causes beyond its reasonable control and not occasioned by its negligence or fault.

Example H

13. (a) If either party is unable to perform any obligation hereunder by reason of any strike, government order or directive, Act of God, or other cause beyond such party's control, such party shall be excused from performance and may terminate this P.O. [purchase order], without liability, by giving notice to the other. In such case the recipient of such notice may elect to defer the time of performance by the length of time such cause may impair the performance of the party who gave such notice. Such election shall be in the form of written notice, given within five (5) business days following the giving of the aforementioned notice of termination.

ASSIGNMENT 1

Draft a contract for the long-term class project. (If you are not doing the long-term project, draft a contract for all the out-of-class assignments.) This is not a contract for a particular grade, but rather a contract stating the rights and obligations of both the student and the professor regarding the work to be completed during the semester. Because these obligations last for approximately four months, this is a long-term contract and should include provisions addressing possible contingencies (such as what happens if computer breaks down, student or teacher become sick and cannot complete one step of the project on time, there is a bus strike on the due date, or the student's dog eats the last draft). Because this is an unusual contract, you will need to do some original thinking about the provisions to include. You will not be able to rely on standard contract clauses to state the bounds of this agreement.

ASSIGNMENT 2

Review the following two contracts. They are typical of those found in form books. Revise each contract to eliminate legalese, unneeded use of redundant verbs, sexist language, and convoluted sentence structure.

A. General bill of sale

Know all men by these presents:

That for and in consideration of the sum of $_____, to _____ in hand paid by _____ of _____ at or before the sealing and delivery of these presents, the receipt whereof is hereby acknowledged, _____, has granted, bargained, sold, released and transferred, and by these presents does grant, bargain, sell, release and transfer unto the said _____ all and singular the _____ mentioned in the Schedule hereunto annexed as "EXHIBIT A":

To have and to hold the said _____ unto the said _____ and his (or her) heirs, executors, administrators, successors and assigns, to and for _____ own proper use, and benefit forever.

And the said _____ and his (or her) heirs, executors and administrators, hereby covenant that he (or she) is the lawful owner of said goods, chattels and property above referred to, and shall and will warrant and forever defend by these presents the same, and every part thereof unto the said _____ and his (or her) heirs, executors, administrators, successors and assigns, from and against all persons whomsoever.

In witness whereof, I have hereunto set my hand the _____ day of _____, 19__.

Signed in presence of

_____

_____

_____

B. Bill of sale of a business with agreement not to compete

Know all men by these presents.

_____ of the _____ of _____, County of _____ and State of _____, the Grantor, for the consideration of _____ Dollars ($_____) received to his full satisfaction of _____ of _____, the Grantee, have bargained, sold and conveyed, and by these presents do bargain, sell and convey unto the said _____, his heirs and assigns, the following described goods, wares, merchandise, chattels and effect, to wit:

All of the _____ [business] _____ equipment, supplies, stock in trade, fixtures and personal property, now owned and used in connection with the _____ business located at _____ Road, _____, _____, whether or not said property is specifically described herein; also the goodwill established by said Grantor in connection with said business at _____ Road, _____, _____.

In consideration of the foregoing and of the sum of the purchase price, the receipt of which is hereby acknowledged, and as an inducement to said Grantee to pay the purchase price aforesaid, said Grantor agrees that he will not open a competing business owned by him, either directly or indirectly, within _____ (_____) miles of the shop located at _____ Road, _____, _____, for a period of _____ (_____) years, and that he will not interfere in any way or manner with the business, trade, goodwill or customers of said Grantee.

It is also understood between the parties that this instrument contains the entire agreement between the parties, and it is expressly understood and agreed that no promises, provisions, terms, warranties, conditions or obligations whatever, either express or implied, other than herein set forth shall be binding upon either party.

To have and to hold the same unto the said Grantee, his heirs and assigns, for their own proper use and benefit forever.

And _____, the said Grantor, does for himself (or herself) and his (or her) heirs, covenant and agree to and with the said Grantee, his (or her) heirs and assigns, that the above described goods, wares, merchandise, chattels and effects are free and clear from any encumbrances whatsoever, and that he (or she) is the true and lawful owner thereof and has good right and lawful authority to bargain and sell the same in manner and form as aforesaid, and that he (or she) will and his (or her) heirs and assigns shall warrant and defend the same against the lawful claims and demands of all persons whomsoever.

In witness whereof I hereunto set my hand at _____, this
_____ day of _____, 19__

Signed in presence of

_____

_____

_____

Bibliography

Bloss, Julie L., *How to Review a Contract,* 91 Case & Comment 38 (May/ June 1986).

Burnham, Scott J., *Drafting Contracts.* Charlottesville: The Michie Company, 1987.

Child, Barbara, *Drafting Legal Documents: Materials and Problems.* St. Paul: West Publishing Co., 1988.

Christiansen, Larry A., *Drafting Contracts.* San Diego: Kensington House Publications, 1986.

Cooper, Frank E., *Writing in Law Practice.* Indianapolis: Bobbs– Merrill Co., 1963.

Crump, David, *The Five Elements of a Contract: Avoiding Ambiguity in Them,* 43 Tex.Bar J. 370 (April 1980).

Cuff, Terence F., *Drafting Agreements,* 15 Barrister 41 (Winter 1988).

Dickerson, Reed, *The Fundamentals of Legal Drafting.* Boston: Little, Brown and Company, 1986.

Felsenfeld, Carl and Alan Siegel, *Writing Contracts in Plain English.* St. Paul: West Publishing Co., 1981.

Goldblatt, Michael L., *Well-drafted Contracts Keep Client and You Out of Court. Here's How!,* 7 Prev.L.Rep. 14 (June 1988).

Goodwin, Rodney L., *Drafting Buy-Sell Agreements to Protect Both Buyer and Seller,* 17 Taxation for Lawyers 124 (September/October 1988).

Haynsworth IV, Harry J., *How to Draft Clear and Concise Legal Documents,* 31 Prac.Law. 41 (1985).

Hurd, Hollis T., *Writing for Lawyers,* Pittsburgh: Journal Broadcasting & Communications, 1982.

Kirshenbaum, Steven L., *Drafting Commercial Agreements.* New York City: Practising Law Institute, 1988.

Llewellyn, Karl N., *Remarks on the Theory of Appellate Decision and the Rules or Canons About How Statutes Are To Be Construed,* 3 Vand.L.Rev. 395 (1950).

Mandel, Ludwig, *The Preparation of Commercial Agreements.* New York City: Practising Law Institute, 1978 edition.

Maxey, David W., *Fundamentals of Draftsmanship—A Guide in Preparing Agreements,* 19 Law Notes 87 (Summer 1983).

McCormack, Mark H., *The Terrible Truth About Lawyers: How Lawyers Really Work and How to Deal With Them Successfully.* New York City: Beech Tree Books, 1987.

Note, *Avoiding Inadvertent Syntactic Ambiguity in Legal Draftsmanship,* 20 Drake L.Rev. 137 (1970).

Perry, Alan R., et al., *Introduction to Drafting California Legal Instruments.* San Diego: Jenkins & Perry, 1983.

Ray, Mary Barnard and Jill J. Ramsfield, *Legal Writing: Getting It Written.* St. Paul: West Publishing Co., 1987.

Samon, Charles S., *Computer-aided Drafting of Legal Documents,* 1982 Am.B.Found.Res.J. 685–754.

Till, Paul H. and Albert F. Gargiulo, *Contracts: The Move to Plain Language.* New York City: AMACOM (American Management Associations), 1979.

Chapter 6

ISSUES

Writing a good issue is like building a bridge.[1] The beginning of the issue is built upon the bedrock of the law. The end of the issue is built upon the bedrock of the facts. The center, which is the core legal question, spans the space between, joining the beginning and end together and making the issue a freestanding element in the memo.

When writing issues and answers, you are focusing intently on one sentence, more so than in most legal writing. In one sentence, an effective issue encapsules the relevant law, the legal question, and the significant facts upon which a case will turn, a discussion that will take pages to explicate and resolve. An effective issue not only communicates the essential elements; it also communicates the nature of the question, which could be a question of which law applies, whether the law applies, or how it applies in this situation. Because the issue communicates so much in one sentence and must communicate it clearly, each word is critical. Similarly, each facet of the issue's sentence structure must communicate how the words relate logically to each other. Each punctuation mark must do its job precisely. This focused writing task provides you with an especially effective opportunity for intensive practice with the small-scale writing skills of word choice and word order.

The most effective sentence structure for an issue will be a variation on a general structure. This chapter teaches you first how to put together that general sentence structure and then how to vary the wording and phrase structures within that structure to serve different purposes. The chapter discusses each component of the issue in turn: the law, the core question, and the facts.

Your task is to choose the most effective way to build each component so the whole issue is a unified, solid structure. This remains your task in writing both objective and persuasive issues. For that reason, this chapter also discusses how to move from objective to persuasive issues, treating these two kinds of writing as variations on a

---

1. Mary Ann Polewski contributed many of the ideas, examples, explanations, and assignments in this chapter.

common theme. The chapter provides specific techniques useful for emphasizing points in your persuasive issues.

Organizing an excellent issue can seem overwhelming at times because writers often feel pulled by contradictory objectives. The issue includes several pieces, each of which can be complex. Yet it is traditionally written in one sentence and it needs to be readable. These objectives seem to be necessarily at odds. To help you master this complexity, this chapter presents a format for the three components of issues (the law, core question, and facts) that allows for substantial complexity while maintaining a readable structure.

STRUCTURING THE ISSUE SENTENCE

When structuring your three components into a one-sentence issue, try putting the law at the beginning and the facts at the end, with the core question as the central subject and verb in between. Although other orders are possible and are commonly used, this order is most useful because it works best logically and grammatically. The three-part nature of the issue means the sentence must include two major dependent phrases (one for the law and one for the facts) and one independent clause (the core question). In turn, this means that one phrase should be placed at the beginning of the sentence and one at the end. Other possibilities are unworkable. In a structure this complicated, making one of the phrases an intrusive phrase within the independent clause would decrease readability too much. The other possibility, putting two phrases in series at the beginning or end of the sentence, would also be too complicated because the two units would blur together visually and grammatically.

The choice then becomes whether the law or the facts should come first. Because the facts often require a list and because lists are most readable at the end of a sentence, placing the facts at the end will usually be more readable. It is also more logical to put the law at the beginning and the facts at the end; this order moves the issue from general to specific, leading the reader from the basic understanding of the law into the particularities of the issue at hand.

For all these reasons, this general structure for an issue is used throughout this chapter:

Under [law], [core question] when [facts].

Although this is not the only way to word issues, we have found it most successful and most easily adapted to the various challenges that the permutations of legal issues can create. It enables you to produce an issue that is both clear and complete, both precise and readable.

THE BEGINNING: THE LAW

The law component provides the context for the whole issue. Memos are written for legal readers; legal readers are trained to interpret information based on the applicable laws. If you do not tell the readers what law applies, you ask the readers to put together a puzzle with a missing piece. To find that piece, legal readers will try to infer what law applies to the issue. They may infer correctly and be able to fully understand the issue. They may infer incorrectly and misinterpret the issue. You will save your readers some work, and quite possibly some error, if you set the legal context from the beginning.

The law is contained in an introductory phrase either alone or accompanied by a modifying phrase. The law component can be as short as four words or as long as thirty. The longer it is, the more carefully it must be written, for any long introductory phrase is hard for a reader to absorb. The law component may set the issue in the context of a broad area of the law, such as contracts, or may set the issue in a specific area of the law, such as a subsection of a particular statute, constitutional provision, or administrative rule. It usually includes the jurisdiction from which the law comes.

Issues Based on Case Law, a Group of Enacted Laws, or Both

The law component of the issue is relatively simple when based on a body of common law. Because a body of common law is based on multiple authorities, no single citation can be included. Similarly, no single title can describe the relevant law without becoming too specific to be accurate. Instead, describe the body of law with a short introductory phrase including the jurisdiction and the general area of law.

[introductory word]	[jurisdiction]	[area]	[law]
Under	Washington	contract	law,
According to	North Carolina	tort	law,
Applying	federal	commodity trade	law,

The area of law described may be as broad as "tort law" or as specific as "the doctrine of res ipsa loquitur," but it should be as specific as is possible. For example, you may be able to specify "negligence," "battery," or "false imprisonment." You may even be able to specify the sub-issue within the broader category, such as "Under the restraint element of Hawaii false imprisonment law, ..." Do not use such overly broad labels as "Under Texas case law," or "Under Ohio common law," because those descriptions are too general to give the reader an adequate legal framework. Be as specific as possible when summarizing the body of law, introducing the legal terms that describe the area applicable to the issue even though you cannot narrow the area down to one particular element or statute.

When describing a body of common law, you may be able to modify your issue's sentence structure somewhat because of the simplicity of the statement of the law. For example, you may incorporate the law into your core question.

Does a city bus driver have a duty of care under Alaska tort law when

This allows you to vary your issues without sacrificing precision or clarity.

Issues Based on a Single Enacted Law

You have more choices to make when writing an issue based on a specific statute or other type of enacted law. In this situation, the law component will usually consist of two of the following three components: citation, title, description. The following examples illustrate some of the possible combinations.

         [citation]   [title, quoted]

Under Wis.Stat. § 895.03, recovery for death by wrongful act,

         [citation]   [description]

Under Wis.Stat. § 895.03, which requires that a wrongful death be "caused in this state,"

         [title, paraphrased]   [citation]

According to the wrongful death statute, Wis.Stat. § 895.03,

         [title, paraphrased]   [description]

Under the Wisconsin wrongful death statute, which requires that the death be "caused in this state,"

Because the citation and title are generally short and easy to comprehend, placing one of them first in the law component improves readability. If a description is used, place it after the citation or title, where it adds more detailed information after the general framework has been clarified.

Using Citations

The biggest decision about the citation is whether to use one at all. Some writers and readers believe the citation provides essential information and must be included. Others believe the citation is distracting or does not provide enough useful information to justify including it. You may hold either of these opinions, but it is best if you do not hold it rigidly. Sometimes the complexity or length of the issue will affect your choice, sometimes your reader will, and sometimes (in briefs) the court's rules will. If your usual inclusion or exclusion of the citation does not seem to be working in a particular issue, try the opposite approach. If you include a citation, be sure to use proper citation form. If more than one form is available, find out which form is either preferred by your reader or your firm, or required by court rules.

In general, do not use a citation alone for the law component of the issue. A citation alone does not give the reader enough information to be useful, even if the reader recognizes the statute number. Also, if your firm maintains a memo bank for reference, someone who has no familiarity with the citation will likely read your memo. Indeed, if the issues are used for indexing the memo bank, the citation may be essential to the retrieval system. Combining the citation with a title or description will provide the necessary information to any reader at any time for any purpose.

Using Titles

Unlike citations, titles can be used effectively alone. Often a title is clear and specific enough to inform the reader of the legal foundation for the issue. The titles in most constitutions, statutory codes, and administrative codes are included as a device to aid the reader, but the wording of the title does not carry any weight when interpreting or analyzing the enacted law.[2] As a practical matter, however, attorneys use them when talking about a law because titles are much more memorable than citations. As a result, using titles enables the writer and reader to communicate easily about the legal foundation of the issue. Use as much of the title as possible, but modify the wording so the title fits in the question.

How much modification you need to make depends on the title itself. Some titles of enacted laws give the reader the needed information and fit without any modification into the law component. Other titles that give the needed information must be paraphrased or restructured before fitting into the law component. Finally, some titles of enacted laws do not provide all of the needed information or provide unnecessary information. You must then add or delete words or restructure the title so it can fulfill its purpose: setting the legal context for the issue.

When the title provides the needed information, simply insert the title into the introductory phrase.

Under the Illinois *kidnapping statute,*

Applying Michigan's *compulsory school attendance statute,*

Under the Georgia statute concerning *judgments docketed in other counties,*

Sometimes inserting the title without modification can create noun strings or other phrases that are hard to read, as happens in the following examples.

Under the Wisconsin buttermaker and cheesemaker license statute,

According to Florida's false, misleading or deceptive insurance solicitation statute,

In this circumstance, the titles are more readable when placed at the end of the introductory phrase.

Under the Wisconsin statute concerning buttermaker and cheesemaker licenses,

2. As discussed in the statutes chapter, the title of a provision is generally not part of the enacted law that it introduces.

Under the Florida statute about false, misleading or deceptive insurance solicitation,

Other titles that give the reader necessary information need to be paraphrased or restructured before inserting them into the introductory phrase. The changes you make in the wording of the title may be as little as adding an article or making a noun or verb plural or singular. At other times, you will significantly restructure the title or paraphrase it. In the next examples, the actual title of a statute is given and then it is paraphrased or restructured in the introductory phrase.

operating vehicle without owner's consent

Under the Kentucky statute concerning operating *a* vehicle without *the* owner's consent,

jurors, how paid

Under the Colorado statute *for paying* jurors,

Many titles will not give all the information the reader needs to understand the legal foundation of the issue, so you will have to add information. Other titles will include unnecessary information, which you will have to delete.

Each of the following titles does not provide enough information for the reader. You can add the needed information following the title.

examinations

Under the New York pharmacist examinations statute,

failure to comply with certain statutes

Under the Montana statute concerning a personal representative's failure to comply with statutes for giving information to interested persons,

Other titles will give more information than is needed for the issue. For these, delete unneeded information and then revise them to make them grammatical and readable.

obedience to traffic officers, signs and signals; fleeing from officer

Under the New Mexico statute requiring obedience to traffic signs and signals,

right of way of funeral processions and military convoys

Under California's right of way statute for military convoys,

Finally, some titles will need both additions and deletions.

applicability to nonresidents, unlicensed drivers, unregistered motor vehicles and accidents in other states

Applying the Vermont statute concerning the applicability of financial responsibility laws to unlicensed drivers,

As the above example illustrates, at some point the title is so changed from the original that it becomes more of a description than a title. At that point, use the next section on using descriptions to see how best to write a description.

Using Descriptions

To a large degree, titles and descriptions are two distant points on one continuum. At one end is the title taken as worded from the enacted law. At the other end is a description that uses none of the language in the title or the law to describe the provision. Any one issue may fall anywhere on this continuum. When a title needs lots of revision or restructuring to make it provide the needed information and to make it fit in the question, then it crosses the line into description. The following example shows a title revised until it becomes a description.

> applicability to nonresidents, unlicensed drivers, unregistered motor vehicles and accidents in other states

> Under the Vermont statute concerning the applicability of financial responsibility laws to unlicensed drivers,

It also shows how a description can be placed in an introductory phrase.

You can place a description in a dependent clause following an introductory phrase containing either a citation or a title. The basic structure for putting the description in a dependent clause is:

> Under [citation OR title], which requires . . .,
>
> > describes . . .,
> >
> > addresses . . .,
> >
> > prohibits . . .,
> >
> > allows . . .,
> >
> > states . . .,

In a description, do not attempt to use the unmodified title. The description may include some words from the title, but the writer's goal is not to be faithful to the title. Rather, the goal is to be faithful to the meaning of the law itself.

Descriptions are most useful when (1) you want to include a lot of information about the law, (2) you want to focus the reader's attention on particular language or on a particular element, or (3) the title of the provision does not give needed information. For example, the following description gives extensive information.

> Under Wis.Stat. § 942.05, which prohibits opening a letter without the sender's or the addressee's consent,

In contrast, the following example focuses the reader's attention on particular language or on a particular element

> Under the Arkansas wrongful death statute, which requires that the death be "caused in this state,"

Finally, the following two examples provide information not given in the title.

> Under Wis.Stat. § 344.19, which concerns the applicability of financial responsibility laws to unlicensed drivers,

According to Oregon's poisons statute, which describes the procedure for delivering highly toxic substances without a prescription,

If you are writing more than one issue about a single statute, often you
can change the description in each question to highlight the focus of the
question.

Inserting the Law Component Into the Issue

There are four possible structures for inserting the law component
into the issue. Which structure you choose depends on what combination of citation, title, and description you use and on what combination
is most readable for that issue.

In the first structure, only the title or description is used in the law
component, and it is placed in an introductory phrase.

Under North Dakota's first-degree murder statute,

Under the North Dakota first-degree murder statute,

Under the North Dakota statute concerning first-degree murder,

This is simple, clear, and useful when this is all the information the
reader needs to identify the relevant law accurately.

The second structure consists of the title and the citation. The
title is in an introductory phrase and the citation follows in an
appositive.[3] In the following examples, the citation acts as a phrase
describing the statute.

Under the highway construction statute, Wis.Stat. § 941.03,

Under the statute concerning judicial administrative districts, Wis.
Stat. § 757.60,

Because the jurisdiction is included in the citation, it is not necessary to
include "Wisconsin" in the introductory phrase. This structure is
useful when you want to include a citation, which follows the title to
make the phrase more understandable.

The third structure reverses the order of the second: the citation is
now in the introductory phrase and the title is in the appositive.

Under Wis.Stat. § 424.501, false, misleading or deceptive insurance
solicitation,

Under Wis.Stat. § 29.427, possession, sale, release and destruction
of live skunks,

This structure works well when the title is long or complex. The
citation tells the reader what type of law is applicable (statute, constitution, administrative rule) and from what jurisdiction the law comes.
The appositive gives the title of the statute, which fills in the details
the citation does not supply.

---

3. An appositive is set off by commas
and is a noun or phrase that comes right
after a noun and describes that noun.

The fourth structure consists of a title in an introductory phrase and a description in a dependent clause.

> According to the Arkansas wrongful death statute, which requires that the death be "caused in this state,"

> Under Wisconsin's opening letters statute, which prohibits opening a letter without the sender's or the addressee's consent,

The combination of an introductory phrase and a dependent clause will bog down the issue if both are long. Therefore, this structure works best when the title is relatively short (five or fewer words).

In summary, your wording of the law component involves choosing between many specific options; nevertheless, your choices will be guided by your objectives of readability and precision.

STATING THE CORE QUESTION

The core of the issue, the span that joins the beginning and end of the issue, contains the central legal question in the subject, verb, and object. Even though this component of the issue is relatively short, it deserves substantial attention.

When choosing the subject for the issue, first consider whether there is a legal term upon whose definition the issue turns. If so, then that term is likely to be the subject. Usually it will be a subcategory of the legal concept introduced in the law component. For example, if the law component was "Under North Dakota's first-degree murder statute, which defines 'intent to kill,'" your core question might zero in on the word "intent." If your law component was "Under Kansas common law regarding intentional tort," your core question might focus on "injury" or "reasonable apprehension."

> Under . . ., is *intent* established by. . . .

> Under . . ., was the plaintiff's *apprehension* that the defendant would strike her *reasonable* when. . . .

Occasionally this term will instead be the object of the verb.

> Under . . ., does the evidence establish *intent* when. . . .

In both situations, by placing this term in your core question, you have focused the reader quickly on the telling legal question. You have gained clarity and conciseness.

The form of the verb you choose is similarly influenced by the issue's focus. If the issue focuses on whether a legal concept applies to the particular set of facts, often you will use a linking verb (usually a form of "to be"), which is the grammatical equivalent of an equals sign. Some other possible links include: "constitute," "equal," and "establish." For example, if the question is whether shouting epithets equals a threat of harm, the core question might be "is shouting sufficient," as the following example illustrates.

> Under . . ., is shouting insults alone sufficient to establish a threat of harm when. . . .

Thus the linking verb often joins a legal term and a word or phrase summarizing the key facts. This core question then bridges the gap between law and facts by pulling the key term from each of those elements and fusing them into a legally significant and grammatical unit. Although using "to be" is often criticized for leading to inactive writing, this use of the verb is anything but passive. Rather, it is the keystone in the arch, which by its very presence unifies and stabilizes the whole structure.

In some cases, the verb may carry the central legal concept. For example, in a negligence case, the following core question might best focus the issue.

> does a landlord *breach* the warranty of implied habitability when. . . .

Here the subject, "landlord," refers to landlord/tenant law and the verb focuses on the critical legal term. The central concern in the core of the issue is that this legal and grammatical center of the sentence expresses the core question of the issue, the exact point where the law and facts meet.

STATING THE SIGNIFICANT FACTS

When moving to the facts component of the issue, you often find yourself structuring a list, because several facts are important to a particular issue. As a result, the techniques you used to structure lists in jury instructions will again be useful: group listed items logically, use clear signals to show the reader how the list is structured, and order items logically. Determining which facts are significant to this issue can also be difficult, and that will be discussed more in Chapter 7 on objective statements of facts. In situations where the issue involves many facts, however, you may use one of the five other options discussed in later subsections.

Structuring Lists Generally

When structuring the list of facts, determine whether those facts fall into groups or whether each fact is logically equivalent to the others. If the facts fall into groups, you may use signals to reflect those groups. For example, the following facts are grouped into the landlord's (1) failure to initiate repairs and (2) failure to respond when others notified him that repairs were needed. These groupings are indicated by the coordinating phrases, "not only" and "but also."

> when the landlord failed not only to inspect the stairs regularly, but also to complete repairs requested by tenants, to answer inquiries from his building supervisor, and to complete the repairs listed by city inspectors?

This grouping adds meaning to the issue, in this example suggesting that the two groups represent different points to be made. Any groupings used should reflect the logical categories created by the relevant law, rather than grouping facts solely for appearance, or because some convenient groups seem possible. That would be more likely to confuse the reader than to help.

You must finally decide how to order the facts or groups of facts. In making this decision, consider two factors: telling a clear story and creating a readable structure. First, make sure the order follows a logical sequence. For example, if you were describing a series of events leading to injury, chronological order might be best.

> when she slipped on the ice, lost her balance and fell sideways, reached out with her left arm to break her fall, and wrenched her left shoulder as the arm twisted beneath her.

Sometimes, however, the facts in the list will not require a particular order. To improve the readability of the following list, consider putting the simpler facts first and the most complicated ones last.

> caused by the failure to turn off the source of the water, to repair the leaking faucet, to post any warning signs, or, given the leak's existence, to take any steps to prevent the ice from building up on the sidewalk.

The longest element is placed last, making the whole sentence more readable because the reader is able to understand the structure and content of the sentence before having to read the more complex component.[4]

Alternative Structures for Issues With Many Facts

This section includes four ways to write issues involving many facts. The first is to tabulate the facts.

> Under Wisconsin contract law, is a liquidated damages clause enforceable when:
>
> (1) the clause was in a standard real estate contract for the sale of a $100,000 home;
>
> (2) the clause required the buyer to forfeit $8,000 when he breached the contract;
>
> (3) the seller incurred over $2,100 in expenses because of the buyer's breach;
>
> (4) the seller lost the opportunity to buy another home on which she had made an offer; and
>
> (5) the seller has not been able to sell her home in the seven months since the breach?

This helps the reader find his or her way through the complicated facts by providing visual signals of the organization.

A second way to handle this situation is to give two or three key facts and indicate that there are more.

> Under the Wisconsin general rule that a liquidated damages clause is enforceable if reasonable under the totality of the circumstances,

4. See Chapter 4 on jury instructions.

is an $8,000 liquidated damages clause reasonable in a standard real estate contract for the purchase of a $100,000 home when the seller suffered losses because of the buyer's breach, *including* $2,100 in out-of-pocket expenses?

A third approach is to state general categories of facts, rather than specifics.

Under the Wisconsin general rule that a liquidated damages clause is enforceable if it is reasonable under the totality of the circumstances, is a liquidated damages clause in a standard real estate contract reasonable when the seller incurred expenses because of the buyer's breach and when the seller lost the opportunity to buy a home she wanted?

The final option is to divide the issue into sub-issues.

Under Wisconsin contract law, which states that a liquidated damages clause meets the test of being reasonable under the totality of the circumstances if three factors are satisfied, does the liquidated damages clause in Ms. Johnson's standard real estate contract for the sale of her home satisfy the three factors?

1. Was the liquidated damages clause not a penalty for breach when it required an $8,000 forfeiture on the sale of a $100,000 home and the parties negotiated the amount of damages at arms length?

2. Was it not possible to estimate accurately the loss from a breach when the parties did not know at the time they negotiated the contract whether Ms. Johnson would offer to buy another home or what expenses she would incur while preparing to move?

3. Did the $8,000 liquidated damages clause accurately forecast the harm to Ms. Johnson when her damages included forfeiting $2,100 in earnest money on the new home she offered to purchase, losing the opportunity to buy a home that uniquely suited her needs, and incurring expenses while preparing to move?

This format is likely to be needed only for extremely complex issues, where both the law and the facts are multi-faceted. Before using this approach, consider whether your issues would be clearer if written separately, rather than as sub-issues.

In summary, when writing the facts, you are basically applying your skills at structuring a list. But because of the many twists facts can take, you may try several options before you find one that communicates your facts clearly and precisely. Nevertheless, a clear focus on the facts will make it much easier for the reader to understand the significance of all the details in your issue and discussion section.

AN ALTERNATIVE PROCESS FOR FORMULATING ISSUES

Apart from deciding how to structure the issues, a central part of the process of writing an issue is clear and precise identification of the issue's content. For some writers, working through the structure does not help them do this. They cannot begin by formulating each component of the issue because they need to begin with a general outline of the overall issue before they can work out the details. If you like to begin with a general outline, we offer the following seven-step process:

(1) ask yourself the general question and write it out;

(2) identify the relevant facts;

(3) ask yourself, "Under what law?" and add the answer to the front of the issue;

(4) look more closely at the relevant law and identify the particular phrases that apply;

(5) if there are several phrases that apply, divide the information into separate issues;

(6) for each of those issues, insert the particular relevant phrase in the law; and

(7) for each issue, select only those facts relevant to that phrase.

The following example shows you how this process would apply in a real situation. Assume the state worker's compensation act provides benefits for all workers who suffer "accidental injuries arising out of and in the course of their employment." Our client, a teacher, was injured when he attempted to put out a fire he discovered while working in the building where he was employed. He applied for benefits, but they were denied by the compensation board on the ground that his duties as an employee did not include attempting to extinguish fires.

Using these facts, begin with step one, asking yourself the general question, "Is our client entitled to benefits?" Then, to identify the relevant facts, make each part of the general question more specific.

Is our client	entitled to benefits?
Teacher injured when attempted to put out a fire that he discovered	because he was at work when it happened, even though he is a teacher, not a firefighter

Next move to the third step by asking yourself, "Under what law?" The answer may be statute or case law. In this situation, you would determine that the answer to the question is "Under the State Worker's Compensation Act." To identify the relevant phrases or parts of the law, the fourth step, describe the law more specifically, employing the techniques discussed earlier in the section on the law component.

Under the State Worker's Compensation Act, which provides benefits for "accidental injuries arising out of and in the course of their employment,"

This provides you with all the pieces needed for your issue.

Now you are ready to put the issue together.

Under the State Worker's Compensation Act, which provides that workers can receive benefits for "accidental injuries arising out of and in the course of their employment," is our client entitled to benefits if the client is a teacher who was injured when he attempted to put out a fire that he discovered in the bathroom while he was working in the school building?

This process should lead you to a solid draft of your issue.

You can then revise this draft for readability.

Under the State Worker's Compensation Act, which compensates workers for injuries "arising out of and in the course of their employment," did a teacher's injury arise out of the course of his employment when he was burned while attempting to extinguish a fire he discovered in the school's bathroom during the school day?

At this stage, you have a good preliminary draft to help you focus as you create first drafts of your facts and discussion.

It is unlikely, however, that you will have successfully drafted a final version of your issue in this one try. It is even unlikely that you can accomplish it in one series of tries. Instead, draft your issues early in the memo writing process. Then return to those issues periodically, revising them as your understanding of the law and facts is revised and sharpening the issue's focus as your research is focused. Drafting your issues is likely to be both the first and last step in your process of writing a memo.[5]

BRIEF ANSWERS

The two main purposes of a brief answer are to answer the question and to give the reader some idea of the main points covered in the discussion. It is generally difficult to accomplish both of those purposes in one sentence, so your brief answer is likely often to take two phrases or sentences rather than one. The first phrase or sentence gives the answer and echoes the language of the question. The second outlines the reasoning behind the answer and echoes the organization of the discussion on that issue.

Under Oklahoma law on superseding causes, which includes foreseeability as an element, was the gang's act of chasing Tommy into the street unforeseeable when gangs had never been present in the neighborhood before, although some parents knew of gang members verbally harassing students?

Probably yes. The gang's act of chasing Tommy into the street satisfies the first element of a superseding cause, which would

---

5. William P. Statsky and R. John Wernet, Jr., *Case Analysis and Fundamentals of Legal Writing* 385 (1977).

relieve the District of liability because it was highly unusual, not likely to happen, and thus unforeseeable.

The most frequent error made when writing brief answers is not including the legal reasoning behind the answer.

> Probably yes. The gang's act of chasing Tommy into the street satisfies the first element of a superseding cause, which would relieve the District of liability.

Without the reasoning behind the answer, the reader must read the discussion section on faith that you will explain the reasoning there. When you include the reasoning in the brief answer, you allow the reader to gain a fuller view of the answer; he or she can read the discussion section with a solid understanding of the analysis you present. An easy way to check whether you have included the reasoning in your brief answer is to look for the word "because" in the answer. If it is there, you have probably included the reasoning; if not, you have probably not. In summary, the brief answer not only answers the issue, but also previews the discussion, serving as a conceptual transition to that portion of the memo.

When writing objective issues, focus on identifying precisely the relevant law, the legally significant facts, and the core question. When you have these components clearly stated and securely joined, your issue will form a single sentence guiding you and your reader through the rest of the memo. Your brief answer then leads the reader from this issue into the discussion by echoing the organization and content of the issue in the first part of the answer and echoing the organization and content of the discussion in the second part.

MOVING FROM OBJECTIVE TO PERSUASIVE WRITING

The difference between objective and persuasive issues is one of purpose rather than of style. For this reason, you change the wording in your issue in response to the changes in your purpose. When stating the law component, for example, word it to emphasize a particular legal concept that favors applying this law to your client. When stating the core question, choose a subject and verb that suggest the justice of the answer you want. When stating the facts, minimize the impact of unfavorable facts and emphasize favorable ones.

To help you adjust your issues to the additional purposes that arise in persuasive writing, this section discusses the general shift in purpose when moving from objectivity to persuasion. The following section then explains specific techniques useful in writing persuasive issues.

As you move from objective writing to persuasion, it is helpful to realize that persuasion depends on your audience, situation, and role in that situation.[6] For example, persuading the legal reader differs greatly from persuading the consumer. In advertising, the problem is to

---

6. Daniel J. O'Keefe, *Persuasion: Theory and Research* 96 (1990).

persuade consumers to purchase a product, but consumers often make purchases without a great deal of deliberation.[7] For example, consumers do not think too much about which bar of soap to use, so appeals to basic drives and pleasant associations may be effective persuasive approaches.

With a legal brief, however, the audience is prepared to deliberate. Indeed its job is to deliberate. Although the judge will want to be efficient, he or she will not make a decision without reflection and careful reasoning. Because of this, appeals that cannot stand close scrutiny will not be persuasive.[8]

Objective and persuasive writing have much in common. For example, much of the same content is needed in both situations. Whether you are informing a senior attorney or persuading a judge, you will still need to explain the relevant law accurately, clearly, and concisely.[9] In both cases, you will need to explain why and how the fact situation before you falls into the category covered by the law, and what the effect of the law is on the outcome.[10] Similarly, you will have to address unfavorable precedent, although the issues you address may vary as you move through the court system. Your need to present your case objectively will also not change, because readers are more readily persuaded by information that seems fair.[11]

Nor will your focus on the reader change. Whether you are informing or persuading, you need to think about what questions the reader will be considering and address them.[12] The information and the structure should lead the reader to ask those questions. The reader of objective writing evaluates the strength of available options to decide whether to proceed; the reader of persuasive writing needs to evaluate the merits of the position taken by the writer. Both situations require the reader to evaluate the reasoning, the sufficiency of the support, and the relevance of the content discussed within the reader's own framework for making the decision.

---

7. When the reader thinks less about the decision, peripheral factors such as credibility of the writer, consensus of the group with which the reader identifies, and liking for the writer become more influential in the decision. *Id.* at 107.

8. "In legal argument, it can be fatal to assume that the judge agrees with your assumptions. If, after inquiry into the hidden assumptions of your position or those of your opponent, you decide that agreement is problematic, you should reckon with those assumptions. Do not presume that if you hide them, the judge or your opponent will remain in blissful ignorance. Just as assumptions are frequently hidden, so implications of deductive arguments are rarely discussed in briefs. While you may choose to forget about the implications of your argument, the judge never does. Because implications are critical to judicial

decision-making, failure to examine all important implications fully may doom your argument." Judith A. Finn, *Writing Briefs for Federal Litigation: The Province of the Elect*, 22 Tulsa L.J. 127, 132 (1986).

9. "Persuasive writing is reader-oriented. This means your briefs should be judge-oriented." Edward J. Devitt and James A. Barnum, *10 Tips for Preparing Better Briefs*, 22 Trial 75 (Oct.1986).

10. Rolf Sandell, *Linguistic Style and Persuasion* 96 (1977).

11. *Id.* at 163.

12. Gerald R. Miller, "Persuasion" in *Handbook of Communication Science* 146 (C. Berger and S. Chaffee, eds., 1987). "Lawyers who write judge-oriented briefs tend to win more frequently than those who write lawyer-centered briefs." Finn, *supra* note 7, at 128.

Finally, your desire to establish and maintain credibility will not change when you shift from objective to persuasive writing, although your reasons for wanting that credibility may shift. For example, you may want to impress the senior attorney with your credibility so he or she will see you as capable and trustworthy. In contrast, you may want to appear credible to the judge in order to be more persuasive and win your case.[13] In both circumstances, however, you are communicating specialized knowledge about a legal question to a skilled reader who has general knowledge but not detailed understanding, and who must make a decision about the question based largely on the information you provide. To do this, the reader must perceive you as a reliable reporter of the information.

What does change as you move from objective to persuasive writing is the question your reader must answer and the context in which your writing appears. For example, the reader of a memo is considering how to proceed on behalf of the client and may have many options, including doing nothing, negotiation and settlement, or litigation. The reader of a brief faces a narrower question; he or she must decide who prevails in the case and for what reason. This reader is generally limited to considering the relief requested by the plaintiff and the defenses offered by the defense. So the question a brief addresses might be quite different than the question addressed by an earlier memo on the same facts. Because of this, the content of the brief may differ greatly from the memo; in comparison, the changes created solely because of the brief being persuasive rather than objective are not as profound.

Although the judge addresses a narrow question, he or she must consider a broader context. The judge has documents from both parties, so your brief will be reviewed in the context of the opposition's brief. Additionally, the judge may consider the broader context of precedent, mandatory authority, and public policy, whether or not the attorneys addressed those concerns in their briefs. For example, a trial judge may consider whether a decision would be appealed, even though the question is not addressed directly in the briefs. A state court of final review might consider what signals its ruling will send to the state bar, even though that issue might not be addressed in the briefs.

If you focus on the reader and his or her needs, you will be able to adjust naturally from objective to persuasive writing without focusing solely on persuasive or objective techniques per se. This should enable you to use persuasive writing techniques with greater subtlety and variety, leading to greater effectiveness.

---

13. "Communicators are more successful at persuading if they are viewed as competent and trustworthy." Miller, *supra* note 12, at 464.

SPECIFIC TECHNIQUES FOR WRITING PERSUASIVE ISSUES

The next examples present ways to write persuasive issues, focusing on how the issues are worded to help the reader see the significance of points central to your argument.

Once you have shaped the issue to address the question argued in your brief, you have done much to make the issue persuasive. Begin by crafting your persuasive issue just as you would the objective issue, developing and refining the three essential parts and fusing them into a whole statement. After you have structured your issue, any of the five following techniques can sharpen your presentation. These include

(1) incorporating favorable, relevant aspects of the applicable law in your explanation;

(2) adjusting the focus and level of specificity in the core question to establish your position;

(3) stating significant and favorable facts in detail and unfavorable ones more generally;

(4) suggesting the logical relationship of facts with skillful use of signals; and

(5) using words with subtle connotations that steer the reader toward your opinion.

Incorporating Favorable and Relevant Aspects of the Applicable Law

If your argument centers on the point that the law you are applying is limited or broad, you can suggest this in your description of the law component. For example, if you were arguing that your client is not liable, you might begin with the following.

Under Wis. Stat. § 48.01, *which limits* liability to . . .,

Although you must take great pains to be accurate in your description of the law, you may still use this description to remind the court of the point you are making.

Adjusting the Focus and Level of Specificity in the Core Question to Establish Your Position

When structuring the core question in objective issues, you focused on presenting the question precisely. When writing persuasively, maintain the focus of your issue, but you may state the core question in slightly more general terms to make the application of the relevant law to the significant facts suggest the result you want. For example, if you were representing a city arguing immunity, you might prefer the following more general core question.

does governmental immunity *prevent*. . . .

In contrast, if you were arguing that the city was liable, your core might focus on the city's responsibility.

does the city's duty to repair its public thoroughfares *extend* to
. . .

If you wanted to counter the opposition's argument directly, you might focus the core more specifically on the interaction of your legal position with the opposition's, that is, which law governs rather than how one law governs.

does governmental immunity excuse a municipality from its duty to . . .

Here the words you choose to be the subject and verb of the sentence have a substantial impact on the focus of the whole issue, just as the subject and verb affect the emphasis of any sentence. This step is often difficult, but its benefits are substantial, because it makes the issue both clearer and more persuasive.

Stating Significant and Favorable Facts in More Detail and Unfavorable Ones More Generally

Although you need to include significant facts whether favorable or not, you can change the way you state those facts. For example, if you are representing a plaintiff who was harmed when a neighbor's pet skunk escaped from its pen, emphasize the significant unpleasantness your client experienced by explaining it in memorable detail.

when the plaintiff, unaware of the skunk's presence, started the car's engine, inadvertently killing the skunk and spreading its odor throughout the engine, requiring the plaintiff to spend several days removing all traces of the unfortunate animal and its odor from the fan, carburetor, pistons, battery, and other affected surfaces within the engine.

If, however, you were representing the defendant in this situation, you might not dwell on these details, but instead emphasize other facts relevant to the question.

when the animal's death resulted from its unprecedented action of climbing under the hood of a car.

Here you use detail and generality in conjunction to focus your reader on the facts you choose, even though you are including other facts as well.

Suggesting the Logical Relationship of Facts With Skillful Use of Signals

This technique involves the connecting signals you use to join the pieces of the issue, usually the facts. These signals tell the reader how to organize the information he or she is reading, and they also signal the relative importance of those pieces of information. For example, within the fact section, you may want to suggest that one fact outweighs another. If so, you might join the facts as follows.

he drove over the speed limit *despite* the narrowness of the road.

If you want to suggest that the facts as a group counter the opposition's claim, you may follow a core question with a signal introducing the supporting facts.

Under . . ., is a municipality immune *even though*. . . .

In this situation, you are developing a question you want the reader to answer "no," something traditionally avoided. Nevertheless, occasionally that structure may be more persuasive than a blander version that can be answered "yes" but does not sharply show the sense of the rightness of your answer that the "no" creates.

Using Words With Subtle Connotations That Steer the Reader Toward Your Opinion

This technique, using slanted language, is often the first one writers turn to when seeking to make an issue more persuasive. It comes last in this list, however, because it is probably best to exercise this option only after the other alternatives have been explored. This option, if misused, can actually detract from the effectiveness of your issue. Slanted language is effective only when it does not destroy the credibility of the question as a fair statement; if it seems to overstate the case, the reader can readily dismiss the issue as dramatic posturing and neglect to see the merits otherwise present. Strong language also has a tendency to overshadow other aspects of writing, especially when it creates a negative response, so use it with care.

Nevertheless, moderate slanting can be effective. For example, the slight emotional charge in the facts below adds clarity and force without seeming unfair.

when, terrified by the noise of the explosion, the thoroughbred crashed into the stable wall, shattered its right front ankle, and subsequently had to be destroyed.

In contrast, the following version seems somewhat uncaring.

when the explosion startled the horse, causing it to run into the stable wall and sustain a critical fracture of an ankle.

And the next version seems unconvincing.

when the explosion shattered the air in the stable, it caused the racehorse to fear for its life so much that it strove in vain to escape, shattering its delicate foreleg against the hardwood wall, ending its possibility to survive and thus needlessly shattering the life of this fine contender, this elegant thoroughbred.

Slanted language can be very effective as long as it maintains accuracy and creates a more vivid picture of the facts themselves, rather than drawing attention to the writer's judgments or literary elaborations about the situation.

In summary, writing a persuasive issue first requires you to focus on the critical content, just as you did with the objective issue. It then requires you to adjust wording and order in many small ways to underscore your point.

CONCLUSION

Writing excellent issues requires an effort that may seem disproportionate in relation to their length, but the effort is not disproportionate in relation to their importance. An effective issue will benefit you throughout the document by making it easier for you to choose content, organization, and even wording throughout your discussion. It will also benefit your image in the eyes of your reader. Senior attorneys and judges alike commonly bemoan the overwhelming absence of useful issues in the memos and briefs they read. With an excellent issue, your document can stand above the rest, an oasis of clarity in the vast desert of words your reader must cross.

EXERCISES

1. Rewrite the following issues.

a. Is a citizen who complains to police about noise made by the occupants of an adjacent apartment and who claims he saw and smelled marijuana when the occupants opened their door, a reliable informant with regard to the use and possession of marijuana where the police also smelled marijuana prior to making an arrest and where the informant was previously unknown by police?

b. Is information, obtained by police from a non-expert informant, regarding the use and possession of marijuana reliable where the informant personally observed and smelled what appeared to him to be marijuana and where such information was corroborated with independent evidence when police entered the suspect's apartment and smelled marijuana?

c. When at the time of a man's death he is living separate and apart from his wife and is not contributing to her support, is she entitled to compensation as his widow under the Worker's Compensation Act?

2. Determine and write the issue(s) for the following situation.

MEMORANDUM

TO: Junior Associate
FROM: Senior Partner
DATE: February 4, 1990
RE: Daisy Alderman file—Intoxicated use of a vehicle charge.

On January 31, 1990, at 2 a.m., Daisy Alderman was stopped by a University police officer as she was driving home from a party. The officer approached her car, stated that she had been weaving back and forth across the center line, and asked to see her driver's license. Daisy misunderstood and thought the officer had asked her to get out of the car. Instead of handing him her license, she threw open the car door, knocking the policeman into the path of an oncoming car. He was taken to the hospital and treated for a fractured femur. Daisy was taken to the police station and given a blood alcohol test, which showed she was intoxicated.

The state has filed charges against Daisy under sec. 940.25. We would like to argue that the state cannot support this charge.

940.25 *Injury by intoxicated use of a vehicle*

Whoever causes great bodily harm to another human being by the negligent operation of a vehicle while under the influence of an intoxicant is guilty of a Class E felony.

ASSIGNMENT 1

Write the issues for the following situation, writing three objective issues and three persuasive ones. You are the attorney representing Fuss and McGovern, the game wardens.

TO: Assistant District Attorney
FROM: District Attorney, LaCrosse County
RE: Liability of Game Wardens for Shooting Dogs

Mr. Vernon Fuss is the resident conservation warden for LaCrosse County, and Mr. Lewis McGovern is a seasonal conservation warden. State conservation wardens are duly licensed law enforcement officers. The wardens are being sued for actual and punitive damages by Mark Gordon for killing one of his trained farm dogs and wounding another.

On November 26, 1990, Fuss and McGovern, acting as state conservation wardens, answered a call on County Highway Q and stopped a motorist to check his hunting license. While they were walking back to their car, which was parked near the driveway of a farm, they saw two dogs run out of the woods and attack a pig in a farm field along the driveway.

The wardens said that the dogs struck the pig simultaneously, one at each end of the animal. Upon being attacked, the pig started spinning and squealing loudly. At one point the pig broke free and the dogs chased it a few yards in the direction of the buildings. Then the pig was knocked flat on the ground, but succeeded in getting back up on its legs. The pig continued to go around with the dogs still attacking until the wardens shot the dogs. The injury to the pig was minor: one scratch on her rump about three inches long that healed in three days.

The wardens have come to us to defend the suit. Please research this situation and determine whether the wardens can be held liable for shooting the dogs.

The relevant cases for this assignment are *Bass v. Nofsinger,* 222 Wis. 480, 269 N.W. 303 (1936) and *Skog v. King,* 214 Wis. 591, 254 N.W. 354 (1934). The two following statutes are also relevant.

Wis.Stat. § 29.05(9)

Exemption From Liability. Each commissioner and each deputy conservation warden, in the performance of his (or her) official duties, shall be exempt from any and all liability to any person for acts done or permitted or property destroyed by authority of law. In any action brought against the commissioner or warden involving any official action, the district attorney of the county in which the action is commenced shall represent such commissioner or warden. No taxable costs or attorney fees shall be allowed to either party in said action.

Wis.Stat. § 174.01

Dogs May Be Killed. Any person may kill any dog, that he (or she) knows is affected with the disease known as hydrophobia, or that may suddenly assault him (or her) while he (or she) is peacefully walking or riding and while being out of the inclosure of its owner or keeper, and may pursue to and upon the premises of the owner or elsewhere, and kill any dog found killing, wounding or worrying any horses, cattle, sheep, lambs or other domestic animals.

ASSIGNMENT 2

Write the issue for the following situation, writing three objective issues and three persuasive ones. You are the attorney representing Susan Ashland.

MEMORANDUM

TO:　　　Junior Associate
FROM: Senior Partner
DATE: November 9, 1990
RE:　　　Susan Ashland, file # 81–386

Our client, Susan Ashland, is a world-class bike-racing champion. On July 24, 1990, as part of her training program, Ms. Ashland left Midville for a twenty-mile bike ride through Dodge County. As Ms. Ashland was riding down County Road Q, which is a two-lane paved road, a large German shepherd dog began chasing her. She was afraid the dog was going to attack her because its ears were laid back and it barked at her. The dog ran up against her and hit her bicycle. The impact knocked her off the bike; she fell, breaking her arm and tearing her clothing. Her bike, a Trek, was badly damaged. A passing motorist took Ms. Ashland to the hospital.

Our investigator has learned that the dog, Ranger, belongs to Doug Bentley, a ten-year-old boy who is spending the year with his uncle and aunt, Mike and Catherine Kelly, who own a large and prosperous dairy farm. The Kellys allow Doug to keep Ranger in one of the outbuildings near the house. Doug pays for most of Ranger's food with money he earns doing chores for the Kellys and a neighboring farmer. Ranger also eats table scraps the Kellys give him after meals.

The investigator found no evidence that Ranger had ever attacked someone before. Mrs. Kelly said the dog is friendly and playful. She has seen Ranger run out to meet neighborhood children riding their bicycles, but she has never seen him bother anyone.

Because of her broken arm, Ms. Ashland was not able to compete in any of the bike races held during the remainder of the summer, and she lost her world-class ranking. Her expenses include $1800 for doctor and hospital bills, $562 for repairing her bike, and $187 for replacing her torn shoes and clothing.

———

Tenn.Code Ann. § 471.20 (1988).[14]

471.20 Owner's liability

The owner or keeper of any dog which has injured or caused the injury of any person or property or killed, wounded or worried any horses, cattle, sheep, ranch mink or lambs shall be liable to the person so injured and the owner of such animals for all damages so done, without proving notice to the owner or keeper of such dog or knowledge by him that his dog was mischievous or disposed to kill, wound or worry horses, cattle, sheep, ranch mink or lambs; but when ranch mink are killed, wounded or worried, it shall be proven that the dog forcibly entered the enclosure in which they were kept.

This statute was first passed in 1873 and has never been amended.

Simon v. Colas, 117 Tenn. 132, 121 S.W. 51 (1911).

Colas owned a dog that bit Simon on the left leg, injuring Simon and ruining the pants Simon was wearing. Simon sued Colas under Tenn.Stat. § 471.20 (1909), claiming $15.00 damages for his injury, great pain and fright, and the value of his pants. The case was tried before a judge, who rendered judgment for Simon and awarded him $8 damages.

Colas appealed the judgment on the grounds that the damages were excessive and that under the statute no damages could be awarded for the value of Simon's pants.

The Tennessee Supreme Court examined the record from the trial court and found that the amount of the damages was not excessive. Even if the damages were given only for the injury to Simon and not for the value of his pants, the record supported the $8 amount. The court also said it did not think section 471.20 should be narrowly construed to allow damages only for injuries to the person. The court believed the liability of dog owners included not only damage to the body of the injured person, but also to the clothes he was wearing at the time of the injury.

Harnett v. Mirr, 175 Tenn. 455, 187 S.W. 871 (1936).

Mr. Mirr owned a three-story building in Knoxville. The first floor of the building was a restaurant, and the second and third floors were a

———

14. All citations are hypothetical.

hotel. Mr. Mirr's brother-in-law and sister, Mr. and Mrs. Ritter, rented two rooms on the third floor of the building. Mrs. Ritter owned three bulldogs that lived with her and her husband. Mrs. Ritter worked as a cook in the restaurant.

On May 20, 1936, the three bulldogs attacked and bit Mrs. Harnett as she was entering the funeral parlor located next door to Mr. Mirr's restaurant. Mrs. Harnett sued Mr. Mirr and Mr. and Mrs. Ritter, alleging that they were keepers of the dogs and therefore liable for her injuries under Tenn.Stat. § 471.20 (1935).

The jury found that Mr. Mirr was the keeper of the dogs and Mr. and Mrs. Ritter were not. The trial court rendered judgment against Mr. Mirr and awarded damages to Mrs. Harnett. Mr. Mirr appealed, arguing that he was not the keeper of the dogs.

The Tennessee Supreme Court reversed the trial court and held as a matter law that Mr. Mirr was not the keeper of the dogs. The court said that to be a keeper of the dogs, Mr. Mirr must have exercised control over the animals and must have harbored the animals, providing them with shelter, protection, or food. The court found nothing in the record that showed that Mr. Mirr had done anything to qualify as the keeper of the dogs. The court also said:

> Where a child is the owner of a dog kept on the premises of the father, who supplies it with food and furnishes it with shelter upon his premises, the father is deemed to be a keeper of the dog. Also, where a dog belonging to a servant is kept upon the premises of the master, with his knowledge and consent, the latter is the keeper. However, where a servant or tenant occupies a distinct portion of the premises of the master, where the dogs are kept, the master is not the keeper.

Severson v. Keating, 182 Tenn. 549, 201 S.W. 417 (1938).

The Keatings were farmers who owned several dogs that ran loose on their farm. One of the dogs attempted to cross a road in front of Severson's car. Severson ran into the dog and lost control of his car. Severson suffered very severe injuries and the dog died.

Severson sued the Keatings, alleging that they were liable for their dog's actions. The case was tried before a jury. At the end of the trial, the judge instructed the jury about the elements of negligence, but did not mention Tenn.Stat. § 471.20 (1937). The jury found that the Keatings did not fail to exercise ordinary care in controlling their dog, and therefore were not negligent. Severson appealed, arguing that although the Keatings were not found to be negligent, they should have been found liable under section 471.20.

The Tennessee Supreme Court upheld the judgment dismissing the complaint. In the opinion, the court discussed the application of section 471.20 at length. The court said that at common law a dog owner was not liable for damages resulting from the vicious act of his dog unless he had prior knowledge of the dog's vicious propensities.

Because the statute dispensed with scienter, it is no longer necessary to a *prima facie* case to show the defendant's previous knowledge of his dog's vicious character. The statute, however, does not fix absolute liability on the owner for damages caused by the innocent acts of his dog, but only for its vicious or mischievous act. The record did not show that the Keatings' dog had been vicious or mischievous at any time before the accident, nor that it was behaving viciously or mischievously at the time of the accident. Therefore, the court found that statute was inapplicable to the case and the only possible grounds for the Keatings' liability were negligence. Because the jury found that the Keatings did not fail to exercise ordinary care, there was no basis for holding them liable.

King v. Cotter, 115 Tenn.2d 50, 62 S.W.2d 526 (1969).

Mr. Cotter's adult daughter, Betty, lived at his home as a member of his family and received all of her support from him. Betty owned a collie that lived with her in her father's home and received its food in the home. Betty took her dog to a park and unleashed it. The dog ran around the park and ran into Mrs. King from behind, knocking her to the ground and permanently injuring her back.

Mrs. King sued Betty and Mr. Cotter under Tenn.Stat. § 471.20 (1967). At the close of the trial, the judge granted a directed verdict in favor of Mr. Cotter. Therefore, the jury considered only the question of Betty's liability; it found Betty liable for Mrs. King's injuries. Mrs. King appealed the granting of the directed verdict in Mr. Cotter's favor.

The Tennessee Supreme Court held that Mr. Cotter was keeper of the dog, but because the dog was not behaving viciously or mischievously, section 471.20 did not apply to the case. Even though he did not care for or control the dog, Mr. Cotter was the dog's keeper because he allowed it to be kept in his home and fed from his table. Mr. Cotter was not liable for the dog's actions, however, because the dog was not behaving viciously or mischievously when the accident occurred. Mere running, which is all the dog did, is neither vicious nor mischievous, and therefore the court held that section 471.20 did not apply to the case. The court affirmed the decision of the trial judge.

Bibliography

Berger, Charles R. and Steven H. Chaffee, Eds., *Handbook of Communication Science.* Newbury Park, CA: Sage Publications, 1987.

Cooper, Frank E. *Writing in Law Practice.* Indianapolis: Bobbs–Merrill Co., 1963.

Dernbach, John C. and Richard V. Singleton, II. *A Practical Guide to Legal Writing and Legal Methods.* Littleton, CO: Fred B. Rothman and Co., 1981.

Devitt, Edward J. and James A. Barnum, *10 Tips for Preparing Better Briefs* 22 Trial 75 (Oct. 1986).

Finn, Judith A., *Writing Briefs for Federal Litigation: The Province of the Elect,* 22 Tulsa L.J. 127 (Winter 1986).

O'Keefe, Daniel J., *Persuasion: Theory and Research.* Newbury Park, CA: Sage Publications, 1990.

Peck, Girvan, *Writing Persuasive Briefs.* Boston: Little, Brown, & Co., 1984.

Porter, Karen C., Nancy L. Schultz, Lauren Scott, Louis J. Sirico, Jr., and Annemich N. Young, *Introduction to Legal Writing and Oral Advocacy.* New York: Matthew Bender, 1989.

Pratt, Diane V., *Legal Writing: A Systematic Approach.* St. Paul: West Publishing Co., 1989.

Sandell, Rolf, *Linguistic Style and Persuasion.* San Francisco, CA: Academic Press, 1977.

Shapo, Helene C., Marilyn R. Walter and Elizabeth Fajans, *Writing and Analysis in the Law.* Westbury, NY: Foundation Press, 1989.

Spears, Franklin, *Presenting An Effective Appeal,* 21 Trial 95 (Nov. 1985).

Statsky, William P. and R. John Wernet, Jr., *Case Analysis and Fundamentals of Legal Writing.* St. Paul: West Publishing Co., 1977.

Tepley, Larry L., *Legal Writing, Analysis, and Oral Argument.* St. Paul: West Publishing Co., 1990.

Weihofen, Henry, *Legal Writing Style.* St. Paul: West Publishing Co., 1980.

Chapter 7

OBJECTIVE STATEMENTS OF FACT

In contrast to the issues or the discussion section, the fact section requires a different focus. When you write an issue, your focus is on condensing the big picture into one sentence; when you write the discussion, your focus is on thoroughly explaining a logical process. In contrast, when you write the objective statement of facts, your focus is on telling a story. Like a reporter, tell the story accurately, clearly, and simply.

> [C]onvey the writer's meaning to the reader with the least possible difference between the effect produced and that intended and with the least possible wear and tear on the reader's capacity and goodwill.[1]

Also like a reporter, you need to be efficient, simply because neither the client nor the firm can afford for you to do otherwise. Finally, be concise. Your reader wants to make sense of the who, what, when, where, why, and how of the facts as quickly as possible before proceeding to the legal issue. Despite these time and space limitations, the statement of facts offers some interesting opportunities for the advanced legal writer to develop his or her own style.

This chapter addresses both these limitations and opportunities while guiding you through the basic tasks involved in writing a fact statement: (1) determining which facts to include, (2) determining how to organize those facts, and (3) writing the facts to be accurate and clear. The section about writing, however, includes only a beginning list of techniques for accuracy and clarity. The next chapter, on persuasive statements of fact, delves more deeply into the wording and sentence structures that affect the way the reader understands your content.

DETERMINING WHICH FACTS TO INCLUDE

Although choosing which facts to include is one of the first questions you consider when drafting your facts, you cannot completely

---

1. Vernon Lee, *The Handling of Words, and Other Studies in Literary Psychology* 40–41 (1968).

answer this question at first. Instead, you will return to this question in revision and throughout the writing process if the question of whether to include a fact is particularly difficult to resolve. You must focus not on whether the fact is favorable, but on whether it is needed. To help you determine whether a fact is needed, consider three categories of facts: legally significant facts, background facts, and emotional facts.

Legally Significant Facts

Your primary obligation in the statement of facts is to communicate the legally significant facts, those facts that, if changed, would change the answer to the issue. For example, include all the highlighted facts when writing the fact section of a memo addressing the following issue.

Under Wis.Stat. sec. 346.11., passing or meeting a frightened animal, did a motorcyclist stop as promptly as she safely could when *the motorcyclist was driving around a curve on a wet gravel road at 40 miles per hour and might have lost control of the motorcycle if she had stopped more quickly?*

If, for example, the motorcyclist had been driving at 20 miles per hour or the road had been dry, the answer you reach in the memo would be different. These are the legally significant facts you should include. To make sure you have included all of these facts, revise your fact statement after drafting your issue and discussion, watching in particular for any omissions of legally significant facts.

Background Facts

Also include any background facts that clarify the story. Names and other details make the picture of what happened more concrete and easier to understand. For example, the first of the following passages presents a clearer picture than the second. Even though the second includes all the legally significant facts, the first gives the reader a more concrete picture.

The balcony, railing, and supports were all made of wood. At the time of the accident, Karen was standing on the right corner of the balcony. She was resting her hands on the railing, which consisted of two horizontal wooden beams supported by vertical beams at the corners and center of the balcony. When the wooden support under the porch fractured into two pieces, the right side of the balcony dropped down suddenly, leaving the floor of the balcony tilted like a slide. Karen fell to the balcony floor, slid under the railing, tried but failed to grab the lower rail, and fell from the balcony fifteen feet to the sidewalk below.

While the plaintiff was standing on the balcony, the support gave way. When the balcony tilted, the plaintiff slid under the rail and fell to the sidewalk below.

Although the first passage is relatively long, the length alone does not indicate wordiness. Wordiness is caused by either the inclusion of unneeded information or the wordy phrasing of needed information. For example, the writer may have used unnecessary prepositional phrases, passive voice, or long transitional phrases. If you need to include many background facts, do not hesitate to do so. Instead, focus on presenting them as clearly and concisely as possible. As you review your fact section, determine when the details are needed for clarity and when they may be omitted for conciseness. When revising for conciseness, consider deleting any details that (1) confuse more than clarify, (2) clarify points of no concern to the legal reader, or (3) signal the reader that an irrelevant point may indeed be relevant. Omitting these should make the statement concise without sacrificing clarity.

Emotional Facts

One decision you will often face is when to include emotional facts. Although these facts may not be legally significant, they may nevertheless prove significant in the actual handling of the case. If so, alert the reader of these facts. Including emotional facts is even more troubling when, in a fair world, they would not be significant. This subsection guides you through the process of handling these difficult facts.

A general question that arises is whether emotional facts have any place in this objective document. The standard wisdom is that they do not. Indeed judgmental labels added by the writer have no place. For example, you would not use the following.

> The *poorly maintained* balcony collapsed *without warning,* sending *young* Karen plunging to the concrete below.

Instead, you would write the following.

> **Karen fell from the balcony when the supports for the balcony collapsed and caused the balcony floor to tilt. The supports, which had not been inspected for three years, had been weakened by dry rot and were**. . . .

The second version states the facts that lead the reader to see the judgments made in the first version, but they do so by giving the detail the reader needs to reach that conclusion. Although in some situations you may need to quote judgmental labels used by others because their use is legally significant, do not introduce them yourself.

Discussions about some emotional facts are more problematic, however, because they are not of legal significance but might be otherwise important to the advancement of the case itself. For example, the handling of a case might be influenced by the fact that your client has a history of bouts with mental disorders that led to violent episodes, even when that fact has no direct legal significance to the question involved.

This is a particularly delicate question because the very source of their importance may lie in the injustice within our society. Examples of facts falling into this category are: age, income, education, sexual preference, sex, race, national heritage, and religion or the absence of religion, appearance, weight, height, mannerisms, and so forth. A few specific examples include the fact that the plaintiff has tested HIV positive, the key expert witness has a lisp, or the defendant has a million dollar insurance policy.

For example, if the client is a defendant professor accused of discriminating against African–American students, is it necessary to include the fact that the professor was born in South Africa? If, after careful consideration, you think an emotional fact will affect the decisions to be made in the case, include the fact, stating it objectively as discussed later in this chapter.

To determine whether an emotional fact should be included, first explain to yourself why this fact may deserve inclusion. Reason out the point, and write out the reasoning if it is at all complex. Then study and evaluate your reasoning. Is it honest? Or is it a rationalization of some of your own biases? This is a hard question, but it is better that you ask it of yourself in private and learn where you stand. You do not want to include the fact without recognizing your reasons and risk having to address this question in front of someone else.

One example of a situation that might require this reflection and evaluation might be whether to include, in a memo addressing whether your client will be liable for damage resulting from a collision, the fact that the plaintiff, the driver of the other car, has a congenitally deformed right hand. This fact might not be legally significant to the issue of liability because no evidence suggests that the condition of the hand affected the plaintiff's driving. It may not be significant to any issue of damages because no injury to the hand is claimed. But would a jury be more sympathetic to this person, so that the deformity might affect the outcome of a trial if the case reaches that point? If so, perhaps the fact is important, and you might be wise to include it as you evaluate the strength of the case. Or if you think the fact could raise a question about the plaintiff's control of his car and thus favor your client, you might decide to include it, even though it may disturb you to do so.

In summary, then, include emotional facts when they may affect the handling of the case. Do not, however, include your own emotions or judgments about those facts.

ORGANIZING THE FACTS

As you move into advanced techniques for organizing the statement of facts, you have an opportunity to add another dimension to your writing of fact statements, your own story-telling style. Often, the constraints of the legal writing task, especially the needs of the client and the reader, force you to set aside your own writing preferences. In the statement of facts, however, you have at least one choice that can be determined by your own style: the way you begin your statement of facts.

This addition of personal story-telling style may make the task not only more pleasant, but also more efficient. Because memos are in-house documents, your writing is not defined by legal rules or traditions, but rather by common sense, an awareness of house rules, and your reader's preferences. In particular, your own process can influence your approach to the organization of the facts.

The most popular organization for facts is chronological, in which the story simply starts at the beginning.

> At 7:30 a.m. on July 12, 1987, Kathryn Archer was waiting at a bus stop on Washington Avenue. While she was waiting, . . .

In general, legal writers organize facts chronologically. This order seems natural for telling a story. The reader can watch the story unfold, seeing how one event leads to another without having to reconstruct the chronology mentally. Chronology simplifies the reader's task in moving through the paragraphs just as active voice moves the reader through a sentence smoothly.

But useful variations also exist. For example, you might begin by stating the general legal situation or the procedural history of the case, if there is one, then return to the chronology.

> Our client, Kathryn Archer, is seeking to invalidate a document she signed. The document may waive her right to sue for damages for an injury she suffered while waiting at a bus stop on July 12, 1987.

This structure helps the reader see the significance of the facts because it clarifies their legal context. In some memos, writers organize the facts into several sections and then organize them chronologically within each section. This is useful if the sequence of facts is hard to follow, as when you need to include facts going to different theories, incidents, or locations. In this case, you may group facts according to issue, incident, or location and then organize them chronologically within those groups. For example, you may place a section on the procedural facts either at the beginning or the end of the fact statement. Placing it at the end allows the procedure to fit into the larger chronological order. Placing it at the beginning may be useful to give the reader a context needed to understand the significance of the chronology. For example, when writing a memo on a *Miranda* issue, you may want to explain the procedural posture first so the reader sees how this issue arises from the facts. In deciding whether to put the procedure at the beginning or the end, choose the location that makes it easy for the reader to understand the entire fact situation.

Another possibility is to begin with a sentence summarizing the facts on which the case turns before beginning the chronology.

> In return for a payment of $5,000, Kathryn Archer agreed to refrain from suing the City of Pleasantview for any additional

damages arising from the injury she suffered while waiting at a city bus stop.

This structure is particularly useful when the chronology is complex and when, without that overview, the reader might wonder where the facts were leading. It is also useful when the facts initially suggest some legal question other than the one that will ultimately arise.

Some other variations of the opening may be particularly useful for certain readers. For example, one staff attorney for an appellate court realized that her judges faced a substantial task just keeping the facts of various cases separate in their minds. To help them, she tried opening her fact statements with a quick, concrete statement orienting the judge and providing a refreshing start. For example, to introduce yet another action in a previously appealed situation, she wrote the following.

> This is the Wilfred Bank Case come back to haunt us yet again.

In a case revolving around a technical question, she opened with a more memorable, concrete fact before introducing the technical details.

> This was a suit over soggy crackers.

Another opening helped the judge quickly see the nature of the case.

> This is a typical *Miranda* question.

Thus she developed a label for each case that she could use in future conferences or other references, so the judge would not have to labor over names, case numbers, and technicalities to become reacquainted with the situation. Although all readers might not appreciate this approach, her readers did. Her change was a welcome improvement in the court's communication habits.

As you try new openings and organizations, much depends on your reader's preferences, and those preferences must supersede your own. When you write a research memo, you are by definition summarizing and providing information to someone whose time you are supposed to save by your work. No matter how clever or skilled your openings and organizations are, they cannot be effective if they distract. They will be effective only if they aid your reader. Nevertheless, within these bounds you can allow your own style to influence the way you open and organize the statement of facts.

WRITING STATEMENTS OF FACT

Two questions arise when drafting statements of fact. The first is how to maintain accuracy and clarity. This question arises not because it is complex or debatable, but because it is central to the statement's purpose. The second is how to handle emotional facts that you must include. This question arises not because it is central, but because it is complex and debatable.

Maintaining Accuracy and Clarity

Whatever choices you make in your openings and organization, you cannot allow your personal style unlimited expression throughout the statement of facts. You must at all times be governed by a concern for accuracy and clarity. Employ the following techniques as you revise: (1) state key points specifically and concretely, even if they are unfavorable; (2) keep labels minimal and consistent; and (3) substitute names for pronouns where needed. Additionally, you can use the emphasis techniques discussed in the next chapter on persuasive facts to add emphasis to the most significant facts.

Stating Key Points Specifically and Concretely, Even If Unfavorable

You must state key points clearly in the memo statement of facts. In a brief you may want to state an unfavorable fact abstractly to minimize it, but you do not want to do this in an office memo. At this point in the process, minimizing the seriousness of a fact could be disastrous. For this reason, avoid unneeded abstractions. State what happened specifically and concretely.

While driving approximately 45 m.p.h. through a school zone with a speed limit of 25 m.p.h., Mr. Protzsky saw a crossing guard step off the curb. He immediately applied his brakes, which caused his car to spin counterclockwise and jump the curb.

rather than

While driving through the school zone, Mr. Protzsky. . . .
When he applied his brakes, the speed of his car caused. . . .

One way to make the facts more specific and concrete is to minimize use of the passive voice, which can obscure the cause of an action. If your client drove into a parked car, say so. You will not state it so bluntly in your brief, no doubt, but here clarity and accuracy are priorities, not tact. If concerns about subsequent discovery exist, you might convey some information to the senior attorney orally rather than in writing. But make sure the attorney somehow receives any information critical to his or her handling of the case.

In a similar vein, avoid using euphemisms. For example, do not say "failed to recollect" if the facts indicate "forgot," "overlooked," or "did not remember to. . . ." Again, the reader must comprehend your meaning with a minimum of effort, and euphemisms only make the reader work harder to get your point.

Keeping Labels Minimal and Consistent

If you have read anything by Tolstoy, you have experienced the struggle of keeping straight a cast of characters, each of whom has several names, nicknames, and titles. To be sure the actors in your facts are clear, choose one name for each person and use that name throughout. You may refer to other roles in some situations, but always accompany any reference with the one consistent label you are using.

> Our client, Evelyn Post,. . . .   Ms. Post. . . .   As a teacher, Ms. Post. . . .   When describing his colleague, Ms. Post, James Lassler said, "Evelyn has always. . . ."

Even though you might be tempted to substitute "the teacher" or "Evelyn" for variety throughout this passage, that change would be more likely to increase the work your reader must do than reduce his or her boredom.

Substituting Names for Pronouns

If you have several "he's" or several "she's" in the facts, clarify the identity of each actor by using names more frequently. Also insert names instead of pronouns when the story shifts the focus to a different actor.

> Carl and Floyd had been working together on this boat for several years. *Carl* had modified the design to suit them better. He also purchased all necessary supplies and equipment and kept the financial records. *Floyd* invested more time in the actual construction of the boat, spending many of his weekends finishing the wooden deck and fixtures. He gave *Carl* an account of the hours he spent working on the boat, but *Carl* did not keep such an account of his hours.

Substitute the names when the scene changes, whether the change is marked by a change in time or location.

> Before they drove the boat out of the garage, Carl checked the hitch to make sure it was properly engaged and checked to see that the safety chains were attached. He did not, however, put any weight on the hitch or in any way check the framing attached to the truck to hold the hitch.

> After *Carl* climbed into the truck, he began studying the owner's manual for the outboard motor they had installed, and so he did not notice that the trailer was swaying back and forth as Floyd drove the truck down the street.

This inclusion of names helps the reader focus on the story without having to sort out who is doing what.

Techniques for Including Emotional Facts

Once you have decided to include an emotional fact, make sure you handle it competently. State the fact objectively and neutrally, eschewing any personal judgment you might have. For example, if you decide to let the reader know that one person in the fact pattern is a supporter of the Irish Republican Army, then do so. But make sure you state the fact respectfully, in no way suggesting any personal evaluation of the fact.

When you state the facts, include the facts that state the emotion. This approach for handling emotional facts is based on research into what makes a writer credible [2] and based on general principles of good storytelling. An effective storyteller will write

He clenched his fists and moved forward, yelling, "I've taken all I plan to from you!"

rather than

He shouted angrily.

You too must give your reader enough facts to reach an independent judgment about what the facts show. You must not force the reader to trust your judgment any more than necessary: "Credibility is just as fragile for a writer as for a President." [3]

Position the emotional fact in the statement to show the reader the fact in context. For example, if the fact would be important only because it suggests possible intent, put it with the others that suggest possible intent. If the fact would be important only at trial, state it in the context of the other facts relevant to a trial.

> Mr. Yeats has asked us to prepare to take this issue to court rather than agreeing to settlement. He believes that the plaintiff's congenitally malformed right hand is evidence that the plaintiff did not have control over his automobile, even though the plaintiff was driving a vehicle with an automatic transmission, which is the only restriction listed on his valid Arkansas driver's license.

Then, in the discussion, communicate to the reader how that fact may be important, just as you do other significant facts.

The Use of Visual Aids

The use of visual aids (charts, tables, maps, and so forth) is gaining popularity. With advanced printer technology, you can now produce visual aids, and their use can enhance the clarity and conciseness of your facts. How much you use visual aids will depend on your own inclinations and abilities in this area. Although effective aids can save time for the reader, preparing them often takes more time than writing. As a result, you will probably choose to use visual aids only when the facts are so complex that the reader needs the extra clarity the visual aid can provide.[4]

When creating a visual aid, observe two principles: (1) keep it as simple and focused as possible and (2) structure it to be read from top to bottom, left to right.

[2]. Research indicates that the reader judges the credibility of the writer based on the reader's sense of the writer's competence in the area addressed and on his or her sense of whether that writer can be trusted to represent the situation fairly. Daniel J. O'Keefe, *Persuasion: Theory and Research* 133 (1990).

[3]. William Zinsser, *On Writing Well* 108 (2nd ed. 1980).

[4]. *See* Kristin R. Woolever, *Untangling the Law: Strategies for Legal Writers* (1987).

Eliminating unnecessary information in your visual aid is a major step in communicating your point. For example, Figure 1 is likely to overwhelm the legal reader.[5]

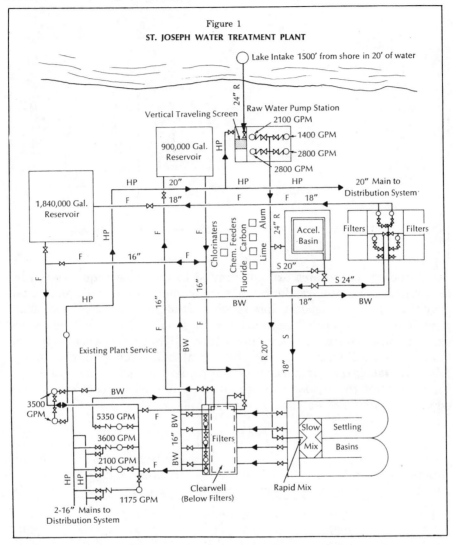

Figure 1
ST. JOSEPH WATER TREATMENT PLANT

Figure 2, in contrast, is a simplified version of the same diagram, providing enough information to leave the reader adequately informed, not overwhelmed. As an extra benefit, it will be easier to understand and produce.[6]

5. J.C. Mathes and Dwight W. Stevenson, *Designing Technical Report: Writing for Audiences in Organizations*, 177 (1976).

6. *Id.* at 176.

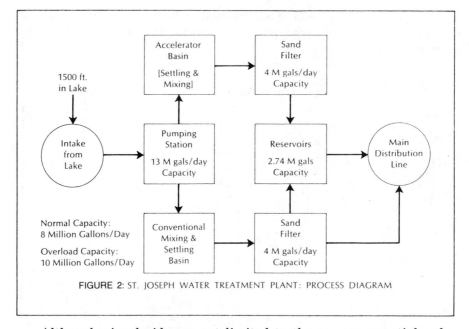

FIGURE 2: ST. JOSEPH WATER TREATMENT PLANT: PROCESS DIAGRAM

Although visual aids are not limited to the same sequential order as English text, the reader who spends more time with text than graphics will bring reading habits when studying the visual aid, scanning it from the top left across, as with a page of text. If you work against these habits, you slow the reader. If you work with them, you help the reader move through the visual aid. For example, in the following table, the comparison of one camera model to another is not the first point the reader will see. Seeing it requires comparing data down a column rather than across a line.

TABLE 1 [7]

Model Number	Year of Origin	Lens f-number	Shutter Speed (maximum in seconds)	Retail Cost New ($)
100	1964	5.6	1/300	82
101	1968	3.5	1/500	89
102	1969	2.8	1/800	104
103	1972	1.4	1/1000	117

If you switch the axes of the table, however, the point becomes clearer. In the following revision, the information from the previous column now appears in a horizontal line.

7. These two tables are adapted from Kenneth Houp and Thomas Pearsall, *Reporting Technical Information* Fourth Edition, 235–236 (1980).

TABLE 2

| | Model Numbers | | | |
Descriptive Data	100	101	102	103
Year of Origin	1964	1968	1969	1972
Lens f-number	5.6	3.5	2.8	1.4
Shutter speed (maximum)	1/300	1/500	1/800	1/1000
Retail cost new (dollars)	82	89	104	117

CONCLUSION

Rather than covering all the writing skills needed when drafting an objective facts section, this chapter has given you a general overview of the tasks you need to fulfill and some ways to address the most common or troubling questions that can arise.

Add to these skills the basic writing concerns of conciseness and readability to round out your expertise when drafting fact statements. Then integrate these skills into your own writing process. To develop your process, study the following sample checklist, which incorporates the techniques and questions discussed in this chapter into an overall checklist. Try this process on the following exercise. Then revise it, adapting the checklist to fit more closely to your natural writing process.

CHECKLIST FOR DRAFTING STATEMENTS OF FACT

1. Include all needed facts.
   a. Legally significant facts.
      (1) Facts that will be used in the discussion section.
      (2) Facts that show that the elements of the cause of action or defenses are met.
      (3) Facts that will be used in the other side's legal argument.
      (4) Any needed procedural facts.
   b. Needed background facts.
   c. Emotional facts you have determined should be included.
2. Organize those facts.
   a. Choose the most effective opening for this fact statement.
   b. Divide into subsections if needed.
   c. Organize each section or subsection chronologically.
   d. Divide facts into paragraphs that group the facts logically.

---

    e.   Use visual aids if appropriate. When using visual aids,

        (1)   keep them as simple and focused as possible, and

        (2)   structure them to be read from top to bottom, left to right.

3.   Draft the facts to be accurate and clear.

    a.   State even unfavorable points specifically and concretely.

    b.   Keep labels minimal and consistent.

    c.   Substitute names for pronouns where needed.

4.   After drafting the discussion, revise the facts. Ask yourself the following questions.

    a.   Are all legally significant facts included?

    b.   Are all unneeded background and emotional facts deleted? Consider deleting any details

        (1)   that may confuse more than clarify,

        (2)   that clarify points that will not concern the legal reader, or

        (3)   that signal to the reader that an irrelevant point may be relevant.

    c.   Are sentences readable?

    d.   Is each word used unambiguous and clear?

    e.   Are all wordy phrases eliminated?

EXERCISE

Write a statement of the case for a bench memo to the Court of Appeals judge you work for, using the two sides' statement of the case given below.

Appellant's Statement of the Case

Christy, a Montana sheep rancher, leased lands adjacent to Glacier National Park from the Blackfeet Indian Tribe. Before entering the lease, Christy checked with the prior lessee about problems with predators. The lessee assured Christy that predators had not been a problem. In June 1982, Christy determined it was safe to leave over 1,700 sheep with an experienced sheep herder on the leased land.

In the previous year, Kenneth Wheeler (Wheeler), an experienced trapper employed by the United States Fish and Wildlife Service (U.S. F.W.S.) live-captured by snare four nuisance grizzly bears near Yellowstone National Park. These marauding grizzlies had been pillaging campground dumpsters and devouring sheep on adjacent ranches. Unknown to Christy, Wheeler relocated the bears just 20 to 40 miles from Christy's leased land. The U.S.F.W.S. has since stopped relocating bears because it was determined that once bears have acquired a taste for sheep, they are more likely to make future attacks on sheep. Grizzlies have been known to travel as far as 400 square miles in search of their acquired food taste.

In the summer of 1982, just after Christy moved his sheep on the leased land, grizzly and black bears began attacking. In just eight days, 20 sheep (worth at least $1,200) were devoured by the bears. Christy's herder tried repeatedly to frighten the bears by building fires and firing shots in the air, but each night the vicious attacks continued. Eager to stop the killings and keep the bears away, Christy sought protection under the Endangered Species Act by notifying the U.S. F.W.S. Accordingly, the government assigned Wheeler full-time to help Christy. Although he told Christy a lot of bears might be in the area, he was sure the vicious attacks were from two grizzly bears and maybe two black bears as well. He set snares baited with sheep in an effort to live-capture the offending nuisance bears. The nightly attacks continued. Wheeler checked the snares twice daily for several days, but did not catch anything. Nothing was working to stop the vicious killings and keep the bears away. Even the dogs were getting worn out from trying to chase the bears away each and every night.

By July 9, 1982, Christy was frustrated and fed up with the futile attempts to keep the bears from his sheep. His herder was fearful for his life and as exhausted as the dogs in trying to protect the sheep. Wheeler could only apologize for the unsuccessful efforts of his snares. That evening when Wheeler was routinely checking one of the snares, he found a black bear that Christy had shot laying by it. Then they both saw two bears coming out of the woods and moving quickly toward the sheep. One was scared away by the sight of the two men; but the other just stood there menacingly. Knowing how many sheep had already been killed and fearing continued relentless attacks, Christy fired one shot at the bear. Wheeler said nothing. The bear staggered, stumbled and eventually fell. Wheeler walked over toward it and fired the second shot. It was a grizzly bear. Wheeler then warned Christy that he could not just shoot grizzly bears because they are an endangered species. After all this, the other bear came back that same night tormenting the sheep repeatedly.

By the end of July, an additional 64 sheep fell prey to the attacking bears. In all, Christy lost over 80 sheep worth at least $5,000. Unable to incur any further loss to his sheep, he finally had to give up his lease. On July 22, 1982, the Tribe agreed to terminate his lease and refund his money. Christy was then forced to move his remaining sheep from the land. After much time and effort, he was unable to find a suitable place. Left with no other alternative, he had to sell a substantial portion of his remaining sheep for slaughter value. The loss he incurred was well in excess of $10,000.

Two years later, a Notice of Assessment for $3,000 was issued against Christy alleging that he violated the Endangered Species Act (1 U.S.C. § 1531, et seq.) (the "Act") and the regulations at 50 C.F.R.

§ 17.40(b) (1984) (the "regulations"). It was not until March 14, 1985, that an administrative hearing was held pursuant to Christy's request. He was ordered to pay a civil penalty of $2,500. Christy's Request for Appeal from the administrative decision was denied. With no other remedy available under the Act, Christy filed this action in U.S. District Court against Defendants–Appellees, Donald P. Hodel, Secretary of the Interior and the United States Department of Interior. He sought declaratory and injunctive relief alleging the Act and the regulations violated his rights guaranteed by the Fifth Amendment to the United States Constitution.

Over a year after Christy's complaint was filed, the district court granted defendants' motion for summary judgment. Christy appealed this decision on multiple grounds to the Court of Appeals for the Ninth Circuit. Summary judgment for defendants was affirmed. Christy then petitioned for rehearing en banc. The decision on whether to hear the case was stayed pending Christy's petition for certiorari to the United States Supreme Court. Certiorari was denied and the Ninth Circuit granted our petition for rehearing.

Review is limited to the question of whether the Act operated as an authorized governmental "taking" of Christy's property in violation of the Fifth Amendment of the United States Constitution.

Appellant's Argument

I. THE GRIZZLY BEARS TOOK CHRISTY'S PROPERTY IN VIOLATION OF THE FIFTH AMENDMENT BECAUSE THEY PERMANENTLY PHYSICALLY OCCUPIED THE PROPERTY AND DENIED CHRISTY THE PROPERTY OWNERSHIP RIGHTS OF POSSESSION, USE AND DISPOSSESSION BY COMING ONTO HIS LAND AND KILLING HIS SHEEP.

    A. The Trial Court Decision To Grant Summary Judgment Was Clearly Erroneous And Should Be Reviewed De Novo By The Appellate Court Because Genuine Issues Of Material Fact Remain As To Whether The Offending Grizzly Bears Are The Same Grizzly Bears That Were Captured And Relocated By The Government.

    B. The Bears Were Owned By The United States Government Because The Government Pursued An Active Policy Of Capturing And Relocating Bears, Exercising Such Control Over The Bears As To Constitute Ownership.

    C. The United States Government Gained A Proprietary Interest In The Bears, And Thus A Duty To Protect Property, Because It Reduced The Bears To Skillful Capture And Actively Regulated The Bear Population.

    D. The Bears' Trespassing And Killing Sheep Effects A Permanent Physical Occupation Of Christy's Property By Denying

Him The Right To Possess, Use, Or Dispose Of His Property And Is Thus A Taking As A Matter Of Law.

E. The Bears' Passing To And Fro Across Christy's Property Constituted A Permanent, Physical Occupation Of His Property Because Their Permanent And Continuous Access To His Land Effectively Created An Easement.

II. THE ENDANGERED SPECIES ACT AND THE REGULATIONS MAKING IT UNLAWFUL TO HARASS, HARM, PURSUE, HUNT, SHOOT, WOUND, KILL, TRAP, CAPTURE OR COLLECT GRIZZLY BEARS EFFECT A REGULATORY TAKING OF CHRISTY'S PROPERTY VIOLATING THE FIFTH AMENDMENT BECAUSE IT SUBSTANTIALLY INTERFERED WITH HIS REASONABLE INVESTMENT–BACKED EXPECTATIONS AS A SHEEP RANCHER AND UNFAIRLY FORCED HIM TO BEAR THE BURDEN OF PROTECTING GRIZZLY BEARS ON BEHALF OF THE PUBLIC.

A. Whether The Endangered Species Act And Its Regulations Effect A Taking Is A Question Of Law For The Appellate Court To Review De Novo.

B. The ESA And The Complementary Grizzly Bear Regulations Went So Far Beyond An Ordinary Regulation As To Effect A Taking Because It Substantially Interfered With Christy's Reasonable Investment–Backed Expectations As A Sheep Rancher By Forcing Him To Rely On Its Provisions To Protect His Property Thereby Denying Him An Effective And Efficient Defense.

C. The ESA And Its Regulations Effect A Taking Because Christy Is Denied The One And Only Profitable Means Of Use Of His Sheep Ranch And Unfairly Forced Him To Bear The Burden Of A Public Good Which Should Be Borne By The Public At Large.

Secretary of Interior's Statement of the Case

The defendant, Richard Christy, is a Montana sheep rancher who owned 1,700 head of sheep. In June 1982, he began grazing the sheep on land leased from the Blackfeet Indian Tribe. The land is located near Glacier National Park, where the United States Fish and Wildlife Service (U.S.F.W.S.) had recently relocated four grizzly bears, classified as "nuisances" for disturbing sheep on nearby ranches and for eating out of campground dumpsters. Even though the national park is known to have a large bear population, and despite bears' known propensity to roam, Christy relied upon the prior lessor's assurances that the ranch was completely safe from predators, and he left his sheep in the hands of a sheep herder instead of watching the herd himself.

Around July 1, 1982, black bears as well as grizzly bears began disturbing Christy's sheep nightly. Between July 1 and July 9, 1982, approximately twenty sheep, at a total value of around 1,200 dollars, were killed by bears. Christy waited until several days after the first sheep were killed before contacting the U.S.F.W.S.

The U.S.F.W.S. dispatched a trapper to work full-time to ameliorate Christy's situation. The trapper concluded that two black bears and two grizzly bears were disturbing Christy's sheep but could not be sure whether they were the nuisance bears relocated by the government because those bears had not been marked for identification. When baited snares were unsuccessful in capturing the bears, the trapper advised Christy to move the sheep to where they would be less vulnerable to attack. In response to the trapper's suggestion, Christy merely told his herdsman to try to frighten the bears by firing shots in the air and by building fires.

Despite continued nightly attacks on Christy's sheep, the herd remained under the supervision of the herder rather than Christy himself. The frightened herder's attempts at scaring the bears were useless. After several nights, the herder became exhausted and fearful for his life.

On July 9, 1982, even though the U.S.F.W.S. trapper was still working full-time to devise a solution to Christy's problem, Christy began killing bears that wandered onto his land. That afternoon, he had killed two black bears even though one was merely twenty feet from the trapper's snares. Later that day, even with the trapper at his side, Christy panicked when he saw two grizzly bears lumber from the forest. One of the bears, apparently frightened by the presence of the two men, quickly retreated. The other bear merely stood watching the men, not acting aggressively toward the sheep. With the bear still one-hundred yards away from the herd, Christy seized his rifle and fired a lethal shot into the animal. After the bear had fallen to the ground, and no longer posed a threat to the sheep, Christy fired another bullet into the animal's body.

The trapper's subsequent efforts to capture any bears were unsuccessful. On July 22, 1982, the Blackfeet Indian Tribe agreed to terminate the lease and to refund Christy's money. Two days later, having lost a total of eighty-four sheep to the bears, Christy removed his flock from the leased land. Deeming no other land suitable for the grazing of his entire herd, he sold part of the herd at slaughter value, at a loss of about ten thousand dollars.

The Department of the Interior assessed a civil penalty of $3,000 against Christy for killing a grizzly bear in violation of the Endangered Species Act (the Act), 16 U.S.C. § 1538(a)(1)(G) (1985) as it is applied to grizzly bears through 50 C.F.R. § 17.11. The regulations forbid the "taking" of grizzly bears except in specific circumstances, 50 C.F.R. § 17.40(b)(1). In August, 1984, the Department held an administrative hearing at which Christy admitted that he knowingly killed a grizzly bear, but said he did so in exercise of his right to defend his sheep. The Department upheld the fine but lowered the amount to $2,500.

Christy appealed the departmental ruling on the basis that the penalty violated his constitutional right to defend his sheep. The appeal was denied on the ground that the Department had no jurisdiction to determine the constitutionality of federal laws and regulations.

In January 1986, Christy initiated the present action in the United States District Court for the District of Montana (Great Falls), seeking a permanent injunction restraining the Department from enforcing the Act and the pursuant regulations against him. Christy alleges that the Act and regulations deprived him of his right to possess and protect property, as guaranteed by the Fifth Amendment to the United States Constitution, that they deprived him of property without just compensation or due process, and that they also deprived him of equal protection of the laws. In addition, Christy seeks a declaration that application of the Act and regulations to him for his defense of his property is unconstitutional.

In July 1986, the Department filed a motion for summary judgment pursuant to Federal Rule of Civil Procedure 56. In May 1987, the district court granted the Department's motion for summary judgment. In ruling that the Department was entitled to judgment as a matter of law, the district court held that damage to private property by protected wildlife does not constitute a taking.

Christy appealed the district court's entry of summary judgment for the Department to a panel of the Court of Appeals for the Ninth Circuit. The Ninth Circuit affirmed the district court's grant of summary judgment, reiterating the district court's ruling that the Act and regulations did not deprive Christy of his property by preventing him from killing intrusive bears. Subsequently, Christy petitioned for rehearing en banc. The Ninth Circuit waited until after the United States Supreme Court denied Christy's petition for certiorari review before granting his petition for rehearing. The Ninth Circuit has limited the scope of Christy's rehearing to the question of whether the Act has operated as a governmental authorization of a "taking" of Christy's property in violation of the Fifth Amendment.

Respondent's Argument

I. THE DESTRUCTION OF SHEEP BY FEDERALLY PROTECTED GRIZZLY BEARS DOES NOT CONSTITUTE AN INVASION OF PLAINTIFF–APPELLANT'S FLOCK OF SHEEP, WHICH WERE GRAZING ON AN ADJACENT INDIAN RESERVATION, BECAUSE THE GOVERNMENT IS NOT RESPONSIBLE FOR THE BEARS AND BECAUSE PROTECTION OF THE BEARS UNDER THE ENDANGERED SPECIES ACT IS A JUSTIFIABLE LAND–USE REGULATION.

A. The Government Is Not Responsible For The Bears' Action Because It Does Not Exercise Adequate Control Over The Bears.

B. The Endangered Species Act And Pursuant Regulations Act As Land–Use Regulations Because The Conditions They Impose Substantially Advance An Important Governmental Interest.

II. THE ENDANGERED SPECIES ACT AND THE COMPLE-MENTING GRIZZLY BEAR REGULATIONS DO NOT EFFECT A "TAKING" OF PROPERTY BECAUSE AN EXPECTATION THAT NO SHEEP WILL BE KILLED BY BEARS IN LIGHT OF THE ACT AND REGULATIONS IS UNREASONABLE, THE ECONOM-IC IMPACT OF THE ACT AND REGULATIONS UPON AN INDI-VIDUAL RANCHER IS LESS SIGNIFICANT, AND THE ACT AND REGULATIONS ARE NOT AN EXTRAORDINARY PRO-TECTION OF THE PUBLIC INTEREST; THEREFORE, A SHEEP RANCHER WHOSE SHEEP ARE KILLED BY BEARS PROTECT-ED UNDER THE ACT AND REGULATIONS IS NOT ENTITLED TO EXEMPTION FROM THE PROHIBITIONS PROMULGATED UNDER THE ACT.

A. Whether The District Court Has Properly Entered Summary Judgment In Favor Of The Department Of The Interior Is A Question Of Law That The Appellate Court Reviews Independently.

B. The Fifth Amendment's Taking Clause Is Invoked When The Endangered Species Act And Complementary Grizzly Bear Regulations Prevent A Sheep Rancher From Killing Grizzly Bears That Are Attacking His Sheep Because The Sheep Are A Tangible Entity Over Which The Rancher Has Control And From Which He Derives Income, Thereby Giving The Rancher A Property Interest In The Sheep.

C. The Endangered Species Act And Complementing Grizzly Bear Regulations Do Not Effect A "Taking" Of Property When They Prevent A Sheep Rancher From Killing Bears That Attack His Sheep Because An Expectation That No Sheep Will Be Killed By Bears In Light Of The Act And Regulations Is Unreasonable, The Economic Impact Of The Act And Regulations Upon An Individual Rancher Is Less Than Significant, And The Act And Regulations Are Not Extraordinary In View Of The Public Interest They Protect.

ASSIGNMENT 1

Memorandum [8]

To: Associate
From: Senior Partner
Date: February 1, 1989
Re: Obtaining a preliminary injunction for Larry Lederhosen under the Lanham Act.

Our client, Larry Lederhosen, is a leading polka musician here in Wisconsin. In early 1987 he signed a record contract with Steven Slimey, president of OOmPA records. OOmPA agreed to release an unedited recording of Larry's La Cross Octoberfest concert, his biggest concert of the year.

OOmPA agreed to record the entire concert and also agreed that Larry would have the right to veto any proposed major changes in how the concert was presented on record.

The record has just been produced and Larry is very upset by it. Upon listening to it, he found that the songs on the record are not in the same order as they were at the concert. In addition, a twenty minute instrumental song featuring Willard Windbag, an acclaimed accordionist, was edited down to five minutes.

Despite these changes, the cover reads as follows: "Larry Lederhosen Presents the 1987 La Crosse Octoberfest Concert: A Live Recording." A sticker on the record reads "This is the record polka fans have been waiting for! Larry, the Mirthmakers, and their many Polka friends captured in concert, just as you remember them." There is also a big picture of Larry on the front cover. On the back cover is a picture of the stage and the crowd during the concert.

Larry does not want this record to be released. I believe that a preliminary injunction may be possible under § 43 of a federal statute called the Lanham Act. 15 U.S.C. § 1125(1). I would like you to research whether Larry's case falls within § 1125(a) and whether a preliminary injunction is possible. In this folder you will find various documents relating to the case.

Because this case involves a musician, copyright issues may well be involved. Do not concern yourself with these issues. I have assigned them to a copyright specialist in our firm's intellectual property group.

Cases relevant to this assignment are: *Rich v. RCA Corp.*, 390 F.Supp. 530 (1975); *Granz v. Harris*, 198 F.2d 585 (2nd Cir.1952); *Yameta Co. v. Capitol Records, Inc.*, 279 F.Supp. 582 (1968); *Benson v. Paul Winley Record Sales Corp.*, 452 F.Supp. 516 (1978); *Gilliam v. American Broadcasting Companies*, 538 F.2d 14 (2nd Cir.1976); *CBS Inc. v. Springboard*, 429 F.Supp. 563 (1976); *Camotle v. Atlantic Records*, 877 F.2d 1403 (9th Cir.1988); *Allen v. Men's World Outlet, Inc.*,

---

8. This assignment was developed by Jake London.

679 F.Supp. 360 (1988); *Grondin v. Rossington,* 690 F.Supp. 200 (1988); *Halicki v. United Artists Communications, Inc.,* 812 F.2d 1213 (9th Cir. 1987).

OOmPA Records
25 E. Wisconsin Ave
Milwaukee, WI 53606
(414) 66-POLKA

November 10, 1986

Mr. Larry Lederhosen
1341 Bluemorrow Street, Ste 310
Oshkosh, WI 53530

Dear Mr. Lederhosen:

As a longtime fan of your music, I have become aware of the growing popularity of bootleg tapes of your live performances. Your annual La Crosse Octoberfest show seems to be a particularly popular target of bootleggers. These bootleg tapes sell for relatively large sums of money, and their sound quality is often very poor. Nonetheless, your fans' appetite for such tapes seems to be insatiable. As fast as the tapes come out, your fans buy them.

My company, OOmPA records, is a nationally recognized company. We specialize in recording and distributing polka music. We would very much like to record your 1987 Octoberfest concert for record release. We believe that a single record highlighting the 1987 show would be a big seller. It could very well create an economically advantageous situation for you. In addition, such a recording would finally reward your longtime fans with a high quality recording of the Octoberfest show.

If you have any interest in pursuing this project, please contact me so that we can set a meeting to begin working out the details.

Sincerely,

Steven Slimey
President, OOmPA Records

Larry Lederhosen
1341 Bluemorrow Street, Ste 310
Oshkosh, WI 53530
(414) THE–BEAT

November 20, 1986

Mr. Steven Slimey
President, OOmPA Records
25 E. Wisconsin Ave
Milwaukee, WI 53606

Dear Mr. Slimey:

Thank you for your letter. I too noticed the rise in bootlegging. I guess the fans must really want to take our music home more than the band and I had thought. I am interested in having your company record the Octoberfest show. However, I am uncomfortable with releasing a one record abridged version of the show. I firmly believe that the joy and power of the concert is in its totality. I have no doubt that a one record album would be a big seller, but to give people one edited record of the Octoberfest concert would be sacrilegious. Therefore, I would only be interested in making a record of the whole concert or at the very least I would want the final right to decide on any major editing.

I will be in Milwaukee on December 10 to play a show. Perhaps we can get together then and discuss this project further.

Sincerely,

Larry Lederhosen

OOmPA Records
25 E. Wisconsin Ave
Milwaukee, WI 53606
(414) 66–POLKA

November 28, 1986

Mr. Larry Lederhosen
1341 Bluemorrow Street, Ste 310
Oshkosh, WI 53530

Dear Mr. Lederhosen:

I would be happy to meet with you on December 10. But before then please reconsider the idea of an abridged album. We would need to do a triple album set to release an unedited version of your concert. Triple albums are very expensive, and I doubt seriously that the Octoberfest project will be financially feasible if you insist on releasing such a large album. I respect your feelings, but OOmPA must also keep track of business concerns.

I look forward to seeing you on December 10.

Sincerely,

Steven Slimey
President, OOmPA Records

MEMORANDUM

TO: File
FROM: Senior Partner
Re: My discussion with Larry Lederhosen

General remarks

At our meeting Larry was rather upset. He had just heard the soon-to-be-released record of the Octoberfest concert. He told me that "Slimey [had] bastardized [his] art." In addition, he was very concerned about the potential damage to his reputation: "I am ashamed to have my name on this record," he said. "I wanted to give people a document to help them remember the Octoberfest concert. But this record is a twisted mess. It totally undermines my artistic vision. The record is a lie! It's not what it claims to be!"

Larry's recollections of his meeting with Steven Slimey

Larry's memory of his December 10, 1986, meeting with Slimey was a bit hazy. He said that Slimey again tried to talk him into a shorter record but he resisted. "I started to get a little hot," Larry said. "Slimey kept laying this bottom line business stuff on me. He said that an unedited recording of the show wouldn't sell, because it would be too expensive. I finally just lost it a little bit. I laid it on the line. I told him that this was the biggest event in Wisconsin polka. I told him he was the businessman and didn't he know that people paid more for the bootleg tapes than a triple record would cost. I wanted to do the record for the fans. But I'm an artist. I can't compromise that. I just don't need the money that badly. I told him to take it or leave it. Slimey backed down and accepted my terms. I think he knew he'd still make a profit, even though the risk might be a little greater."

MEMORANDUM

TO: File
FROM: Senior Partner
DATE: January 14, 1989
Re: Lederhosen Music Contract

Although we have yet to receive a copy of the final contract between Mr. Lederhosen and OOmPA Records, we do have a copy of the initial draft Mr. Lederhosen and Mr. Slimey wrote at their December 10, 1986, meeting. The final contract was written from the draft produced at the December 10, 1986, meeting. Mr. Lederhosen gave his copy of the final agreement to his accountant. At this time, his accountant is in the process of changing offices; many of Mr. Lederhosen's papers are currently in a rather disorganized state. The accountant will attempt to deliver the more complete agreement ASAP. However, both Mr. Lederhosen and his accountant told me that to the best of their recollection the contractual clauses below do not differ materially from the corresponding clauses in the final draft. Therefore, in doing research on this case, please assume that the clauses below accurately represent the intentions of the parties. I will put a memo in the file if anything should change.

December 10, 1986

RECORD PRODUCTION AND DISTRIBUTION
AGREEMENT

1. Steven Slimey of OOmPA Records hereby agrees to record, produce, and distribute audio cassettes and phonodiscs of Larry Lederhosen and the Mirthmakers' Octoberfest polka concert. This is officially called the 1987 La Crosse Octoberfest Concert, featuring Larry Lederhosen and the Mirthmakers.

2. The Octoberfest polka concert described above will be recorded in its entirety. Cassettes and phonodiscs documenting the entire Octoberfest concert will be produced from this recording.

3. OOmPA Records retains the right to do minor editing of the final product. However, no major editing of the final product is to be done without the expressed written consent of Larry Lederhosen.

The Wisconsin Musician
September, 1987

"Larry Lederhosen: Over 30 Years of Rolling Out the Barrel"

It's 11:00 on the second Friday night in June. The Steinhaus bar in Eau Claire is packed with polka fanatics bouncing up and down to the infectious beat of Larry Lederhosen and the Mirthmakers. Regulars in the crowd are readying themselves for the Lederhosen Limbo, an institution twenty years in the making. As the more faint at heart look on, the thrillseekers in the crowd attempt to hurdle over a large foam rubber barrel as it rolls towards them. Those who succeed are rewarded with a free glass of their favorite beverage. Those who fail, get off the ground and just keep on dancing.

"I heard that it all started with a big wooden barrel," explains one member of the crowd. "One of the bartenders who used to work here was a pretty crazy guy from down south. The only tip he'd accept was a shot of Dickel Whiskey. One night he'd done pretty well with the tips. He stumbled over this big wooden barrel in the back room while he was coming back from the bathroom. Before anyone knew it, he'd pulled the damn thing out onto the dance floor and was offering people a free drink if they could hurdle the barrel as he rolled it towards them. Larry and the Mirthmakers were playing that night just like they are tonight. When the bartender rolled the barrel at someone he'd scream at the top of his lungs, 'Let's see if you can do the Lederhosen Limbo!' People have been doing it during Larry Lederhosen's monthly show ever since. But we had to give up the wooden barrel a while ago; too many people were breaking bones and getting concussions."

The crazy bartender who started the monthly ritual at the Steinhaus retired to Florida about ten years ago. But Larry Lederhosen— his inspiration for the "Limbo"—just keeps chugging along. He and his band the Mirthmakers have been bringing big beat polka music to bars throughout Wisconsin for over thirty years now. Judging from that June night in the Steinhaus, Larry hasn't lost a step; he's picked up steam. "I just stick with the polka wherever it leads me," Larry explains matter of factly. "Hairstyles have changed, the Kennedys, Martin Luther King and Malcolm X were killed, Elvis died, and now my grandchildren stare at MTV all day. But polka just keeps moving along on its own course. It's always evolving, but at the same time it retains a certain consistency and tradition. I like this balance. Some guy I met at a show down in Madison compared it to the eastern Zen religions and their concept of ying and yang. I liked that description— or at least what I understood of it—because I've always tried to incorporate both change and continuity into my music. Maybe that's why I'm still able to make a living."

. . .

When he was a young boy, few observers would have predicted that Larry Lederhosen would ever succeed at "making a living," as he calls it. He seemed destined instead for nowhere fast. The son of a dairy farmer, Larry was born and spent his younger years in the country north of Oconomowoc. He was a troublemaker from the word go. "When I was eleven," says Larry "I had some bottle rockets that I'd bought at a roadside stand. I was having a jolly time shooting them at the neighbors' barn while I hid in the bushes. I hadn't thought much about how there was a lot of dry straw inside the barn. Anyway, a spark from one of the rockets set the straw on fire and burned down the barn. It killed five prime dairy cows. I got caught and my dad ended up having to make restitution to the neighbors. Later on, he got his restitution out of my hide."

In the late 1930's, the Lederhosen's farm fell on hard times and Larry's family moved to Kenosha. Larry's father took a job in the Chrysler factory, and Larry found deeper trouble in the city. "Kenosha was a pretty wild place in the late 1930's and early 1940's," Larry remembers. "It was a real melting pot. You had blacks from the south, people from Appalachia, recent immigrants from southern and eastern Europe, as well as people like my family, farmers of German descent who came from rural Wisconsin. I started running with a pretty fast crowd. We didn't like to work: our motto was 'why earn it for yourself when you can take it from someone else.' I was pretty young then, about sixteen. A lot of the other guys were older. But I was wild. I wouldn't back down to nobody, even though I was a little guy. I'd fight at a moment's notice."

Things began to change for Larry when he was sixteen. He was arrested for stealing a car, after leading police on a forty-five minute high speed chase all over Milwaukee. Because he was still a minor, he was not sent to prison. Instead, the judge required that he go to a home for delinquent boys.

It was during this time that Larry became obsessed with polka. "I first encountered polka in a serious way at Father O'Mally's youth home. I'd definitely heard it before while I was growing up, but this was the first time that it really touched me. O'Mally played the banjo and the saxophone. He organized some of the boys into a band and he showed them the polka standards. At first I thought it was stupid. It didn't really seem very cool to me—I was a real badass back then. But the Father was a real fan of all types of music. He knew I liked swing, so he'd talk to me about it and show me how swing wasn't as different from polka as I thought. They're both very rhythmic musics, and by talking to the Father I began to see that—I've always had a fascination with rhythm. Pretty soon the Father had me learning to play the drums. I became obsessed with it. I'd go down in the basement of the home and beat on those things for hours. I got pretty good in a pretty short time, and when the drummer in the Father's band left the home I took his place."

Upon leaving Father O'Mally's home in 1946, Larry entered the army for two years. He played in the army band and picked up any side gigs he could get. "I'd play any job. It didn't matter what kind of music. I learned a lot during that period," Larry explains. But Larry's passion remained polka. Upon leaving the service in 1948, he returned to Milwaukee and joined the Happy Tones as their drummer and sometime singer. The Happy Tones weren't the most successful band in Milwaukee during this period, but they were among the most innovative, integrating many other musical styles into their sound. Their only recording shows a polka music influenced by samba, swing, blues, country, and occasionally even bebop. For Larry the group was perfect: "I've never been a narrow minded musician," explains Larry. "I love polka, but I also love many other kinds of music. The members of the Happy Tones shared my eclectic tastes, and I developed a great deal as a musician while playing with them."

Although the Happy Tones were innovative, they never broke through to commercial success. In 1955, the leader of the Happy Tones, Bud Hefferandson, died when his car hit a tree in rural northern Wisconsin. Some observers believe that Bud committed suicide, a contention Larry doesn't deny but can't confirm. "Bud was a volatile person. He had the power to move people with his music, but he wasn't always stable. Our lack of commercial success grated on him. We were all pretty poor, but Bud became increasingly down about it. When they found his body his blood alcohol level was three times the legal limit. It might have been suicide. But I can't be sure, because Bud could really put down the bourbon and beer. He might have just been drowning his sorrows before he got in the car, not planning to kill himself."

Following Bud Hefferandson's death, the Happy Tones disbanded. Larry thought about joining another band but eventually decided that the time had come to strike out on his own. The Mirthmakers were born. From the beginning the Mirthmakers attempted to carry on the eclectic tradition of the Happy Tones. Rock and Roll music was beginning to become popular, and Larry was intrigued by it. "The beat really got to me. It was big and right up front. I really liked that beat. Polka is also a beat oriented music, but it was still pretty timid in 1955. When I started the Mirthmakers I wanted to get rid of that timidity. I wanted polka for the industrial age. Polka where you really felt the beat. Big Beat Polka!!"

At first the Mirthmakers didn't meet with much success. Polka traditionalists were a bit shocked by their hard driving sound. But as the 1960's began, the band began to hit stride. Their take-no-prisoners approach began drawing sell-out crowds at places like the Steinhaus throughout the state, and they've been at it ever since. Now even the traditionalists respect their work, a compliment which Larry finds gratifying: "Whenever one of those people pays me a compliment I look up in the sky, think of Bud, and hope he's up there listening in on the conversation. Those kind of compliments are really for him. He was a true pioneer—a man ahead of his time."

As we near 1990, there is no doubt that Larry and the Mirthmakers have become a Wisconsin institution. Their annual show at the La Crosse Octoberfest is like a polka rite of passage: Polka fanatics from throughout the state routinely travel up to six hours to see the show. Larry, the elder statesman, presides over the festivities. He and the Mirthmakers are on stage the most of the night, but over the course of the night many polka luminaries join the band on stage. The spontaneous "jam sessions" have become legendary. And in recent years poor quality bootleg tapes of the Octoberfest show have begun to circulate, fetching high prices from polka fans who want something to remember the show by.

In view of this growing demand for recorded music, Larry says that he has agreed to have OOmPA Records record and release a full length record of this year's Octoberfest show. "I'm very excited about it," he explains. "We've never been a big recording band. Our art is our live performance. That's where we made our reputation. Until recently we didn't think that most fans were interested in hearing us in their homes. But the rise in bootleg tapes demonstrates that we were wrong about that. We care about our fans and while I don't have a moral problem with those bootlegs, they really have awful sound quality. By releasing a high quality recording of the show we can give a little something back to our fans. They deserve it, and I'm really looking forward to October because I think we're going to have some really excellent players joining us on stage. I'm thinking of it as sort of a career retrospective. I want to show our fans where we've been. But I don't want to just glory in the past either. I think we may take the fans a few places that they've never been with polka. You know, polka for the 1990s."

.   .   .

Back at the Steinhaus things have reached a fever pitch. People are lined up twenty deep to do the "Lederhosen Limbo." On stage, Larry and the Mirthmakers are busy formulating their polka for the

1990s. The changes are subtle so far but every now and then you hear something new. "My grandson played me some of that rap music," Larry explains. "Now that's a beat. It got me thinking. Maybe polka could use a beat like that. I'll have to think about that."

We're not sure what hip hop polka would sound like. But history says that if Larry Lederhosen is responsible for it, Wisconsin polka fans won't be let down. The barrel will roll on.

—Peter Firstmier

La Crosse Times   **October 27, 1987**

Lederhosen Wows Octoberfest Crowd

By Jack Long

Excitement reigned at Larry Lederhosen and the Mirthmakers' La Crosse Octoberfest concert last night. Spurred on by the fact that the show was being recorded for a live record, the boys were especially spirited, putting on a concert that Wisconsin polka fans will never forget.

From the first "roll out the barrel" it was clear that something special was happening. The Mirthmakers presented a show unlike anything they have every done.

The show was like a retrospective of Larry Lederhosen's entire career, including some songs from his tenure with the Happy Tones, a first. At the same time, Larry and the Mirthmakers also demonstrated their ongoing vitality, extending and transforming familiar songs from their large repertoire while the sold out crowd roared back at them with approval.

The band opened its set with the crowd favorite, "Here Comes the Big Beat." Regularly a three-and-a-half minute song, the band extended it out to more than six minutes with a lengthy jazz-inflected saxophone solo in the middle.

The pounding beat of the song cranked up the energy level of the crowd about four steps, and they appeared ready for anything by the time the song ended. They were not to be disappointed.

The next number was totally unexpected. As the opening passage of "the Happy Tone Shuffle" began, only the most diehard Larry Lederhosen fans appeared to understand what was going on. Here was the signature tune of the Happy Tones, Larry's first band. Larry had not played a Happy Tones song on stage since the untimely death of Happy Tones leader Bud Hefferandson in 1955.

Three decades have not eroded the power of the "Shuffle." It was truly polka ahead of its time, incorporating the rhythm and blues feel which has become one of the hallmarks of the big Mirthmaker sound. Longtime Mirthmaker guitarist Chester Buklocovilstokol really made an impression on this one, demonstrating once again his gift for playing the blues without abandoning the rhythmic sensibility of polka. One could almost imagine Bud Hefferandson smiling down from heaven as he heard how good Chester made his song sound.

The rest of the hour-and-forty-five minute concert showed clearly the stylistic breadth and longevity of Larry Lederhosen's career.

There were the slow songs like "Sweetness in the Evening," "The Girl from Whitefish Bay," and "The Bluest Blue Moon."

There were upbeat numbers like "Please, Please, I Need You More Than You Could Know," "Rhythm of Life," and "Wash Me in the Water."

Larry and the boys also performed "Oompa Ornithology," a polka reading of the Charlie Parker bebop classic, featuring some able sax work by Dale Rosterhaaft.

ASSIGNMENT 2

Write an objective statement of facts for a bench memo to a Court of Appeals judge.[9] Base your statement of facts on the point headings and statements of fact from the following briefs presented in the case.

RHONDA FISHER, a minor
by Jeffrey Wade, her
guardian ad litem,
     Plaintiff–Appellant,
        vs.
WALTER FISHER and
KAREN FISHER, husband and
wife, and LIFE INSTITUTE FOR
ENLIGHTMENT, an unincorpo-
rated association,
     Defendants–Respondents.

Appellant's Brief

THE TRIAL COURT ERRED IN GRANTING RESPONDENT'S MOTION FOR SUMMARY JUDGMENT BECAUSE THERE IS A TRIABLE ISSUE AS TO WHETHER LIFE'S CONDUCT EXCEEDED THE BOUNDS OF DECENCY TOLERATED IN A DECENT SOCIETY.

A. Where There Is A Question Of Fact As To Whether Respondent's Conduct Is Outrageous, Appellant Is Entitled To Have That Question Decided By A Jury.

B. A Jury Could Reasonably Conclude That LIFE's Conduct Is Outrageous Because LIFE Subjected Appellant To Its Extreme Practices Involuntarily.

9. This assignment was developed by Maureen Arrigo and Irwin Miller.

C. A Jury Could Reasonably Conclude That LIFE's Conduct Is Outrageous Because LIFE Subjected Appellant To Its Extreme Practices Knowing She Was Susceptible To Emotional Distress.

D. A Jury Could Reasonably Conclude That LIFE's Conduct Is Outrageous Because LIFE Abused Its Position Causing Appellant's Injuries.

STATEMENT OF CASE

Appellant Rhonda Fisher, a minor, filed suit through her guardian ad litem, Jeffrey Wade, in the Superior Court of San Diego. She alleged two causes of action.

The first cause of action, based on a theory of intentional infliction of emotional distress, was against Life Institute For Enlightenment (LIFE) for damages she incurred resulting from her presence at a camp owned and operated by LIFE.

The second cause of action, based on the tort of child abuse, was against her parents, Walter and Karen Fisher, for damages she incurred resulting from her parents sending her to camp and continues to incur from their neglecting her condition since her return.

Respondents LIFE and Walter and Karen Fisher filed a motion for summary judgment, stating that there was no genuine issue of material fact and they were entitled to prevail on both causes of action as a matter of law. On February 19, 1990, the trial court granted the motion, holding as a matter of law that LIFE's conduct was not outrageous, and that Walter and Karen Fisher acted within the scope of appropriate parental discipline and authority. (R. 3.)

The appellant appeals from the summary judgment as to the first cause of action against LIFE for intentional infliction of emotional distress, and as to the second cause of action against Walter and Karen Fisher for the tort of child abuse.

STATEMENT OF FACTS

Until Rhonda was seven, she was sickly and had trouble relating to peers. She played alone and made up stories which she told to her dolls. (R. 10.) Fortunately, she recovered and by last summer Rhonda was a slightly overweight but emotionally well-adjusted thirteen year old. (R. 11.) After harassing Rhonda to lose weight, the Fishers insisted, over her objections, that she attend a summer camp for "overweight teens" run by LIFE, an organization to which the Fishers belonged (R. 11.) LIFE advocates "eating for transcendence" in order to "purify the mind and heart." (R. 18.) A transcendent diet consists of raw vegetables and small amounts of partially cooked grains with no animal fat or protein. LIFE also advocates renouncing the "normal" world and living in a community of other transcendent people in harmony with each other and all living things. (R. 14.)

Feeding her only transcendent meals and awakening her each day at 4:00 a.m., LIFE forced Rhonda into a rigorous routine of cleaning, gardening, counseling sessions, graphic films of animals being slaughtered, lectures, and drills on what LIFE taught. The movies and lessons were designed to indoctrinate Rhonda in LIFE's philosophical principles. LIFE personnel routinely screamed at Rhonda if she lagged in her chores or lessons. At evening drills, LIFE forced Rhonda to stay awake as late as midnight until she had answered all questions correctly. (R. 15.)

Before Rhonda went to camp, her parents told her she could leave if she wished. (R. 13.) When Rhonda asked to leave, however, LIFE strongly discouraged her by threatening her with her parents' disappointment. Rhonda wrote her parents several letters asking to leave. She received no replies. (R. 15.) The head counselor admitted not mailing letters the children wrote, "so the outside world did not interfere" with the program. (R. 18.) The camp kept the Fishers fully informed, however, on Rhonda's daily routine, diet, weight, and planned activities. (R. 11.)

Since camp, Rhonda has suffered severe physical and emotional distress including extreme weight-loss, anemia, depression, lethargy, withdrawal, anger, and fear. She is unable to eat normal foods or function in school. (R. 7.) She continues to lose weight, now weighing only eighty-five pounds. (R. 15.)

The Fishers' reaction, however, was "delight" that she had lost 30 pounds. (R. 11.) The Fishers' are unconcerned about her condition and are unwilling to consider that she was seriously abused by LIFE's and their conduct. Despite Rhonda's profound injuries the Fishers have sought no medical or psychiatric treatment for her. (R. 21.)

Respondent's Brief

THE TRIAL COURT CORRECTLY HELD THAT A WEIGHT LOSS CAMP CANNOT BE LIABLE FOR INTENTIONAL INFLICTION OF EMOTIONAL DISTRESS WHEN ITS CONDUCT DOES NOT EXCEED ALL BOUNDS OF DECENCY TOLERATED BY A CIVILIZED SOCIETY.

A. The Activities Of A Teenage Weight Loss Camp May Be Deemed Strict, Supervised And Disciplined, But Do Not Constitute Outrageous Conduct Because They Lack The Elements Of Fraudulent Inducement Or Abuse Of A Known Susceptibility.

B. Conduct Furthering A Person's Well–Being Cannot Give Rise To Liability For Intentional Infliction Of Emotional Distress Because The Foundation Of Outrageous Conduct Is Action Meant To Cause Harm.

STATEMENT OF CASE

Plaintiff–Appellant Rhonda Fisher, a minor, through her guardian ad litem, Jeff Wade, filed suit in Superior Court of California, County of San Diego, on February 19, 1990 against Defendants–Respondents Life Institute for Enlightenment ("LIFE") and her parents, Walt and Karen Fisher. (R. 5–9.)

In her first cause of action, Appellant alleges she was injured through LIFE's intentional infliction of emotional distress. This is based on the conduct of LIFE while she was attending its summer camp. (R. 2.) The trial court granted LIFE's motion for summary judgment, ruling that as a matter of law, Defendant's conduct was not outrageous. (R. 3.)

In her second cause of action, Appellant alleges that she was injured by her parents' tortious child abuse. This was grounded on her parents' actions in sending her to the camp and their subsequent failure to treat her alleged emotional and physical injuries. (R. 2.) The trial court granted Walt and Karen Fisher's motion for summary judgment, ruling that as a matter of law, their conduct was not unreasonable as it was within the scope of parental discipline and authority over their child. (R. 3–4.)

Plaintiff–Appellant now appeals the summary judgment on both causes of action. (R. 1.)

STATEMENT OF FACTS

Life Institute for Enlightenment ("LIFE") operates a summer weight loss camp in a beautiful rural area. They have run the camp for 3 years, helping over 300 young people. (R. 17.) This is the camp where Rhonda overcame her eating disorder and reduced her weight to a healthy level. (R. 11–12).

The camp's daily activities are structured to provide a safe, supervised, and disciplined environment conducive to learning and growing. The vegetarian meals consist of a nutritious variety of vegetables and grains. (R. 7.) The children adjust quickly to their new diet. (R. 18). As a pedagogical technique, they are counseled with lectures and films on vegetarianism, community living, and spiritual growth. At night they are sent to bed promptly upon completing their lessons. (R. 18.)

The children at the camp are also provided with new clothes. Any distracting personal items they bring with them are safely stored. (R. 14.) Direct contact between the children and their parents is discouraged. (R. 18.) This is all done to keep the children from being distracted from the LIFE experience. The camp sends regular reports home to the parents describing the progress of their child. (R. 11). As with any group of teenagers, occasional disobedience is not unusual and is handled solely with verbal corrections. (R. 15.)

Walter and Karen Fisher have been members of LIFE since 1987 and believe in its philosophy. After personally visiting the camp and receiving recommendations from their friends, they decided to enroll Rhonda for the summer of 1989. (R. 6, 11, 13.)

Rhonda, who is 5'1", was 13 years old and weighed 130 pounds when she went. She lost 30 pounds at the camp and has lost 15 more since. (R. 11–12, 21.) She faithfully follows the LIFE diet she learned there. (R. 15.) Walt and Karen were very happy about Rhonda's weight loss. Though Rhonda was a little distant, they considered it to be little more than a teenage mood change. (R. 11.)

Rhonda's experience has left her somewhat confused. (R. 15.) In January of 1990, Rhonda moved in with her grandmother. Her parents are heartbroken that she has left home. (R. 12.) They felt that Rhonda's overeating was detrimental to her social and emotional well being. This eating disorder had existed since Rhonda had overcome her childhood illness at age 7. (R. 10–11.) They believed they were acting in Rhonda's best long-term interests when they sent her to a camp whose basic goals were to help children enhance their physical and mental health and to live in harmony with each other and all living things. (R. 11, 14.)

If you want to read further on the relevant law, see the Arguments included in Assignment 1, Chapter 9.

Bibliography

Acuna, Frank R., Daniel E. Casa, Claire P. McGreal, John Ossiff, and Roger M. Rosen, *Handbook of Appellate Advocacy*. St. Paul: West Publishing Co., 1986.

Dernbach, John C. and Richard V. Singleton, II, *A Practical Guide to Legal Writing and Legal Method*. Littleton, CO: Fred B. Rothman and Co., 1981.

Lee, Vernon, *The Handling of Words and Other Studies in Literary Psychology*. Lincoln: Univ. of Nebraska Press, 1968.

Mathes, J.C. and Dwight W. Stevenson, *Designing Technical Reports: Writing for Audiences in Organizations*. Indianapolis: Bobbs–Merrill, 1980.

O'Keefe Daniel J., *Persuasion: Theory and Research*. Newbury Park, CA: Sage Publications, 1990.

Pearsall, Thomas E. and Kenneth W. Houp, *Reporting Technical Information*. New York: Macmillan Publishing Co., Inc., 4th ed. 1980.

Porter, Karen C., Nancy L. Schultz, Lauren Scott, Louis J. Sirico, Jr., and Annemick N. Young, *Introduction to Legal Writing and Oral Advocacy*. New York: Matthew Bender, 1989.

Pratt, Diane V., *Legal Writing: A Systematic Approach*. St. Paul: West Publishing Co., 1989.

Shapo, Helene C., Marilyn R. Walter, and Elizabeth Fajans, *Writing and Analysis in the Law*. Westbury, NY: Foundation Press, 1989.

Weihofen, Henry, *Legal Writing Style.* St. Paul: West Publishing Co., 1980.

Woolever, Kristin R., *Untangling the Law: Strategies for Legal Writers.* Belmont, CA: Wadsworth Publishing Co., 1987.

Zinsser, William, *On Writing Well.* New York: Harper and Row, 2d ed. 1980.

Chapter 8

PERSUASIVE STATEMENTS OF FACT

If briefs to the court were gymnastics events, the statement of facts would occur on the balance beam. Writing a persuasive statement is accomplished not by following one set of rules, but by balancing your use of various techniques to maintain credibility while achieving the stance needed to highlight favorable facts. It does not require the brute force of emphatic language so much as a subtle blend of strength and control of structure and detail. It involves much thought, consideration of alternatives, and monitoring the interactions of various techniques.[1] Yet an excellent statement of facts looks natural and effortless, just as a complex routine looks easy when completed by a skilled gymnast.

The statement of the case is critical to the brief.[2] It tells the story that makes the fairness of your client's position evident. Judges want to make a decision that is legally valid, but they also want to make a decision that is fair. Although the court must decide the case based on the law, a sense of fairness about your case can make the judge more willing to accept the argument that follows. This situation is congruent with that of all persuasive writing: a reader is more fully persuaded if both head and heart are convinced.[3] Linguistically, the fact section is the part of a brief most likely to help the reader develop a general opinion and feeling about which party ought to prevail. It provides the specific, concrete facts the reader needs to generalize to the preferred legal result. Many practitioners even claim the fact statement is the most important part of a brief, eclipsing even the argument in its ability to persuade the court.[4]

1. See the discussion of studies by Thistlewait (1955) and Sharp and McClung (1966) in Rolf Sandell, *Linguistic Style and Persuasion* 79 (1977).

2. Irving M. Mehler, *Effective Legal Communication* 96 (1975).

3. Gerald R. Miller, "Persuasion," in *Handbook of Communication Science* 454 (C. Berger and S. Chaffee, eds. 1987).

4. For example, "[t]he statement of facts is the most important part of any appellate brief, for no matter how much substantive law the judge may know, he or she knows nothing about the facts of the case before reading the appellant's brief." Thomas R. Newman, *Writing Briefs— Statement of Facts*, 200 N.Y.L.J. 3 (1988).

Writing a persuasive statement of facts presents a writing situation rare in the larger world of writing. Like a short story, a good statement of facts tells a story, complete with plot, characters, and setting. As a result, many of the techniques discussed in this chapter are drawn from the skills of the storyteller. Unlike the writer of fiction, you are not free to invent facts. Your discretion rests in your selection—of details, of words, and of order. Making effective selections is a complex process involving many factors. This chapter helps you make those selections by giving you general guidelines for making choices.

To make the best selection, you must also be aware of your options. Accordingly, this chapter introduces possible persuasive writing techniques individually before integrating them into the larger process of writing a statement of facts. It explains each technique and its potential uses. The table summarizing these techniques at the end of the section can help you coordinate these options.

The chapter then moves to ways to incorporate these techniques into the larger writing process. It illustrates how to use the techniques by commenting on two example statements and, finally, provides a chance to apply the techniques.

If you are tired of following rules in your writing, stating the facts persuasively offers a fascinating opportunity to balance competing concerns, try different techniques, and make judgment calls. If you enjoy the security that comes from rules, writing a persuasive fact statement presents some frustration and uncertainty. For most writers, it presents a little of both.

GUIDELINES FOR MAKING CHOICES

When looking at all the ways you can shape the facts to favor your client's position, remember both what you can and cannot do. The following rhyme incorporates those constraints, offering some guidelines for making effective choices and avoiding ineffective ones.

When the news is bad, frame it.

If it's not true, don't claim it.

When the news is good, be bold.

When it's too much, break the mold.

State essentials, every one.

But please stop writing when you're done.

These guidelines will help you use, and not misuse, the many specific techniques for emphasis and de-emphasis discussed in this chapter.

First, you cannot ignore any major unfavorable facts, or bad news. To do so would be to allow the other side's presentation of those unfavorable facts to stand unchallenged. Just as you could not avoid giving unfavorable-but-needed information to a senior attorney when writing a memo, here you cannot avoid discussing unfavorable information with a judge who may be apprised of it by your opposition. Additionally, including unfavorable facts will probably increase your credibility with the judicial reader.[5] Research in persuasion has found that a "both-sided" approach has greater success persuading listeners who were initially undecided or in opposition, were better educated, and were later exposed to counter-arguments.[6] Instead of excluding unfavorable facts, employ one of the de-emphasizing techniques discussed later in this chapter to place the unfavorable fact in a context that is less detrimental to your position. For example, you may put the unfavorable fact in a dependent clause so the reader sees the fact in the context of more favorable information. In this way you frame the bad news just as a storyteller frames the setting for a story to create the appropriate mood.

Second, you cannot lie. This ban includes misinterpreting the record, stating an opinion not supported by the evidence, and presenting a disputed fact as undisputed. The ethical reasons for this guideline are obvious.[7] Even if there were no code of professional responsibility, misrepresenting the facts would be ineffective for many pragmatic reasons.

> We rely on our images, caring about our image not for an immediate purpose, but like money in the bank to use when needed.[8]

For example, a misrepresentation, even a small one, would most likely be caught by the opposing attorney, the court's law clerks, or the judges themselves. One such lapse could call all of your statements into question, not only in this brief but in your future submissions to that court.[9] Neither you nor your client can afford such a threat to your credibility, so state your facts persuasively but with circumspection. Aim for a fact statement the court could use in its opinion if it finds in your favor.

Third, you cannot emphasize a fact simply by restating it in several ways; restating can easily bore the reader. It can also suggest you are uncertain of the point's effectiveness and are restating it to give it another try. Instead, be bold. Use a strong technique to highlight those facts so the reader will not miss them. Remember that your reader, although dedicated and conscientious, has many briefs to read. Make the main facts stand out, then let the reader move ahead.

5. Communicators are more successful at persuading when viewed as competent and trustworthy. Miller, *supra* note 3, at 454.

6. Carl I. Hovland, Irving L. Janis, and Harold H. Kelley, *Communication and Persuasion* 105–111 (1953).

7. Model Rules of Professional Conduct Rule 7.1(a) (1989).

8. Herbert W. Simons, *Persuasion: Understanding, Practice, and Analysis* 77 (1986).

9. For example, one opinion censuring counsel for misrepresenting facts states, "A brief of this character, instead of being an aid to the court in determining the questions involved, furnishes no aid whatever, because suspicion must naturally rest upon every statement asserted as a fact in it and little reliance be placed upon a brief so made, and the counsel submitting it is deserving of the severest censure." *Ryan v. Courtland Carriage Goods Co.*, 133 App. Div. 467, 470, 118 N.Y.S. 56, 58 (1909).

Fourth, you cannot depend on only one or two techniques for emphasis. Any technique, if overdone, loses its effectiveness. If too obvious, it draws attention away from the content to the writing itself. This in turn reduces persuasiveness by reducing the reader's acceptance of the message.[10] Develop your favorite techniques and then develop the discretion to avoid overusing them. For example, you may repeat a key word you want to emphasize, but avoid repeating it too much. Try other techniques instead, such as putting a word to be emphasized at the beginning or end of a sentence. Break the mold before the mold gains more attention than the content.

Fifth, you cannot expect the reader to fill in the gaps in your presentation; you must provide all the information needed. Most of us have occasion to say, "you know what I mean"; a statement of facts, however, is not one of those occasions. If you use a fact in your argument, include it in the fact statement. If the previous record documents a fact, cite the record. If you need a fact to present the overall situation, even though it is not essential to the legal argument, include the fact for clarity's sake. Also include what you need for persuasiveness. Do not let a blanket concern for conciseness lead to bland, ineffective statements. Just as with objective facts, where you included enough specifics to be clear, here include enough detail to be interesting. Especially you need to include the detail needed to present vividly the fairness of your client's position.

Finally, you cannot claim an unlimited amount of the reader's time. State everything that is needed and state it clearly. But minimize repetition of content. Repetition that does not provide effective emphasis can make you appear uncertain and can make the story become boring. Avoid unnecessary embellishment. Obvious, emotion-creating techniques and clearly biased words draw more attention to the writing than the content. You do not want the reader to say at the end, "Weren't those facts persuasively written?" or "Didn't the writer get a little carried away?" Rather you want the reader to focus sympathetically on the reasonableness of your client's position.

This elimination of unneeded repetition and embellishment will make the statement sound more confident and will get your brief off to a more assertive start. It will also make your fact statement more concise, for which the reader will be grateful.

[A]ll depends on what you can get the Reader[s] to do; if you confuse [their] ideas or waste [their] energy, you can no longer do anything with [them].[11]

SPECIFIC TECHNIQUES

With the six general guidelines in mind, and having chosen the facts to include, you can apply specific techniques to present the

10. Sandell, *supra* note 1, at 163.

11. Vernon Lee, *The Handling of Words and Other Studies* in *Literary Psychology* 10 (1968).

content so it has the desired effect on the reader. Although the possible ways to word any given set of facts are almost endless, all those ways involve only three variables: how you group the information, how you order it, and how you word it. Grouping and ordering are choices you make when organizing the whole statement, when organizing paragraphs, and when structuring sentences. As you study the following list of techniques, you will see they are all variations of these options. The techniques involve four areas of writing: overall organization of the statement of facts (large-scale organization), organization of individual paragraphs (small-scale organization), structure of sentences, and word choice.

Techniques Involving Overall Organization

Sometimes you can emphasize facts when you set up the overall organization of your fact statement. For example, you may be able to put a fact you want to emphasize in the opening paragraph, when you explain the nature of the case. To do this successfully, you must have a fact that can logically fit in the opening statement: it must be a fact that is central, either legally or emotionally, to the question the case presents.

> **On March 3, 1980, the defendant was charged with second-degree sexual assault upon an eleven-year-old girl who was going home from school.**

Making that fact part of the reader's first impression of the case ensures the reader will notice the fact. Inserting a fact that is emotionally but not legally significant would not be as effective. This sample opening does this.

> The defendant, a sixty-five-year-old widow, pled no contest to a charge of driving while under the influence.

Similarly, you can reprise the fact in the summarizing paragraph to drive the importance of the point home.

> The defendant now argues his rights were violated during the course of the trial at which he was found guilty of sexually assaulting the child.

As always, make sure that repeating this fact underscores the point without boring or irritating the reader. For example, if the statement of facts is only two pages long, repeating a fact may seem more redundant than emphatic.

To de-emphasize a point through organization, place the point one-half to two-thirds of the way through the fact section, if it is possible to do so without confusing the chronology. The beginning of a section gets attention because the reader is working to understand the situation, to become oriented to the story. By the time he or she has reached the middle of the fact narrative, the content is more familiar and the reader is more likely to skim information quickly. Thus, putting a point in the middle puts it in a position that encourages the reader to skim the point quickly, with less involvement.

In summary, emphasize a point by placing it near the beginning or end of the statement of facts, or state it early in the facts and remind the reader of it later. In contrast, minimize unsympathetic points by moving them away from the beginning or end.

Techniques Involving Paragraph Organization

Another variation of using organization to emphasize a fact is to state it in the opening sentence of a paragraph. Each time the reader starts a new paragraph, the slight pause and the white space around the new paragraph give the reader a break. The reader comes to the new paragraph slightly refreshed, as one is slightly refreshed after taking a breath. Additionally, some readers skim information by noting the opening of each paragraph, and you can use this habit to provide the reader with an outline of your main points. By placing your main point in the first sentence of the paragraph, you communicate it even to a reader who is skimming. You can maximize this technique's effectiveness by putting the key words in the first half of the first line.

You can also put a point to be emphasized in the final phrase of a paragraph, although in legal writing this does not get quite as much emphasis as the beginning of a paragraph. You can combine these two techniques with particular effectiveness. You can introduce an important concept at the end of a paragraph and then address the fact in the next paragraph, giving the fact the emphasis of both positions. This technique not only provides you with a strong, smooth emphasis on the point, but it also provides a smooth transition between the paragraphs.

One final organizational technique you can use for emphasis is to place a fact in a separate paragraph. Although it is often useful in the argument section, this is less frequently useful in fact statements because few facts make sense without the surrounding context. To write a one-sentence paragraph, you need to use a fact that suggests its legal significance even when standing alone. Usually, rather than a one-sentence paragraph, you will want to state a point and then support it with specific facts. A strong opening to a paragraph supporting the fact will probably be more effective.

Techniques Involving Sentence Structure

Sentence structure is a versatile and useful tool in fact statements, and its use involves many more options than does organization. Structure, more than word choice, influences how most readers read a text and how much of the text they read.[12] This section shows you how to use short sentences, choice of subjects and verbs, active voice, place-

12. V.H. Yngve, *A Model and an Hypothesis for Language Structure,* 104 Proc. Am.Phil.Soc'y 444–466 (1960).

ment of dependent clauses, and unusual order of sentence parts to create emphasis or de-emphasis.

Short Sentences

At a general level, there are only three positions in a sentence: the subject of the main clause, the predicate of the main clause, and the dependent clauses or other phrases that add detail. Every sentence has to have a main clause, which is usually the main point of the sentence. If the clause is set off by itself, with no distractions, it gets all the attention, like a musician playing a solo.

    subject   predicate

      ↓   ↓

He followed her instructions.

You can give a point the attention of an entire sentence by making it all there is to the sentence, and you do it by stating the point in a simple, short sentence.

Short is strong.

One might think adding more words would underscore a point, but the reverse is true.

> A sentence is much stronger when it is written so that its length is relatively short.

This longer sentence dilutes its point with more words. Therefore, if you want to play down a point, do not use a short sentence. This is the rare place where you might even use a little wordiness to reduce the effectiveness of a point.

> The strength of a statement can be increased by reducing its length.

One drawback of the short sentence is that it does not have room for much detail. If the short sentence is temporarily misleading, so your reader misunderstands the point, then your credibility might be at risk. Therefore, make sure the point is clear within the sentence or within the sentences around it.

> Short sentences are strong sentences.

> or

> In sentences, length does have an impact on emphasis. Short is strong.

A word of caution: avoid overusing short sentences. You do not want to fall into the pattern described in the following dialogue.

> Cleander: I find his style convenient for short Lungs; and, methinks, of all things, you cannot complain his Periods put you out of breath.

Eudoxus: They seem indeed to be generally made in favour of Readers that are troubled with an Asthma; and I fear, his are as much too short as those others are too long.[13]

Subjects and Verbs

One technique involving the subject and predicate you can use most of the time is to use the main subject and verb to carry the main point. The basis of the sentence's structure is the subject and verb, so it should express your main point.

subject   verb
   ↓   ↓

Blackie had bitten another child one year before this incident and under similar circumstances.

This technique increases clarity and often adds conciseness by eliminating empty words, as in the following example.

subject   verb
   ↓   ↓

Blackie had bitten another child one year before this incident (R. 17–25).

rather than

subject verb
   ↓   ↓

There was a previous incident in which Blackie had bitten another child one year earlier. (R. 17–25).

This technique tends to add either a natural variety or a natural emphasis through repetition to your fact statement. For example, you may repeat a central concept to add emphasis.

Blackie *attacked* a smaller dog owned by neighbors across the road (R. 17–18). Several years earlier, Blackie's *attack* on a large stray dog had resulted in that dog's death (R. 19–21).

Similarly, as the important concepts vary, your subjects and verbs will also vary, and you will avoid unintended emphasis.

For example, write

The Anderson's *German shepard*, Blackie, attacked a smaller *dog* owned by neighbors across the road. (R. 17–18). Several years earlier, Blackie had bitten a large *stray* so severely that it eventually died. (R. 19–21).

rather than

The Anderson's dog attacked a smaller dog owned by neighbors across the road. (R. 17–18). Several years earlier, the Anderson's dog had bitten a large stray dog so severely that the dog eventually died. (R. 19–21).

13. John Constable, *Reflections upon Accuracy of Style* 7 (1731).

Active Voice

Another structural technique you can use for emphasis is to put the verb in the active voice.[14] Using active voice emphasizes the action by making the sentence more interesting and easier to read.

According to Helmsley, Acker offered to sell a small amount of marijuana for $40.

rather than

According to Helmsley, an offer was made by Acker to sell a small amount of marijuana for $40.

Active voice is useful for emphasizing a sympathetic action by your client. Because the subject of the sentence is the natural focus, the reader is likely to focus on your client when he or she is the subject of the sentence. The reader's position of emphasis structurally becomes the point of view of the sentence.

Because he believed drug trafficking presented a serious problem in the neighborhood, Helmsley agreed to help the police by working as an informant.

Active voice can emphasize an unfavorable action by the opponent.

According to Helmsley, Acker had boasted frequently that he could provide a variety of drugs.

In contrast, the passive voice can remove attention from the actor.

The exchange was made later that evening.

The effectiveness of this technique is limited. Because it is so frequent in bureaucratic language, readers assume it is a way to avoid naming the responsible party.

A decision has been made that your services are no longer needed.

As a result, sophisticated readers can readily see the passive structure as an attempt to avoid responsibility, and the ploy may be ineffective if used too often or too obviously.

Placement of Dependent Clauses

Once you have determined what information belongs in the main clause, you can relegate a less important point to a dependent clause to de-emphasize it. This puts that point structurally in the background and encourages the reader to focus on the point stated in the main subject and predicate. This placement is particularly useful when you are explaining away an unfavorable fact.

Blackie had never bitten a person before this incident, *although she had gotten into fights with other dogs.* In fact, one of Blackie's

---

14. Active voice is the use of the verb form that allows the subject to act, "He sold the car." In contrast, passive voice reverses the order of the nouns so that the subject becomes the thing acted upon, as in "The car was sold by him." Passive voice thus allows the actor to be left unidentified until after the verb, and even to be left unidentified in the sentence, as in "The car was sold."

attacks on another dog occurred because she was defending her master against the large stray.

This technique is the converse of setting a point in a separate sentence for emphasis. This technique cannot help de-emphasizing the point. To adapt a quotation from Vernon Lee, "If you want Tom to seem less a villain, put a bigger villain, Dick, by his side." [15]

The next decision is where to put the dependent clauses. This also affects emphasis. There are three possible places: the beginning, the middle, and the end. It sounds simple, but is not simple in practice. The parts of the sentence interact, and sentence structure interacts with word choice and other elements in the sentence. To guide you through these interactions, this section discusses the placement of clauses in detail, noting how you can use clauses for emphasis or de-emphasis as needed.

The principle that the beginning gets more attention than the middle applies to sentences as well as paragraphs and documents. A dependent clause at the beginning of a sentence will get some emphasis, even though it is not the main clause. Following an introductory phrase by a main clause creates a sentence with two opportunities for emphasis: the set-up and the punch line. This structure is especially effective if the introductory phrase is slightly long, creating suspense, and the main clause following it is rather short. For example,

> **Clifford had not yet been trained to operate the stamping machine when his supervisor, Morris, asked him to fill in at the machine.** *But, anxious to make a good impression on his first day at the job, Clifford agreed.*

rather than

> Clifford had not yet been trained to operate the stamping machine when his supervisor, Morris, asked him to fill in at the machine. But Clifford agreed because he was anxious to make a good impression on his first day at the job.

This structure has many uses. You can use it to set up a contrast,

> *Unlike the defendant,* the plaintiff had little experience operating tractors.

to establish the context of an event,

> *Because there was no commingling of funds or sharing of proceeds,* the defendant believed no conflict of interest existed.

> *Soon after beginning this medication,* Ms. Rodriquez began suffering frequent headaches.

to dismiss an opponent's point,

> *Although the defendant was advised of his Miranda rights,* he was not in a position to understand the advice. At the time, he was

---

15. Lee, *supra* note 11, at 7.

bleeding from a cut above his left eye and was in substantial pain caused by a broken arm.

and to build a stronger emotion.

> *Even after these warnings,* after two employees became ill while working and after other employees had complained of dizziness, the management still took no action to notify employees of the danger.

You will not add much emphasis, however, when you use a short introductory phrase as a transition. When the introduction is short and rather commonplace, the emphasis of the beginning is muted.

> *In the morning,* Stacy left the breakfast table early.

> *For example,* Harrison called Valencia three times earlier in the day.

Here the placement emphasis is overridden by other techniques, such as putting the main point in the subject and verb and using more arresting word choice. The break in the ordinary pattern is also overcome by the familiarity of the wording and the fact that the reader moves quickly to the subject.

Another place to put a dependent clause is in the middle of the main clause, where it will be an interruption, or an intrusive phrase. Even though it comes in the middle, an intrusive phrase can create emphasis: it claims a share of the attention from the main point, as a child does when interrupting a parent who is talking.

> The defendant, *unlike her predecessor,* did not review the daily balances.

This technique may seem to contradict other techniques, such as putting the point to be emphasized in the beginning or end of a sentence. But an intrusive phrase claims attention because it is out of the ordinary, like an unexpected interlude within a piece of music. This unusualness, when combined with content that draws attention to itself, outweighs the general disadvantage that comes from being in the middle.

> The patch of ice, *shaded by the overhanging tree,* was not seen by the driver.

Like a short sentence within a group of longer sentences, an interruption can stand out in a crowd of phrases. A short, rather routine interruption will not stand out too much.

But an intrusive phrase of more than a few words puts a burden on the reader. It asks the reader to stop what he or she is doing and do something else. This burden can quickly become overwhelming and the reader can rebel, so avoid long interruptions.

> **At approximately 9:00 a.m., the defendant was taken from her cell and, *without an opportunity to consult an attorney,* was again interrogated. She was not advised of her Miranda rights even during this second interrogation.**

rather than

> At approximately 9:00 a.m., the defendant was taken from her cell and, *without an opportunity to consult an attorney as she had requested earlier and without being advised by any officer of her Miranda rights,* was again interrogated.

The burden on the reader can also be overwhelming if the sentence as a whole is long or complex.

> **In connection with his wholesale bedding and potted plant business, Mr. Gray purchased pre-cut, pre-drilled and shaped metal tubing from out-of-state retailers.**

rather than

> Mr. Gray *in connection with his wholesale bedding and potted plant business* purchased pre-cut, pre-drilled and shaped metal tubing from out-of-state retailers.

For this reason, the usefulness of intrusive phrases is somewhat limited. You can use them, however, to point up an irony.

> The dealer, *despite his promise,* did not order the needed replacements.

They can also add an important explanation.

> The defendant, *believing the prison term would be shorter,* agreed to plead guilty to this charge.

Using intrusive phrases makes the tone somewhat more formal because it requires coordinating two thoughts at once. It is associated with prepared statements, such as a written speech or other document. Intrusive phrases are hard to use well and easy to use poorly. Use them infrequently, not as the dominant technique in your repertoire.

> Do not, again, break off in the midst of some event unless you wish that event to become important in the reader's mind and to react of future events: if, for instance, you have had to introduce a mysterious stranger, but do not wish anything to come of his mysteriousness, be sure you strip off his mystery as prosaically as you can, before leaving him in the Reader's charge.[16]

In marked contrast to intrusive phases, dependent clauses added to the end of the sentence are easy to read and more likely to create a relaxed tone. This may be desirable if you want the reader to see the situation you are describing as routine and not requiring heightened sentiments.

> The preliminary examination was held before Hon. Hillary Anderson, of the Wold County Circuit Court, on October 1, 1979, at the close of which the court found "reasonable grounds to believe the offense charged in the complaint was committed and was committed by this defendant." (R. 33–40)

16. *Id.* at 7–8.

The end of the sentence may therefore be the best place for information you want to play down or present as support.

Using a dependent clause at the end of the sentence signals that the content is detail that fills out the picture once you have established the main point.

> Garrison shoved Wagner into the car *after Wagner told him that he did not have a driver's license.*

In this example, the point is made and the framework established in the reader's mind. The phrase at the end then adds detail. Notice how much more emphasis the point would get in an introductory phrase.

> *After Wagner told Garrison that he did not have a driver's license,* Garrison shoved Wagner into the car.

It would also gain more emphasis in an intrusive phrase.

> Garrison, *after hearing that Wagner did not have a driver's license,* shoved Wagner into the car.

One interesting combination of several techniques is to put a fact to be de-emphasized in the middle of a list within a sentence.[17] In the following example, the *underlined* fact is de-emphasized because it is placed in the middle of a list that is itself a dependent clause.

> Kevin Wagner testified that he was 16 years old, was a freshman at Central High School, *had been drinking on the night of August 21, 1979,* and was walking home when Garrison offered him a ride.

Use a sentence with information added in a dependent clause at the end as your routine sentence structure. If each sentence has a dramatic structure, you would overdo the techniques and they would lose effectiveness because they compete for attention. Instead, choose the facts you want to emphasize, put those facts in specially crafted sentences, and then use this workhorse sentence structure for most of the other information. One exception to this use of de-emphasis is the last sentence in a paragraph or section. In this case, the end of the sentence gets the emphasis of the climax; the end of the last sentence is a place for emphasis.

Unusual Order

Another sentence structure technique is to put the elements of the sentence in an unusual order. Because something different tends to get the reader's attention, this technique will draw attention to the content of the sentence. For example, you might put the predicate, or some phrase from the last part of the sentence, before the verb.

> *Embracing,* the couple was observed by many witnesses as the couple stood by the entrance to the lounge.

---

17. Clear structuring of lists was discussed in the chapter on jury instructions earlier. This use adapts and builds on the skill you developed earlier.

You might use multiple introductory phrases,

> *At 5:00 p.m. on Friday, June 2, as they had done on many previous Fridays,* the complaining witness and the defendant left work together and walked to the Backroom Tap.

multiple phrases at the end of the sentence,

> At the trial, Ms. Harrison testified the defendant forced her to the floor, forced her to remove her clothes, forced her to have intercourse.

or a longer, looser structure.

> They stayed at the Backroom Tap until approximately 7:00 p.m., drinking several alcoholic drinks each and laughing with other patrons over some suggestive jokes told by the complaining witness.

You might even omit some needed words, as long as they are clearly implied by the structure of the sentence.

> The complaining witness was the defendant's secretary, eighteen, a high school graduate. The defendant was wealthy, forty-two, an attorney.

These unusual structures are dramatic and complex to construct, so use them with restraint. Structure an unusual sentence well and choose content that is easy to follow. The reader must not be overburdened or confused by the structure. Nevertheless, when used well, the unusual structures can make a fact stand memorable and interesting in the reader's mind.

Techniques Involving Word Choice

When legal writers first attempt persuasive writing, they often change their word choice, and with good reason. English offers a wealth of words. "[O]ne [person's] bandwagon is another [person's] reasoned consensus." [18] For example, a senator who refused to change her vote even after some political arm-twisting might be labelled by various camps as "loyal," "unwavering," "resolute," "unchanged," "resistant," "rigid," "stubborn," or "pig-headed." In fact, it is usually by word choice that speakers or writers first reveal their biases.

> Senator, do you plan to persist with this plan despite the President's request that you reconsider?

or

> Senator, to what do you attribute your impressive ability to resist White House pressure in this situation?

Therein lies the main limitation of word choice: it easily projects the writer's bias, and obvious bias lessens the legal writer's effectiveness.[19] It can also lapse into semantic gyrations.

18. Wayne C. Booth, *Modern Dogma and the Rhetoric of Assent* 146 (1974).

19. Sandell, *supra* note 1, at 163.

Semantic argument tries to make a persuasive point not by presenting or arranging evidence, but by using impressive language. It should convince no one.[20]

For maximum effectiveness, restraint is essential. The challenge of effective word choice lies in its multidimensional aspects.[21] Words vary not only in meaning (denotation), but also in emotional association (connotation), degree of detail (specific or general), terms of address (concrete or abstract), unusual wording (familiar or unfamiliar), repetition, and rhythm.[22] Each of these dimensions can affect the persuasive impact of the word, and each factors into the writer's choices. Words have an additive effect; one word's impact is colored by the words around it, so word choice often creates repetition and rhythm. No wonder legal writers find those techniques difficult to master. But not impossible. By considering each of these dimensions, you can build your understanding so that interrelating the various dimensions is easier.

Emotional Association

Stirring the reader's emotions will increase the likelihood that the reader will remember the fact generating the emotion.[23] Yet you want that memory to be appropriate to your goal, and the content must be what is remembered, not that you tried to create a feeling. Emotional association can be effective when managed well. To avoid showing bias, avoid words with strong connotations, either positive or negative.[24] Instead, choose a word that is slightly positive or negative. For example, to describe a push you might use "shove" for a negative slant or "nudge" for a positive one, but you would use "bulldozed" or "escorted" only if the facts supported the label.

Another useful technique is to put the emotional association in the verb, rather than as adjectives or adverbs, because the verb has more impact. For example, "the group's leader shoved the woman into the car" is stronger than "the group's leader roughly pushed the woman into the car."

Degree of Detail

A technique related to both organization and word choice is to explain favorable facts in greater detail, less favorable ones in less detail. A more specific picture makes the fact stand out as more

---

20. Daniel McDonald, *The Language of Argument* 128 (3rd ed. 1980).

21. Lyle E. Bourne, Jr., *Human Conceptual Behavior* 22 (1966).

22. For more on the dimensions of word choice, *see* Theophil Spoerri, "Style of Distance, Style of Nearness" in *Essays in Stylistic Analysis* 62–78 (H. Babb ed. 1972).

23. Dean Hewes and Sally Planalp, "The Individual's Place in Communication

Science," in *Handbook of Communication Science* 164 (C. Berger and S. Chaffee, eds. 1987).

24. Euphemisms are words with positive emotional loading; perjoratives are words with negative loading. For a rhetorician's discussion of emotionally loaded words, *see* Simons, *supra* note 8, at 314.

memorable: [25] "to be interesting, you must be specific." [26]   For example, the following sentence creates a clear picture.

The plaintiff, who is 6′ 3″ and weighs 210 pounds, strode toward the defendant, who is 5′ 10″ and weighs 160 pounds.

A more general statement would render the fact less memorable.

The plaintiff, who is larger than the defendant, moved toward him.

One of the reasons specific language is more effective is that it gives the reader more information, so the reader knows more clearly what the writer had in mind.   For example, "tree" could refer to a white pine, a cypress, or a dogwood.   Because "tree" is so general, the reader has to think either of a specific kind of tree, which may or may not be the one the writer meant, or maintain the general idea of tree by keeping various possibilities open.

For example, if the defendant's fear was the favorable fact, you might word it as follows.

When he heard the defendant's question, the plaintiff did not answer.   Instead he grasped the iron handle of the jack he was using and wrenched it loose.   Still saying nothing, the plaintiff, who is 6′ 3″ and weighs 210 pounds, strode toward the defendant's car.   The defendant rolled up the window and fumbled with his keys, meaning to start the engine.   In his nervousness, he removed his foot from the clutch.   His only thought was to secure his escape.

The abrupt release of the clutch caused the defendant's car to lurch forward unexpectedly, ...

If the fear was a fact to be minimized, the description of the situation might be much more general.   Instead focus the passage as follows.

When the plaintiff approached the defendant's car, the defendant attempted to drive away as quickly as possible.   In his hurry, he released the clutch abruptly, causing the car to lurch forward unexpectedly.

Terms of Address

Similarly, you can adjust the closeness with which the writer views the people involved by careful use of names (Ms. Milkowski, Adam), labels (mother, child, etc.), or legal terms (plaintiff).   Just as a film director can pull the camera back to show the audience the larger view, more abstract terms of address pull the reader back from the individuals involved by suggesting the larger view.   If you want the reader to focus on a ruling's effect on future cases, for example, it is logical and natural to use the label for the larger conceptual group.

---

25.   "[T]he example seems to be a particularly powerful form of information, especially when compared to information in statistical summary form."   Daniel J. O'Keefe, *Persuasion: Theory and Research* 169 (1990).

26.   *Id.* at 247.

Appellant was stopped by the Wold County Deputy Sheriff on August 10, 1981, in Wold County at approximately 8:30 p.m. after the officer observed a defective headlamp, but no erratic driving.

rather than

Jessica Birdsong was stopped by Deputy Sheriff Frank Buschman on August 10, 1981, at approximately 8:30 p.m. after Officer Buschman observed a defective headlamp, although he did not observe Ms. Birdsong driving erratically.

If the sympathy of the situation runs in your favor, focus the reader by using names of the parties.

On January 1, 1984, while struggling with Roger Green over a loaded gun Green was using to threaten Evans' sister, Will Evans was shot. Mr. Evans died from the resulting loss of blood.

rather than

The victim was shot on January 1, 1984, while struggling with the defendant over a loaded gun the defendant was using to threaten the victim's sister. The victim subsequently died from loss of blood.

Unusual Wording

A word slightly out of the ordinary can add emphasis if it is not so unusual that its meaning is lost to the reader. For example, the wording of the following sentence is unusual and eye-catching, but its meaning is likely to elude the reader.

To adumbrate a rhetoric of assent butters no parsnips.

The level of formality must also be appropriate to the situation (what linguists identify as the "register scale").

Although Mr. Green carried a loaded gun into the trailer, he said he did not intend to harm anyone. Although he had not been threatened, he said he took the gun in self-defense.

If it is not, the result will be humor.

The defendant, 68 years old and semi-retired, was driving home from work as a semi-pro baseball field manager when an officer pursued the defendant's car with lights flashing. The defendant pulled over to the side of the road. The officer asked the defendant for his license, but he refused. The officer then asked the defendant to exit his vehicle, but he refused. The officer asked the defendant to unlock his door, but he again refused. After the defendant refused to unlock the door, the officer reached through the open window and unlocked the door.

You can use humor to belittle a fact.

The dog was not startled by the child. The dog ran up to the child while she was playing with a ball. He came. He saw. He bit.

This is occasionally effective, but it is more likely to reflect poorly on the writer.[27] Use extreme care when incorporating humor in persuasive writing.

Similarly, slang is out of place in an attorney's language to the court. Its presence would be unusual and somewhat startling. Thus, quoting a witness's description that includes slang might be effective in the context of a formal document to the court.

> Mr. Jones denied being drunk and denied hitting his wife, stating, "I'd remember if I'd whacked her."

Slang has a stronger emotional impact on the reader, so use it rarely and only when that emotion will work in your client's favor. When the emotion does not need to be heightened, use a more formal term.

> Mr. Jones denied being intoxicated and denied striking his wife (R. 4–7).

But avoid stating the facts so formally that they sound artificial.

> Mr. Jones protested that he was not inebriated. Furthermore, he repudiated any intimation that he may have assaulted his wife physically.

Despite the seriousness of the setting, you are telling a story of something that happened, and that story should not be hidden.

Repetition

Repetition is obvious in concept but subtle in mastery. It requires a faithful ear, a sense of the level of drama and formality appropriate to the situation, and a balance of courage and restraint. Repetition creates a sense of heightened drama, an increased formality elevating the value of the content repeated. When using repetition, make sure the item repeated deserves emphasis. If the point repeated is minor, repetition can be distracting.

You can repeat many elements. The most obvious are words. Also effective is the repetition of a phrase's structure.

> During preliminary questioning, the defendant admitted that he had used marijuana in the past. (R. 14–15) During the trial, he denied this. (R. 30)

The writer can also repeat larger structures, such as those of whole sentences, paragraphs, or paragraph blocks. Repetition can be subtle, as in the following example.

> The dealer promised to have the brakes tested on the car, but this promise was not kept.

Or it can be bold.

> The clerk, Jerry Vance, fumbled with the cash drawer and coins clattered on the floor. Silent, the defendant pointed the gun at

---

27. Humor can increase the reader's liking for the writer, but does not increase the reader's estimation of the writer's competence. Humor can also decrease the reader's liking for the writer. *Id.* at 139–140.

him. Silent, he pulled the trigger. Silent, he turned from the slumping body to gaze at the customers huddled behind the shelving.

In either case, the writer needs to be vigilant against going one step too far. One repetition too many can lead the reader to snicker or become irritated, either of which is a distraction from the content at hand.

Rhythm

Rhythm, a combination of structure and word choice, focuses on controlling the pace and vocal emphasis in the text, as the pace and intensity of music varies. In prose this is a subtle force; nevertheless, it can be useful to convey a certain mood while describing a set of facts.

> Later in the evening, while walking along the still, calm, lighted pathway, Mr. Hill heard a small cry. He stopped to listen. Hearing another cry, he moved in the direction of the sound. Pushing aside the heavy underbrush, he found the victim. The boy moaned again. Hill knelt beside him.

This sample slows the reader by placing three stressed syllables together "still, calm, light" which creates a touch of anticipation just before stating the event of hearing the small cry. When Hill stops, the reader is stopped by the rhythm of the short sentence, "He stopped to listen." The pace then increases with the faster, galloping rhythm of a series of phrases "hearing another cry," "in the direction," "of the sound," and "pushing aside the heavy underbrush." The reader can sense the rush here, and then is brought up suddenly by a short phrase with more stressed syllables: "he found the victim." The reader is held at this slower pace with two more short sentences that have more stressed than unstressed syllables. The reader reads slowly, quickly, then slowly again, lingering on the passages of greatest emotional impact. To use rhythm effectively, it is important not to be too heavy-handed. A rhythm that is too strong can draw the mind away from the content to the writing, and in this circumstance the writing is likely to look rather silly.

The use of rhythm is much more art than science and will be developed through experiment, experience, and evaluation. Metaphor may be the best way to explain the workings of rhythm in English.

> [T]he movement is neither a rise nor a fall, but an easy progress, a punctuated comfortable swing, in which there is a combination of both [a rise and fall of stress]. The orchestra leader, who beats time exaggerating greatly the force of stress, and the motion of the sea waves are in some ways better parallels to musical rhythm than the thrusts of a piston rod.[28]

Word choice can sharpen the focus of your presentation when used effectively, but can distort it if used without skill or restraint. Be

---

28. Morris W. Croll, *Style, Rhetoric, and Rhythm* 371 (1966).

interesting, but always be accurate and thorough. Use emotional association, degree of detail, terms of address, unusual wording, repetition, and rhythm not solely to sound persuasive, but to emphasize the facts that are themselves persuasive.

Putting Persuasive Techniques to Use

Because of the complexity of word choice, sentence structure, and small-scale and large-scale organization, you cannot constantly consider each of these dimensions while writing a statement of facts. Instead, first concentrate on the concerns discussed in the chapter on objective fact statements: choosing your facts, organizing them, and writing your story clearly and accurately. As you rewrite the section, identify the fact you want to emphasize or de-emphasize. Then turn to persuasive techniques and choose the ones that best suit your purpose. After you have rewritten the text for emphasis, you can revise it further for conciseness, omitting unneeded phrases and wordy structures. Making a fact statement persuasive involves adding a step to the middle of the legal writing process, rather than shifting to a completely different process. The summarizing checklist at the end of this chapter illustrates this by mimicking the checklist for objective statements of facts, but adds the steps needed to state the facts persuasively.

The following table summarizes the persuasive techniques discussed in this chapter.

SUMMARY OF TECHNIQUES FOR PERSUASIVE STATEMENTS OF FACT		
WRITING ASPECT	TO EMPHASIZE	TO DE–EMPHASIZE
OVERALL ORGANIZATION	Put the fact in as early as possible. Reprise the fact in the summary.	Put the fact in the middle to two-thirds of the way through the fact statement. Include less detail on the fact than on others in the fact statement.
PARAGRAPH ORGANIZATION	Put the fact at the beginning of a paragraph. Put the fact at the end of a paragraph. Set the fact off in a separate paragraph.	Place the fact within a paragraph on a more favorable point. Place the fact with other facts that establish a mitigating background.

WRITING ASPECT	TO EMPHASIZE	TO DE–EMPHASIZE
SENTENCE STRUCTURE	Put the fact in a short sentence.	Put the fact in a longer sentence.
	Make the fact part of the main subject and verb.	Use a linking verb to move the fact out of the main subject and verb.
	Use active voice to emphasize an action.	Use passive voice to de-emphasize an action.
	Put the fact in the first few words of a sentence.	Put the fact in the middle of a list at the end of a sentence.
	Put the fact in an intrusive phrase.	Put the fact in a dependent clause, usually at the end of a sentence.
	Put the fact in an unusual structure.	Put the fact in a sentence with very routine structure, such as subject, verb, elaboration.
WORD CHOICE	Use a word with a favorable connotation.	Use a word with an unfavorable connotation.
	Describe it in detail.	Summarize it in general terms.
	Characterize parties in sympathetic roles.	Characterize parties in unsympathetic roles, but not insulting or inaccurate.
	When the facts are sympathetic, use personal names or roles for the parties.	When the facts are unsympathetic, use legal terms rather than personal names.
	When a legal concept is favorable, use the legal terms to describe the parties.	When the legal concept is not particularly favorable, describe your situation as unusual, not fitting in the general mold.
	When the relationship of the parties is significant and favorable, use the significant relationship as a label.	When the relationship of the parties is an unfavorable fact, avoid using the relationship as a label.

WRITING ASPECT	TO EMPHASIZE	TO DE–EMPHASIZE
WORD CHOICE Cont'd	Use a slightly unusual word.	Use common words, nothing unusual.
	When the emotions of the situation are favorable, use slightly more informal wording.	When the emotions are not favorable, use slightly more formal words.
	Repeat a key word.	Use synonyms if needed to avoid repeating a word.

Incorporating These Techniques Into the Writing Process

Although the previous summary of techniques helps organize options for you, you still must work these techniques into the larger process of writing the statement of facts. Focus on a few tasks at once, rather than all of them simultaneously. Proceed through the steps for writing an objective statement of facts and then revise the fact statement to make it persuasive, incorporating some of the techniques discussed in this chapter. As you do this, consider changes in content and organization first and sentence structure and word choice later.

To help you see the interrelationship between this checklist and the one for objective statements of fact, the changes from the objective checklist are in boldface.

A CHECKLIST FOR A PERSUASIVE STATEMENT OF FACTS

1. Include all needed facts.
   a. Include legally significant facts:
      (1) facts that will be used in the argument section,
      (2) facts that show that the elements of the cause of action or defenses are met,
      (3) facts that will be used in the other side's legal argument, and
      (4) procedural facts.
   b. Include needed background facts.
   c. Include emotional facts you have determined should be included.
2. Organize those facts.
   a. Choose most effective opening for fact statement.
   b. Divide the facts into further sections if needed.
   c. Organize each section chronologically.
   d. Divide facts into paragraphs that group the facts logically.

e. Use visual aids if appropriate **or when they emphasize a favorable point.** When using visual aids,

   (1) keep them as simple and focused as possible, and

   (2) structure the visual aid to be read from top to bottom, left to right.

3. Draft the facts to be accurate and clear.

   a. State **necessary** unfavorable key points specifically **but not concretely.**

   b. Keep labels minimal and consistent.

   c. Substitute names for pronouns where needed **or where they add sympathy for your client.**

4. **Either before or after drafting your argument, review the facts to determine which specific facts should be emphasized.**

5. **Focusing on the facts you have chosen, experiment with different techniques until you get a sentence, phrase, or word that creates the effect you want. (Refer to the previous table for a list of these techniques.) Then revise the rest of the fact statement to frame your emphasized points effectively, revising sentence structure, word choice, and other small-scale concerns.**

6. After drafting the argument, revise the facts. Ask yourself the following questions.

   a. Are all legally significant facts included?

   b. Are all unneeded **and unfavorable** background and emotional facts deleted?

   c. Consider deleting any details

      (1) that may confuse more than clarify,

      (2) that clarify points that will not concern the legal reader, or

      (3) that create red herrings, or signals to the reader that an irrelevant point may indeed be relevant.

   d. Are sentences readable?

   e. Is each word chosen unambiguous and clear?

   f. Are all wordy phrases eliminated?

EXERCISE

The following excerpts from two statements of the case show you how two attorneys presented facts related to a case contesting the validity of a will. The plaintiff, James Hart, argues the will signed by Julia Hart, his stepmother, was invalid. The defendant John, Julia's son, argues the will was valid. The excerpts included show how each party described (1) Julia's health, (2) her medications, and (3) some unusual circumstances surrounding the signing of the will. Both excerpts make good use of various persuasive writing techniques, but neither is perfect.

Read the following statements of fact and locate examples of the writer's use of persuasive writing techniques. Then determine whether you think each technique is used effectively. Rewrite the passages, discussing the pluses and minuses of each revision. Also note other places where the writer could have used persuasive techniques to handle a point better.

Plaintiff–Appellant's Facts

As the picture from the Colonel's 1956 birthday party shows, time and chronic illness had ravaged Julia's health, so that Julia was prematurely old eighteen years before she died.

In 1973, Julia's health was terrible. She had always suffered from excruciating tension headaches (R. 925, 928–53) and in her late seventies and early eighties suffered from increasing cardiovascular problems, cataracts, arteriosclerosis, and many other problems (R. 928–53). So bad was Julia's health that, even though he was battling cancer at the time, Colonel Hart insisted that Julia never be left alone (R. 484, 710, 889). Julia was surrounded by many servants during the day (R. 454) and was watched by a baby-sitter at night (R. 484, 710, 889).

Julia was also on a large and complex daily regimen of drugs (R. 454). Daily she took three kinds of barbiturates—Tuinal (R. 1115–16), Fiornal (R. 113), and Fiornal with Codeine (R. 1113–14)—one of which included an opium derivative (R. 115). In addition to these drugs, she took greater-than-normal daily dosages (R. 1114–15) of Triavil, a specialized compound tranquilizer formulated and normally prescribed for mental depression (R. 1148–49).

Triavil was misprescribed for Julia. Dr. Desmond, Julia's personal physician in Adams, continued the prescription from one given to Julia by a Dr. Simmons, whom she had seen while on vacation in Florida (R. 454). Dr. Desmond continued the use of strong dosages of Triavil four times daily for Julia's tension headaches, which he had long feared would drive both Julia and himself out of their minds (R. 925). Dr. Desmond, in attempting to explain Julia's heavy medication, said that he later forgot that he had continued the use of Triavil for his patient. (R. 954–58).

Triavil offered no treatment or cure for tension headaches, as testified by Dr. Paul Wyles (R. 1149), a psychiatrist and former anesthesiologist with great knowledge of drugs used for both tension headaches and mental disorders (R. 1130, 1109–10). The Physician's Desk Reference 1083 (30th Ed.1976) concurs that Triavil is not used for headaches.

The only effect Triavil could have had on Julia's headaches, however, lay in its powerful tranquilizing effects (R. 113). Dr. Wyles testified in detail that, solely by reason of the drugs she took, Julia was susceptible to influence. He also testified that he normally prescribes taking Triavil only before retiring, so that the person taking it will be alert and functional during the day (R. 1117).

On November 1, 1973, five months before she died, Julia signed a new will in the presence of John Hart, Jr. (her sole heir under the new will), Sidney Green (the attorney John had urged her to hire), and Bill Wilson (Sidney Green's law partner) (R. 525, 630). The will, distributing over $8 million and allegedly taking three weeks to draft, was just three pages long. Despite its abolition of her estate plan of over twenty years, and despite the fact that it appointed a marital trust worth $6 million in addition to disposition of her own $2 million estate, a copy of the new will was never sent to Julia for her review and consideration.

Julia did not see the will until one-half hour before she signed it (R. 835). On November 1, Sidney Green and his partner arrived at Julia's home and read and summarily discussed the new will for twenty to thirty minutes (R. 836–37).

But Julia did not sign the will until John arrived. After John arrived, she signed the will within ten minutes. Sidney Green and his partner then departed immediately. This document not only reversed her twenty-year estate plan to the detriment of James and his sisters; it also disinherited Julia's own grandchildren from the $2.5 million trust that had been provided for them. . . .

Defendant–Appellee's Facts

Julia was uniformly described by all the witnesses who had personally known her as a strong-willed, positive, and independent woman who knew her own mind (R. 710, 719–20, 917–18). James Hart himself characterized Julia as an "independent and abrupt person" (R. 994).

Many witnesses who knew Julia for years and who observed her both before and after her husband's death testified that her personality and character were unchanged. They also testified that her mental faculties were unimpaired at the time of the execution of her last will, except that she was understandably sad over Colonel Hart Sr.'s recent death. Ms. Meyer stated that Julia's composure was "wonderful" at her husband's funeral (R. 1091). Dean Higgins, the family chauffeur and handyman for 27 years, testified that following John Sr.'s death "she was practically her old self" (R. 903).

Before his death, John Sr. had insisted on having someone present in the house when he was out of town because he was concerned about Julia's eyesight and was afraid she might fall (R. 746–47). As a result, since May 1973, Julia had aide-companions who stayed with her at night (R. 484). Dr. Desmond, Julia's personal physician, testified that the companions were traditionally used by wealthy persons in the community as aides, and that their presence therefore did not imply that Julia was incapable of caring for herself (R. 977).

Dr. Desmond and others have testified that Julia's medication had not affected her alertness (R. 918, 974, 984–87). Her doctor's opinion, based on his observations of Julia over the years, was that she was not susceptible to being influenced (R. 973–74). Because Julia had a history of osteoarthritis, tension headaches, thyroid deficiency, and cardiovascular disease (R. 984–85), she was and had been for many years taking a variety of medications. Nevertheless, no direct testimony from any witness shows that this schedule of medication affected Julia's mental alertness, independence, or forcefulness.

Shortly before executing her new will, Julia met twice with her attorney, visited the family office in the First National Bank of Adams building, and appeared at social functions. Angie Miller, who saw Julia frequently during this period and who accompanied her to Florida earlier, testified that during the period around November 1, 1973 (when Julia executed her last will), Julia was "remarkably peppy and alert" (R. 707).

Julia and her attorney, Sidney Green, had arranged for her to execute her will on the morning of November 1, 1973. Because of a conflict, however, Mr. Green asked Julia if they could meet in the afternoon, and Julia suggested that they meet at 5:00 p.m.

Attorneys Sidney Green and Bill Wilson drove to Julia's home together a little before 5:00. Julia greeted them at the door (R. 832). After they retired to the living room, Mr. Green briefly reviewed Julia's assets and then presented copies of the will for himself and attorney Wilson (R. 883, 638–39). Mr. Green then read through the will provision by provision (R. 471, 639). When they came to the language exercising the power of appointment over the marital trust established under Colonel Hart's will, Mr. Wilson explained the power of appointment to Julia. He made clear that, through the exercise of her power, all of the assets of the marital trust would be distributed to John Jr. (R. 639–40). At this point, Julia expressed her satisfaction with the provisions being read or explained to her (R. 639–41).

During the reading and discussion of the will, John Jr. arrived for his customary evening visit at his mother's home (R. 834, 630). He asked if he should come into the living room, and Julia indicated that he could (R. 1052). When he did so, he sat on the opposite side of the room until the attorneys completed their reading and discussion with Julia. Julia and the two attorneys then signed in the presence of each other (R. 446, 641–42). Both attorneys testified that in their opinion Julia was competent to execute the will at the time she did so (R. 466, 643–44).

ASSIGNMENT 1

Write a persuasive version of the following facts, favoring one of the two parties, which would be part of briefs filed to the administrative law judge hearing this matter. The Truehart Insurance Company wants to show Howard Haskell was not "engaged in performing a service growing out of and incidental to his employment" when he was injured. Howard Haskell wants to show he was so engaged. The following objective statement provides extensive facts; choose the facts that are needed and persuasive and then organize and word them effectively. The relevant law and several cases are included to help you determine what facts will be persuasive or legally significant. You should be able to write this statement without doing further research.

Objective Statement of Facts for Revision

Howard Haskell filed an application for workers' compensation with the Wisconsin Industrial Commission after he was injured on January 18. His employer is the Fresh Fruit Market in Milwaukee, Wisconsin, and his injury occurred as he was stepping from a bus on his way to the Market's premises.

The Fresh Fruit Market operates an open-air retail fruit and vegetable market on a seasonal basis. From November through May, the telephone number for the Market is disconnected, but a toll phone in the Market is left operational. The Market has electric heating available, but the heat is not sufficient to heat the office to a temperature adequate for work in the winter. During subzero weather, the water is shut off to prevent freezing pipes. Water service from the city is available at all times, however. Mail is delivered to the market throughout the year, but packages and special deliveries are delivered to Haskell's home from November to May. The Market's premises are leased from year to year from the Clark Oil Company, but Fresh Fruit installed and owns the structures and equipment used in the operation of its business upon those premises.

The Fresh Fruit Market is a Wisconsin corporation. Of the 100 issued shares of capital stock in this corporation, Haskell and his wife jointly own 73 shares; his brother-in-law, Donald Davies, owns 10 shares; and his mother, Hilda Haskell, owns 17 shares. The Fresh Fruit Market has employed Howard Haskell for ten years, since the founding of the Corporation. Mr. Haskell's title is president and general manager of the Fresh Fruit Market. He is not under the directional control of any superior officer. The insurance carrier's description of Haskell's duties states:

> Howard H. Haskell, general manager, buyer, and president—operates fruit market—maintaining and managing, buying and selling, approximately 25 percent to 50 percent of time away from premises in conduct of administrative duties.

More specifically, Mr. Haskell was the buyer from May to November. Mr. Goetz, the market supervisor, stated the following in a deposition.

Mr. Haskell purchased the produce the Market handled. He also took care of the advertising. Most of his work was away from the premises. He came there in the morning about 8:00 a.m. and usually left between 12:00 noon and 1:00 p.m., went out to the tracks to inspect fruit and vegetables, and went over on Broadway to buy our produce and also to take—went down to the Journal and different newspapers to take care of the advertising. Then he returned usually about 7:30 or 8:00 p.m. because that was when we have our heaviest business, and he was there through the evening until about 11:30 p.m. or so when the heaviest business would finish off, and then he would leave again at that time and go back over on Broadway at 12:00 midnight or 1:00 a.m. to look at produce. Trucks came in then. We had lots of trucks come in at 1:00, 2:00 a.m. Many times we would get caught and help unload trucks until 2:00 a.m., or maybe go over and leave notes for deliveries for the next morning.

From November to May, Mr. Haskell is the only employee on the Company's payroll. During that time he takes care of the bookkeeping, checks the building most evenings to make sure it is secure, and takes care of the mail. He also does any maintenance work needed on the building, such as replacing light bulbs and shoveling sidewalks. During these months, he also purchases new equipment as needed, sees to insurance and income tax matters, takes inventory, and calls past employees to see if they will be willing to work in the following season.

In a deposition, Haskell described his job during the off season as follows.

I take care of everything that we cannot take care of during our work season because we opened 16 to 18 work hours and don't have time to sacrifice all that and do it either before the season or after.

From November to May, Mr. Haskell works out of his home. During the winter of the accident, Haskell moved current files and account ledgers to his home. He also moved a typewriter and other office supplies, such as paper, a stapler, etc. to his home. He did not move other items, such as the telephone, cash register, or older files. He also did not move the desk, filing cabinets, or other office furniture.

During this time, Mr. Haskell gave his home address and phone number to people with whom he worked. He met with a representative of the Fresh Fruit's largest supplier of produce to settle the year's account, and they met at Mr. Haskell's home. During the year, this supplier would also call Mr. Haskell at home to inform him of future crops. Mr. Haskell was also called by the landlord who owned the market premises, by the insurance agent, by other seasonal employees who came to talk about personal matters, and by members of the Board of Directors. When any of these people needed to meet with Mr. Haskell, they met in his home.

The Board of Directors, which included the four family members who held stock, knew of this relocation of the company's office to Haskell's home during the off-season. They had never discussed the move at a meeting, either to agree or disagree about the arrangement.

During January, the month when the injury occurred, Mr. Haskell was dealing with the following matters for Fresh Fruit:

(1) the bag supplier's mistaken duplication of a year's order of mesh orange bags, and

(2) the terms for the renewal of the year-to-year lease for the Market's premises, which included

    (a) the amount of the rent for the next year,

    (b) whether Fresh Fruit would receive credit for permanent improvements to the premises, and

    (c) Fresh Fruit's right to remove mobile walk-in refrigerators upon termination of the lease.

Fresh Fruit had ordered mesh bags printed with the name of the company, but the provider of the mesh bags had mistakenly sent twice the number ordered. Haskell was considering whether to keep the extra bags or return them and ask for a refund. The lessor had increased Fresh Fruit's rent in the previous year and Fresh Fruit had spent money on repairs of benefit to the lessor, for which Haskell wanted to obtain credit. Fresh Fruit had by its previous lease reserved the right to remove the sheds and equipment it had installed on the premises. Fresh Fruit had installed walk-in refrigerated rooms, and the terminology of the lease made it unclear whether these refrigerators were included in the equipment that could be removed. The refrigerators were large units that would have to be dismantled to be moved.

Haskell had tried unsuccessfully for two days to contact his attorney, Ms. Melan, to determine whether the refrigerators were included in Fresh Fruit's equipment. He wanted to know about this matter before meeting with the landlord, Mr. Dawes. On January 18, the day of the injury, Haskell made an appointment to meet with Mr. Dawes at 10:00 a.m. the next day.

To prepare for this meeting, he decided he would need to get files of bills that had been paid for improvements and copies of the leases from previous years, which were in the files at the Market. He again tried to contact Ms. Melan, but she was in court and unavailable. He then determined he would also visit the public library to learn about Fresh Fruit's right to remove improvements. He also thought he would check California newspapers to get information about the orange crop, so he could determine whether to keep the extra bags. If the crop was expected to be plentiful, he believed the prices would be lower next year and he would keep the bags because he thought he could sell more oranges at lower prices. If the crop was not promising, he would return the extra orange bags.

He planned to leave after dinner, and accordingly he changed his clothes and put on long underwear because of the frigid weather. At dinner, they discussed the weather and his wife mentioned a sleet storm was in progress on the West Coast that could affect the orange crop. Haskell mentioned to his wife that he was going to the library and then to the market. Before leaving, Haskell telephoned his brother-in-law, Donald Davies, and asked him whether he had not only turned off the water at the market but also drained the pipes. Haskell wanted to make sure the pipes did not freeze, as had happened in previous years. Davies assured him that he had drained the pipes.

After making the call, Haskell took a bus to the library, read the California newspapers, and then found a real estate book and another book on merchandising. He found some helpful information in the real estate book regarding the law of fixtures, which he believed resolved his question. He then began reading the book on merchandising and became engrossed in the section on the principles of marketing. He continued reading until the library closed at 10:00 p.m.

When the library closed, he went across the street to a Walgreen's drugstore and had a cup of coffee and a doughnut. Snow was falling and the roads were becoming quite slick. At about 10:20 p.m. he left the drugstore for the bus stop. He boarded a bus and obtained a transfer, which he needed to get to the market. While waiting for the second bus, he decided to stop in a tavern next to the bus stop, Joe's Place. He had one beer. He then left the tavern and returned to the bus stop. After waiting for ten minutes, he decided he would try to get a cab, and called for one from a nearby phone booth. Before the cab arrived, the bus came. Haskell boarded the bus. As he was crossing the street after leaving the bus, about one block from the market, a speeding car struck him. The car sped away and the car and driver were not subsequently identified. He suffered a broken leg and elbow, which caused the disabilities for which he now seeks workers' compensation.

The relevant statutes are the following. Section 102.03 Conditions of Liability.

"(1)(c) . . . Every employee going to and from his or her employment in the ordinary and usual way, while on the premises of the employer, shall be deemed to be performing service growing out of and incidental to his or her employment; . . . The premises of the employer shall be deemed to include also the premises of any other person on whose premises service is being performed."

"(1)(f) Every employee whose employment requires him [or her] to travel shall be deemed to be performing service growing out of and incidental to his [or her] employment at all times while on a trip, except when engaged in a deviation for a private or personal purpose. . . . Any accident or disease arising out of a hazard of such service shall be deemed to arise out of his [or her] employment."

Section 102.18 Findings and Award.

"(1) After final hearing the commission shall make and file its findings upon all the facts involved in the controversy, and its order, which shall state its determination as to the rights of the parties. . . ."

Section 102.23 Judicial review.

"(1) The findings of fact made by the commission acting within its powers shall, in the absence of fraud, be conclusive; . . . ."

The relevant cases are *Hills Dry Goods Co. v. Industrial Com'n.*, 217 Wis. 76, 258 N.W. 336 (1935); *Motor Transport Co. v. Public Service Com'n*, 263 Wis. 31, 56 N.W.2d 548 (1953); *Milwaukee Toy Co. v. Industrial Com'n.*, 203 Wis. 493, 234 N.W. 748 (1931); and *Bitker Cload & Suit Co. v. Industrial Com'n*, 241 Wis. 653, 6 N.W.2d 664 (1942).

ASSIGNMENT 2

Draft the persuasive facts for a brief to the court supporting the Jones' claim against the Chevrolet plant and dealership. Consider the following memos, statute, and cases in drafting your statement.

SMITH AND GRANDINE

Attorneys at Law
975 Bascom Mall
Madison, Wisconsin

To: Associate
From: Jane Williams
Date: March 1, 1984
Re: Howard Jones, Case No. 84–15

On December 10, 1983, our client, Howard Jones, and his wife Anne Jones were driving on Interstate 90 outside Janesville, Wisconsin. Mrs. Jones was a passenger in the car driven by Mr. Jones. She was six months pregnant with her first child. The Jones car collided with one driven by James Carson. The Jones' seat belts broke. Mr. Jones wasn't injured, but when Mrs. Jones's seat belt broke, she was thrown against the dashboard. The Jones child was stillborn a few hours after the accident and Mrs. Jones died two days later. According to the doctor who treated Mrs. Jones, the fetus, a girl, was "viable" (i.e., alive and capable of life outside the womb) before the accident. The doctor also said that the death of Mrs. Jones and the fetus were a direct result of the internal injuries received when Mrs. Jones's seat belt broke.

Mr. and Mrs. Jones bought their car, a new Chevy Chevette, on December 1, 1983, from Andrews Auto Dealership, Inc., 950 Maple Street, Madison, Wisconsin. The car was equipped with seat belts when purchased. The entire car, including the seat belts, was manufactured in Janesville, Wisconsin. No one at Andrews Auto Dealership, Inc., or at the Chevrolet plant tested the strength of the seat belts. The warranty on the car and all parts, including the seat belts, is for twelve months.

The Chevrolet plant and dealership admit fault (i.e., negligence), but refuse to accept liability for the death of the fetus on the ground that Wisconsin's wrongful death statute does not provide for the recovery of damages for the death of an unborn infant.

Mr. Jones wants to bring a wrongful death action for his child, as well as for his wife. Therefore, please examine the wrongful death statute and the case interpreting it. After you have thoroughly analyzed the problem, write an office memorandum indicating whether Mr. Jones can maintain an action under the Wisconsin wrongful death statute for the death of his child. Do not discuss damages, Mr. Jones's standing, or the application of the wrongful death statute to Mrs. Jones.

MEMORANDUM

STATEMENT OF FACTS

The wife and fetus of our client, Howard Jones, were both killed in a car accident when the car's seat belts broke. Mr. Jones wants to receive damages for their deaths from the auto dealer and manufacturer involved. This memo discusses the application of the wrongful death statute, Wis.Stat. § 895.03 (1981–82), to the death of the fetus.

Mr. and Mrs. Jones bought their car, a Chevy Chevette, on December 1, 1983, from Andrews Auto Dealership, Inc., 950 Maple Street, Madison, Wisconsin. The car was equipped with seat belts when they purchased it. The warranty on the car and all parts, including seat belts, was for twelve months. The entire car, including seat belts, was manufactured in Janesville, Wisconsin. No one at Andrews Auto Dealership or at the Chevrolet plant tested the strength of the seat belts.

Mr. Jones and his wife were driving their new car on Interstate 90 on December 10, 1983, outside Janesville, Wisconsin. Mr. Jones was driving, and Mrs. Jones was a passenger. Mrs. Jones was six months pregnant with her first child. The right-hand lane was clear but the left-hand, or passing, lane was snow-covered and slippery. James Carson, who was passing the Jones's car, lost control of his car, which collided with the Jones's car. Mr. Carson was injured only slightly. During the collision, however, the Jones's seat belts broke. Mr. Jones was not injured, but his wife was thrown against the dashboard. The fetus she was carrying, a girl, was stillborn a few hours after the accident, and Mrs. Jones died two days later. The doctor who treated Mrs. Jones after the accident, Dr. Bernhardt, has informed us that the fetus was viable before the accident. He based this decision on several factors. First, the weight of the fetus was 1 lb. 13 oz., which is 2 oz. larger than the average fetus at this stage of development. Second, the fetus's lungs were more well developed than most this stage; lung development, he explained, is a major factor in a premature baby's chances of survival. He said he could not, however, give specific odds on the chances of survival of this fetus had it been born alive at this time. He has also stated that the deaths of Mrs. Jones and the fetus were a direct result of the internal injuries that occurred when Mrs. Jones's seat belt broke.

The Chevrolet plant and dealership admit that they were negligent, but refuse to accept liability for the death of the fetus on the ground that Wisconsin's wrongful death statute does not allow recovery of damages for the death of a fetus.

QUESTIONS PRESENTED

Under Wis.Stat. § 895.03 (1981–82), which covers wrongful death actions, is a fetus considered a "person" when the fetus died during the sixth month of gestation, but the physician said it was viable at the time of its death?

BRIEF ANSWER

Yes. The Wisconsin Supreme Court has specified that when a fetus is viable, it is a "person" within the meaning of the wrongful death statute. The court has not specified that a fetus must reach a particular age before the court considers the fetus to be viable.

DISCUSSION

A fetus is a "person" within the meaning of Wisconsin's wrongful death statute if that fetus is "viable" at the time of the injury causing its wrongful death. *Kwaterski v. State Farm Mutual Automobile Insurance Co.,* 34 Wis.2d 14. In *Kwaterski,* a viable fetus died as the result of an automobile collision, and the parents sued the driver at fault for damages. The defense argued that no cause of action existed for the death of an unborn infant. The court held, however, that a cause of action did exist because "a viable infant who receives an injury and by reason thereof is stillborn is a 'person' within the meaning of sec. 331.03, Stats.1963 (now sec. 895.03, Stats.)" *Kwaterski,* 34 Wis.2d at 22. Mr. Jones may argue that his situation is analogous to the Kwaterskis'. Like the Kwaterskis' fetus, the Jones's fetus can be considered viable, based on Dr. Bernhardt's testimony. Dr. Bernhardt's testimony can also establish that, as in *Kwaterski,* the fetus's death was a result of the automobile collision.

The crucial factor in making this analogy, however, is the certainty of the fetus's viability. The court in *Kwaterski* did not answer the question of whether a cause of action exists for the death of a nonviable fetus: "We are not here concerned with a nonviable fetus and we, therefore, do not decide whether such a nonviable infant . . . is such a person. . . ." *Kwaterski,* 34 Wis.2d at 22. The automobile plant and dealer argue that *Kwaterski* should not apply because the Jones's fetus was not viable. In *Kwaterski,* the fetus was in the eighth month of gestation, while the Jones fetus was only in the sixth month. This two month difference is critical to viability. The plant and dealer may support this distinction with the testimony of other experts, who will state six-month-old fetuses usually do not survive outside the womb. The court in *Kwaterski* did not specify a required age for the fetus, however, and therefore Dr. Bernhardt's testimony that the fetus was viable may be sufficient to show that the court's holding in *Kwaterski* should apply to the Jones fetus. The facts given by Dr. Bernhardt may establish viability of this fetus even if six-month fetuses in general are not viable: the fetus was larger than average and had better-than-average lung development. If the court finds that these facts distinguish the Jones' fetus from six-month fetuses in general, the age of the fetus may not bar recovery.

Wis.Stat. § 895.03 (1981–82)

895.03 Recovery for death by wrongful act. Whenever the death of a person shall be caused by a wrongful act, neglect or default and the act, neglect is such as would, if death had not ensued, have entitled the party injured to maintain an action and recover damages in respect thereof, then and in every such case the person who would have been liable, if death had not ensued, shall be liable to an action for damages notwithstanding the death of the person injured; provided, that such action shall be brought for a death caused in this state.

Bibliography

Bereiter, Carl and Marlene Scardamalia. *The Psychology of Written Composition.* Hillsdale, NJ: Lawrence Earlbaum Associates, 1987.

Constable, John. *Reflections upon Accuracy of Style.* New York: Garland Publishing Co., 1970 (facsimile edition of original printed in 1731).

Corbett, Edward P.J. *Classical Rhetoric for the Modern Student.* New York: Oxford University Press, 1965.

Fowler, Roger, *Essays on Style and Language: Linguistic and Critical Approaches to Literary Style.* London: Routledge and Kegan Paul, 1966.

Hovland, Carl I., Irving L. Janis, and Harold H. Kelley. *Communication and Persuasion.* New Haven: Yale University Press, 1953.

Lee, Vernon. *The Handling of Words, and Other Studies in Literary Psychology.* Lincoln: University of Nebraska Press, 1968.

McDonald, Daniel. *The Language of Argument.* New York: Harper and Row, 3d ed. 1980.

Mehler, Irving M. *Effective Legal Communication.* Denver: Philgor Publishing Co., 1975.

Patrick, J. and Robert O. Evans, eds., *Style, Rhetoric, and Rhythm.* Princeton, NJ: Princeton University Press, 1966.

Rieke, R.D. and M.O. Sillars. *Argumentation and the Decision Making Process.* Glenview, IL: Scott, Foresman and Co., 1984.

Rybacki, Karyn C. and Donald J. Rybacki. *Advocacy and Opposition: An Introduction to Argumentation.* Englewood Cliff, NJ: Prentice–Hall, Inc., 1986.

Sandell, Rolf. *Linguistic Style and Persuasion.* San Francisco: Academic Press, 1977.

Sebeok, Thomas A., Ed. *Style in Language.* Cambridge, MA: M.I.T. Press, 1960.

Simons, Herbert W. *Persuasion: Understanding, Practice, and Analysis.* New York: Random House, 2d ed. 1986.

Chapter 9

DISCUSSION SECTIONS OF
RESEARCH MEMOS

Most beginning legal writers learn to follow a specific format for writing office memos, which includes a format for organizing the discussion section.[1] This format helps the writer achieve a standardized level of quality, conforming to what is usually recognized as acceptable work. This approach provides a sound basis for writing memos. Rather than learning more about these standard approaches, however, in this chapter you will study three tasks for organizing the discussion section and explore alternative approaches for accomplishing them, including a variety of specialized approaches to choosing and organizing your content. Just as getting the basics involved learning some standard forms and techniques, getting beyond the basics will involve learning how to move from those forms into a broader variety of organization plans. As always, the goal is to communicate your point clearly.[2]

Although good research and writing skills are important in excellent memos, this chapter focuses on medium- and large-scale organization. Organization is central to an excellent memo for many reasons.[3] First, resolving organization questions helps you resolve remaining content questions, because organization and content are interdependent.[4] Second, busy readers want research memos they can read easily; logical organization increases readability by increasing clarity and conciseness. Finally, readers can read and comprehend information much more readily when you organize it in a way that makes sense to them.[5]

1. This format, known as IRAC, which stands for issue-rule-analysis or application-conclusion, is taught in most 1st year legal writing courses. We have no objection with the IRAC method of organization but this chapter moves beyond that basic format.

2. Dean E. Hewes and Sally Planalp, "The Individual's Place in Communication Science" in *Handbook of Communication Science* 147 (1987).

3. William L. Rivers, *Writing: Craft and Art* 15 (1975). Carl Bereiter and Marlene Scardamalia, *The Psychology of Written Composition* 156 (1987).

4. Lil Brannon, Melinda Knight, and Vara Neverow–Turk, *Writers Writing* 5 (1982).

5. Hewes and Planalp, *supra* note 2, at 160.

To help you adapt your organizational skills, this chapter focuses on three parts of the organizing process. The first two sections discuss organizational tools that offer the advanced writer an opportunity to address the more sophisticated questions organization raises: (1) choosing the content your reader needs and (2) organizing the building blocks of the content, the presentation and application of individual cases or subissues. The third section discusses five patterns you can use to organize these building blocks into an effective whole.

CHOOSING CONTENT FOR YOUR READER

When choosing what content to include, start with the basic requirements with which you are familiar: answer the issues, include the relevant law, and explain how the law applies to the factual circumstances. Nevertheless, some questions may remain: how thorough should the explanation of the reasoning be? should you raise other issues not now considered by the senior attorney? These questions arise because of your uncertainty, not so much about your research skills as about your reader's needs.

When researching a question for a senior partner or for a judge, you usually feel two contradictory pressures: one for doing a thorough job and one for getting done in the allotted time. The pressure for thoroughness comes from your desire to impress the boss and do a good job. The pressure for efficiency is also immediate. Conflict is likely. Fortunately, some of the thinking necessary to resolve this conflict may be done once in general, rather than done for each research assignment. Because you will often write more than one memo for the same reader, you can develop a default model for memos to that reader, varying the model only as the situation warrants.[6] These specialized models for memo discussions function like the form clauses you developed for contracts because you will use them repeatedly when writing memos. You can also adapt the writing system you have been developing since Chapter 2 to create a helpful routine for organizing.

Central to your development of this default model is the question of what your reader wants from the memo.[7] All readers have an optimum amount of information they find desirable,[8] but what that amount is varies from one reader to another. For example, some attorneys value conciseness greatly and want a memo to state the points general-

6. Just as a computer program has a default setting that it chooses unless told to do otherwise, you can have a default pattern of organization that you choose unless circumstances dictate a change.

7. Joseph N. Cappella, "Interpersonal Communication: Definitions and Fundamental Questions," in *Handbook of Communication Science* 212 (C. Berger and S. Chaffee, eds. 1987).

8. Their response can be analogized to that of consumers in general. One study in consumer research found that, when the amount of information about a product increases, the consumer will increase the time spent studying that information, but only up to a point. After that point, the consumer's response to more information is to spend less time studying the information, not more. (Jacoby, Speloler, and Knon, 1974). Scott Ward, "Consumer Behavior," in *Handbook of Communication Science* 659 (C. Berger and S. Chaffee, eds. 1987).

ly, not dwelling on specifics or supporting details. Others want more detail and more support. After you have fully researched and analyzed each issue, you will be able to choose the amount of detail and support that each attorney wants without compromising the quality of the conclusions you reach. The following paragraphs sketch other common preferences legal readers have and outline ways you can organize to provide those readers with effective discussion sections.

Some attorneys prefer for clerks or associates to write a cut-and-paste memo, which means including long passages from cases they have found relevant. This sometimes happens because the attorney does not want to trust the analysis of cases to the clerk or associate and prefers to do it personally. This approach may not reflect the attorney's view of the writer's personal abilities, but rather how the attorney likes to work. This attorney wants the writer to complete the research, organize it, but leave the task of making conclusions to him or her.

For this attorney, your main writing task will be to provide clear, concise signals that show the purpose of each inserted quotation. One way to do this is to explain why the quotation is included. For example, if a case has been reversed but is quoted to develop some needed history about the issue, let the reader know that. Alternatively, if the case is the one most applicable to the client's situation, state that. These signals, which you can communicate in one sentence, are a tremendous help to the reader, who can then adjust his or her reading to obtain the information most efficiently. Signals also help the reader place the information in context. If some phrases in a long passage are particularly important, underline these key phrases so they will not be overlooked. This allows the reader to see your point without reading the whole passage. Readers who want cut-and-paste memos may want the extended quotation, but may prefer not to read all of it.

Other attorneys have the opposite view, looking with disgust at pages with long passages of single-spaced, indented text. These readers view the major function of the memo to be analysis and application of the research, and they do not expect to do this work themselves. For these attorneys, include quotations only when the particular language is central to your point or when it is so well stated that it will be pleasant reading for your reader. One way to determine when to include a quotation in this circumstance is to consider whether you would quote it in a brief. If so, you probably should include it in the memo. If not, you probably should paraphrase it and include a pinpoint citation instead.

Some attorneys fall between these extremes. In addition to wanting the writer to analyze and apply the law, these attorneys want the writer to communicate the answer quickly, stating it up front followed by a quick, clear explanation of the reasoning behind it. This attorney does not want to be instructed on the law, nor does he or she want long quotes. The attorney wants an answer that provides a clear framework for the memo, so he or she can evaluate the following support. This attorney does not want to read the history behind the law unless and until it is relevant. He or she does not want to follow the complexities of a cited case unless and until the need to understand those complexities is apparent. For this attorney, boil down the information. This means conciseness, but it also means focus. Rather than leading your reader through each step of your research or analysis, digest the research for the reader and present your findings as clearly and directly as possible. State the point of each section and paragraph as quickly as possible.

Most likely your reader will be a combination of these three models. Your default pattern for that reader may combine elements of the three models previously discussed.

While developing your default pattern, also consider whether your reader will question you about other alternatives beyond those covered in the memo. In some situations, the reader wants a concise memo focused on the issues most likely to arise, but he or she expects you to be prepared to address other possibilities if asked. In this situation, you may want to note your thoughts on those possibilities in a separate memo to your file. You can then discuss the matters intelligently if they do arise. For example, as you eliminate unworkable theories, jot down your reasons for the theory not working and keep these notes in your file. Specifically, if you wrote a memo determining that negotiation should be pursued because litigation would not be worth the expense, list the possible theories for litigation in the memo. In your own notes, note the cases and details you discovered in your research into possible approaches for litigation. This way you can recall your answer without too much work if a senior partner asks you to pursue it. In contrast, if you determine that a theory will not succeed but you expect that the answer will surprise the reader, include the theory in your discussion and explain your conclusion to the reader.

Also consider tone. Some readers prefer a down-to-earth tone, and a straightforward opening can sharpen the clarity of the whole memo for these readers. For example, consider the following opening sentences from two memos.

> This case is far less complicated than the size of the complaint would indicate.

> I have great difficulty with this argument. This certainly doesn't look like a frivolous case to me.

These sentences are refreshing, yet they communicate important information about the memo, information worth the emphasis of the opening sentence of a discussion section. This opening may help you build on the style you developed for your objective statement of facts in Chapter 7.

In summary, develop a default model adapted to your reader. If you have different readers, develop different models. As soon as you start a job, begin working out these default models for memos, and refine them until you receive positive feedback.

ORGANIZING YOUR CONTENT

After you have chosen the content, organize the components of that content. This organization occurs at two levels: organizing the presentation and application of individual cases and organizing the cases within each issue.

For each case you use to explain how the law answers the issue, construct three elements: the legal foundation for your point, the logical steps in your reasoning that arise from the foundation, and the landing leading from that point to the next point to be developed, eventually leading to the answer.[9]

The Legal Foundation

Presenting the legal foundation is basically a task in expository writing,[10] explaining the law that you will use to resolve the question at hand. It includes (1) a statement of the legal principle or rule that you will apply later and a citation to that rule, (2) the facts that are critical for interpreting that rule, (3) a statement of how that court used the rule to resolve this issue, and (4) an explanation of the reasoning the court used when applying the rule. Sometimes, the logical foundation is rather straightforward, as in the following example.

> In 1988, the Wisconsin Court of Appeals held that "highways" as used in the Wisconsin highway defects statute included sidewalks. *Bystery v. Village of Sauk City,* 146 Wis.2d 247, 251, 430 N.W.2d 611, 613 (Ct.App.1988). In *Bystery,* the plaintiff was injured when the bicycle she was riding overturned on a sidewalk. The court decided that a village could be liable under the Wisconsin highway defects statute if the facts established the sidewalk was not repaired. The court reasoned that it was legislative policy that "municipalities are to keep their highways and sidewalks in repair and are liable for injuries caused by want of repair and dangerous conditions. . . ." *Bystery,* 146 Wis.2d at 247, 430 N.W.2d at 613.

Sometimes, however, the presentation is more complex.

> The third requirement to obtain a temporary injunction is that the plaintiff must show lack of an adequate remedy at law. When the damages are compensable by a monetary award, the courts will not grant a temporary injunction. *Werner v. Grootemaat,* 80 Wis.

---

9. Some of you have used the IRAC formula (Issue, Rule, Application, and Conclusion) for organization at this level. This way of looking at the organization does not contradict that formula, but presents an alternative way to view what is basically the same logical process. Similarly, this is an alternative approach to the Toulmin model, which is outlined in Karyn C. Rybacki and Donald J. Rybacki, *Advocacy and Opposition: An Introduction to Argumentation* 63–64 (1986).

10. In other words, it presents and explains ideas, rather than telling a story (narrative).

2d 513, 259 N.W.2d 310 (1977). In *Werner*, the plaintiffs were seeking a temporary injunction to prevent the defendants from honoring drafts under a letter of credit. The court denied the injunction because the plaintiffs could have amended their complaint to include the monetary equivalent of the drafts honored. *Werner*, 80 Wis.2d at 524, 259 N.W.2d at 315.

Conversely, when an action for damages would not afford the plaintiff relief from the injury, there is no adequate remedy at law. *American Mutual Liability Insurance Co. v. Fisher*, 58 Wis.2d 299, 306, 206 N.W.2d 152, 156 (1973). In *Fisher*, the appellant-defendants were trying to terminate a permanent injunction. The injunction forced them to provide the plaintiff with eighteen parking places, as set forth in their lease. The appellants argued that because each space had a value of $10, there was an adequate remedy at law. However, even though each space had a monetary value, there were no available parking spaces in the vicinity of the plaintiff's business. The court affirmed the injunction after reasoning that because the money could not be used to obtain any suitable, substitute parking spaces, there was no adequate remedy at law.

In a bench memo, or a memo written to an appellate judge about a case to be reviewed, often the foundation is actually the arguments made by the parties.

Briefly, Patient and Doctor Service (PDS) is arguing that sec. 636.10(1) does not apply to them. The statute requires insurers to pay a covered loss within thirty days after written notice, or pay simple interest at the rate of twelve percent per year. But PDS argues that it is a "service insurance corporation," and not a direct insurer. Because PDS makes payments to health providers whose patients are insured, rather than making payments to the insured individuals who received the services, it claims that there is no loss to be covered. Because there is no loss, the statute's 30 day limit does not apply to PDS and therefore it is not required to pay interest.

Your reasoning rests on this foundation, so it must be solid. For example, you would not write the following paragraph, because it omits a simple fact (that Bystery was riding a bicycle) needed to make the analogy clear.

In 1988, the Wisconsin Court of Appeals held that "highways" as used in the Wisconsin highway defects statute included sidewalks. *Bystery v. Village of Sauk City*, 146 Wis.2d 247, 251, 430 N.W.2d 611, 613 (Ct.App.1988). Bystery was injured when she fell on a city sidewalk. The court decided that the village may be liable under the Wisconsin highway defects statute. The court reasoned that it was legislative policy that "municipalities are to keep their highways and sidewalks in repair and are liable for

injuries caused by want of repair and dangerous conditions. . . ."
Bystery, 146 Wis.2d at 247, 430 N.W.2d at 613.

As in *Bystery,* Timothy Murphy was riding a bicycle when he was injured. . . .

A more common error here is for writers to include unneeded detail that obscures the main point. To avoid this problem, keep the focus on the issue at hand. For example, if the focus of your issue was the point stated in the topic sentence of the following paragraph, you would focus on that aspect of the case. The following paragraph illustrates this by focusing on the concept of "subjective intent."

> **The recreational status of an activity, and therefore whether immunity attaches, is not based upon the subjective intent of the actor. *Bystery v. Village of Sauk City,* 146 Wis.2d 247, 254, 430 N.W.2d 611, 614 (1988). Ann Bystery was bicycling on a Sauk City sidewalk and suffered injuries when her bike overturned. Bystery conceded that her travel was recreational. But the court reasoned that the legislature did not intend for immunity to be determined by the specific motivation for the activity, because liability would turn solely on the subjective intent of the actor. *Id.* Instead, they reasoned that bicycling is generally recreational, and for that reason Bystery's activity was recreational.**

You want to avoid rambling to related but distinct points, as does the following, less focused version.

> The recreational status of an activity is based on the nature of the activity rather than the actor's subjective intent. *Bystery v. Village of Sauk City,* 146 Wis.2d 247, 254, 430 N.W.2d 611, 614 (Ct. App.1988). Ann Bystery was bicycling on a Sauk City sidewalk and suffered injuries when her bike overturned. The court reasoned that the legislature did not intend for immunity to apply whenever the activity was recreational, for liability would then turn solely on the subjective intent of the actor. *Id. The legislature created the immunity statute to promote the recreational use of property by encouraging owners to permit access without fear of liability. Id.* at 247, 430 N.W.2d at 613. Bicycling is generally recreational and, therefore, Bystery's activity was recreational. The court held that Bystery's activity was recreational, regardless of her subjective intent.

The foundation gives the reader the information he or she needs to understand the following reasoning and to have confidence in its reliability. For this part of your presentation, focus on giving the reader all the important information. Omit any unneeded information related to other points made in the memo, but not focused here.

The Logical Steps That Explain Your Reasoning

The second part of your discussion of the case, explaining the steps, does not involve explaining so much as taking the reader through a series of syllogisms. At this stage, apply the rule stated in the foundation to the facts of your case and lead your reader step-by-step through the application. The rhetorical stance of this paragraph is somewhat different from the preceding legal foundation, and this portion usually begins in a new paragraph.

[the foundation]

> In 1988, the Wisconsin Court of Appeals held that "highways" as used in the Wisconsin highway defects statute included sidewalks. *Bystery v. Village of Sauk City*, 146 Wis.2d 247, 251, 430 N.W.2d 611, 613 (Ct.App.1988). In *Bystery*, the plaintiff was injured when the bicycle she was riding overturned on a sidewalk. The court decided that the village may be liable under the Wisconsin highway defects statute. The court reasoned that it has been legislative policy that "municipalities are to keep their highways and sidewalks in repair and are liable for injuries caused by want of repair and dangerous conditions." *Id.*

[the steps]

> In our case, pedestrians routinely used the footpath to travel between a large residential area and a small commercial district. Therefore it performed the function of a sidewalk, and should be included in the definition of a highway just as the concrete sidewalk in *Bystery* was included. If included in the definition of highway, then it will come under the statute and our client will probably be able to recover for her injuries. Furthermore, because of the policy encouraging cities to keep sidewalks in repair and free of dangerous conditions, the court should decide that it would be appropriate for the city to be liable for any dangerous conditions allowed to exist on the path.

Here you must discern the essential logical steps and include all of them. For example, the following paragraph omits a logical step that the revision includes.

> Just as a homeowner's electrocution was the precise injury foreseeable due to SDG & E's negligence, a child being hit by a car while walking home from school was the precise injury foreseeable from the District's negligence in not informing parents of the school's early closing. Tommy's being hit by a car then is the type of injury that could be foreseen as a result of the District's negligence.

Revise to include all logical steps.

> **Just as a homeowner's electrocution was the precise injury foreseeable due to SDG & E's negligence, a child being hit by a car while walking home from school was the precise**

> injury foreseeable from the District's negligence in not in-
> forming parents of the school's early closing. Three miles is a
> long way for a child to walk, especially when alone and for
> the first time. Most people are afraid to allow their young
> children to cross streets and walk alone precisely because a
> car might hit them. A child being hit by a car then is the
> type of injury that could be foreseen as a result of the
> District's negligence.

Similarly, do not include supporting information necessary in the
memo but not in this series of logical steps.

Besides including all needed steps in the right order, also make
sure the movement from step to step is clear. One way to clarify these
steps is to use transitions ("thus," "as a result,"), but a subtler technique is to repeat sentence structure or key words, or both. These
techniques allow you to show how the logical progression arises from
the content itself.

When writing the logical steps leading from your legal foundation
to your conclusion, focus on including each step and stating it clearly.

The Landing

This final step is small, and perhaps for that reason is often
overlooked. But the landing, or the concluding statement, states the
reason why the reader has followed your steps, and is also the platform
leading to the next point. This element tells the reader the significance of the logic to the broader issue you are addressing in that section
of the memo. It answers the question, "So what?" that appears in the
reader's mind after he or she has made the effort to follow your
reasoning. For example, the final sentence of the previous example is
the landing.

> A child being hit by a car then is the type of injury that could
> be foreseen as a result of the District's negligence.

Although the landing may be only a sentence, make sure it is present.
Once you have mastered the organization of each piece of logical
reasoning, you can use these organized units to construct the larger
organization of the issue.

ORGANIZING THE INFORMATION WITHIN EACH ISSUE

One of the most challenging steps in writing is the large-scale
organization. It is also one of the most crucial, because organization
makes a huge difference in the speed and ease with which the reader
can comprehend the content.

> In a case of bad construction the single items might be valuable,
> but the Reader was obliged to rearrange them. Such rearrange-
> ment is equivalent to rewriting the book. . . . When the badly
> arranged items are themselves good, one sometimes feels a mad

desire to hand them over to someone else. It is like good food badly cooked.[11]

As this quotation suggests, poor organization forces the reader to read a document several times, thinking about the information and recombining it in his or her mind until the logical connection of the individual points becomes clear. This consumes too much of the reader's time and energy, which is why poor large-scale organization is one of the most serious flaws a memo discussion can have.

Comprehension is also increased by using the readability techniques you have studied in earlier chapters, such as using clear sentence structures, crafting sentences of reasonable length, using familiar words, and handling lists carefully. When you write a discussion section, employ all the skills you have mastered in these areas.

Most practitioners develop a default pattern when writing memos. This pattern is useful because it reduces stress and increases efficiency. But when the pattern does not suit the task at hand, you must move to another more appropriate pattern. Understanding the following patterns provides you with the resources to do this. Usually this need for change arises from the nature of the issue, although it can also be caused by changes in the tastes of the reader or writer. The challenge for the advanced writer of memos is to use your default pattern appropriately and effectively and to know its limitations.

Five of the most common patterns are discussed below: the trial format, the analytical pattern, the bifurcated analysis, the educational approach, and weighing possibilities. Note which one is most like your default pattern, so you can watch for overuse of that pattern. But also read the other patterns carefully, so you understand the different options for organizing when your default pattern does not work.

Trial Format

In the trial format, the writer explains one party's position, then the other's, and then weighs the two to reach a result. This pattern, organized around the two sides, has the advantage of creating a concrete picture of the argument. It is often a natural choice for bench memos, because it provides the reader with the foundation of the two parties' arguments before moving into the writer's analysis. Because it does not organize around the abstract ideas of the law, it may seem simpler.

> *We could argue that* Tommy should have known, even at his age, that it was too dangerous to walk home from school. He should have gone to the nearest phone booth and called his parents or a neighbor to pick him up at school. *The plaintiff, however, could respond that* perhaps there were not any nearby phone booths, that Tommy did not have any money to make a phone call

11. Vernon Lee, *The Handling of Words, and Other Studies in Literary Psychology* 11 (1968).

or did not know the phone number, or that he should not have been expected to decide on the least dangerous alternative for getting home.

In conclusion, *a California court will probably decide that* Tommy's injuries from the car accident were foreseeable by the School District. The risk of a student's injury by a motorist was a foreseeable risk created by the School District's negligence in not notifying parents of the early closing.

However, the trial pattern has limitations that can create problems with more complex subjects. First, it can lengthen the presentation. If you present one position, you may need to refer to it when presenting the other side's position. This tends to add explanatory phrases that would be unneeded if the two positions were combined in one description of the law.

A more serious problem is that the comparison of the two positions, which in essence answers the issue, does not appear until after much preliminary information, so the reader gets the answer relatively late in the memo. This is not a problem when the comparison comes after one focused description, as in the previous example. But if each position takes several pages to explain, a reader can get impatient or confused.

The trial format also requires the reader to read quite a bit of information without a larger framework of understanding. This adds to the reader's burden, because it is generally easier to remember information if you know how to file it in your mind, rather than hold unprocessed information in your mind until its relevance becomes clear.

For these reasons, if you decide to use the trial format, you can offset some of its disadvantages. First, add topic sentences to communicate the main point.[12]

The first question here is whether the corporation is entitled to a Class one or a Class two hearing. If it is entitled to a Class one hearing, then the request for a hearing is premature. If, however, it is entitled to a Class two hearing, then. . . .

The corporation argues that. . . .

Second, divide issues so the reader gets to the conclusion as soon as possible. Finally, consider using one of the following alternative organizations for more complex issues.

Analytical Pattern

A second possible pattern is the analytical one, or organizing by subissue. This is often useful if the issue has clear elements. In this pattern, begin by identifying the subissues in an overview, which

---

12. To help you focus on the organization structure, these examples omit much of the specific context.

usually contains a list. You then discuss each listed item in turn. If several cases are needed to explain a listed item, organize them to work together to make a point, rather than organizing around the cases themselves. Similarly, if one case develops several of those listed points, split your presentation of the case, using the relevant parts of the case in each place needed. The following excerpt shows one way to organize one case to support several points.

> St. Justine's can be held liable for Hanba's injuries under Wisconsin's apparent agency law. Under apparent agency (also called apparent authority), a hospital can be held liable for injuries caused by an independent contractor if:
>
> (1) . . . ;
>
> (2) . . . ; and
>
> (3) . . . .
>
> *Pamperin.* . . .
>
> In *Pamperin,* . . . . The patient sued the hospital under the theory of apparent authority.
>
> Addressing the first element of liability, the court found that . . . . Most people believe . . . , the court reasoned, and this hospital had not . . . . Thus, the hospital had . . . .
>
> The court could make a similar finding in the Hanba matter. St. Justine's . . . , which could lead a patient to assume that . . . . St. Justine's did not expressly or implicitly inform Hanba that . . . . Although St. Justine's had . . . , because Hanba was seeking emergency care it is doubtful that . . . . A court would probably rule, therefore, that . . . .
>
> The second element of liability under apparent agency, . . . , does not have to be proven where . . . . *Pamperin* . . . . Similarly, the court will probably not require that Hanba prove . . . because . . . .
>
> *Pamperin* does examine the third element of apparent authority, whether . . . . According to *Pamperin,* . . . . The court found that . . . . Because . . . , the hospital was therefore held to have met the third test for liability under apparent authority.
>
> It also can be shown that Hanba relied upon St. Justine's . . . . While the court will have to determine whether . . . , it should not be difficult to demonstrate that . . . . St. Justine's should therefore be held liable for Hanba's injuries by Stone.

The analytical pattern allows you to divide information into discrete points that can each be handled in a page or so, which means that the reader does not have to juggle many pieces of information at one time. In general, this is a very readable and concise form of organization. It is helpful in situations that include disjunctive and conjunctive elements. For example, there may be three required elements, but two of them could be met in either of several ways. Dividing the text by elements permits you to address each element in relative isolation, so you can apply each element without worrying that the reader does not know where he or she is in the analysis.

The following extended example illustrates the use of organizing by elements in a more complex situation, where there are elements within elements, some disjunctive and some conjunctive. The memo discusses how a group of nonprofit organizations can argue that a house in a single-family residential area should be rezoned to provide group housing for the Children with AIDS Project (CAP). The group reasons that this is an allowable use of spot zoning (rezoning one parcel of land without changing the zoning of the surrounding area). The segment begins in the middle of the memo, after the writer has established that spot zoning is the applicable theory.

> Spot zoning is legal in Wisconsin if it is . . . and is not . . . . *Ballenger* . . . . In addition, spot zoning may be legal if it satisfies one of the following three criteria. First, spot zoning may be legal if it . . . . *Howard* . . . . Second, spot zoning may be legal if . . . . *Eggebeen* . . . . Third, spot zoning may be legal if . . . . *Ballenger* . . . . The CAP spot zoning is legal because . . . , . . . , and . . . .
>
> Spot zoning is legal if it is done in the public interest and is not solely for the benefit of the property owner. *Ballenger* . . . . In this case, ...
>
> The court upheld the zoning amendment, reasoning that it was not spot zoning because . . . . The court further elaborated that even if . . . .
>
> Improvement of services was the Ballenger ferry line's goal when it sought to . . . . Similarly, CAP sought to improve its services . . . .
>
> Second, spot zoning is legal if it is in the public interest, even if . . . . *Howard* . . . . In this case, ...
>
> The court granted summary judgment in support of the Village Board's authority to spot zone the parcel. The court reasoned that . . . . Likewise, although CAP had . . . , there was a . . . , so the spot zoning is legal . . . .
>
> Spot zoning is illegal, however, if there is . . . and . . . . *Cushman* . . . . In *Cushman*, ...
>
> In our case, by contrast, CAP is . . . . Therefore, based on these distinctions, the CAP spot zoning is not illegal because . . . .
>
> The first of the three additional criteria by which spot zoning may be judged legal is whether . . . . *Howard* . . . . The property owners in Howard . . . . The court granted summary judgment, reasoning this was legal spot zoning because . . . .

In *Howard,* the rezoning sought was consistent with . . . , even though . . . . In our case, rezoning to allow the hospice as a residence for orphans is consistent with . . . , even though . . . . Zoning for the hospice is also consistent with . . . . Based on this similarity with the facts of *Howard,* the spot zoning for CAP is legal because . . . .

Spot zoning is illegal if it does not . . . , even if rezoning . . . . *Cushman* . . . . In *Cushman,* . . . . The court held this was illegal spot zoning because . . . .

In *Cushman,* the planned dental clinic was . . . . The hospice, by contrast, is . . . . Based on this distinction, the spot zoning for the hospice is not illegal because . . . .

The second of the three additional criteria by which spot zoning may be judged legal is whether . . . . *Eggebeen* . . . . In *Eggebeen,* . . . . The court held that zoning the parcel was legal spot zoning, reasoning that . . . .

In *Eggebeen,* the specific characteristics of the property in question were the factors that made the spot zoning legal. A similar situation occurs in CAP's case, where . . . . Thus it was in the interest of the community to rezone the property . . . . If the property had not been rezoned, ... Based on these similarities, spot zoning of CAP's property is legal because . . . .

The third additional criterion by which spot zoning may be judged legal is whether . . . . *Ballenger* . . . . In this case, ... The court upheld the amendment, reasoning that . . . .

As in *Ballenger,* where . . . . , so in our case . . . .

Although the hospice is not . . . . *Browndale* . . . . In *Browndale,* the court emphasized that . . . . Because . . . , the hospice is functionally equivalent to . . . . Therefore, as in *Browndale,* CAP's case is legal spot zoning because . . . .

But the analytical pattern has limitations, too. It can be cumbersome when several elements need little discussion, because the structure may require too many transitions to make the organization clear. It may also be cumbersome when one case is being used for several elements, leading you to repeat the same facts or holdings too much. In this situation, you might be self-conscious about restating all the information just stated for another element; yet you know omitting it would delete logically necessary steps. Additionally, this pattern may not help when several elements overlap or when your question concerns which set of criteria should be applied.

In short, you find yourself facing an organizational dilemma: a choice between a boring and awkward structure and one that provides inadequate support. At that point, consider other possible patterns.

Bifurcated Analysis

A third pattern, the bifurcated analysis, combines trial format and the analytical pattern and can be useful for more complex discussions that the previous two patterns cannot handle well. This pattern divides the discussion of the issue into parts (elements, subquestions, etc.), then for each part discusses first one side, then the other, and finally weighs the two. In essence, this pattern inserts the trial pattern within a looser version of the analytic pattern.

Bifurcated analysis lets the reader focus on one task at a time, while still allowing the integration of a complex set of ideas. First organize the larger issue into subissues.

> The first prong of the test for superseding cause centers on
> . . . .
>
> The second prong of the test centers on . . . .

Then begin your discussion with an overview of how these subissues fit together to answer the larger issue.

> The test for superseding cause has two prongs, each focusing on a different aspect of foreseeability: (1) . . . and (2) . . . .

After you have provided this overview, focus on each subissue separately, discussing each subissue individually as in the trial format.

Finally, after you have organized the subissues so they fit together and have discussed each subissue, revise the total discussion, adding transitions and interim summaries between the subissues to remind the reader periodically where he or she is in the larger analytical framework.

> The test for superseding cause has two prongs, each focusing on a different aspect of foreseeability: (1) . . . and (2) . . . .
>
> The first prong of the test for superseding cause centers on the foreseeability of the intervening act. An intervening act that is highly unforeseeable, not likely to happen, and uncommon is unforeseeable and satisfies this prong. *Bloomberg* . . . .
>
> The plaintiff could argue that the District should have foreseen the gang's acts because . . . .
>
> We can respond that the District was unaware of the gang because . . . .
>
> In conclusion, the court will probably decide . . . .
>
> The second prong of the superseding cause test centers on the foreseeability of the type of injury caused. When the injury caused by the intervening act is precisely and directly the injury to be expected from the defendant's negligence, then the injury is foreseeable. *Pappert* . . . .
>
> The defendant may assert that . . . .

The plaintiff, however, could respond that the injury was foreseeable because Tommy should not have been expected to choose the least dangerous alternative . . . .

In conclusion, the court will probably decide . . . .

Step by step, you have guided your reader smoothly through an organization that is sufficiently complex to communicate the logic of the analysis and yet sufficiently clear to be understood quickly.

Educational Approach

A fourth pattern sometimes used is the educational approach. Here you begin by teaching the reader about the development of a legal theory or rule through a line of cases, leading to the current point and then addressing the current issue. This pattern can be useful when the historical development is central to the reasoning you are presenting. It can also teach the reader the basics of a specialized area of law that is unfamiliar to the reader. The following example comes from an unusually complicated research question that required a lengthy answer. The first issue was whether an employer was personally liable for pension benefits not provided by a pension fund, despite contractual provisions in the fund agreement that limited the employer's liability to providing its defined contributions. To answer the question, the writer applied some sophisticated analysis to various interpretations of a "termination liability provision" within one title of a complicated body of law, the Employee Retirment Income Security Act (ERISA). But first, the writer showed the reader where this provision fit in the larger context of the law, because that larger context was critical to later analysis.

ERISA's primary goals are twofold: (1) . . . , and (2) . . . . ERISA contains four titles; each is designed to correct problems that had previously resulted in . . . . Title I established . . . . Title II established . . . . Title III imposed . . . .

To encourage pension plan growth, ERISA . . . . Implicit in the statutory scheme of Titles I through III is . . . . Employee interests are protected by the requirements in Titles I through III, and as part of . . . .

Although ERISA's statutory language does not directly address . . . , Title IV of ERISA does . . . . In Title IV, Congress chose to . . . . Under Title IV, ... This Title IV provision is . . . .

This organization is not useful, however, if that development is not central, because it will either overemphasize an unimportant point or look as if you have lost track of the purpose of the memo. In the middle of a memo, a lawyer does not want to learn for the sake of learning; he or she is concerned with how the law applies to a specific set of facts. But if a historical overview or explanation is needed to help the reader understand that application, this organization is effective. This pattern is very useful for particular kinds of questions, but avoid overusing it out of habit.

Weighing Possibilities

A final organizing pattern, weighing possibilities, is useful when the heart of the issue is how two large bodies of information as a whole interact, rather than how they compare on particular points. This may occur when the issue will be resolved based on broad policy issues, rather than specific applications of the law. It is also likely to arise when the question is neither whether nor how the law applies, but rather which law applies. This pattern is complex, but that very complexity facilitates understanding when simpler patterns are inadequate.

Begin with an overview of the problem explaining why the issue boils down to how two bodies of information or theory interact. This may seem unusual because you are explaining the why before the what. Yet the order is logical because the reader needs to know why the preliminary information is necessary. At this point, let the reader know what position you think will prevail and perhaps hint at your ultimate reasons, but do not go into those reasons in detail. By using this structure, you are signalling that the reader cannot fully understand the reasoning without the background, so it would be futile to present it.

After introducing the content and structure of your analysis, discuss one of the possible theories or policies and explain the result if the theory or policy prevailed. Then take the other and play that one out. Sometimes one of your possibilities blends several theories or policies. If so, explain that blend and its result. After you have presented each possibility separately, you are ready to begin weighing them.

To do this, you will compare options, often organizing in ways similar to those you use when comparing cases. As part of your comparison, explain thoroughly the reasoning that led you, step by step, to your conclusion. If you weighed one policy against another, state that and then explain how you reached your conclusion. Finally, summarize your comparison section. You return, naturally, to restating the point you made in the overview, but stating it with more detail and elaboration now that the reader has the context. This becomes a natural conclusion for the issue, and the organization, even though protracted and complex, seems intuitively clear.

CONCLUSION

This chapter has introduced a process for choosing and organizing the content for your discussion. Choosing involves considering content and the reader's needs. Organizing addresses the individual cases and the larger issues. To organize each case, present the legal foundation, logical steps, and the landing to which these steps lead. To organize the issues, choose one of the available patterns: trial format, analytical pattern, bifurcated analysis, educational approach, and weighing possibilities.

EXERCISE

Because these large-scale concerns require you to work with much information, providing a realistic, original, in-class discussion exercise is not feasible. Instead, study a memo you have written in the past, analyzing the structure you used and discussing how one or more of the other available structures might suit that content.

ASSIGNMENT 1

Write a discussion section for a bench memo based on the facts in Assignment 2 of Chapter 7 on Objective Statement of Facts and these excerpts of two briefs presented to the California Court of Appeals.

Appellant's Brief

I. THE TRIAL COURT ERRED IN GRANTING RESPONDENT'S MOTION FOR SUMMARY JUDGMENT BECAUSE THERE IS A TRIABLE ISSUE AS TO WHETHER LIFE'S CONDUCT EXCEEDED THE BOUNDS OF DECENCY TOLERATED IN A DECENT SOCIETY.

A. A Jury Could Reasonably Conclude That LIFE's Conduct Is Outrageous Because LIFE Subjected Appellant To Its Extreme Practices Involuntarily.

Under California law, the elements of intentional infliction of emotional distress are "(1) outrageous conduct by the defendant, (2) intention to cause or reckless disregard of the probability of causing emotional distress, (3) severe emotional suffering, and (4) actual and proximate causation of the emotional distress." *Molko*, 46 Cal.3d at 1120, 762 P.2d at 61, 252 Cal.Rptr. at 137. Conduct is outrageous when it goes beyond the "bounds of decency usually tolerated by a decent society." *Wollersheim v. Church of Scientology of California*, 212 Cal. App.3d 872, 881, 260 Cal.Rptr. 331, 336 (2d Dist.1989).

In *Wollersheim*, the defendant subjected the plaintiff to "auditing" where the defendant conducted one-on-one encounters designed to coercively persuade Wollersheim to adhere to defendant's principles. *Id.* at 891, 160 Cal.Rptr. at 343. Auditing was carried out within a rigorous nineteen-hour daily regimen of morning cleaning, afternoon study or auditing, and evening meetings. *Id.* at 894, 160 Cal.Rptr. at 345. Despite Wollersheim's attempts to leave the organization, the defendant forced auditing on Wollersheim through physical coercion, verbal threats and pressure tactics, and the threat of retribution. *Id.* at 896, 260 Cal.Rptr. at 344.

The court in *Wollersheim* ruled that, while employing practices like auditing to pressure persons into accepting the organization's beliefs and practices may not be outrageous in themselves, employing such practices against the person's will is. *Id.* at 896–897, 260 Cal.Rptr. at 346–347. The court held that coercing Wollersheim to suffer auditing despite his objections exceeded the "bounds usually tolerated by a decent society," and thus was "manifestly" outrageous. *Id.* at 881, 260 Cal.Rptr. at 337.

Like the defendant in *Wollersheim,* LIFE subjected Rhonda to a disciplined program to indoctrinate her in its beliefs. LIFE employed several techniques designed, like auditing, to coerce Rhonda into embracing its doctrines. Like the defendant in *Wollersheim,* LIFE carried out its program within a strenuous daily regimen including morning cleaning and gardening; afternoon counseling; and evening films, lectures and drills. Also like Wollersheim's, Rhonda's days lasted up to twenty hours. Finally, like Wollersheim, Rhonda submitted to this coercion wholly involuntarily. Besides threatening Rhonda with her parents' disappointment when she expressed a desire to leave, LIFE kept her from contacting her parents, and confined her to an isolated rural compound, making escape impossible.

As the jury in *Wollersheim* found, a jury in this case could also conclude that by forcing Rhonda to endure its coercive practices against her will, LIFE's conduct was manifestly outrageous. Thus, there is a disputable issue of material fact on an essential element of Rhonda's cause of action against LIFE which is, under *Molko,* the proper province of the jury.

B. A Jury Could Reasonably Conclude That LIFE's Conduct Is Outrageous Because LIFE Subjected Appellant To Its Extreme Practices Knowing She Was Susceptible To Emotional Distress.

The trial court distinguished *Wollersheim* in that Wollersheim was susceptible to mental illness. Under the law, "behavior may be considered outrageous if a defendant . . . knows the plaintiff is susceptible to injuries through mental distress . . . ." *Id.* at 881, 260 Cal.Rptr. at 337. Knowing Wollersheim's susceptibility to mental illness, the defendant in that case prevented Wollersheim from seeking professional help and continued to subject him to auditing. *Id.* at 881, 160 Cal. Rptr. at 337.

There is evidence that Rhonda is also susceptible to emotional illness. While Rhonda was well-adjusted emotionally before attending LIFE camp, she has a history of emotional problems. Her father admits that until Rhonda was seven, she was sickly, had trouble relating to peers, played alone, and made up stories which she told to her toys. As agents of the parents, LIFE knew or should have known of this history. Yet, LIFE subjected Rhonda against her will to the same kind of coercive environment as in *Wollersheim.*

Whether Rhonda is also susceptible to emotional distress, as was Wollersheim, is thus another disputable issue of fact which should have been placed before a jury.

C. A Jury Could Reasonably Conclude That LIFE's Conduct Is Outrageous Because LIFE Abused Its Position, Causing Appellant's Injuries.

"Behavior may be considered outrageous if a defendant (1) abuses a relation or position which gives him power to damage the plaintiff's interest; (2) knows the plaintiff is susceptible to injuries through mental distress; *or* (3) acts intentionally or unreasonably with the recognition that the acts are likely to result in illness through mental distress.'" *Id.* at 881, 260 Cal.Rptr. at 337 (emphasis added).

The use of the disjunctive in the tests of outrageous conduct implies more than one basis upon which a jury could find LIFE's conduct outrageous. Thus, even if a jury did not find Rhonda susceptible to emotional distress, it could find LIFE's conduct outrageous on the alternative basis that LIFE abused its relation to Rhonda which gave it power to injure her.

LIFE stood in a particularly strong relation to Rhonda giving it significant power to damage Rhonda's interest in a healthy life free from mental distress and malnutrition.

First, LIFE has not denied that it was the agent of Rhonda's parents. (R. 6). As an agent of the Fishers, LIFE stands in a special relation to Rhonda through which the Fishers authorized LIFE's control over their daughter. As an agent, LIFE is also liable for its wrongful acts *as a principal* (i.e., as the Fishers). Cal.Civil Code Section 2343 (Deering 1986). Thus, if LIFE's conduct is tortious, it stands in the same relation to Rhonda as do her parents.

Second, the policy of this state is that one who has the care or custody of any child shall not endanger that child's health. Cal.Penal Code, Section 273a(2) (Deering 1984). The policy is supported in the statutes requiring child care custodians to report suspected abuses of children. Cal.Penal Code Section 11166a (Deering 1989 Supplement). Thus, the policy is clear that those who have the care and custody of children have a special relationship with them and a duty to ensure that they are not abused. It would be wholly inconsistent with that policy to hold that LIFE did not have such a special relationship with Rhonda.

There is considerable evidence that LIFE did indeed abuse its relationship with Rhonda. LIFE abused it by forcing Rhonda to eat a wholly inadequate diet, to live on four hours sleep a night, to watch films of animals being slaughtered, to accept its beliefs through repetitious drilling and verbal abuse, and to endure all of this against her will.

This evidence is more than enough for a jury to conclude that LIFE's conduct was outrageous because it abused its relationship with Rhonda as her parents' agent or one having the care and custody of a minor. Therefore, the trial court erred in denying appellant the opportunity to present this evidence to a jury.

Respondent's Brief

I. THE TRIAL COURT CORRECTLY HELD THAT A WEIGHT
    LOSS CAMP CANNOT BE LIABLE FOR INTENTIONAL INFLIC-
    TION OF EMOTIONAL DISTRESS WHEN ITS CONDUCT DOES
    NOT EXCEED ALL BOUNDS OF DECENCY TOLERATED BY A
    CIVILIZED SOCIETY.

    A. The Activities Of A Teenage Weight Loss Camp May Be
        Deemed Overly Strict, Supervised, And Disciplined, But Do
        Not Constitute Outrageous Conduct Because They Lack The
        Elements Of Fraudulent Inducement Or Abuse Of A Known
        Susceptibility.

    The elements of a cause of action for intentional infliction of
emotional distress are extreme and outrageous conduct which intentionally or recklessly causes mental harm. *State Rubbish Collectors
Ass'n v. Siliznoff,* 38 Cal.2d 330, 240 P.2d 282 (1952). Conduct is
deemed outrageous when it *"exceeds all bounds of decency* usually
tolerated by a decent society *and* is of a nature which is especially
calculated to cause, and does cause, mental distress." *Molko* at 1122,
763 P.2d at ___, 252 Cal.Rptr. at ___ (emphasis added).

    This standard requires conduct to be atrocious and utterly intolera-
ble. *Harris v. Jones,* 281 Md. 560, 380 A.2d 611 (1977). While the
standard has been met on occasion in this state, the courts have
continuously found that certain damaging and often times hateful
conduct is not, as a matter of law, outrageous. The Appellant contends
that LIFE's conduct towards her was so extreme and reprehensible that
it meets this standard. She cites *Molko* and *Wollersheim v. Church of
Scientology,* 212 Cal.App.3d 872, 260 Cal.Rptr. 331 (1989) to support her
position.

    On a purely factual basis, Respondent agrees that the activities at
the camp were somewhat similar to the activities present in *Molko* and
Wollersheim. Those activities include occasional limited sleeping
hours, a disciplined work requirement, and the promotion of a specific
way of life. Additionally, the Oregon case of *Christofferson v. Church
of Scientology,* 57 Or.App. 203, 644 P.2d 577 (1982) also involved similar
activities. Although these cases involved a claim of intentional infliction of emotional distress, the activities themselves (as distinguished
from overall conduct) were not deemed outrageous.

    The *Wollersheim* court held that non-outrageous activities, when
coupled with the abuse of a known susceptibility, become outrageous
conduct. *Wollersheim* at 882, 260 Cal.Rptr. at 337. In *Wollersheim,*
the Church coerced the plaintiff into continuing the activities even
though his sanity was in question and he contemplated suicide. This
abuse and disregard of a known danger gave rise to a prima facie case
of outrageous behavior.

The *Molko* court held that the use of *fraudulent inducement* to recruit the plaintiff into an "intensive religious practice," which primarily benefited the inducer, established prima facie outrageous conduct for a jury to consider. *Molko* at 1122, 763 P.2d at ___, 252 Cal.Rptr. at ___. In *Molko,* the Unification Church "witnessed," or recruited, members of the public by misrepresentations. These recruits were then taught the ways of the Unification Church for the purpose of selling flowers to benefit the Church at the expense of the defrauded member.

In both *Wollersheim* and *Molko,* the critical elements of abuse of a known susceptibility and fraudulent inducement were essential to finding the conduct outrageous. In contrast, the *Christofferson* court found no evidence of outrageous conduct. There, the plaintiff, free from any known susceptibility, knowingly joined the Church of Scientology. The fraudulent inducement, so important in the *Molko* case, and the known susceptibility, so important in the *Wollersheim* case, were missing. The court held that lacking any special circumstances, the conduct was as a matter of law not outrageous. *Christofferson* at ___, 664 P.2d at 583.

In contrast to *Molko* and *Wollersheim,* and analogous to *Christofferson,* LIFE used neither fraud to induce Rhonda or her parents into enrolling Rhonda into the camp, nor exploited a known susceptibility while Rhonda was at the camp. Rhonda's parents visited the camp and were informed of all the activities and rules prior to her enrollment. While Rhonda may not have been privy to all that was going on around her, LIFE was completely honest with Rhonda's parents.

Additionally, LIFE did not know of Rhonda's possible susceptibility. Although Appellant may claim that all children are susceptible to harm by virtue of their age and experience, children are more accurately described as impressionable. Rather, it is the person who has a mental illness or a physical handicap who is correctly considered susceptible. LIFE agrees that children are impressionable. For that very reason it is appropriate to teach proper habits and discipline at this eary age.

California courts set the standards of outrageous conduct extremely high. The conduct must "exceed all bounds of decency." It must be atrocious and utterly intolerable. In contrast to *Molko* (fraudulent inducement) and *Wollersheim* (abuse of known susceptibility), and analogous to *Christofferson* (voluntary participation), LIFE did not violate that standard. In short, LIFE's conduct was a matter of law, not outrageous.

    B.   Conduct Furthering A Person's Well–Being Cannot Give Rise To Tort Liability Because The Foundation Of Outrageous Conduct Is Action Meant To Cause Harm.

An examination of successful lawsuits involving the tort of intentional infliction of emotional distress reveals a single unifying theme: the advancement of the interests of the defendant at the expense of the plaintiff. See, e.g., *Godfrey v. Steinpress,* 128 Cal.App.3d 154, 180 Cal.

Rptr. 95 (1982) (fraudulent inducement of plaintiff to buy termite infested home to procure real estate commission); *State Rubbish Collectors Ass'n v. Siliznoff*, 38 Cal.2d 330, 240 P.2d 282 (1952) (vexatious threats against plaintiff for not assisting with corrupt business practices benefiting defendant's business); *Alcorn v. Anbro Engineering, Inc.*, 2 Cal.3d 423, 86 Cal.Rptr. 88, 468 P.2d 216 (1970) (humiliation of plaintiff by attacking his race to induce compliance with defendant's unlawful activity); *Moore v. Greene*, 431 F.2d 584 (9th Cir.1970) (sending letters threatening bodily harm to discourage valid lawsuit against defendant); *Guillory v. Godfrey*, 134 Cal.App.2d 628, 286 P.2d 474 (1955) (destroying plaintiff's competing business through unlawful trade practices).

In contrast, the Ninth Circuit Court of Appeals, applying California law, held conduct benefitting the plaintiff was not outrageous. *Higson v. Pacific Southwest Airlines*, 743 F.2d 1408 (9th Cir.1984). In *Higson*, a blind passenger suffered severe mental distress when he was unwillingly escorted out of an airplane. The airline cited the safety of the passenger as the motive for its conduct.

Similar to *Higson*, LIFE's conduct was meant to benefit Rhonda. Although the activities were regimented and somewhat strict, they were undertaken in Rhonda's best interest. Rhonda lost the weight she desperately needed to lose. After learning to be more disciplined and to have better eating habits, Rhonda went home. And, rather than disconnect Rhonda from her family, she was taught to live in harmony with others, especially with people who believe in LIFE's philosophy. People like her parents. LIFE did not attempt to advance its own interests while Rhonda was at the camp or contact her in any way once the camp ended.

Conduct cannot be outrageous when it is done in the plaintiff's best interest. Acting to help someone can never "exceed all bounds of decency" because acting to help is what decency is all about. LIFE's conduct was intended to benefit Rhonda. Finding LIFE liable under these circumstances would distort the meaning of outrageous conduct and impose liability every time someone's well meant act goes awry.

ASSIGNMENT 2

Write the discussion section for the Larry Lederhosen problem. The materials for this are in Assignment 1 in Chapter 7.

Bibliography

Beardsley, Monroe C., *Thinking Straight: Principles of Reasoning for Readers and Writers*. Englewood Cliffs, NJ: Prentice–Hall, Inc., 4th ed. 1975.

Bereiter, Carl and Marlene Scardamalia, *The Psychology of Written Composition*. Hillsdale, NJ: Lawrence Earlbaum Associates, 1987.

Berger, Charles R. and Steven H. Chaffee, eds., *Handbook of Communication Science.* Newbury Park, CA: Sage Publications, 1987.

Brannon, Lil, Melinda Knight, and Vara Neverow–Turk, *Writers Writing.* Montclair, NJ: Boynton/Cook Publishers, Inc., 1982.

Eisenberg, Anne. *Effective Technical Communication,* New York: McGraw–Hill Book Co., 1982.

Houp, Kenneth W., and Thomas E. Pearsall. *Reporting Technical Information.* New York: Macmilliam Publishing Co., Inc., 4th ed. 1980.

Lannon, John M. *Technical Writing.* Boston: Little, Brown and Co., 2d ed. 1982.

Lee, Vernon, *The Handling of Words, and Other Studies in Literary Psychology.* Lincoln: University of Nebraska Press, 1968.

Rivers, William L., *Writing: Craft and Art.* Englewood Cliff, NJ: Prentice–Hall, Inc., 1986.

Rybacki, Karyn C. and Donald J. Rybacki, *Advocacy and Oppositions: An Introduction to Argumentation.* Englewood Cliff, NJ: Prentice–Hall, Inc., 1986.

Chapter 10

ARGUMENT SECTIONS

When many legal writers think of writing a brief,[1] they think of presenting their adversarial position to defeat the opponent's logic. They organize their argument as they would for a debate [2] and treat the brief as different from a memo. They also view the reader's role as passive, more like an audience than a participant. But the changes when writing a brief are subtler than this.

For this reason, this chapter focuses on the many smaller adjustments made when moving from objective to persuasive writing. It does not address new aspects of writing, but instead explains additions and changes you can make to the techniques you learned in the previous chapters. The first change is how you view the advocate's role when writing the argument.

THE PURPOSE OF THE ARGUMENT SECTION OF A BRIEF

The reader of this document is a judge who is constrained by the law in what he or she can do. The task presented in the brief, as in a memo, is still helping a busy reader decide how to resolve a problem. The reader is actively involved [3]; indeed the reader's action is the focus of the whole document. What has changed is identity of the reader and the context in which the document is written. The attorney is not the judge's adversary, and the judge, not the opposition, is the primary reader to whom the brief is addressed.

Rather than focusing on the adversarial role, think of your role as that of an advisor or expert helping the reader solve a problem.[4] As you write a brief, think of yourself as an aide to the court when choosing what content to include, what arguments to make, and how to

---

1. This book uses "brief" to include what is called in some states "memorandum of points and authorities."

2. "Students or young lawyers may have the impression from their own experience that an oral or written argument is a kind of verbal combat, whereas it is in fact an exercise in artful salesmanship." Girvan Peck, *Writing Persuasive Briefs* xv (1984).

3. Daniel O'Keefe, *Persuasion: Theory and Research* 28–117 (1990).

4. "Unless you settle first the questions that are on your readers' minds, they won't listen to a thing you want to say." Eugene R. Hammond, *Critical Thinking, Thoughtful Writing* 80 (2d ed. 1989) (quoting Herbert Miller of the Nuclear Regulatory Commission). *See also,* Rolf Sandell, *Linguistic Style and Persuasion* 229–236 (1977).

221

order the arguments you do make. Consider how to help the reader
and in the process help your client.[5]

Persuasion affects organization subtly. For example, the following
passage focuses on the reader's needs by organizing to give the reader
the information he or she needs to make the decision. Its organization
is similar to that used in a memo discussion.

> **The test for determining whether a document is subject to
> the qualified immunity from discovery under the work prod-
> uct rule is whether** . . . . **Wright & Miller,** *Federal Practice
> and Procedure* . . . .

> **This document meets this test. The litigation to protect
> Hammond's interest** . . . . **Thus,** . . . .

> **To compel production of material subject to qualified
> immunity, defendant debtors must at least make a showing of**
> . . . .

> **They have not done so** . . . . **Moreover,** . . . .

In contrast, the following passage organizes around the writer's debate
with another attorney. This creates a defensive tone, rather than a
confident one. It also makes the organization of the writer's own line
of reasoning more obscure. This is not desirable. In this excerpt, the
reader has to infer the plaintiff's opinion from the response to the
defendant's position.

> Despite their extensive arguments, the defendant's attorneys
> have failed to show the necessity of obtaining the requested docu-
> ments, which were . . . . Litigation to protect Hammond's inter-
> est . . . . As a result, ...

> The defendant has not shown that the documents requested do
> not meet the test for determining qualified immunity, so the
> documents should not be discoverable. Documents are subject to
> qualified immunity when . . . .

The plaintiff has yielded the stage to the defendant.

This organization also affects the point of view the writer uses, as
evidenced in the opening phrases, subjects, and verbs of the topic
sentences.

advisory point of view	*adversary point of view*
the test is	despite arguments, attorneys have failed
this document meets the test	
to compel, debtors must	defendant has not shown
they have not done so	

The focus in the more effective version is primarily on persuading
the reader that your position is valid. Although doing this often entails

---

5. For discussion of individual persuasion processes and the way they are affected by the style of the persuasive message,
see, id. at 110–143.

explaining why the opposition's position is invalid, the counterargument is not your focus.

The context of writing also changes when moving from a memo to a brief. A memo is an in-house document, read by a few; a brief is a public document read by the opposition, the judge's clerks, and sometimes even the press. This leads most writers to use a more formal tone for the brief and certainly requires following any rules or conventions used in briefs in your area. To find out what these rules are, contact the clerk of the court, who is usually happy to see an attorney making an effort to follow the rules. If writing for a jurisdiction with which you are unfamiliar, such as a federal circuit or the U.S. Supreme Court, you can also consult practitioners' guides in law libraries.[6]

The purpose of a brief also differs from a memo. A memo is the main document upon which the reader will depend when making his or her decision. But a brief will be read along with the other counsel's brief, and it will be read by opposing counsel. This may mean you organize your document or choose content in the context of what will be presented in the other document, especially in a reply brief. This often gives you organizing options beyond those you have in a memo.

The rest of this chapter helps you explore how your organization choices may be affected by the subtle effects of reader, context, and purpose. It discusses the techniques you can use to enhance the persuasiveness of your argument beyond those learned in previous chapters. It explores organizational techniques, including choosing content appropriate to your reader's role, choosing content to exclude, presenting emotional facts, and grouping and ordering your content. It covers small-scale organization techniques useful for maintaining a focus on your position, presenting and answering opposing arguments, and blending policy into your argument. It discusses how sentence structure techniques can be used in argument and shows you how to combine and extend these techniques to add new dimensions to your repertoire. It also addresses imagery, conciseness, and humor. It then reviews polishing details of particular importance. Synthesizing these discussions of particular techniques, the chapter finally explains how to maintain balance and focus in your argument and summarizes the process in a checklist.

This discussion focuses on the reader's needs. This habit of focusing the reader on how your clients' objectives are congruent with the reader's objectives is central to persuasive writing. It is probably more important than all the persuasive techniques you learned in the earlier chapters. This basic focus, combined with the tools taught earlier, will make you a formidable adversary in litigation.

---

6. For example, one useful source is Robert Stern, Eugene Gressman, and Ste- phen Shapiro, *Supreme Court Practice* (6th ed. 1986).

TECHNIQUES FOR STRUCTURING A PERSUASIVE ARGUMENT

Persuasion is not a point of view added in revision, but a goal addressed throughout the process of preparing an argument. Accordingly, this section addresses persuasion as it applies to large-scale organization, paragraph organization, sentence structure, wording, and polishing.

Large–Scale Organization

Organization is particularly critical for persuasive writing. So consider your persuasive goals when (1) choosing content appropriate to your reader's role, (2) choosing content that resolves the issue, (3) determining how to handle emotional facts, and (4) grouping and ordering the content into paragraphs and sections. In each of these tasks, the choices you make will depend upon the court you are addressing.

Choosing Content Appropriate to Your Reader's Role

Choose the content that will lead the reader to take the action you request. Consider what kind of authority will meet this reader's needs and what legal criteria this reader is obliged to apply.

When writing for a trial judge, choose the mandatory authority that will lead to a favorable ruling for your client. A trial judge cannot change the law if mandatory authority exists resolving the issue; he or she must follow this authority. For this reason, you are less likely to use persuasive authority that contradicts mandatory authority. Concurring persuasive authority may also be extraneous. Use persuasive authority only when it adds substantial support, such as when no mandatory authority exists to support your case. Furthermore, do not choose many cases when one or two will do because the judge may not have a clerk to assist in checking research. Attach copies of any out-of-state cases used and include pinpoint cites. These two considerations can save the judge much work, which can never hurt your case.

The trial judge reading your brief will probably have a specific purpose in mind when requesting a trial brief or have a particular issue to determine when your brief is in support of a motion. When writing a brief, focus on the procedural or substantive criteria the court must apply to resolve your motion. For example, if requesting that a pleading be dismissed for failure to state a claim, focus on how the facts cannot establish the cause of action claimed rather than on what the facts are.

If the question is which legal standard the court should apply when resolving the case, include the standard you believe should be used and explain why it applies. For example, if the question were whether in-home child care providers are covered by either the zoning ordinances for day care centers or by ordinances for single family dwellings, you would focus on the criteria the court should consider, which might include the governing definitions of day care centers and family dwellings, the intent behind the zoning ordinances, or other criteria. In sum, when choosing content for a trial brief, include all that is needed to support the action you want, but do not include extraneous cases or arguments that may support your conclusion but are not relevant to the trial judge's criteria for deciding the matter.[7]

Like the trial court, the appellate court has specific criteria for deciding the issues it faces, but these criteria differ from those used by the trial court. When writing an appellant's brief for an error-correcting court, look first to the standard of review the court must apply. It will not retry the case on the facts, but will review the case to see if the trial judge exercised his or her discretion appropriately and if the judge applied the right law. To sustain the trial court's decision, you must show that no error was made. To win reversal, you must show that the trial judge made an error. Do not include harmless errors, because these will not support an appeal. Show that the trial court made errors and show how those errors are substantial and justify reversal, modification, retrial, or the other relief you are requesting. Do not focus on eroding the reader's opinion of the trial judge or the opposing counsel because that will not reflect well on you, nor will it get your job done.

Expect to write the appellate brief from scratch. Because the appellate court is essentially reviewing the events of the preceding legal action rather than the original conflict between the parties, you may need to include different cases and statutes, different facts, and different reasoning.

For example, if you were arguing that the trial court abused its discretion when granting a judgment because the judgment was based on an error of law, you might state the following supporting assertions.

1. The trial court erred by grounding its decision on an erroneous view of the law of unjust enrichment.

2. The trial court granted judgment based upon the theory of unjust enrichment.

3. Unjust enrichment requires a showing of a benefit being conferred by the party making the claim.

4. Here the party making the claim did not confer the benefit, but rather a third party did.

5. Thus the party has not established all the needed elements.

6. The judgment is therefore based on an erroneous view of the elements of unjust enrichment.

An error-correcting court is constrained in what it can and cannot consider, so you must not waste the court's time arguing points it does not have the discretion to resolve. Appeal decisions challenging the

---

7. "The factfinder's lack of attention is caused not so much by the recitation of numerous details, but from the recitation of irrelevant details." Paul Bergman, *Trial Advocacy in a Nutshell* 51 (1979).

court's factual findings only when those findings are not supported by the great weight and clear preponderance of the evidence.[8] Do not appeal those decisions where the court weighed the evidence and made a finding against your client that is supported by the evidence.

If your reader is the supreme court in your jurisdiction that reviews constitutional issues and other broad questions,[9] consider what issues your case presents that are worth the court's time to consider. You know that this court will be looking at the policy concerns and the development of the law beyond your case. You also know that this court will consider how trial courts and appellate courts will use this decision to resolve future cases.

When writing to a supreme court requesting review, consider the grounds upon which the court will review a case and choose the grounds appropriate to your situation. When choosing content, you must first include why the case you present merits review. Is it a wrong that cries out to be rectified? Is it a case that provides an opportunity to address something the court wants to address? Is it an opportunity to address a common societal problem and therefore provide a tool to resolve future cases? For example, if its decision in a custody case will resolve an unsettled aspect of "best interests of the child," include that point. Find the main reason the court should address this case and include it. Choose also to address the larger picture of the development of the law and let the court know how this case will address some issue you think the court would like to address. If it addresses an issue the court would like to avoid, show why justice here compels this review. Focus your argument on why this court needs to review this case.

If you are writing for an administrative law judge in a government agency, you must first learn how the agency makes decisions and what your administrative judge can and cannot decide. Learn what the agency's criteria are for determining the issue that exists in your case. Each agency has its own rules and legal guidelines, and even within an agency there can be variety from department to department.

Sometimes these criteria are quite specific. For example, if you are arguing that a firing was discriminatory, you may need to show that the firing was based on illegal criteria. Even if the judge personally disapproves of the employer's practices, he or she will decide the case based on whether the evidence meets the criteria for illegal discrimination. Sometimes administrative law judges have broader guidelines, so you have somewhat more latitude in your argument. For example, if you are writing a brief to a public service commission arguing that a rate increase is not in the public interest, you could probably choose

8. *See, e.g., Cogswell v. Robertshaw Controls Co.,* 87 Wis.2d 243, 249, 274 N.W.2d 647, 650 (1979).

9. Not all the highest courts are called "supreme" courts. For example, New York's highest court is called the Court of Appeals. The court we are referring to here is the court of last resort in your jurisdiction, but for simplicity we will use the term "supreme court" throughout.

from a variety of facts, including economic issues, general public interest, policies behind regulation, and so on. Similarly, some agencies may want you to spell out the relevant law, but with others you may not need to explain the law to the judge, because this judge is a specialist. Here, your brief may move quickly to show how your facts and reasoning fit the law to be applied, with little time spent outlining the applicable law. Whether your argument is broad or narrow, keep the argument organized around the issues you address. As you address those issues, show how the result you request is fair. Generally, agency law judges, like trial judges, see the people involved and the results of their decisions, and can see the human side of the case more readily.

When writing for a specialized court, such as a bankruptcy or admiralty court, you will probably be addressing a judge who is well aware of the law you are applying. You can again focus on how the law applies to your case without a lengthy description of the law. If, however, you are arguing a new interpretation of the law, you may need to set up the history or theory supporting your interpretation.

When writing to a federal court, begin by establishing that this court has jurisdiction.

A. THE CIRCUIT COURT HAS JURISDICTION TO HEAR AN ACTION REQUESTING A DECLARATION OF THE RIGHTS OF MENTALLY RETARDED ADULTS CONCERNING THE EXERCISE OF PROCREATIVE DECISIONS BECAUSE THIS DECISION AFFECTS THEIR CONSTITUTIONAL RIGHT TO PRIVACY.

If you have exhausted other possible areas of relief, explain that to the court. Address the preliminary argument addressed first. Then move to the issue you want the court to resolve.

With all courts, avoid dwelling on distracting points. Was the other side's brief filled with grammatical errors that destroyed its credibility and made it an insult to the court? No need to comment on it; the court will have noticed and the factor will not directly affect the outcome of the case. Even if it does affect the outcome, let the court initiate any sense of irritation or outrage. If sympathy favors your client but you are writing to an appellate court where facts are not at issue, do not waste the court's time with impassioned pleas that will not matter. Instead, weave these facts into your argument where appropriate, so the court is aware of them without being forced to address whether they are relevant. By weaving the facts into your legal argument, you can use them to support your position while maintaining your focus on the legal issues that will form the basis for the court's resolution.

Choosing Content That Resolves the Issue

Four particular questions frequently arise when deciding what content to include in your brief. The first two are whether to include authority unfavorable to your position and whether to anticipate and counter the other side's arguments. A third is how to include supporting information. A final question is when and how to include emotional arguments that do not go specifically to legal questions.

First, you must include authority, whether helpful or not, if it is mandatory authority on the issue. You may need to include the case if it is an essential link to another point. But when you cite unfavorable argument, distinguish the case from yours and explain why the unfavorable authority does not control this decision. For example, use language such as "While the defense argues that this case resolves the issue in favor of her client, a closer reading reveals that the facts of the two cases differ in significant ways . . . ."

You may also want to include your answer to an issue if you believe the other side will focus on it. Some writers argue that this may be dangerous because (1) you may give the other side the idea for an argument it overlooked or (2) you will reveal your answer early and give the other side a chance to counter it.[10] These concerns are valid, but they are countered by other factors. People are more resistant to subsequent counter-arguments if they have been exposed to answers to those arguments previously.[11] Furthermore, the reader's opinion of the advocate's competence and trustworthiness will be enhanced by its inclusion.[12]

The best solution may lie in the middle. If an issue is so obvious that you are sure the opposition will discuss it and if your counter for the issue is strong, offer your alternative reasoning in the initial brief. Showing that your position is strong is seldom a disadvantage in litigation or negotiation. Do not, however, address an issue that would be harder to defeat or that is not obvious. Save that battle for the reply brief. Be realistic in deciding to address the issue. If the issue must be resolved to decide the case, address it regardless of the strength of your argument.

Include the best cases supporting your arguments, but do not include all possible supporting cases or cases that duplicate a point already made. "Two or three decisions directly on point are worth a dozen which are not, or in most cases, a dozen which are." [13]

Handling Emotional Facts

When determining when and how to include emotional aspects of the case, try to include favorable aspects, but you must handle them carefully. Courts not only want to apply the law properly; they also want to do justice.

10. Peck, *supra* note 2, at 169.

11. Both-sided approaches to persuasion have greater success with listeners who were initially undecided or in opposition, who were better educated, and who were later exposed to counter arguments. Herbert Simons, *Persuasion: Understanding, Practice, and Analysis* 67–68 (2d ed. 1986); Daniel O'Keefe, *supra* note 3.

12. A communicator whom the receiver perceives as having only biased knowledge will presumably be viewed as less competent. *Id.* at 133.

13. Goodrich, *A Case on Appeal* 17 (4th ed. 1967).

> Counsel should hesitate to rest [a] case on mere technicalities, however strongly they may be embedded in earlier decisions. [Counsel] should never feel safe unless he [or she] can and does demonstrate the reasonableness and utility of the rule . . . .[14]

However, an impassioned plea alone is not convincing. What is convincing is when the heart and mind unite behind the same conclusion. Therefore, through the cloth of your argument, weave the golden threads of common human fairness.[15] Make the reader want to see the legal strength of your argument and want to find in your client's favor. Avoid setting up a separate section within your organization to deal with the emotions of your claim.

Grouping and Ordering Content

Generally, your issues will determine how you group your cases and other authorities, and your grouping will not differ from that of a memo. Start with your strongest argument unless logic requires you to modify this approach. Although some research suggests that readers remember the point most recently read,[16] this advantage pales in this situation, because you have no assurance that the reader will read your document just before making the decision. You cannot be sure that recency will occur just because an argument comes at the end of your brief.

When deciding what issue to present first, your choice may differ from the one you would put first in a memo. In a memo, you may have started with the argument that would gain the largest award for your client, with the argument suggested by your senior partner, or some other point. But in an argument, you want to start with your strongest point because you are making an important initial impression about the merit of your argument. Starting with the strongest point is supported by research in persuasion.[17]

Do not, however, violate the logical order of your argument. If you must address an issue regarding standards of review, for example, address it before moving to the merits of your case. In general, always follow the pattern the court will need to follow to resolve the question.[18] Choose the stronger of two points only when the court may address either of several issues first.

Whatever organization you choose, convey the organization in clear headings that communicate your assertions. This will help the reader understand your logical development and your point. Also consider

---

14. Peck, *supra* note 2, at 80 (quoting Chief Justice Vanderbilt of the New Jersey Supreme Court).

15. O'Keefe, *supra* note 3, at 158–161.

16. Some research suggests that listeners remember the last point because it is the most recent, but results on this are divided, and readers are in a different situation than listeners, in that readers may reread if they choose. Simons, *supra* note 11, at 140–148.

17. *Id.* at 151–157.

18. "The writer not only determines what the reader thinks, but also how." Vernon Lee, *The Handling of Words, and Other Studies in Literary Psychology* 190 (1968).

dividing larger sections with subheadings. Subheadings give the eye a respite and the mind a map, and can encourage your reader through the document. When subdividing, moderation is the key. Avoid headings that fragment, rather than organize, your text.[19]

Organize to guide your reader through the logical process, showing how it leads to the result you want. Include all the information needed to answer the reader's questions, but exclude irrelevant information. Then mark the path clearly for your reader, using an order that seems natural and headings that communicate the progression of your argument.

Small–Scale Organization

For small-scale organization, your focus remains on choosing and ordering information to guide the reader. You simply move your attention from the choice of issues to address to a choice of sentences, from which cases to use to what amount of explanation is needed, and from ordering sections to ordering sentences.

Keep the reader focused on your point.[20] To do this, begin each paragraph block or paragraph with an affirmative statement of your position.[21] For example, write

> **A parolee's reasonable expectation of privacy is less than that of other citizens. *Latta v. Fitzharris,* 521 F.2d 246, 249 (9th Cir.1975), *cert. denied,* 423 U.S. 897 (1975).**

rather than

> Generally a citizen has a reasonable expectation of privacy in his or her home. Jason Harrow's reasonable expectation, however, is lower because he is a parolee.

The affirmative opening states your topic and shows your reader how you intend to develop your reasoning. For example, if sympathy runs in your client's favor, you may add a sentence mentioning the point.

> Furthermore, Officer Washington's warrantless search was essential to determining if Harrow was again selling drugs to high school students.

But more likely you will use language throughout your paragraph that suggests sympathy.

> To perform his or her duties, a parole officer needs to be able to conduct a warrantless search of a parolee's apartment. So it was that Officer Washington needed to search Harrow's apartment to determine if Harrow was indeed violating parole by again selling drugs. The parole system is designed to help the parolee reintegrate into society while preventing further anti-social behavior.

---

19. "[A] great number of divisions, far from rendering a work more solid, destroys its coherence. To the eye the book seems clearer; but the author's design remains obscure." *Essays in Stylistic Analysis* 14 (H. Babb, ed. 1972).

20. Persuaders need to let the audience know what it is they will be discussing and why, not leaving it to the end. Daniel O'Keefe, *supra* note 3, at 160.

21. *Id.* at 150.

Officer Washington was furthering this prevention when he conducted the warrantless search in response to information that Harrow was using his home as a base for selling drugs at a nearby high school.

Weave themes through your argument, but do not allow them to draw you away from your main focus.

Presenting and Answering Opposing Arguments

Generally, if you decide to address the opposition's arguments, you may refer to them while stating your position. But do not focus on them. For example, state the other side's position in the middle of the paragraph, not at the beginning. Keep the focus on your affirmative position, using the other side's argument as a backdrop for your reasoning, rather than presenting its argument and putting yourself in a defensive position. Arrange your phrases and choose your language carefully. For example, you might refer to your opponent's position in a dependent clause, rather than giving it a sentence of its own. For example, compare the following two versions of the same argument. The first takes an affirmative stance.

> **The standard of reasonable cause is the appropriate standard by which to evaluate warrantless searches by parole officers. Because they have a special relationship with the parolees they supervise and because of the special circumstances of parole, the standard should be "flexible enough to give the parolee meaningful protection and to preserve the functions of parole." *Latta v. Fitzharris*, 521 F.2d 246 (9th Cir.1975) (dissenting opinion). Thus the reasonable cause standard, rather than a stricter standard, is necessary for and consistent with the purposes of parole. Although a later case did require a warrant before a search by a parole officer, that court did not clearly define what showing of cause would justify that warrant. *United States v. Bradley*, 571 F.2d 787, 789 (4th Cir.1978). Indeed, the court in *Bradley* concluded that the strong governmental interests in maintaining a viable parole system require a standard not as rigorous as that applied in an ordinary case. *Bradley* at 790. Thus . . . .**

The second focuses on the opponent's position.

> Opposed to the *Latta* rule is the view that a warrantless search by a parole officer is acceptable only when it falls under a judicially recognized exception to the warrant requirement. *United States v. Bradley*, 571 F.2d 787, 789 (4th Cir.1978). Proponents of this position contend that a warrant requirement for parole officers would not hinder the rehabilitative and law enforcement process of the parole system. *Id.* at 790. They fear that parole officers may be tempted to abuse their discretion in conducting a search if they are not first required to obtain a warrant. *Id.*

> To the contrary, a warrant requirement would be destructive to the goals of the parole system and particularly to the special relationship between the parole officer and his client. Officer Washington was a professional. He was uniquely qualified to determine when to conduct a search of his client's home. Parole officers need the latitude to conduct warrantless searches and to do so spontaneously if necessary. The reasonable cause criterion for searches by parole officers is consistent with the purposes of parole.

These small-scale changes accumulate throughout the passage affecting the focus and tenor of the whole passage.

In a reply brief, you may organize around your opponent's argument if doing so shows the strength of your position. But if your position counters the opposition on a broader scale, such as on the relative importance of issues, use your own organization and refer to the opposing argument only when needed to explain your point.

To attack the opposing argument, you must find an error in its position. Perhaps you can assert that the argument is based on cases not applicable to this situation because they turn on facts not analogous to this situation. Even if the facts are similar, you may state that the issue in this case is not the same. Or you may state that the reasoning used in that case does not apply to this situation. Perhaps the case is not mandatory, and need not be considered. Perhaps another equally relevant case states a position favorable to you, which may let you establish that the law is not clearly running against your position. Moreover, it may be that the law is stated correctly, but the logical steps flowing from that statement are flawed. Perhaps the opponent states logically inconsistent points, overgeneralizes, or misapplies the law so it would work against the original purpose for which the law was promulgated. By explaining how the opposing argument is faulty, you can interrupt its progress, so it cannot lead to the outcome your opponent desires.

If you must concede a point, do so by saying that it is not important to the case, that it is overshadowed by some other point, or that it is countered in some other way. Rather than conceding a point in a separate sentence, concede it in a dependent clause that brushes the reader's mind away from the concession and right into another point you present as more important.

> Although other jurisdictions have broadened their interpretation of this phrase, Idaho has not. As recently as . . . , the Idaho Supreme Court has held that . . . .

Thus the position that "other jurisdictions have broadened" is never given full focus, but is overshadowed by "although," signalling to the reader that the forthcoming counterargument is the main focus.

Blending Policy into Your Reasoning

Beginning legal writers often include policy in a paragraph, after the case law has been reasoned to its conclusion. But this structure treats the policy as an extra. For example, in the following passage, the policy is introduced in a separate paragraph after the logical progression through the case law is completed.

> The rule from these two cases is that sexual conduct must be shown to affect the child adversely before it can be considered relevant to a child custody determination. There must be a demonstrable nexus between the conduct and the best interest of the child. In the present situation, the trial court presumed Devon's sexual conduct would adversely affect Erica absent any evidence in the record. This is contrary to the precedent of *Gould* and *Schwantes.*
>
> The trial court's presumption against lesbians in child custody cases is also against Wisconsin policy toward homosexuality
>
> . . . .

If the policy is introduced within the reasoning as a broader level of support, it can appear integral to the precedent itself.

> The rule from these two cases is that sexual conduct must be shown to affect the child adversely before it can be considered relevant to a child custody determination. There must be a demonstrable nexus between the conduct and the best interest of the child, **just as there must always be demonstrable relevance before a person's sexual conduct can be a factor in a legal decision.** In the present situation, the trial court presumed Devon's sexual conduct would adversely affect Erica absent any evidence in the record. This is contrary to the precedent of *Gould* and *Schwantes.*

In this way, policy appears as it applies throughout the reasoning, rather than a concept apart from the law itself. By explaining how policy also supports the reasoning, you underscore the reader's sense that your position is congruent with the law on many levels. The position appears not only legal, but also just.

In summary, effective small-scale organization is often a matter of maintaining your logical progression and focus. Address the opposing arguments, the emotions of the situation, and other facets of the case that come into play, but keep the reader's eye fixed on the logical path you have blazed to your conclusion.

Structuring Sentences

Because persuasive sentence structures are discussed at length in the chapter on persuasive fact statements, refer to that chapter for techniques to use here. This section presents some general aspects of sentence structure that are particularly useful in arguments and ways to combine and extend them.

General Uses of Sentence Structure to Enhance Arguments

In general, identify points you want to emphasize and use structural techniques to draw attention to those points. Then identify points you want to minimize and structure those to achieve your goal. Beyond emphasizing and de-emphasizing points, use sentence structure throughout your argument to signal how your points fit together. Most writers have learned the importance of transitions, but may not realize that structure, as much as transition words, is also useful. For example, the structure of the following two topic sentences subtly suggests a logical relationship between the two.

> In *Eberhardy,* the supreme court carefully specified the limits of its jurisdictional holding in each of the four places in the opinion where it defined the issues . . . .

> The supreme court's jurisdictional holding is therefore limited to . . . .

The first sentence focuses on the court's action by making the subject and verb "the supreme court . . . specified." But the second topic sentence uses passive voice when discussing the current case ("holding is . . . limited"), suggesting that the decision has already been made by the previous action.

Repeating a structure alerts the reader to logically parallel points and makes them easier to remember.

> Language serves three functions. The first is to communicate ideas. The second is to conceal ideas. The third is to conceal the absence of ideas.[22]

The following example uses parallel structure to show how the facts support the same conclusion.

> Jane performed academically at the second or third grade level. When asked a question, she could respond in short, articulate sentences, but her communication skills were substantially below normal. Jane could feed herself, but could not cut her own food. She could bathe herself, but could not regulate the temperature of the bath water. She could put on a dress, but could not button it.

Finally, structure can be used to emphasize a word within a sentence that provides a critical link between ideas.

> The defendants both expected the plaintiff to disagree on this point, *an expectation that* . . . .

Combining and Extending Structural Techniques

As you refine your sentence structure to emphasize points in your argument, you need not employ one technique in isolation but can combine several techniques to get a particular effect. The following

---

22. Richard Hatch, *Business Communication: Theory and Technique* 1 (1977).

examples show four ways to word the same point with differing levels of emphasis. The example used introduces a distinction between the precedent and the current facts. These variations use structural repetition, short sentences, and careful placement of phrases.[23] They also apply wording techniques such as using concrete and abstract terms and stronger verbs. By combining these techniques in different ways, the sentences achieve noticeably different effects.

[the original, with no particular emphatic techniques employed]

> First, there is no "right to be let alone" in a customs search at a nation's borders, which is very different from a police search through a private library.

[the old one-two]

> First, the "right to be let alone" does not apply to this situation. A customs search at a border is very different from a police search through a private library.

[the quick jab]

> First, the "right to be let alone" does not apply here. A customs search of one's baggage does not equal a police search of one's library.

[the butterfly and the bee]

> First, the "right to be let alone" does not apply to these facts. Suitcases are not like books, and international borders are not like private libraries.

[the heavy weight]

> The "right to be let alone," however, does not fit this body of facts. International borders are not private libraries, nor are suitcases books.

As you read these examples, you probably found you preferred some, disliked others. Balancing the interplay of emphasis techniques and the subtlety or boldness of their use involves personal judgment.

EXERCISE

After reviewing the four examples, choose your favorite and least favorite. Then rewrite the following sentence twice, using the two structures you have just chosen.

> Second, the customs procedures here are procedures strictly against the materials (which *Stanley* does not protect) and not against the individual seeking to import them.

---

23. These examples are labelled with boxing terms, because this is sometimes referred to as adding "punch" to your writing.

In summary, sentence structure is a tool with many possible uses in the argument, as in the persuasive statement of facts. To master sentence structure, experiment and reflect on the results of your experiments, combining and recombining phrases until you arrive at a sentence with just the effect you want. Then, when you craft an effective sentence, study it so you know how to replicate its structure when you need a similar effect. Bit by bit, you will build your expertise and expand your capacity to control not only the content of your argument, but even the way the reader will remember it and the way your reader will feel about it.

Wording

Content and clarity should anchor your argument, but an attractively worded presentation is also important. Although the judge wants to make a just decision regardless of how well the advocates plead their cases, it is immensely helpful if the advocates make this job more pleasant. Do not create in your reader the feeling described below.

> [The text was] presented in such a way as to give the minimum of interest with the maximum of fatigue. It is a thing to make one cry merely to think of.[24]

A well-written brief will stand out in the judge's memory of the day's readings.

To help your brief stand out, you can use the techniques discussed in Chapter 8 on persuasive facts. You may also use some other techniques not available within the constraints of the fact statement, which are discussed next.

Imagery

Metaphor, simile, and other figures of speech can enliven your argument, especially in introductions or conclusions.[25] For example, the following sentence promises a text that will be fun to read, and yet not be frivolous.

> Precedent has reached, but not grasped, this question.

Careful selection of imagery can also introduce the emotional aspect of your message.

> The writer seems to be bludgeoning a butterfly.[26]

Although the way imagery enhances persuasion is not clear, it does enhance an argument.[27] Imagery creates a more concrete picture in the reader's mind, and concreteness increases memory.[28] Additionally, because you are dealing with an educated reader, these rhetorical devices may be appreciated as adding grace to your writing.

---

24. Lee, *supra* note 18, at 223–224.

25. For some useful examples and further discussion of figure of speech, *see*, Simons, *supra* note 11, at 223–224.

26. William L. Rivers, *Writing: Craft and Art* 81 (1975).

27. Sandell, *supra* note 4, at 75.

28. *Id.* at 182.

Because imagery is an attention-getting and an emotion-inducing device, make sure you use it on worthwhile points. Drama for its own sake can be distracting rather than emphatic,[29] or embarrassing rather than impressive. You do not want to be remembered by the judge as the following speaker was remembered by a fellow member of the House of Lords.

> The late Duke of Argyle, though the weakest reasoner, was the most pleasing speaker I ever knew in my life. He charmed, he warmed, he forcibly ravished the audience; not by his matter certainly, but by his manner of delivering it . . . . I was captivated like others; but when I came home, and coolly considered what he had said, stripped of all those ornaments in which he had dressed it, I often found the matter flimsy, the arguments weak . . . .[30]

As with any technique, you also need to guard against overuse.

> If a writer will seem to observe no decorum at all, nor pass how he [or she] fashions [the] tale to [the] matter, who could doubt but he [or she] may in the lightest cause speak like a Pope, and in the gravest matters like a parrot, and find words and phrases enough to serve both turns, and neither of them commendably.[31]

Conciseness

Although conciseness is considered a virtue in itself, it can also serve other purposes, especially in argument. A short sentence, combined with effective wording, can drive a point home with unusual force.

> Discretion was not abused; it was exercised.

A sentence using an active, strong verb instead of longer prepositional phrases can add energy to a whole paragraph.

> The beam plummeted to the pavement.

When the verb also packs an appropriate emotional punch, you can again weave equity into your logical argument.

> He *assumed* he could handle the large machine without further training, and in so doing he *assumed* the risk.

The conclusion is an excellent place to be concise because the groundwork for your points has already been laid. But be concise throughout your argument. If you can present your side more effectively in forty pages than the opposition can in fifty, your position will

---

29. "Nothing is more inimical to this warmth [of effective style] than the desire to be everywhere striking; nothing is more contrary to the light which should be at the center of a work, and which should be diffused uniformly in any composition, than those sparks which are struck only at the cost of a violent collision between words, and which dazzle us for a moment or two, only to leave us in subsequent darkness." *Essays in Stylistic Analysis, supra* note 19, at 15.

30. *Classics in Composition* 100 (D. Hayden, ed. 1969) (from a letter from Lord Chesterfield to his son in 1749).

31. *Id.* at 41 (quoting George Puttenham's "Of Stile").

be stronger.[32] If you can do it in thirty, you will gain the court's admiration.

Humor

Humor is refreshing for a reader, but risky to use in persuasive writing.

> The person who attempts to use humor in a persuasive message is usually asking for trouble. Humor frequently is not understood and may well backfire.[33]

Humor may enhance the reader's liking for you, which can enhance trustworthiness, but it will not generally enhance the reader's view of your competence.[34] If you decide to use humor, make sure it is appropriate to the mood and message you are communicating, and make sure the reader will understand it.

> A little drama, or a little humor, is welcome in a final argument. But the purpose of the argument is to persuade, not to entertain. Therefore the gist of the argument should appeal to the factfinder's reasoning process.[35]

When you ask yourself if the humor is worth it, the most likely answer will be "no." If the answer is yes, craft the humor carefully, test it on someone whose judgment you trust, and if he or she says delete it, take the advice.

Wider Vocabulary

Although a reader will usually be put off by being forced to consult a dictionary to read your brief,[36] correct and skillful use of a broader vocabulary may be a pleasant diversion. For one thing, variety is more interesting. For another, using a varied vocabulary improves your chances of choosing the best word. Widening your vocabulary does not always mean using more multisyllabic words. As Justice Jackson said, a skillful advocate will "master the short Saxon word that pierces the mind like a spear and the simple figure that lights the understanding. He [or she] will never drive the judge to the dictionary." [37]

In summary, in wording, as in the use of sentence structure, expertise comes with practice, with balancing and combining different writing techniques until you get the effect you want.

---

32. Albert Tate, Jr., *The Art of Brief Writing: What a Judge Wants to Read* 4 Lit. 11, 12 (Winter 1978).

33. William M. Schutte and Erwin R. Steinberg, *Communication in Business and Industry* 57 (1983).

34. O'Keefe, *supra* note 3, at 139–140.

35. Bergman, *supra* note 7, at 330.

36. "Using language readers do not understand invites them to stop reading." Rivers, *supra* note 26, at 38.

37. Robert Jackson, *Advocacy Before the Supreme Court: Suggestions for Effective Case Presentations*, 37 A.B.A.J. 801, 863 (1951).

Polishing Details

Improving the readability of the content will also be appreciated by your reader, so do all you can to make it appealing to the eye and easy to understand. Polishing aids persuasion by increasing the reader's comprehension of the point you are making.[38] Polishing reduces distractions.

> Readers see misspellings as oddities—like a troop of bald Boy Scouts—and must give their attention to them. Distracted by the oddities, readers find it impossible to follow the sense of the writing.[39]

It also helps by increasing your credibility.

> God does not much mind bad grammar, but God does not take any particular pleasure in it.[40]

Consider your audience when polishing. Observe any requirements the court has, making especially sure that forms, numbers in citations, and other small mechanical details are correct. An error here may seem small, but it might loom quite large in the time it takes the judge to discern what you meant to do. Include parallel cites, so the judge may easily find a case in whatever reporter series that is available. In appellate briefs, cite to the page in the record that supports your point, use headings to help the reader refer to the part of the brief needed, and use the parties' names to help the reader understand the facts. In agency briefs, follow any specific form or content requirements of the agency. In short, take pains with the details of your brief, so your reader does not have to.

ACHIEVING BALANCE AND FOCUS

An effective persuasive message is greater than the sum of the techniques used. The most memorable and effective writing smoothes the individual persuasive techniques into a flawless whole, so that the result you want the reader to reach seems logically inevitable. As with excellence in dancing, singing, and other performance arts, an excellent piece of persuasion seems natural and effortless, even though it is neither.

> Every work of enduring literature is not so much a triumph of language as a victory over language; a sudden injection of life-giving perceptions into a vocabulary that is, but for the energy of the creative writer, perpetually on the verge of exhaustion.[41]

38. Comprehension in persuasion has been studied extensively. Sandell, *supra* note 4, at 82–101.

39. Rivers, *supra* note 26, at 7.

40. Hatch, *supra* note 22, at 135 (quoting Erasmus).

41. J. Middleton Murry, *The Problem of Style* 85 (1976).

Its craft is subtle, and best exercised with restraint.

Consider, for example, the following two versions of a passage from Abraham Lincoln's inaugural address. The first is the draft he was given by W.H. Seward for consideration.[42]

> I close. We are not, we must not be aliens or enemies but fellow-countrymen and brethren. Although passion has strained our bonds of affection too hardly, they must not, I am sure they will not be broken. The mystic chords which proceeding from so many battle fields and so many patriot graves pass through all the hearts and all the hearths in this broad continent of ours will yet again harmonize in their ancient music when breathed upon by the guardian angel of our nation.

Lincoln revised this, making a series of small changes. First, he lengthened the first sentence to "I am lothe to close." This softened the strength of the sentence, reducing the focus on this transition and personal reference. At the same time, it added a note of personal emotion by changing the verb of the sentence from "close" to "am loth," focusing on regret instead of action. These simple changes made the paragraph open with a different feeling.

He then simplified the next sentence, eliminating the insistent tone of "we must not be" and the repetition of "aliens or enemies" and "fellow-countrymen and brethren." Instead of repeating words, he chose the simple "enemies" and substituted the logical and simple opposite, "friends." This simpler wording strengthened the sentence, making it shorter and clarifying the contrast. But the revisions also warmed the tone of the sentence, maintaining the feeling established in the opening sentence.

Then Lincoln repeated the idea, "We must not be enemies," using several short sentences for emphasis, unlike the original, which added more words to one sentence. Here he used the insistent "must," but only after the personal tone had been established. This made "must" seem more a personal request, less an edict.

He simplified the next sentence, omitting modifiers ("too hardly") and putting the sentence in parallel structure: "Though passion may have strained, it must not break our bonds of affection." He also created some syntactical suspense by stopping the introductory phrase with "strained," and leaving the reader waiting for the completion of the phrase until the end of the sentence when the object of "strained" ("our bonds of affection") appeared, at that point also the object of the verb "break." It is a streamlined sentence, with each word, each omission of a word, and each structure communicating a part of his meaning.

The final sentence of the paragraph, although still long, moves smoothly to its conclusion. The subject was simplified; "the mystic

42. Henry Weihofen, *Legal Writing Style* 324 (1980).

chords which proceeding from so many battle fields and so many patriot graves pass through all the hearts and all the hearths in this broad continent of ours" became "the mystic chords of memory," with modifying information put in a supporting phrase set off with commas. The predicate, "will yet again harmonize in their ancient music" was changed to "will yet swell the chorus," becoming a concrete image stated more concisely. The intervening phrase also became more concrete, so the reader could see more clearly the picture Lincoln was painting. For example, "proceeding from" was replaced by "stretching from" and the plural "battlefields" became the singular and more concrete "battlefield." "Breathed" became the more physical "touched." Finally, he revised "the guardian angel of our nation" to "the angels of our nature," choosing the more personal image over the nationalistic one.

Each change was small. Each was a detail many writers would have been tempted to overlook. And yet the overall change was anything but small. To appreciate it, reread the original version aloud, and then read Lincoln's following revision.

> I am loth to close. We are not enemies, but friends. We must not be enemies. Though passion may have strained, it must not break our bonds of affection. The mystic chords of memory, stretching from every battlefield and patriot grave to every living heart and hearthstone, all over this broad land, will yet swell the chorus of the Union, when again touched, as surely they will be, by the angels of our nature.

Persuasive communication is an imprecise art, but that does not reduce its power. The cause you are advocating may not be as moving as that of President Lincoln, so the eloquence required may not be as great. Yet, having seen the potential that word choice and word order have to move the human spirit, you know what is possible. You can reach toward the goal as much as your abilities, time, and cause allow.

CONCLUSION

When moving from writing the memo to writing the argument, the needs of the reader remain central. Adjust for the differing demands placed on trial, appellate and supreme courts, and agencies and specialized courts. Then, throughout your writing, make the subtle changes required to advocate effectively. As you make these changes, pay attention to both the specific techniques and the general impression you want to create.

Practice. Expect to gain expertise through trial and error, then through trial and success. As you become comfortable with those techniques, you will reach for the right technique unconsciously. You will be able to see beyond the task of choosing the word and constructing the sentence or paragraph to the larger task of writing the brief.

CHECKLIST FOR WRITING THE ARGUMENT SECTION

Organization

1. Choosing content.

   a. Choose points within the court's discretion.

   b. Choose points on which your objectives can be met while also meeting the court's concerns.

   c. Choose legally compelling reasons why you should prevail.

   d. Omit unneeded points. To determine when to exclude information, consider whether you must include it for any of the following reasons:

      (1) if mandatory authority on the issue,

      (2) if other side will definitely make it seem central, or

      (3) if it is an essential link to another point.

      If it is unfavorable and none of the above, exclude it.

2. Organizing content.

   a. Follow the pattern that the court will need to follow to resolve the question.

   b. If you have several options, start with your most persuasive point, or with the one in the reader's mind after reading issues.

Small–Scale Organization

1. Dealing with opposing arguments.

   a. Generally, refer to them while stating your position, but do not organize around them.

   b. In a reply brief, you may organize around the opposition, addressing each of the opposition's points in turn.

   c. Keep reader focused on your point.

2. Dealing with unfavorable points.

   a. Show that they are not unfavorable.

   b. Show how they are outweighed by other factors that are more important.

Sentence Structure

1. Identify important points and restructure to emphasize.

2. Identify unfavorable points and restructure to minimize.

3. Repeat structure as necessary to show links between points.

Wording

1. Use wording to increase interest as well as clarity, including the following possible techniques:

    a. imagery,

    b. concise wording,

    c. humor, and

    d. broader vocabulary.

Polishing

1. Make sure all cites are accurate and in proper form.

2. Observe all court rules.

3. Eliminate grammatical, spelling, and other mechanical errors.

EXERCISE

The following two excerpts are from briefs written to appellate courts. They are somewhat better than average, but they could be much better. They use some of the persuasive techniques discussed in this chapter, sometimes successfully and sometimes not. As you read the excerpts, note persuasive techniques used, determining whether you think the use is effective. Then select two passages from the text (each passage being one to three sentences long) and rewrite those to make them more persuasive, experimenting in particular with some of the techniques you have learned in this chapter.

Excerpt A

III. THE RED MASK WAS PROPERLY ADMITTED AS EVIDENCE BECAUSE THE CIRCUMSTANCES UNDER WHICH IT WAS FOUND AND TAKEN DID NOT VIOLATE THE FOURTH AMENDMENT PROTECTION AGAINST UNREASONABLE SEARCHES AND SEIZURES.

   A. The Trial Court Correctly Decided The Question Of Law Of Whether The Facts Of This Case Violated Fourth Amendment Protection.

The issue in this case is whether Fourth Amendment protection applies in a situation where a private person turns over criminal evidence to the police in response to information he learned about the crime from publicity asking citizens for their help in finding the criminal, and the police accept the evidence without first obtaining a warrant. Deciding whether these facts meet the standard of "unreasonable search and seizure" which invokes Fourth Amendment protection is a question of law. The standard of review for questions of law is "whether the facts fulfill a particular legal standard . . . ." *Nottelson v. ILHR Department*, 94 Wis.2d 106, 116, 287 N.W.2d 763, 768 (1980). The lower courts here correctly decided that the Fourth

Amendment was not violated, and for the reasons stated below this Court should find that appellant cannot meet the burden of showing that this case violated the Fourth Amendment.

B. The Evidence Was Found And Taken By A Private Individual Not Acting As A Government Agent, And Is Therefore Outside The Scope Of Fourth Amendment Protection.

The case of *Burdeau v. McDowell* established that the Fourth Amendment protection against unreasonable searches and seizures applies only to governmental action and not to actions of private individuals without the knowledge or participation of government officials. *Burdeau v. McDowell,* 256 U.S. 465 (1921). This holding has been repeatedly affirmed since then throughout the United States, in both the U.S. Supreme Court and many state Supreme Courts.

According to this mainstream interpretation, in order for an individual to be considered a police agent, two factors must be shown: that the police instigated, encouraged, or participated in the search, and that the person engaged in the search with the intent of assisting the police in their investigative efforts. *United States v. Lambert,* 771 F.2d 83, 89 (6th Cir.1985). In *Lambert,* the defendant's housekeeper turned over to the FBI inculpatory evidence of narcotics use that she had picked up while carrying out her housekeeping duties. The court held it was a private search because the factor of sufficient police involvement was lacking. Although the FBI had knowledge of her activities, they had neither instigated, encouraged, or participated in them—the housekeeper was acting on her own initiative.

Applying this majority understanding to the situation before this Court confirms that Joe Roberts was acting privately rather than as a government agent when he found and reported the evidence in Tuttle's locker. There was no police involvement in Roberts' actions. The police knew nothing of him or his activities until he called them on his own initiative after accidentally discovering the mask. Furthermore, there was no intent on Roberts' part to act as an agent when he opened and looked into Tuttle's locker. One of Roberts' duties as locker room attendant at SERF (Southeast Recreation Facility) is to open the members' lockers and replace used towels with clean ones. Roberts had simply picked up a dirty towel from Tuttle's locker, and in so doing happened to see the red mask which was also in the locker.

The publicity about the rape, including the local "Crimestoppers" show in which a policeman asked for citizen assistance in solving the crime, gave Joe the background information he needed to realize he had found incriminatory evidence and to report it. But it would unduly stretch the imagination to determine that this general citizen-wide alert constituted direct state involvement in Joe's activities in the SERF's locker room.

The idea that Joe was not a government agent is further buttressed by the fact that, even in situations where the government pays individuals to be informers, it is widely held that there is not enough government participation to consider that individual a government agent. *United States v. Valen*, 479 F.2d 467 (3rd Cir.1973). In *Valen*, an airline employee had been told by a Customs agent to notify Customs officials if he came across any suspicious packages. He had been paid in the past for such information, and in this case was paid $100 for reporting his suspicions about Valen's suitcase. The court determined that this payment did not make the airline employee into a government agent.

It is therefore even less likely that a generalized offer of a reward for information about a criminal could be considered sufficient government involvement to call the individual who earns that reward a government agent. The fact that Joe may receive the reward in this case is merely incidental to the discovery of the mask—Joe was not looking for the mask in response to an offer for payment.

The appellant raised two other factors to question Roberts' status as a private individual. Decisions from several states suggest that using these factors to try to portray Roberts as a government agent is an approach which lacks merit. First, the fact that Joe was employed by a state university is too tenuous a government contact to make him an agent of the state. A North Carolina court held that a resident advisor in a state university dormitory had neither the status nor the authority to make him a quasi-law-enforcement officer or agent of the state. *State v. Keadle*, 51 N.C.App. 660, 277 S.E.2d 456 (1981). Joe's position as a locker room attendant has even less status and authority. Second, the fact that Joe is a retired policeman does not give rise to the presumption that he is, therefore, acting in collusion with the police. An Idaho court found that an off-duty policeman who opened an envelope containing marijuana was not automatically acting in concert with government officials simply because he discovered contraband. *State v. Castillo*, 108 Idaho 205, 697 P.2d 1219 (1985). Joe, as a retired policeman now engaged in alternate employment, would be even further removed from such an automatic assumption.

In summary, the facts of this case establish that Roberts' discovery and reporting of the mask in Tuttle's locker was a private act. Because Fourth Amendment protection applies only to actions by the state, it does not apply here, and therefore the trial judge properly admitted the mask into evidence.

Excerpt B

I.   A DEPENDENT CHILD HAS A RIGHT TO RECOVER FOR THE WRONGFUL DEATH OF HER MOTHER WHEN THE RECOVERING HUSBAND HAS TAKEN NO RESPONSIBILITY FOR THE CARE OF THE CHILD; THEREFORE THE COURT OF APPEALS ERRED IN REVERSING THE TRIAL COURT'S RECOGNITION OF THIS CAUSE OF ACTION.

     A.   Existence Of A Cause Of Action Is A Question Of Law, And Is Therefore Entitled To Independent Review By This Court.

The existence of a cause of action, whether based on the common law or statutory interpretation, where the facts are undisputed, is a question of law. *State v. Williams,* 104 Wis.2d 15, 310 N.W.2d 601 (1981). Plaintiff–Petitioner does not dispute any factual determinations made by the trial court. Plaintiff–Petitioner asserts only her right to recover for the wrongful death of her mother under the state's wrongful death statute or, alternatively, under the common law. The Supreme Court must decide questions of law independently, without deferring to the Court of Appeals, if it is to fulfill its function as a developer of principles of common law and statutory interpretation. *Ball v. District No. 4, Area Bd. of Vocational, Technical and Adult Ed.,* 117 Wis.2d, 529, 345 N.W.2d 389 (1984), *Levy v. Levy,* 130 Wis.2d 523, 388 N.W.2d 170 (1986).

    B.   When A Statute Is Ambiguous, The Ambiguity Must Be Interpreted To Avoid Unreasonable Results; Therefore, The Court Must Interpret The Wrongful Death Statute To Allow Recovery By A Dependent Child When The Surviving Spouse Has Not Taken Responsibility For The Care Of The Surviving Child, And When The Child Has No Other Means Of Recovery.

Twenty years ago, the Supreme Court interpreted the Wisconsin wrongful death statute, secs. 895.01–895.04, Stats., to bar recovery for surviving children when the decedent is survived by a spouse who will support the child. *Cogger v. Trudell,* 35 Wis.2d 350, 151 N.W.2d 146 (1967). In *Cogger,* plaintiffs, Ronald Cogger and September Trudell brought suit for the wrongful death of their mother, Darla Trudell. Darla had been killed when their car, driven by her husband, Joseph Trudell, collided with a car driven by Paul Jensen. Defendants included Paul Jensen, the insurance company, and the plaintiff's father, Joseph Trudell. The court held that the Wisconsin wrongful death statute did not give Ronald Cogger and September Trudell a cause of action for the wrongful death of their mother, because their mother was survived by her husband, Joseph Trudell.

The *Cogger* court began its analysis with the statutory language prior to the 1961 amendment. In 1940, the court had interpreted the pre–1961 statute as creating a series of priorities regarding the ownership of a cause of action for wrongful death. Under this priority scheme, surviving children had no cause of action if a spouse survived. *Lasecki v. Kabara,* 235 Wis. 645, 294 N.W. 33 (1940). Although the statute was amended in 1961 to provide increased protection to minors, the *Cogger* court determined that the amendment did not intend to modify the pre–1961 priority scheme. Therefore, the *Cogger* court held that a dependent child did not have a cause of action for the wrongful death of a parent, when the decedent was survived by a spouse.

Despite the important factual distinction between *Cogger* and the case before this Court, the Court of Appeals rigidly held that the *Cogger* decision was controlling. Whereas the surviving spouse in *Cogger* was also the natural parent of the surviving children, Hans Nelson is not the natural parent of Amanda. This distinction is crucial because it bears directly on the policy behind the 1961 amendment of the wrongful death statute: protection of minor children. While it can be assumed that the natural parent of the surviving child will provide adequate care for the child, this assumption is unreasonable when the surviving spouse is not the child's parent and has never assumed any responsibility for the child's care.

Because the facts of this case are significantly different from *Cogger,* the analysis in *Cogger* must be reconsidered to take into account the peculiar facts of this case. Although reference to prior statutory language, used in *Cogger,* is often a legitimate method of statutory interpretation, courts must also construe statutes to avoid unreasonable results. *Keithley v. Keithley,* 95 Wis.2d 136, 289 N.W.2d 368 (1980). Denying Amanda a cause of action would be unreasonable because it would vitiate the policy of protecting dependent minors explicit in the 1961 amendment, and would result in an outcome which the legislature could not have intended.

A rigid application of *Cogger* is especially unreasonable in light of *O'Leary v. Porter,* 42 Wis.2d 491, 167 N.W.2d 193 (1969). The court in *O'Leary* ruled that children of divorced parents have a cause of action for the wrongful death of the supporting parent, even if the decedent is survived by the ex-spouse. In *O'Leary,* the surviving child, Kevin O'Leary, was allowed a cause of action for the wrongful death of his mother, Janice O'Leary, even though Mrs. O'Leary was survived by her ex-husband. The court held that Kevin did have a cause of action for the wrongful death of his mother. In reaching its decision, the *O'Leary* court stressed that past support of the mother was sufficient proof of actual pecuniary loss by the child.

Our case is more factually analogous to *O'Leary* than *Cogger.* Just as Kevin O'Leary was dependent on his mother for support, Amanda was dependent on her mother. Furthermore, just as the surviving ex-spouse, Patrick O'Leary, has assumed no responsibility to care for Kevin, Hans Nelson has not assumed any responsibility to care for Amanda. Our case is distinguishable from *O'Leary* only by the remarriage of the supporting parent prior to the accident. Unlike the differences between *Cogger* and our case which are important because of their close relation to the policy of protecting minor children, the distinction between our case and *O'Leary* rests only on the parent's marital status, which in this case bears no relation to the policy goals advanced by the statute.

It is unreasonable to deny Amanda recovery simply because Amanda's mother and Hans Nelson chose to marry. Had Karen and Hans Nelson merely lived together, Amanda would have had a cause of action for wrongful death under *O'Leary.* In both cases, the legal relationship between Amanda and Hans Nelson is the same. Therefore, it is unreasonable to interpret the wrongful death statute to forbid Amanda recovery.

Because this Court has a duty to interpret statutes to avoid unreasonable results, the *Cogger* decision must be modified to permit recovery where the surviving spouse has not assumed any responsibility to care for a surviving child. This is necessary to realize the legislative purpose of the post–1961 wrongful death statute: the protection of dependent minors.

ASSIGNMENT 1

Write a short brief based on the facts and the law supplied in the following. Your brief will have only three sections: Statement of Facts, Issue Presented, and Argument (with at least one point heading). Assume that you are writing the brief to the trial court. The court has required both parties to file briefs before the final divorce hearing on the one unresolved issue in the case.

Included are:

(1) a senior partner's memo telling an associate to write a memo about a client's situation,

(2) the associate's memo explaining how the law applies to the client's situation, and

(3) citations for three cases: *Hartung v. Hartung,* 102 Wis.2d 58, 306 N.W.2d 16 (1981); *Broms v. Broms,* 353 N.W.2d 135 (Minn. 1984); and *Marriage of Auld,* 72 Or.App. 747, 697 P.2d 220 (1985).

You may use any of the information in these materials when you write your brief. You should focus, however, on rewriting and maybe reorganizing the information in the associate's memo to make it persuasive. You need not spend much time thinking of new arguments to include in the brief. This assignment emphasizes persuasive writing, not creative analysis.

TO: Whizbang Associate
FROM: Impressive Senior Partner
RE: Murphy Divorce: Length of Maintenance Payments
DATE: November 7, 1989

Our client, Helen Murphy, is seeking extended maintenance payments in divorce proceedings. Helen and Timothy J. Murphy are getting a divorce after ten years of marriage. Tim is a 39–year–old pediatrician and Helen is a 31–year–old housewife. Before marrying Tim, Helen had completed high school and one year of nursing school to become a licensed practical nurse (LPN). Tim met Helen when he was completing his internship and she was working as an LPN in the same hospital.

They married after Tim finished his internship and went into practice. Helen continued to work as an LPN for eight years, earning $9,000 a year. Meanwhile Tim practiced with a small medical group; he began at $30,000 a year and worked up to $60,000 two years ago. At that time he became a full partner and began earning $80,000.

After his promotion to partner, the Murphys decided to start a family, so Helen left her job, which was paying her $12,000 per year. She did not become pregnant, however, and they discovered that Helen could not bear children. These previously undiagnosed complications were caused by the IUD she had used during their marriage. This mutual disappointment destroyed the relationship; Tim became irritable, and they began to bicker constantly.

Tim asked for a divorce so he could "leave the rancor behind and get on with life." Although Helen did not ask for a divorce, she does not think they have much chance of overcoming their problems and thus is willing to agree to it.

They have agreed on a property settlement. Helen will keep the Chevy they bought her a year ago from Tim's income, valued at $10,000. He will keep his three-year-old Porsche, valued at $15,000. She will also keep the $120,000 house they bought from his income. She wants to sell the house but expects that it will take a long time to sell and that she may lose money on it. He will keep the $100,000 savings they have, which was saved from his income. She will keep $6,000 that she saved from her income and kept in a separate account.

They have not agreed, however, on maintenance (alimony). Tim has offered $1,500 a month for six months while she finds work as an LPN. Helen agrees to this amount but wants maintenance for six-and-one-half years while she obtains training as a medical technician. Tim is adamantly opposed to paying maintenance for this long and is not willing to settle out of court. He insists that six months is long enough.

Helen's skills as an LPN are up-to-date and the local demand for LPNs is high, so she probably could find work within six months. As an LPN, her income would peak at $15,000 per year.

To become trained as a medical technician, Helen will need to earn a Bachelor of Science degree, which she can do in four or four-and-one-half years, and complete one year of specialized training. There is a demand for medical technicians locally, although there are not as many positions available as there are for LPNs. As a medical technician, Helen would begin earning $20,000 per year and her income would peak at $32,000 per year.

Neither party is willing to compromise on this issue. I want to know if the law supports Helen's request for longer maintenance.

MEMORANDUM

TO: Impressive Senior Partner
FROM: Whizbang Associate
RE: Murphy Divorce: Length of Maintenance Payments
DATE: November 14, 1989

I. STATEMENT OF FACTS

Helen Murphy, our client, and her husband Timothy are trying to reach a maintenance settlement. They have agreed on a property settlement and an amount for maintenance, but disagree on the length of time that maintenance should be paid.

The Murphys are seeking a divorce after ten years of marriage. When they married, Tim was beginning his practice as a pediatrician and was earning $30,000 per year. Helen was working as an LPN and was earning $9,000 per year. Tim's income rose over the years. After eight years, Tim was promoted to partner and began earning $80,000 per year. At that time, the Murphys agreed that Helen should quit her job so they could start a family. After two years, however, they discovered that Helen could not bear children. Subsequently, Tim requested a divorce and Helen agreed.

Both parties agree on a property settlement and on the amount of maintenance Tim should pay Helen, but they disagree on the length of time that maintenance should be paid. Helen wants to receive maintenance for six-and-one-half years while she becomes trained as a medical technician and finds a job. To become a medical technician, she would need to attend undergraduate school for four to four-and-one-half years to get a Bachelor of Science degree and then attend a postgraduate program for one year to become certified as a medical technician. She then estimates that she would need up to one year to find employment.

Tim believes maintenance should only be continued for six months, until Helen can find work as an LPN. He does not believe that he should be responsible for paying for her training as a medical technician.

II. APPLICABLE STATUTES

Section 767.26, Stats., provides:

> Maintenance payments. Upon every judgment of annulment, divorce or legal separation, or in rendering a judgment in an action under § 767.02(1)(g) or (j), the court may grant an order requiring maintenance payments to either party for a limited or indefinite length of time after considering:
>
> 1. The length of the marriage.
>
> 2. The age and physical and emotional health of the parties.
>
> 3. The division of property made under § 767.255.
>
> 4. The educational level of each party at the time of marriage and at the time the action is commenced.
>
> 5. The earning capacity of the party seeking maintenance, including educational background, training, employment skills, work experience, length of absence from the job market, custodial responsibilities for children and the time and expense necessary to

acquire sufficient education or training to enable the party to find appropriate employment.

6. The feasibility that the party seeking maintenance can become self-supporting at a standard of living reasonably comparable to that enjoyed during the marriage, and, if so, the length of time necessary to achieve this goal.

7. The tax consequences to each party.

8. Any mutual agreement made by the parties before or during the marriage, according to the terms of which one party had made financial or service contributions to the other with the expectation of reciprocation or other compensation in the future, where such payment has not been made, or any mutual agreement made by the parties before or during the marriage concerning any arrangement for the financial support of the parties.

9. Such other factors as the court may in each individual case determine to be relevant.

III. QUESTION PRESENTED

Under Section 767.26, Stats., which lists factors the court must consider when awarding maintenance payments, will the court award maintenance payments to cover the time needed for a spouse to become self-supporting at a higher standard of living when the spouse is already employable but wants to obtain training for a different but related job that would increase the spouse's earning capacity?

IV. BRIEF ANSWER

Yes. The court will grant maintenance for an extended period of time if the additional education is for the purpose of allowing the spouse seeking maintenance to become self-supporting at a standard of living reasonably comparable to that which the spouse enjoyed during marriage.

V. DISCUSSION

When determining the length of maintenance payments, a Wisconsin court must consider a set of statutory criteria listed in Sec. 767.26, Stats., to ensure that the final award is not arbitrary. If a court awards maintenance without stating why or how it applied these statutory criteria, the award may be overturned as an abuse of discretion. *Hartung v. Hartung,* 102 Wis.2d 58, 69, 306 N.W.2d 16, 22 (1981). In *Hartung,* the supreme court reversed an award granting $200 a month for eighteen months to a spouse with custody of the couple's three minor children. The supreme court stated that the trial court must consider, among other things, the feasibility of the party seeking maintenance becoming self-supporting at a standard of living reasonably comparable to that enjoyed during marriage. Id. at 67, 306 N.W.2d at 19–20. Because the trial court did not explain how the award reflected these criteria, its decision was reversed and remanded. Thus, when the trial court considers Helen's request for six-and-one-half years of maintenance, it must determine whether that period of maintenance is needed in light of the statutory criteria.

Under these statutory criteria, a spouse may be granted maintenance for the length of time the court finds it will take that spouse to become self-supporting at a standard of living reasonably comparable to that enjoyed during marriage. Sec. 767.26(6), Stats. In Helen's case, the trial court must determine whether the income of an LPN will allow her to attain this reasonably comparable standard of living. Before the divorce, Helen and Tim shared an income of $80,000 per year. The court will grant the longer period of maintenance if it decides that an income of a medical technician, at $32,000 per year, will allow Helen to attain a reasonably comparable standard of living but the income of an LPN, at $15,000, will not.

The court may grant a spouse maintenance for a period of time long enough to allow that spouse to pursue an advanced degree if the spouse has some education in a particular field but not enough to be employable in that field. *Broms v. Broms,* 353 N.W.2d 135, 138 (Minn. 1984). In *Broms,* the spouse seeking maintenance had a Bachelor of Science degree but needed a master's degree to pursue a career in social work. Although the appellate court reduced the trial court's award from ten to five years, it did state that the trial court could award maintenance for the purpose of furthering a spouse's education so that he or she could pursue a career. Id.

Helen may use this persuasive authority to support her request for extended maintenance while she pursues an additional degree. Like Ms. Broms, Helen is pursuing a degree that is necessary for a career that is somewhat established. If the court views receiving training to be a medical technician as necessary for Helen to support herself at a reasonably comparable standard of living, then it may find the length of maintenance is appropriate under the law.

If, however, the court views Helen's training as a medical technician as a career change, then it may not grant maintenance for the duration of the training. A court may decide not to grant maintenance for an extended period of time if it finds that the spouse seeking maintenance does not need further education to become self-supporting at a standard of living reasonably comparable to that enjoyed during the marriage. *Marriage of Auld,* 70 Or.App. 747, 751, 697 P.2d 220, 222 (1985). In *Auld,* an Oregon court concluded that Mr. Auld could not be required to pay for Ms. Auld's career change. Ms. Auld was already employable as a real estate agent and a school teacher, and Mr. Auld had already supported her through one career change. Shortly before the separation, Ms. Auld had decided to enroll in a five-year program to become an interior designer, and she requested maintenance to support her during this five-year period. The lower court awarded her maintenance for the period of time necessary to complete the program. The court of appeals reversed, however, reasoning that she did not need the further education to become self-sufficient at a standard of living reasonably comparable to that enjoyed during the marriage. Id. When doing this, the Oregon court applied a factor similar to that listed in the Wisconsin statute:

> the need for education, training or retraining to enable a party to become employable at a suitable work or to enable the party to pursue career objectives to become self-supporting at a standard of living not overly disproportionable to that enjoyed during marriage to the extent that is possible.

Or.Rev.Stat. 107.105(1)(d)(E). Under this reasoning, Helen would have to show that the future education was necessary to attain a reasonably comparable standard of living.

Tim may argue that Helen is asking him to finance a career change, like Ms. Auld's, and that therefore the court should not grant maintenance for the extended time that the training will take. Tim may reason that if the training were to update Helen's skills or to enable her to work as a nurse, then the training would be covered. Training to become a medical technician, however, would be a career change.

Helen may counter that the training is necessary because she could not attain a reasonably comparable standard of living as a LPN. Therefore her situation is distinguishable from that of Ms. Auld, who could earn as much as a teacher as she would as a designer. Helen's situation is also distinguishable from that of Ms. Auld because Tim has not previously financed any of Helen's education. Because of this, he cannot argue that he has already helped her improve her ability to attain a reasonably comparable standard of living on her own.

VI. CONCLUSION

The court will grant Helen Murphy maintenance for six-and-one-half years if she can show that the extended maintenance period is needed to allow her to become self-supporting at a standard of living reasonably comparable to the standard she enjoyed during marriage. There is a good chance that the court will probably grant her extended maintenance if Helen can convince the court that becoming a medical technician is not a change of career but rather an extension of her training and that this training is necessary to attain a comparable standard of living.

ASSIGNMENT 2

Write the argument section of a brief based on the facts and the law supplied in Assignment 2 on Chapter 8: Persuasive Facts on Howard Jones' claim for the wrongful death of his unborn child. Assume that you are writing the brief to the trial court. Your brief is in response to a motion to dismiss for failure to state a claim upon which relief can be granted under sec. 802.06(2)(f), Stats.

You may use any of the information in these materials when you write your brief. You should focus, however, on rewriting the information in the associate's memo (# 2) in a persuasive manner. You should not spend much time thinking of new arguments to include in the brief. This assignment emphasizes persuasive writing, not creative analysis.

But you should recognize that to be fully persuasive, you would have to make two alternative arguments.

    (1) The 6–month fetus is viable and so a cause of action for wrongful death exists under the statute.

    (2) Even if the 6–month fetus is not viable, the court should decide that a wrongful death cause of action exists because the Wisconsin Supreme Court has not said that it is precluded under the statute.

Bibliography

Benson, Robert W. and Joan B. Kersken, *Legalese v. Plain English:* An Empirical Study of Persuasion and Credibility in Appellate *Brief Writing,* 20 Loy.L.A.L.Rev. 301 (Jan. 1987).

Board of Student Advisers, Harvard Law School, *Introduction to Advocacy.* Mineola, NY: The Foundation Press, Inc., 1985.

Cooper, Frank E., *Writing in Law Practice.* Indianapolis: Bobbs–Merrill, 1953.

Dernbach, John L. and Richard V. Singleton, III, *A Practical Guide to Legal Writing and Legal Method.* Littleton, Co: Fred B. Rothman & Co., 1981.

Eble, Timothy E. and Mary M. Molloy, *Ten Commandments of Appellate Advocacy,* Case & Comment 16 (Jan.–Feb. 1986).

Grey, Lawrence, *Writing a Good Appellate Brief,* 57 N.Y.B.J. 24 (Feb. 1985).

Kaplan, Lueithe R., *Writing That Persuades: No Quick Fix for The Advocate,* 20 Trial 44 (June 1984).

Peck, Girvan, *Writing Persuasive Briefs.* Boston: Little, Brown, & Co., 1984.

Pittoni, Mario, *Brief Writing and Argumentation.* Brooklyn: The Foundation Press, Inc., 3rd ed. 1967.

Porter, Karen, Nancy Schultz, Lauren Scott, Louis Sirico, and Annemick Young, *Introduction to Legal Writing and Oral Advocacy.* New York: Matthew Bender, 1989.

Re, Edward D., *Effective Legal Writing and the Appellate Brief,* 89 Case & Comment 9 (July–Aug. 1984).

Spears, Franklin, *Presenting An Effective Appeal,* 21 Trial 95 (Nov. 1985).

Wydick, Richard, *Plain English for Lawyers.* Durham, NC: Carolina Academic Press, 2nd ed. 1985.

Chapter 11

PLEADINGS

Many new associates in law firms are dismayed when asked, often within the first month of practice, to draft pleadings. They have had little or no practice during law school. In addition, they quickly learn that pleadings can be difficult to write because of the analytical, tactical, and writing concerns arising when drafting these documents. But drafting pleadings is an integral part of the practice of law. Although most attorneys do not have a litigation practice or even try cases, virtually all draft pleadings during their careers.

Pleadings are the documents that initiate a lawsuit and, although ninety percent of cases settle before trial, all of them start with pleadings.[1] In the complaint, the plaintiff alleges the actions by the defendant that are the basis of the plaintiff's claims. The complaint describes the damages the plaintiff has incurred and states the remedies desired. In the answer, the defendant responds to the allegations contained in the complaint.[2] The answer states which of the plaintiff's allegations the defendant admits are true and which he or she denies. The answer also raises affirmative defenses to the plaintiff's claims and can raise counterclaims against the plaintiff as well. This chapter discusses the drafting of both of these documents, after discussing the general writing concerns that come into play with both complaints and answers, and the process needed to address those concerns.

GENERAL CONCERNS

Pleadings have many purposes. Filing the complaint commences the action.[3] It gives the other party notice of the claim pending against him or her.[4] When filed, it stops the running of the statute of

1. Menkel–Meadow, *For and Against Settlement: Uses and Abuses of the Mandatory Settlement Conference*, 33 U.C. L.A. L.Rev. 485, 488 n. 19 (1985–1986). Cases that are resolved through alternative dispute resolution (ADR) may or may not start with pleadings, depending on whether ADR is chosen before the complaint is filed.

2. Before answering the complaint, the defendant must decide whether to bring any motions challenging the complaint. Fed.R.Civ.P. 12(b). For a fuller discussion of the role motions play, see Chapter 12, Notices of Motion, Motions, and Orders.

3. Fed.R.Civ.P. 3.

4. Fed.R.Civ.P. 8(a). This rule states that the complaint should be "a short and plain statement of the claim showing that the pleader is entitled to relief." Additionally, in federal court, the complaint must

limitations. Together, the complaint and answer focus the disputed facts and issues between the parties. Either document can encourage the opposing side to settle and may establish a dollar amount for settlement negotiations.[5] Both documents also provide discovery of the facts underlying each side's arguments and the legal theories on which they rely.

When you consider the important role pleadings play in most attorneys' daily practice, it is surprising that most attorneys spend little time on drafting these documents. Many simply copy language from form books or sample pleadings found in the office, making only those changes required by the different fact situations. We believe, however, that these documents deserve careful preparation. Much valuable attorney and court time would be saved if these documents were drafted with more attention.

Because the pleadings establish the substance of the lawsuit, you must be thorough and precise. Thoroughness is necessary to present your client's cause of action, which will form the legal basis for negotiation or trial. You must include all elements of the cause of action and allege the facts necessary to establish each element. You must allege the facts establishing a particular element even if they appear undisputed because, without them, you will fail to present every element of the cause of action. If you do not include every element of each cause of action, it is vulnerable to a challenge for failure to state a claim upon which relief can be granted. It may be dismissed.[6]

Precision is necessary when stating the allegations in the complaint and the admissions or denials in the answer. You will be unable to narrow the issues for trial if these documents are not precise. By precisely stating the allegations of each cause of action, you indicate to your opponent exactly what your view of the facts is, and you force your opponent to answer your allegations specifically. If your allegations are precise, your opponent must admit those that are true, which reduces the facts you must prove at trial and strengthens your case for settlement. The same holds true for the answer: if your responses are precise, you can eliminate undisputed issues and focus on defending your client on the issues that are in dispute.

state the basis for the court's jurisdiction and a demand for judgment for the relief sought. *Id.*

5. The federal rules do not require that specific dollar amounts be pled. However, Rule 54(c) only permits relief in the amount requested in the demand for judgment in the case of default judgments, thus encouraging specific dollar amounts to be included in case of default. Some state rules forbid specific dollar amounts to be pled in some instances. For example, Cal.

Civ.Pro. § 425.10(b) provides that you may not allege a specific dollar amount in a personal injury complaint and Cal.Civ. § 3295(e) provides that you may not allege the amount of punitive damages sought.

6. In the federal courts, this challenge would be brought as a motion under Fed.R. Civ.P. 12(b)(6). Some states refer to this challenge as a demurrer to the complaint, but the result is the same: if the challenge is granted, your complaint is dismissed.

PROCESS FOR ACHIEVING THOROUGHNESS AND PRECISION

The need for thoroughness and precision begins even before you begin drafting. Just as you must research before writing a memo or a brief, you must obtain the information you need to write pleadings. You will interview your client and investigate the facts, research the procedural and substantive law, and make many tactical decisions. Only after completing these initial steps will you be prepared to begin drafting, a process also requiring several steps.

Interview Your Client and Investigate the Facts

The basis for writing a thorough pleading comes from knowledge of the client's situation, so the interview is the usual place to begin. In the interview, obtain as much information as possible with an eye toward framing the cause of action. Although your client will know that he or she wants to bring a lawsuit, you must determine what cause of action to pursue. A good framework to begin the interview with is to ask reporter's questions: who, what, when, where, why, and how. Elicit the dates, times, places, parties, documents, events, and any other relevant information. Be sure to ask the hard questions: those questions that may challenge the client's version of what happened or that may put the client in a harsh light. For example, if your client is describing a traffic accident, ask whether he or she was driving too fast for conditions or broke any other traffic rules. While you need to ask these questions with tact and understanding, you do need to ask them.[7]

After completing the interview, verify the information you have and obtain other information. For example, rather than assuming that your client was correct in her statement that the president of the company refused to provide the contracted-for items, you may want to contact the company and verify who the president is and whether that person did, in fact, refuse to provide the items specified under the contract. This investigation may help you avoid bringing a breach of contract action because of an error in the shipping department.

Also obtain relevant documents and witnesses' statements when possible. This additional information can help fill out the facts that you learned during the client interview and help you make decisions about how to proceed. For example, if your client told you she was injured in an automobile accident, you would contact the police department to obtain a copy of the police report and contact the insurance company to obtain a copy of the applicable policy. Then you might check with the witnesses listed on the police report and try to obtain a brief statement from each of them regarding their views of the accident. It is preferable to find out whether any of them consider the

---

7. For additional information on interviewing techniques, *see* Binder and Price, *Legal Interviewing and Counseling* (1977).

accident to be your client's fault before filing a negligence action against the defendant.

Research the Procedural and Substantive Law

After gaining a thorough understanding of the situation by interviewing your client and investigating the facts, the next step is to research the procedural and substantive law controlling lawsuits in your jurisdiction. Before you can draft a complaint or respond to one, you must understand both the procedure that controls the lawsuit and the underlying substantive law. This is because pleadings are based on legal theories, even though those legal theories are usually not explicitly stated within the pleading.

Start your research by determining the procedural requirements for your jurisdiction. Each jurisdiction has different rules controlling pleading practice, and each court within a given jurisdiction may have additional local rules controlling that practice. Usually the code of civil procedure for your jurisdiction will contain the general rules, and the clerk of court can provide the local rules. The appearance and content of your pleading will be controlled by these rules.

For example, most states have very specific rules regarding the format of the caption of your documents. Federal Rule of Civil Procedure 10(a) specifies that the caption must state the name of the court, the title of the action, the file number, and the name of the document.[8] While these details may seem insignificant, they are not. Many court clerks reject documents that do not conform to these rules.

These procedural rules also control the content of the document. For example, California rules state that a general denial may be used only for those complaints that are unverified or for verified complaints alleging less than $1000 in damages.[9] When answering a verified complaint alleging more than $1000 in damages in California, you must use the special denial form and respond to each allegation of the complaint specifically, rather than use the general denial form that denies all the allegations of the complaint.[10]

In contrast, the Federal Rules of Civil Procedure virtually preclude the use of the general denial form even though many states do use it. Rule 8(b) requires the person answering to deny specific allegations, unless he or she intends "in good faith" to controvert all the allegations of the pleadings.[11] Thus, in federal court you must admit any of the

---

8. This rule requires that, in the complaint, all the parties must be included, but subsequent pleadings can simply include the first party on each side, with an indication that other parties exist. Fed.R.Civ.P. 10(a). Similar rules exist in most states. *See, e.g.,* Mass.Civ.P. 10(a); N.Y.C.C.P. 2101(c); Pa.R.C.P. 1018; Utah R.Civ.P. 10(a).

9. Verified complaints must be signed by the complaining party. Cal.Civ.Pro. § 431.30.

10. Cal.Civ.Pro. § 431.40. A general denial to verified complaints is allowed in municipal court. Cal.Civ.Pro. § 431.30(d).

11. Fed.R.Civ.P. 8(b). Federal R.Civ.P. 11 states that an attorney's signature at the bottom of a pleading indicates that it is well grounded in fact and law and not

allegations in the complaint that are true. A few states also require the answer to include "the substance of the matters on which the pleader will rely to support the denial." [12] In these jurisdictions, you would be required to state the factual basis for your denial.

The procedural rules also control some substantive aspects of pleading. For example, the federal rules state that, when pleading the performance or occurrence of conditions precedent, it is sufficient to allege that all the conditions precedent have been performed or have occurred.[13] The same rule requires that the denials in the answer "be made specifically and with particularity." [14] The federal rules also require that all affirmative defenses be set forth when responding to a preceding pleading.[15]

To draft a thorough and precise complaint, you must also understand the legal theories underlying the document. You cannot simply state the facts and expect the court to allow your pleading to withstand a demurrer motion or motion to dismiss for failure to state a claim.[16] To avoid such a motion, you must include every element necessary to state a cause of action against the defendant within your complaint's allegations, even if those facts are not disputed. Otherwise, your complaint will not withstand scrutiny. Some sources for determining the elements of specific causes of actions include your state's jury instructions, restatements, form books containing sample complaints and counterclaims, encyclopedias and hornbooks, cases decided in your state, and statutes within your jurisdiction.

You must complete the same research before drafting an answer. For example, most jurisdictions require that all affirmative defenses be stated in the answer.[17] While you can amend your answer freely,[18] the better practice is to include all defenses within the original answer, so you need not spend the time and money filing an amended answer.

To help ensure that their pleadings include all possible causes of action or affirmative defenses, many attorneys use checklists. A sam-

---

imposed to cause unnecessary delay, harassment, or increase in litigation cost.

12. Michigan Court Rules 2.111(D)— Form of Denials. Irwin Alterman, *Plain and Accurate Style in Lawsuit Papers*, 2 Cooley L.Rev. 243, 281 (1981).

13. Fed.R.Civ.P. 9(c).

14. *Id.*

15. Fed.R.Civ.P. 8(c). These affirmative defenses include accord and satisfaction, duress, estoppel, laches, and statute of frauds. The rule also states that when a party has "mistakenly designated a defense as a counterclaim or a counterclaim as a defense, the court, if justice so requires, shall treat the pleading as if there had been a proper designation." *Id.*

16. Different jurisdictions use different names to refer to their motions to dismiss

for the legal insufficiency of the complaint. For example, in the federal system, a motion to dismiss is controlled by Fed.R.Civ.P. 12(b)(6) and is called a motion to dismiss for failure to state a claim upon which relief can be granted. In California, the same challenge is raised by a demurrer motion. Cal.Civ.Pro. § 430.10(e).

17. Fed.R.Civ.P. 8(c), Tex.T.R.C.P. 94, Cal.Civ.Pro. 431.30, M.C.P. 2.111(F)(3).

18. Fed.R.Civ.P. 15(a) allows you to amend a pleading once as a matter of course any time before the responsive pleading is served, or if no responsive pleading is required, within twenty days after the pleading is served. Otherwise, you may only amend the pleading with leave of the court, which is to be freely given.

ple checklist is included in the section below on drafting the body of the complaint. Although you cannot draft a checklist that will list everything needed for every pleading, you can draft one that includes the standard causes of action arising in your area of practice and the usual affirmative defenses made in response to those causes of action. You can then compare your checklist to the facts involved in a particular case to determine which causes of action or defenses are available.

Tactical Considerations in Drafting Pleadings

Many new associates move right from interviewing and researching into drafting. Without making tactical decisions, they skip an important step taken by more experienced attorneys. When associates ask for advice from other attorneys in their firm, they find that most have definite opinions about how pleadings should be written based on tactical considerations. Experienced attorneys often cannot take the time to discuss these considerations, so the associates are left to struggle on their own. By reviewing the tactical considerations discussed in this section, you will be better prepared to draft your pleadings.

Several tactical considerations arise when drafting the complaint. The first is who should be named as defendants and what claims should be joined. After you have interviewed your client and completed your factual and legal research, you must analyze this information to determine the possible defendants and causes of action. Also consider which of these defendants to sue and which claims to join. You may want to include all defendants in your complaint and join all possible claims. Other tactical considerations, however, may militate against this.

> The presence of remote defendants might irritate the jury. Extensive briefings on sophisticated jurisdictional issues relating to another defendant might not be worth the aggravation. Difficulty of proof might render another cause of action virtually useless. You might want helpful testimony from someone who would not be friendly if named as a defendant. Now is the time to decide whom to sue and for what.[19]

The second tactical consideration involves what legal theories to allege. Consider which legal theories will be easiest to prove, which will best provide the relief desired, and which will reach defendants who have the most resources to contribute. Also consider what theories your evidence will support. Many attorneys allege different causes of action to ensure that at least one will be established by the evidence that is admitted by the court and presented by the witnesses. If your complaint supports several causes of action, then your client may achieve the desired result even if the evidence does not support the main theory you expected to advance when the lawsuit began.

19. Karla Wright, *A Seven Step Process for Preparing Non–Routine Complaints,* 77 Ill.Bar J. 662, 663 (August 1989).

The third tactical consideration concerns where to file your complaint. Jurisdiction and venue requirements will significantly affect your decision in this matter. But you may have some choices and you should carefully consider what location will be most favorable for obtaining your client's desired result. For example, consider the situation of conflicting federal court of appeals decisions, some of which support your legal theory, some of which destroy it. You have the choice to bring your action either where the defendant resides or where the accident occurred.[20] Your research indicates that the court of appeals where the defendant resides has decided a case contrary to the argument you must make, while the court of appeals where the accident occurred has not decided any cases on this particular issue. You may decide to bring the action where the accident occurred to avoid direct case law against you, depending on other considerations, such as ease of movement for yourself, the plaintiff, and your witnesses; local court rules; and jury considerations.

The fourth tactical consideration involves how much information to provide in your complaint if notice pleading is allowed in your jurisdiction. The federal rules state that a pleading need only include "a short and plain statement of the claim showing that the pleader is entitled to relief."[21] This is known as notice pleading and requires only that the complaint give the defendant enough information to provide notice of the claim against him or her. A majority of the states also allow notice pleading.[22] You may want to provide only enough information to give the defendant notice, so you can avoid informing your opponent of your strategy or assisting him or her in discovery. On the other hand, providing additional information establishing a strong case for your client at the outset can induce settlement negotiations and may require the defendant to admit or deny information that will assist you with discovery.

The fifth tactical consideration involves what types of relief to request and what amount of damages to allege. Many attorneys try to include as many types of relief as possible so that, once trial has been completed, the judge or jury will have as many options as possible in granting relief. Additionally, including multiple claims for relief may make the incentive for settlement stronger.

The final tactical consideration concerns whether to rebut anticipated affirmative defenses. Under the federal rules, no pleading is required beyond a complaint and an answer.[23] Thus you have no

---

20. 28 U.S.C. § 1391 (1988).

21. Fed.R.Civ.P. 8(a).

22. Friedenthal, Kane and Miller, *Civil Procedure* § 5.2, at 238–239 (1985) [hereafter Friedenthal]. *See, e.g.,* Mass.Rule of Civ.Pro. 8(a), Wis.Stats. § 802.02(1), Ill. Code of Civ.Pro. § 2–603. A number of states still use code pleading. Drafting code pleadings is more difficult than drafting notice pleadings because of controversies that arise concerning what constitutes a "cause of action" and an "ultimate fact" as compared to evidentiary facts or conclusions of law. For further discussion of these problems, *see, Friedenthal,* at §§ 5.4–5.5.

23. Fed.R.Civ.P. 7(a). Rule 7(a) also permits a reply to a counterclaim, an answer to a cross-claim and a third-party complaint and answer.

opportunity to reply to an answer. While the court may order a reply to a third-party answer, do not assume that permission will be granted to respond to a standard answer.[24] If you do not anticipate affirmative defenses, you may be precluded from responding to them until the motions are filed or the case goes to trial. You must weigh the desire to respond to the defendant's affirmative defenses against the fact that you do not want to provide your opponent with defenses that he or she may not have considered. It can be dangerous to outline your responses to anticipated defenses because, without your assistance, your opponent might not have raised those defenses.

Different tactical considerations arise when drafting the answer. The first is whether the answer is the best response to the complaint. Before responding to the complaint, you may want to raise defenses to the plaintiff's claims for relief.[25] In federal court, the defenses that may be raised by motion before answering include (1) lack of subject matter jurisdiction, (2) lack of personal jurisdiction, (3) improper venue, (4) insufficient process, (5) insufficient service of process, (6) failure to state a claim upon which relief can be granted, or (7) failure to join a party under Rule 19.[26] Although you can raise these defenses in your answer, you may decide to raise them by motion before answering. Then you do not admit or deny your opponent's allegations while raising defenses that may eliminate the lawsuit completely. You will waive some of these defenses if you do not raise them immediately, either in a motion or in your answer.[27]

The second consideration is whether to raise any affirmative defenses and whether to present any counterclaims. You must make these decisions when preparing your answer or you may be precluded from doing so. The federal rules require you to raise all the affirmative defenses you have when answering.[28] Generally, a failure to plead an affirmative defense results in that defense being waived and excluded from the case.[29] Compulsory counterclaims are waived if they are not raised in the answer. Compulsory counterclaims are those that arise out of the same transaction or occurrence and do not include third parties outside the court's jurisdiction.[30] Additionally, you may include

24. *Id.*

25. Fed.R.Civ.P. 12(b). See Chapter 12: Notices of Motion, Motions, and Orders for a fuller discussion.

26. *Id.*

27. Fed.R.Civ.P. 12(g)–(h). Those that are waived are a defense of lack of personal jurisdiction, improper venue, insufficient process or insufficient service of process. Fed.R.Civ.P. 12(h)(1). The defenses of failure to state a claim upon which relief can be granted, to join an indispensable party under Rule 19, or to state a legal defense to a claim may be made up to the trial. Fed. R.Civ.P. 12(h)(2).

28. Fed.R.Civ.P. 8(c) states that a party must set forth any matter constituting an avoidance or affirmative defense in the answer to the complaint.

29. 5 Wright and Miller, *Federal Practice and Procedure* § 1278, at 339 (1969). *See also, Dole v. Williams Enterprises, Inc.,* 876 F.2d 186, 189 (D.C.Cir.1989) and *U.S. v. Continental Illinois Nat. Bank and Trust,* 889 F.2d 1248, 1253 (2nd Cir.1989).

30. Fed.R.Civ.P. 13(a). These counterclaims do not need to be presented if (1) at the time the action was commenced, the claim was the subject of another pending action, or (2) the opposing party brought suit upon the claim by attachment or other

any permissive counterclaims against any opposing party. Permissive counterclaims are those that do not arise out of the transaction or occurrence on which the complaint is based.[31] If you do not include a permissive counterclaim, you may amend the pleading to raise it.[32]

After gaining some experience with these tactical considerations, most attorneys develop strong opinions about what should and should not be included in pleadings. The attorneys you work for will likely have their own views and you must learn these preferences when drafting pleadings for them. Talk with other attorneys about their tactics in drafting pleadings and vary your pleading practice accordingly.

DRAFTING THE COMPLAINT

Having completed your factual and legal research and considered your tactics before drafting, now draft the complaint. Maintain your focus on thoroughness and precision. A complaint usually has six main parts: (1) the caption, (2) the commencement, (3) the body or charging part, (4) the prayer or demand for judgment, (5) the signature, and (6) the verification. This section discusses each of these parts, including drafting considerations that apply to each part and to the complaint in general.

The Caption

The caption includes the jurisdiction, the name of the court, the venue, the title of the case including the names of the parties and their positions, the case number, the file number or the docket number, and the name of the document.

STATE OF KENTUCKY CIRCUIT COURT FAYETTE COUNTY

Branch 11

SUSAN G. BLACK and DAVID R. BLACK,	
Plaintiffs,	NOTICE OF MOTION TO DISMISS AND MEMORANDUM
vs.	OF POINTS AND AUTHORITIES IN SUPPORT
STEWART PROPERTIES, INC.,	
Defendant.	Case No. 90 CV 10

This caption is repeated on all the documents filed with the court; the only change is in the name of the document. Consider naming the document to ensure clarity, even if your jurisdiction does not require it. Many rules also require the first pleading to include the names of all

---

process by which the court did not acquire jurisdiction to render a personal judgment on that claim and the pleader is not stating any counterclaim under Rule 13. *Id.*

31. Fed.R.Civ.P. 13(b).

32. Fed.R.Civ.P. 13(f). Amendment is allowed when the counterclaim is excluded through oversight, inadvertence, excusable neglect, or when justice requires.

parties, while subsequent pleadings can simply state the first party for each side and an indication, such as "et al.," that other parties exist.[33]

The Commencement

The commencement follows the caption and introduces the complaint, but is set off from the body of the complaint. Legalese is often included, which indicates to the court that additional legalese will likely follow. For example, the following commencements are often found in form books.

> Now comes Mollie Anderson by her attorney Henry Frank and alleges as follows:

OR

> Comes now the plaintiff Mollie Anderson and for cause of action and complaint against the defendant herein alleges:

Many users of form books feel compelled to include this legalese as magical "fairy dust," because they are afraid that, without this language, the judge may reject their complaints as incorrect. But the judge will more likely applaud your decision to eliminate this legalese.

In addition to including legalese in the commencement, most attorneys also err by punctuating the commencement with a colon at the end.

> NOW COMES Mollie Anderson, by her attorney Henry Frank:

By ending the commencement with a colon, the attorney must either state each allegation as an incomplete sentence or misuse the colon.[34] Stating each allegation as an incomplete sentence makes the complaint difficult to read. Instead, rewrite your commencement as a complete sentence and, while rewriting it, eliminate the legalese.

> **Plaintiff, Mollie Anderson, represented by her attorney Henry Frank, states the following as a cause of action against defendant, John Hopkins.**

OR

> **Mollie Anderson, plaintiff, by her attorney Henry Frank, complains against John Hopkins, defendant, and asserts the following in support of her claim.**

These commencements include the same information as the traditional ones above, but are more readable.

The Body or Charging Portion

This is the main portion of the complaint and consists of the numbered paragraphs in the complaint. The paragraphs comprising this part must be broad enough to give you flexibility in proving your case at trial. They must also be sufficiently precise to give notice of the

---

33. Fed.R.Civ.P. 10(a).

34. Mary Barnard Ray and Jill J. Ramsfield, *Legal Writing: Getting It Right and Getting It Written* 42–43 (1987).

claims against your opponent; they must be thorough by including all the elements of the cause of action you are alleging. Remember that the opposing counsel, before answering, will consider whether to bring a demurrer or motion to dismiss for failure to state a claim. You must write your complaint with a view toward preventing or surviving that demurrer or motion.

Using a checklist is often helpful when drafting complaints, defensive motions, and answers. A checklist that includes procedural and substantive elements is most useful because it reminds you of both procedural concerns and substantive causes of action that may be raised.[35] How general or specific the checklist will be depends on the variety of cases you handle in your practice. The following excerpt shows the checklist's usefulness.

SAMPLE CHECKLIST

[The first section raises procedural and documentation questions that you may be likely to forget if not reminded.]

I. Related documents and questions.

Required statement and cover sheet.

Court fee.

Service fee.

Proper jurisdiction?

Proper venue?

All *proper* plaintiffs named. (Name individuals in partnership or fictitious entity. Name guardians, if necessary.)

Proper defendants and all defendants?

Proper service on all defendants.

. . .

Demand for jury trial.

[The second section raises broad questions about both substantive and drafting concerns for the body of the complaint.]

II. Allegations

   A. Jurisdiction over each defendant and capacity and jurisdictional amount or other basis of jurisdiction. Is corporation "in good standing"?

   B. Conformity of allegations to general rules of pleading.

     Sufficient ultimate facts to show each type of relief sought.

     All elements of each type of relief sought have been included.

---

35. See, for example, the checklists contained in Nancy Schleifer, *Complaint and* *Defensive Checklists,* 61 Fla.Bar J. 23 (July–Aug. 1987).

Separate statements—single set of circumstances per paragraph.

Elimination of all "and/or" terms.

. . .

G. Special Damages—allege specifically in addition to compensatory damages. (Some of these may go in body of complaint rather than in plea for damages or costs.)

Pain and suffering.

Emotional damages (impact rule).

Consequential damages limited by contract?

Loss of use.

Rental Value.

Punitives/trebles.

Cost of cover.

Lost profits.

Cost in collection (in contract?).

Cost of receiver (in contract?).

Costs of accounting (in contract?).

Costs of investigation (in contract?).

Prejudgment/postjudgment interest.

Attorneys' fees.[36]

Developing a checklist will take time because it should be specifically annotated to include your local procedural rules and should include as much information as possible concerning possible causes of action and defenses. Developing a checklist will help you feel more assured that you have considered the available options when drafting complaints or answers.

You must be careful, however, not to become overly dependent on your checklist so that you overlook other options available to your client. One way to avoid this lapse in thoroughness may be to have the last item or section of your checklist refer to brainstorming or researching other possible causes of action or defenses. Or your last item may refer to discussing these matters with your colleagues to help you recognize other options.

The first paragraphs of the complaint's charging part identify the parties. If there are only two parties, paragraph one identifies the plaintiff and paragraph two identifies the defendant.

36. *Id.* at 23–24. Schleifer also has checklists for defensive motions and answers, which can serve as a starting place for writing your own. She includes references to Florida statutes and rules, which have been omitted from the excerpt. Consider also including similar references for your jurisdiction.

1. Mollie Anderson, the plaintiff, is an adult residing at 1234 Happy Valley Lane, Smalltown, Wisconsin 53098.

2. John Hopkins, the defendant, is an adult residing at 5678 Mountain View Avenue, Village, Wisconsin 53704.

Include a separate paragraph for each additional plaintiff or defendant. These paragraphs should state each individual's name and address, whether he or she is an adult or minor, and perhaps the person's occupation. If a party is a business, state the type of business (sole proprietorship, partnership, or corporation) and its principal business address. For corporations, consider including under what state law it is incorporated. If you do not know the names of all the defendants, many states and some federal courts allow you to allege them fictitiously using the name "Doe 1" or "John Doe." [37]

After identifying the parties, you will state the allegations that support your cause of action. Depending on your tactical decisions, you may include all or only some of the causes of action arising under the facts that concern the named defendants. You will probably include most of the possible causes of action, because those not raised when an incident is being litigated may be precluded by res judicata.[38] If you have several counts arising under each cause of action, organize your complaint with headings that specify each cause of action and then state Count I, Count II, and so on under each. Using headings helps to clarify the organization of your complaint. Some attorneys shy away from naming the specific cause of action in the headings and, instead, use headings that state Claim I, Claim II, and so forth. They do this because the allegations may satisfy the elements for more than one cause of action and they do not want to be precluded from pursuing any cause of action raised by the facts. Doing this is fine as long as you ensure that you have stated all the elements of the cause of action you intended to raise.

While you must include allegations for every element of each cause of action, you may not need to include all of your evidence supporting the existence of any particular element. You may withhold favorable facts unnecessary to state the cause of action and use them for some tactical advantage later. On the other hand, you may include these favorable facts if you believe they demonstrate the strength of your case to the defendant and increase the possibility of obtaining a good settlement.

37. *See e.g.,* Mass.Gen.Laws Ann. ch. 223, § 19.

38. Res judicata means that a final judgment on the merits of a cause of action is conclusive on the parties' rights and has binding effect on all subsequent lawsuits arising from the same cause of action. How "cause of action" is defined determines whether subsequent lawsuits arising from the same incident can be litigated.

The federal rules broadly define cause of action and allow for liberal joinder of claims, so that all claims arising from one incident should be litigated in the same lawsuit. If joinder of claims is restricted, then the cause of action is restricted and the judgment will not be res judicata on other claims. Friedenthal, *supra* note 22, at § 14.4, at 619–621.

Drafting allegations requires you to understand the difference between evidentiary facts, ultimate facts, and conclusions of law so that you will include the right combination of each to state your client's cause of action thoroughly and precisely. The following example explains the differences between each type of information. Evidentiary facts are those facts that tell the story of the incident.

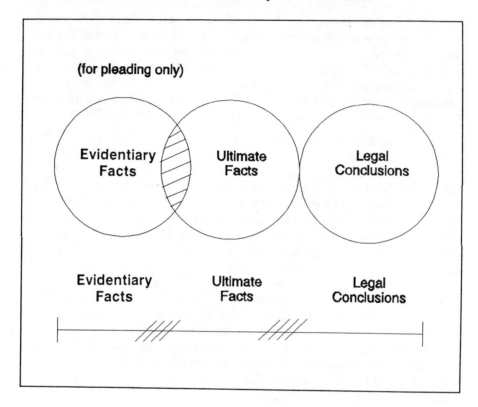

Evidentiary facts:

      Joan saw Fred driving very fast down the street.

      Joan wrote down the car's license plate number.

      Fred was driving a red car.

      The posted speed limit was 25 m.p.h.

      Snow was falling and the wind was blowing.

      The roads were icy.

      Fred hit Sally while she was crossing the street.

An ultimate fact is a fact that establishes one element of your cause of action.

      Ultimate fact:

      Fred was driving too fast for conditions.

A conclusion of law is a statement of an element of the cause of action.

Conclusion of law:

Fred breached his duty of care to Sally.

In your cause of action, you must allege those evidentiary facts that establish the ultimate fact. You may want to allege that Fred was driving faster than the posted speed limit of twenty-five miles per hour, that the roads were icy, that snow was falling, and that the wind was blowing. You probably do not need to allege that Fred was driving a red car, unless the allegation is needed for identification. You should plead the ultimate fact that Fred was driving too fast for conditions because this is the factual basis supporting your allegation that Fred breached his duty of care, which is a required element in bringing a cause of action for negligence. You need to allege conclusions of law because they establish the elements of your cause of action and must be included to withstand a motion to dismiss your complaint. Conclusions of law will be routinely denied in the answer, however, because the defendant presumably will challenge the legal conclusion, even if he or she admits some or all of the facts supporting the conclusion.

Because conclusions of law will be routinely denied, you need to separate your factual allegations from your conclusions of law so the defendant cannot deny the existence of a fact simply because it is contained in the same allegation as a conclusion of law. For example, do not state your allegations as follows.

7. Snow was falling, the wind was blowing, and the roads were icy. Fred was driving too fast for conditions and thus breached his duty of care to Sally.

Instead, rewrite your allegations to separate evidentiary facts from ultimate facts from legal conclusions.

7. Snow was falling, the wind was blowing, and the roads were icy.

8. Fred was driving too fast for conditions.

9. By driving too fast for conditions, Fred breached his duty of care to Sally.

By separating your allegations, the defendant will have to admit allegation 7 if those facts are true.[39] The defendant will probably deny allegations 8 and 9, but you will have gained an admission so you do not have to prove the facts contained in allegation 7 at trial.

State your facts precisely and unemotionally. Hyperbole and generalities make it easy for the defendant to deny allegations containing them. If your allegations are precise and brief, the defendant will be forced to admit them. Being precise means using objective words, rather than coloring your evidentiary facts or ultimate facts. Saying that Fred drove "recklessly" or "carelessly" would probably result in a

---

39. However, the defendant may try to file a general denial to the complaint in this situation, if allowed under the procedural rules, so that he or she does not have to admit any allegation. Fed.R.Civ.P. 8(b) seems to preclude this practice if the defendant knows that some facts are true.

denial by the defendant. In contrast, it would be harder to deny that Fred drove "faster than the speed limit."

Finally, do not allege more than you actually know. In the example above, it would be easy to allege that Fred drove "his" car too fast for conditions. However, you probably do not know whether it was his car or not. By using "a" car, you avoid having Fred deny the allegation solely because it was not his car. In the same way, do not allege that a defendant "owned, operated, controlled, and managed" the restaurant. If the defendant simply managed it, he or she will be able to deny the allegation because three-quarters of your allegation is incorrect. The need to state facts precisely underscores the importance of investigating the facts after interviewing your client. Good investigation allows you to draft your allegations precisely and thus obtain the defendant's admissions.

Similarly, be precise about the dates, amounts, facts, and circumstances you do include. Oftentimes, attorneys answering complaints are able to deny allegations that otherwise would have to be admitted because a date or amount is incorrect. This denial by the defendant may lead you to believe that the substance of the allegation is being challenged when, in fact, the allegation was denied because of imprecise facts. If the primary factual basis for your complaint is found in a document (contract, letter, etc.), you can attach the document and incorporate it by reference. For example, you could state: "attached as exhibit A and incorporated in its entirety into this complaint."

The last paragraph of the body or charging portion of the complaint describes the plaintiff's injuries and damages. In jurisdictions where you can plead the amount of damages, the charging portion may end on an "ad damnum" clause, which means "to the damage." [40] This clause states "all to his [her] damage in the sum of $_____.___." But many attorneys prefer not to include a specific statement of the amount of damages unless that amount can be readily computed. Otherwise, stating a specific amount may cause the defendant to request that you itemize and explain each item of damage leading to the amount. If the amount claimed is large and unsubstantiated, the ad damnum clause makes it appear that the plaintiff is inflating his or her demand.

The Prayer or Demand for Judgment

The federal rules require you to include in the complaint a demand for judgment for the relief desired and allow you to demand several different types of relief.[41] This demand for judgment is not numbered. It usually starts with "Wherefore," which indicates that the demand results from the allegations stated in the complaint's body, although "wherefore" can be eliminated. Here the plaintiff lists all the types of relief he or she believes are appropriate. Different types of relief

40. *Black's Law Dictionary* 35 (5th ed. 1979).

41. Fed.R.Civ.P. 8(a)(3).

include equitable relief, consequential or special damages, punitive damages, or specific performance.

Plaintiff requests that the court:

(1) declare the defendant has tortiously interfered with plaintiff's contract;

(2) permanently enjoin defendant from tortiously interfering with plaintiff's contract;

(3) award plaintiff the entitled amount of damages plus interest;

(4) award plaintiff its costs and attorney fees; and

(5) grant plaintiff any other relief the court considers equitable.

The demand for judgment usually ends with the catchall phrase "and any other relief the court considers equitable and just." The rules do not require this additional phrase in most situations; Rule 54(c) states that final judgments should include the relief to which the winning party is entitled, even if the party did not request that relief in the pleadings.[42] This phrase is important, however, in default judgment situations because default judgments may not be different in kind or exceed the amount requested in the demand for judgment.[43] Thus your demand for judgment limits the relief granted in default situations. In anticipation of those situations, adding "and any other relief the court considers equitable and just" may allow the court to provide relief beyond that explicitly requested in your demand.

Also request interest and costs in your complaint; request attorney's fees if there is some basis for doing so. Some statutory causes of action (such as Title VII) provide for attorney's fees for the successful complainant.[44] Most causes of action for frivolous suits or for frivolous motions also provide for attorney's fees. Many contract actions involve a request for attorneys' fees, if the contract provides for them. You should include these requests if you want your fees included as part of the damages awarded to the plaintiff.

Some attorneys place the demand for judgment at the end of the complaint, after all the causes of action have been stated. Others make a demand for relief at the end of each cause of action, believing that each cause of action may require different types of relief and that separating them will clarify matters.

Signature and Address

The final required section of the complaint is the seemingly formalistic requirement that the attorney who prepared the pleadings must sign them, or the plaintiff must sign them if he or she does not have an attorney.[45] Include your business address with your signature.

---

42. Fed.R.Civ.P. 54(c).

43. *Id.*

44. *See, e.g.,* 42 U.S.C. § 2000(e)(5)(k) (1988).

45. Fed.R.Civ.P. 11.

HANRAHAN & HOWARD, P.C.

BY: _____

Jude Hanrahan

AND: _____

Dara Howard
Attorneys for Plaintiff
210 Main Street
Lexington, Kentucky 40511

While it seems formalistic, your signature has a strong substantive component as well. Your signature at the bottom of any document filed in the federal courts indicates that you have read it, that it is well grounded in fact and law, and that it is not filed for any improper purpose.[46] If you sign the pleading in violation of the rule, then the court will impose sanctions, including the expenses and attorney's fees that the opposing party incurred because of the document.[47] Even if your jurisdiction does not place a substantive restriction on your signature, treat your signature as if it did. This will help you ensure that you are not wasting your client's or the court's time in presenting documents that are unsubstantial or frivolous.

Verification

Under the federal rules, complaints need to be verified by the party or accompanied by an affidavit only when specifically required under the rule or statute upon which the complaint is based.[48] States vary on whether they require verification. Some attorneys prefer to include a verification by their clients, regardless of whether it is required, to impress upon their clients the seriousness of the step they are taking.

Carefully draft each aspect of the complaint so you will not waste time and money defending your complaint from challenges by your opponent. The time spent on careful drafting is minimal compared to the time it takes to respond to motions raised by your opponent or to bring motions to amend defects in your complaint.

DRAFTING THE ANSWER

An answer is a response to the complaint and simply indicates which of the complaint's allegations your client, the defendant, admits, denies, or is unable to answer because of insufficient information. Answers help narrow the issues for trial because the defendant may admit some things, which do not then need to be established at trial.

---

46. *Id.* A large amount of controversy has surrounded Rule 11 since its amendment in 1983. For a fuller discussion of this controversy, *see* Arthur Miller, *The New Certification Standard under Rule 11,* 130 F.R.D. 479 (1990); William Schwarzer, *Rule 11 Revisited,* 101 Harv.L.Rev. 1013 (1988).

47. Fed.R.Civ.P. 11.

48. *Id.* Among those that must be verified are derivative actions by shareholders under Fed.R.Civ.P. 23, depositions taken before an action or pending appeal under Fed.R.Civ.P. 27, requests for injunctions under Fed.R.Civ.P. 65, and requests for receivers appointed by federal courts under Fed.R.Civ.P. 66. *See,* Coyne, *Federal Rules of Civil Procedure for the United States District Courts* 120 (1990).

The format of an answer is quite simple. If you are making a general denial, you need only state: "The Defendant denies each allegation contained in plaintiff's complaint." If you are making a special denial, you should indicate which paragraphs you admit and which ones you deny. If you do not have enough information to admit or deny an allegation, state your lack of information, which acts as a denial.

> 1.   Defendant admits the allegations in paragraphs 1, 2, 3, 4, and 8 and admits the allegations in paragraph 10 except to state (or to deny . . .).

> 2.   Defendant denies the allegations in paragraphs 5, 6, 7, and 9 (or denies paragraph 9 except that portion that states) (or denies paragraph 9 and adds (version of facts).

> 3.   Defendant is without sufficient information or facts to admit or deny the allegations in paragraphs 11, 12, 13, and 14 and puts plaintiff to his (or her) proof on these matters.

One question that arises in answering a complaint is when an allegation must be admitted or when it can be denied. The federal rules require the attorney responding to admit that portion of the allegation that is true.[49] Many attorneys believe that the answer must admit any portion of an allegation that is true.

Complaint:

> 5.   Defendants wrongfully entered the Happy Trails Convention Center on June 25, 1989, by misrepresenting themselves as authorized to enter and videotape the workshop.

Answer:

> 5.   Denies paragraph 5, except admits that defendants entered Happy Trails Convention Center on June 25, 1989.

Other attorneys prefer to deny an allegation that is untrue in any part, however small. They would interpret the federal rule to allow them to deny entirely the preceding allegation because part of it can be denied as untrue.[50] But the federal rules state that the pleader will be responding "in good faith," so if you know that the defendants did enter the convention center on June 25th, you would be obliged to admit that information.

One way you can prevent this problem when you draft a complaint is to separate the evidentiary facts from the ultimate facts. The above example could be redrafted as follows.

> 5.   The defendants entered the Happy Trails Convention Center on June 25, 1989, and videotaped the workshop.

> 6.   The defendants entered the Convention Center on June 25, 1989, by misrepresenting themselves as authorized to videotape the workshop.

49. Fed.R.Civ.P. 8(b). Alterman, *supra*   **50.** *Id.*
note 12, at 280.

These allegations require different responses from the attorney drafting the answer. The allegations of paragraph 5 are factual in nature and, if the attorney knows that they are true, he or she must admit them. The answer will presumably deny paragraph 6 because the dispute probably revolves around whether the defendants were misrepresenting their authority. But the complaint drafter will have obtained admissions on two important points: the defendants did enter the center and they did videotape the workshop. These admissions have thus eliminated plaintiff's need to prove these facts at trial and have focused the litigation on the issue of misrepresentation, not on the factual question of whether the event was videotaped by defendants.

Once you are finished responding to the complaint, you should include any affirmative defenses or counterclaims that you need to raise. These resemble the allegations in the complaint. Allege the ultimate facts that provide the basis for your claim, those evidentiary facts that are necessary to provide a context, and the conclusions of law establishing each element of the defense or claim.

CONCLUSION

Drafting excellent pleadings requires you to concentrate on thoroughness and precision. Thoroughness requires considering (1) all the possible causes of actions, affirmative defenses, and counterclaims and (2) all the allegations needed to establish each element of the causes of actions, defenses, or counterclaims you raise. Precision requires drafting the documents to comport with the procedural and substantive rules of your jurisdiction and the allegations or responses so they are most helpful to your client.

EXERCISE 1

Using the criteria below, improve the following set of allegations. Do not concern yourself with the caption, names of the parties, or the request for relief. If you think they are necessary, supply additional facts for the allegations in each complaint.

A complaint must state a *prima facie* case against the defendant. In addition, it can narrow subsequent litigation and provide a preview of the defense by compelling the defendant to admit some parts of the plaintiff's case. Each numbered allegation in a complaint should be a brief, objective statement of one element of the case.

Part A.

The law:

> 471.20 Owner's Liability. The owner or keeper of any dog which
> has . . . killed, wounded or worried any . . . cattle
> . . . shall be liable to . . . the owner of such animals
> for all damages so done.

The allegations:

1. That Bozo, a large yellow beast, cornered plaintiff's cow Annabelle and worried her.

2. That plaintiff recognized said Bozo on the basis of previous familiarity with him.

3. That the incident happened in plaintiff's fenced pasture.

4. That as a result of said worrying by said Bozo, said Annabelle was off her feed for several days and stopped producing milk.

EXERCISE 2

Write a complaint for our client, Herbert Lanz. Lanz is a dairy farmer in Green County. Lanz has a large herd of Brown Swiss cows and they produce a high-quality milk for making cheese. Two weeks ago, on the morning of June 24, Lanz put a dozen of his cows in a small fenced-in pasture about half a mile from the farm yard.

About an hour later, Lanz was working on his tractor in the farm yard when he heard a commotion from the small pasture. He looked across the fields and saw the twelve cows running around the pasture and heard them bellowing and mooing. He could see a smaller animal running around the pasture behind the cows, but he was not close enough to see it clearly. Lanz ran across the fields toward the pasture. As he got closer, he could see that the smaller animal was a large, black-and-white spotted dog. The dog was barking at the cows and chasing them. When Lanz reached the pasture, he threw a couple of stones at the dog and chased it away. The dog ran to the north.

Lanz is certain that the dog belongs to a neighbor, Mr. Randall Crosby, who lives about three miles north of Lanz's farm. On several occasions, Lanz has seen a large dog with distinctive black-and-white spots riding in the back of Crosby's pickup truck. Crosby is a corn and alfalfa farmer, not a dairy farmer, so Lanz assumes that Crosby has not trained his dog not to chase cows.

The twelve cows that the dog chased did not eat much for five days after the incident. Their milk production dropped sharply and is still only about half of what it was before. Lanz estimates that his losses will be at least $5,000.

Write a complaint for Lanz alleging that Crosby is liable for his dog's behavior and for Lanz's loss of income. Wis.Stat. § 471.20 (1979–80).

471.20   Owner's liability

The owner or keeper of any dog which has injured or caused the injury of any person or property or killed, wounded or worried any horses, cattle, sheep, ranch mink or lambs shall be liable to the person so injured and the owner of such animals for all damages so done, without proving notice to the owner or keeper of such dog or knowledge by him that his dog was mischievous or disposed to kill, wound or worry horses, cattle, sheep, ranch mink or lambs; but when ranch mink are killed, wounded or worried, it shall be proven that the dog forcibly entered the enclosure in which they were kept.

ASSIGNMENT 1

You represent Mark Gordon, a farmer who owned two dogs shot by game wardens. The facts on which the complaint is based are included in Assignment 1 in Chapter 6, Issues. Write a complaint suing the wardens for actual and punitive damages for damaging Gordon's property. The fact situation provides a start on writing the complaint, but do not assume that the allegations given in the facts are complete or in the best order.

ASSIGNMENT 2

You are the attorney representing Susan Ashland. Write a complaint in her behalf, using the facts in Assignment 2 at the end of Chapter 6. Allege that the Kellys are liable under Tenn. Code Ann. § 471.20 (1988), for Ranger's actions that resulted in Susan's accident, and that they should pay for Susan's damages.

Bibliography

Alterman, Irwin, *Plain and Accurate Style in Lawsuit Papers,* 2 Cooley L.Rev. 243 (1981).

Bender, Matthew, *California Forms of Pleading and Practice.* New York City: Times Mirror Books, 1990.

Binder, David A., and Susan C. Price, *Legal Interviewing and Counseling.* St. Paul: West Publishing Co., 1977.

Black, Henry Campbell, *Black's Law Dictionary.* St. Paul: West Publishing Co., 5th Ed. 1979.

Cooper, Frank E., *Writing in Law Practice.* Indianapolis: Bobbs–Merrill Co., 1963.

Coyne, Thomas A., *Federal Rules of Civil Procedure for the United States District Courts.* New York City: C. Boardman Co., 1990.

Friedenthal, Jack H., Mary Kay Kane, and Arthur R. Miller, *Civil Procedure.* St. Paul: West Publishing Co., 1985.

Koffler, Joseph H., and Alison Reppy, *Common Law Pleading.* St. Paul: West Publishing Co., 1969.

Mehler, Irving M., *Effective Legal Communication.* Denver: Philgor Publishing, 1975.

Menkel–Meadow, Carrie, *For and Against Settlement: Uses and Abuses of the Mandatory Settlement Conference,* 33 U.C.L.A. L.Rev. 485 (1985–1986).

Miller, Arthur R., *The New Certification Standard Under Rule 11,* 130 F.R.D. 479 (1990).

Neubauer, Mark A., *Check–The–Box Pleadings,* 11 Litigation 28 (Winter 1985).

Owens, William Brownlee, *California Forms and Procedure.* Los Angeles: Parker & Son Publications, Inc., 1990.

Porter, Karen K., Nancy L. Schultz, Lauren Scott, Louis J. Sirico, Jr., and Annemiek N. Young, *Introduction to Legal Writing and Oral Advocacy.* New York: Times Mirror Books, 1989.

Ray, Mary Barnard, and Ramsfield, Jill J., *Legal Writing: Getting It Right and Getting It Written.* St. Paul: West Publishing Co., 1989.

Schleifer, Nancy, *Complaint and Defensive Checklists,* 61 Fla.Bar.J. 23 (July–August 1987).

Schwarzer, William W., *Rule 11 Revisited,* 101 Harv.L.Rev. 1013 (1988).

Wright, Charles Alan, and Arthur R. Miller, *Federal Practice and Procedure.* St. Paul: West Publishing Co., 1969.

Chapter 12

NOTICES OF MOTION, MOTIONS, AND ORDERS

Like pleadings, motions play a central part in many attorneys' practices. While many law students anticipate exciting jury trials and rousing closing arguments, upon joining a law firm, they soon realize that most litigation practice is completed long before the case reaches trial. Thus your opportunity to persuade a court to rule favorably for your client may occur most frequently during "law and motion" practice at your local courthouse. Even before the pleading stage of the lawsuit has been completed, you will need to know how to use motion practice to protect your client. In Chapter 11, you learned to draft both the complaint and the answer. But before drafting the answer, you must split your focus between the possibility of taking the suit to trial and the probability of making motions because you will have to decide whether to raise any preliminary motions before answering. Once you have served the answer, you will be precluded from raising numerous motions that may best serve your client.[1] You may need to make several other motions after answering and before trial. These may include motions to compel discovery, motions for a continuance, motions in limine to exclude specific testimony from trial, and other pretrial motions. Thus, learning to draft these motions will help you throughout your practice.

Motions are requests for assistance from the court. If the judge grants your request, he or she will issue an order explaining the assistance being granted. Due process concerns within our legal system, however, require that, before a judge can issue the order in most cases, your opponent must be given an opportunity to respond to your request.[2] To meet these due process requirements, a hearing will be

---

1. Fed.R.Civ.P. 12(b) lists the motions that must be raised before or when answering or the right to raise these motions is waived. The next section of this chapter describes these motions in detail.

2. U.S. Const. amend. V and XIV. Additionally, Fed.R.Civ.P. 6(d) requires notice of all motions except ex parte ones, as do many state statutes. *See, e.g.,* Cal.Civ.Pro.

§ 1005.5. Ex parte motions are those requesting orders in the absence of interested parties and without notice of the hearing. An example of an ex parte order is a temporary restraining order granted when "great or irreparable injury" is established. 3 *Cal.Forms and Procedure* § 30.04(E)(iii) (1986). Ex parte motions are granted in extremely rare circumstances.

held on your motion, although it may be an informal conference in the judge's chambers. The document informing your opponent of this hearing is the notice of motion. Before preparing the notice of motion, you must make arrangements for the judge to hear your motion and provide notice to your opponent of the date, time, place, and content of the hearing.

For example, suppose that the trial in your client's personal injury accident case is set for October 16th and, one week before the trial, your chief witness calls and tells you that one of his parents has been hospitalized and he needs to go home. Your first step will be to contact your opponent to see if he or she would agree to a continuance. In routine matters, always attempt to reach an informal agreement or stipulation with opposing counsel before proceeding into court to make formal motions to resolve the issue.[3] If your opponent agrees, you will then simply call the judge's chambers, inform the clerk of the problem, indicate your opponent's agreement, and determine whether the judge has any objections.[4]

If your opponent opposes the continuance, perhaps because that is the only week his or her chief witness can be present, then you will apply to the judge for an order resetting the trial date. You will then call the judge's clerk and determine when a hearing could be held on the matter. Next you will send a Notice of Motion and Motion for Continuance to your opponent, stating the basis for your motion and requesting the desired relief. You might also attach an affidavit from your witness stating the need for the continuance and prepare the order granting your motion, so the judge can simply sign the order if he or she decides to grant the motion.[5] At the hearing, both sides will present their arguments for and against the continuance and the judge will issue an order granting or denying the motion.

This motion process can repeat itself before the trial, during the trial, and even after trial. Some motions will be made orally during trial, such as motions for directed verdict, and others will be made after trial, such as motions for judgment notwithstanding the verdict or for

---

3. Besides saving valuable attorney and court time by not having to prepare or defend the motions and argue them in court, these conversations with opposing counsel increase communication between opposing parties. This communication may lead to informal resolution of nonroutine matters or to settlement. 1 *California Points and Authorities* § 1.02(2) (1990).

4. The judge may very well object. In some jurisdictions, he or she may be virtually prohibited from granting a continuance in this type of situation. For example, regardless of the opposing party's problem of his or her witness's availability, Cal.Rules of Court 375(a) states that continuances are disfavored and the date set for trial is firm.

5. You might also consider sending a memorandum of points and authorities containing legal support for your motion, although the factual nature of the motion in this example might make legal argument unnecessary. These memoranda are known as trial briefs in some jurisdictions. Local court rules may require the filing of memoranda of points and authorities regardless of the motion's nature. *See* Cal. Rules of Court 313(a), which requires a party filing a notice of motion, except a motion for a new trial, to file a memorandum of points and authorities with the notice of motion. The court considers the absence of the memorandum to be an admission that the motion is not meritorious and thus cause for its denial.

reconsideration. Your litigation practice will return continuously to drafting, defending, and arguing motions.

The documents involved in motion practice are usually rather short and simple to draft. The writing concerns involved in these drafting tasks are being clear and eliminating legalese. Because they tend to be short, most attorneys choose to copy form documents from form books or files within their law firm. This practice perpetuates overlong sentences and legalese, which makes these otherwise simple documents difficult to comprehend. Your goal is not to avoid using forms, but to revise them or develop forms that increase clarity and decrease legalese.

This chapter divides drafting motions into two sections. The first section concerns the procedural, strategic, and ethical concerns of presenting motions to the court, as well as the general rules governing motion practice. The second section concerns the drafting requirements for notices of motion, motions, and orders. Together, these sections will prepare you to join the attorneys whose work revolves around the "motion calendar" at the local courthouse.

PROCEDURE, STRATEGY, AND ETHICS OF MOTION PRACTICE

This section addresses (1) the general procedural rules and timing requirements controlling motion practice and (2) the strategic and ethical considerations governing this aspect of practice. By becoming acquainted with these rules and considerations, you will more effectively achieve your client's desired goals.

Rules Controlling Motion Practice

Both the federal courts and the state courts have statutes regulating motion practice. Becoming familiar with these statutes will help you understand how your jurisdiction regulates motion practice. For example, Rule 7(b) requires attorneys to file motions when requesting orders from a judge and requires most motions to be in writing; it also permits the notice of motion and motion to be made in the same document if the notice of motion states the legal grounds for the motion.[6] The substantive argument supporting the motion is contained in the brief or memorandum of points and authorities supporting your motion.[7]

These rules may also control substantive aspects of your documents. For example, Rule 7 requires that motions include the particu-

---

6. Fed.R.Civ.P. 7(b). These rules are the same in many states. For example, *see* Cal.Civ.Pro. § 1010; Fla.R.Civ.P. 1.100; Or.R.Civ.P. 14; Tex.R.Civ.P. 21.

7. This brief or memorandum of points and authorities is a persuasively written document that presents the legal argument

for the court ruling in your favor. A full discussion of drafting these documents is contained in Chapter 6 on Persuasive Issue Statements, Chapter 8: Persuasive Statements of Fact, and Chapter 10: Argument Sections of Briefs.

lar grounds on which they are based.[8]   Motions have been dismissed simply for failure to state the particular grounds for the motion.[9] When bringing a motion, you are asking the court for a specific remedy. Therefore, you must provide enough information for the court to understand your request, while avoiding presenting so much information that you outline your overall strategy for your opponent.[10]

These procedural rules may also control which motion you are making. For example, the federal rules differentiate between a motion to dismiss and a motion for summary judgment, depending on which documents support the motion. If the motion is based on the pleadings alone, the federal rules will treat it as a motion to dismiss for failure to state a claim upon which relief can be granted under Rule 12.[11] On the other hand, if the motion is based on matters outside the pleadings, the federal rules will treat it as a motion for summary judgment under Rule 56.[12] Thus your understanding of the procedural rules controlling motion practice must extend to recognizing the interplay between the rules and the motions you make.

Similarly, local federal court rules control many aspects of motion practice.[13]   Local rules control numerous details, including (1) time limits, (2) page limits for memoranda of points and authorities,[14] (3) meet-and-confer rules requiring the attorney bringing the motion to meet with opposing counsel before filing the motion,[15] and (4) requirements for documents supporting the motion.[16] To be successful in your motion practice, you must be aware of and understand how your jurisdiction regulates these documents.

Just as the federal rules and local court rules regulate federal court motion practice, state statutes and local court rules regulate state court motion practice. These state rules cover many of the same details covered by the federal rules. These rules can regulate even the organization of your documents. For example, the California Rules of

---

8. Fed.R.Civ.P. 7(b)(1). Despite the clear language of this rule, the courts have not explained what degree of specificity is required to fulfill this rule. Herr, Haydock, and Stempel, *Motion Practice* 15 (1985).

9. For example, *see, Lynn v. Smith*, 193 F.Supp. 887, 888 (W.D.Pa.1961).

10. In this regard, motions strategy is similar to pleadings strategy, such as when drafting a complaint, you may prefer to make your allegations as narrow as possible to avoid providing your opponent with your overall plan.

11. Fed.R.Civ.P. 12(b)(6).

12. Fed.R.Civ.P. 12(b).

13. *See,* Herr, Haydock, and Stempel, *supra* note 8, at 12 n. 1, where they list the federal courts that regulate motion practice by local rule.

14. *Id.* at 83 n. 1, where the authors list the federal courts that have imposed page limits on memoranda of points and authorities supporting motions. For example, the Eastern District of California imposes a ten-page limit while the Utah District Court imposes a thirteen-page limit, except for summary judgment motions, which are given 32 pages. *Id.*

15. *Id.* at 25 n. 22. The California Judicial Council has considered adding Rule 310 to the Cal. Rules of Court "which would require a reasonable attempt to resolve disputed issues prior to hearing on certain motions." California Points and Authorities, *supra* note 3, at § 1.02(2).

16. Herr, Haydock, and Stempel, *supra* note 8, at 12.

Court require the opening paragraph of the notice of motion to state the nature of the order requested and the grounds supporting it.[17] Thus, in California, if you place the time, place, and location of the hearing in the first paragraph of your notice, you will have violated a court rule. This error probably will not result in the dismissal of your motion or sanctions imposed against you. But organizing your motion differently would interfere with the judge's expectations, and the judge would have to take a few moments to determine how the organization of your motion differs from the others he or she is reading. While you want your motion to be noticed by the court, this is not the kind of attention you should seek.

As you learn these rules, also determine who handles motion practice in your jurisdiction. Some jurisdictions assign the entire responsibility for a case to one judge who addresses all matters arising in the case from the pleadings through the post-trial motions. If that is your situation, find out from the particular judge's clerk how motion practice is run in that courtroom.

In contrast, other jurisdictions rotate judges into "law and motion" practice.[18] These judges hear all motions pending in the jurisdiction for a specific amount of time. If this is your situation, your motions must follow that judge's dictates in all your currently pending cases, and you will want to learn as much as possible about that judge's predilections. Knowing his or her views on specific aspects of motion practice will help with your litigation strategy. For example, if the judge grants a continuance only when a party is hospitalized, you would be well advised to remove that motion from your bag of tricks. To learn these predilections, talk to other attorneys or listen to the judge resolve several motions and see whether you can determine any patterns the judge has. This may provide you with a clear advantage in deciding how your litigation strategy should proceed.

The timing of motions is also controlled by the statutes and local court rules in your jurisdiction. For example, Rule 12(f) requires that a motion to strike be made by a party either before responding to the pleading or within twenty days after service of the pleading if no responsive pleading is permitted.[19] Rule 56 states that a motion for summary judgment may not be made until twenty days after beginning the action or after service of the adverse party's motion for summary judgment.[20] Rule 6 requires that notice of the hearing be served no later than five days before the hearing, unless specifically fixed by the court.[21] Successful motion practice thus requires knowledge of these timing rules and conformity with them.

---

17. Cal. Rules of Court 311(a).

18. *See* Cal. Rules of Court 307, which states that the presiding judge or a judge designated by him or her will hear all proceedings in law and motion.

19. Fed.R.Civ.P. 12(f). The Rules do allow for a motion to strike at any time on the court's own initiative.

20. Fed.R.Civ.P. 56.

21. Fed.R.Civ.P. 6.

State statutes correspond to the federal rules, and you must consult them when practicing in the state courts. Local court rules also regulate the timing of motions. In California, for example, most motions and supporting papers must be served and filed fifteen days before the hearing, and all opposing papers must be filed five days before the hearing.[22] Additionally, the moving party must file a memorandum of points and authorities within ten days of filing a motion for a new trial.[23] If the memorandum is not filed within ten days, the court may deny the motion without a hearing on the merits.[24]

You can lose options for your client during litigation by not knowing the procedural rules governing motion practice; you can be liable for malpractice also.[25] As these restrictions on motion practice indicate, you must be aware of the procedural rules governing practice in your jurisdiction.

Ethical and Strategic Considerations of Motion Practice

Besides learning the rules regulating motion practice, also learn the ethical and strategic aspects of motion practice. Do not use motions to harass your opponents, delay the movement toward trial, or force the opposing side to expend resources. Ethical questions "include limitations on the nature, scope, and frequency of motions made, on the authorities cited or not cited in support of any motion, or the underlying purpose of motions." [26] Related to these ethical concerns are the numerous strategic questions that arise during motion practice. These include decisions on using motions "to control the timing of various events in litigation, to shape the issues to be decided by the court, to dispose of claims and defenses that are not meritorious, and to seek specific relief." [27] Before you begin drafting your motions, consider these questions to ensure that you use motions to your client's best advantage.

The Federal Rules of Civil Procedure were amended by Congress in 1983 due to concerns about inappropriate motion practice. Rule 11 now requires that all motions be signed by the attorney of record, except when a party is unrepresented.[28] This signature

> constitutes a certificate by the signer that the signer has read the pleading, motion, or other paper; that to the best of the signer's knowledge, information, and belief formed after reasonable inquiry it is well grounded in fact and is warranted by existing law or a good faith argument for the extension, modification, or reversal of existing law, and *that it is not interposed for any improper purpose, such as to harass or to cause unnecessary delay or needless increase*

---

22. Cal. Rules of Court 317. Summary judgment motions need to be filed 28 days before the hearing. Cal.Civ.Pro. § 437(c).

23. Cal. Rules of Court 203.

24. *Id.*

25. Model Code of Professional Responsibility DR 7–1–101(A)(1) (1989).

26. Herr, Haydock, and Stempel, *supra* note 8, at 145.

27. *Id.* at 35.

28. Fed.R.Civ.P. 11.

in the cost of litigation. If a pleading, motion, or other paper is not signed, it shall be stricken unless it is signed promptly after the omission is called to the attention of the pleader or movant.[29]

By submitting motions to the court, you are certifying that you are bringing them for valid purposes. This rule attempts to prevent attorneys from interposing numerous motions whose main purpose is to harass or delay.[30] If you sign a pleading, motion, or paper violating this rule, then Rule 11 requires the court to impose sanctions, which may include the costs incurred by the other side due to the improper filing of the document.[31]

The Model Rules of Professional Conduct, passed by the American Bar Association in 1983, also address the ethical issues arising during motion practice.[32] The most pertinent of these are Rule 3.1, which requires you to bring only meritorious motions, and Rule 3.2, which requires you to expedite litigation to the extent consistent with your client's needs. These rules recognize that motion practice can be the major cost of litigating and encourage you to make only those motions that will ultimately minimize the time spent by you and the court.[33] Your roles as an advocate for your client and as an officer of the court require you to spend time judiciously in pursuing a lawsuit.

Spending your time judiciously also requires you to make strategic decisions so you do not file motions at random. At the beginning of the lawsuit, before filing your complaint or responding to it, establish your litigation strategy. Consider the motions needed to implement your strategy and file those. Then anticipate the motions your opponent may raise and prepare for those. Remember, however, that all the motions your opponent files may not require opposition. Some may even help you achieve your goals, so do not immediately challenge them just because your opponent has filed them.[34]

Throughout the lawsuit, you can use motions strategically to inform the judge about numerous aspects of the case, including your theories of the case. For example, bringing a motion to strike irrelevant portions of the complaint tells the judge what you think are the actual issues in the suit. Bringing a motion for a protective order tells the judge that your opponent has promulgated twice as many interrogatories as are permitted under the local rules.[35] Bringing a motion in limine explains why you believe a particular witness's testimony needs

---

29. *Id.*

30. While this was never acceptable practice, the rule amendment indicates that the federal court system will no longer ignore this problem. For a fuller discussion of Rule 11 and the controversy surrounding its amendment, *see*, note 46 in Chapter 11 on Pleadings.

31. Fed.R.Civ.P. 11.

32. Herr, Haydock and Stempel, *supra* note 8, at 148. Chapter 7 of Herr,

Haydock and Stempel discusses these ethical aspects in depth and is highly recommended to all attorneys starting or involved in motion practice.

33. California Points and Authorities, *supra* note 3, at § 1.02(1).

34. *Id.* at § 1.02(1).

35. See Chapter 13, Interrogatories, on local rules imposing numerical limits on interrogatory use.

to be restricted at trial. While you would not bring these or any other motions solely for educational purposes, the judge who resolves them will be more acquainted with the parties and attorneys in the pending suit than if he or she knew nothing more than what the pleadings stated. This increased knowledge about the case can work in your favor because informing the judge about your case may help you reach the result your client desires, especially if you are raising novel theories or require unusual evidentiary proceedings.[36] On the other hand, the judge who must find time to hear and decide your motions will be unfavorably disposed toward you if your motions are questionable or frivolous. In summary, bring motions that will further your client's case and will educate the judge along the way. But avoid having the judge throw his or her hands up in dismay when yet another time-consuming motion related to your lawsuit crosses his or her desk.

Additionally, the rules controlling motion practice will help you to use motions strategically to preserve your client's procedural rights.[37] For example, Rule 35 requires a motion for good cause before the court can order an examination of a party whose physical or mental condition is in controversy.[38] Rule 50 requires that a motion for directed verdict be made at the close of the opponent's case in order to bring motion for judgment notwithstanding the verdict.[39] Rule 51 requires a motion to the court to request particular jury instructions and a motion objecting to the judge's instructions in order to appeal from those instructions.[40] Knowing the rules is vital to protecting your client's options and must remain an integral part of your long-range strategy.

Considering the ethical concerns of motion practice will lead you to use motions to protect your client but not to harass your opponent or delay the movement toward trial. Considering the strategic concerns of motions practice will lead you to plan your litigation strategy and use motions as an integral part of that strategy. Having mastered these rules governing the procedure, timing, ethics, and strategy of motion practice, you will be ready to draft your notices, motions, and orders.

DRAFTING THE DOCUMENTS FOR MOTION PRACTICE

There are five main documents in motion practice: notices of motion, motions, affidavits or declarations, briefs (or memoranda of points and authorities), and orders.[41] The three documents discussed in this chapter are notices of motion, motions, and orders.

36. For example, *see,* Elizabeth Schneider and Susan Jordan, *Representation of Women Who Defend Themselves in Response to Physical or Sexual Assault,* 4 Women's Rts.L.Rep. 149 (1978) where the authors discuss the importance of educating the judge and jury when raising "battered women's syndrome" as a defense in a murder trial.

37. Herr, Haydock, and Stempel, *supra* note 8, at 36.

38. Fed.R.Civ.P. 35.

39. Fed.R.Civ.P. 50.

40. Fed.R.Civ.P. 51.

41. Techniques for drafting memoranda of points and authorities or briefs are discussed in Chapter 10: Argument Sections

In drafting these documents, the primary writing techniques involve being clear and eliminating legalese. Remember that you want your motion to be granted and you want the judge to be kindly disposed toward doing so. Keep in mind the judge's heavy workload. Law and motion practice at the local courthouse often resembles a cattle call, with your motion placed on the judge's calendar along with all the others currently pending. He or she will be moving from one pressing matter to another, trying to keep an overburdened court system running as smoothly as possible, and will be reading your motion and supporting documents between attending to other matters. Therefore, you must do everything possible to help the judge understand your motion quickly so the relief you request will be granted.

Most documents for motion practice are rather short and straightforward and, unlike many of the other documents discussed in this book, they do not require a great deal of time to draft. But the judge will scrutinize your motion, so avoid making that scrutiny difficult. If you simply turn to in-house forms or to form books, the needed clarity will not be forthcoming because these sources frequently provide examples full of legalese and obtuse sentence structure. Instead of using them as they are, revise these forms to eliminate this legalese and clarify the sentence structure.

Many attorneys are hesitant to remove the legalese from these forms because they feel that the language is a magical "fairy dust." They are afraid that, by changing the language, they may eliminate some part of the document vital to its success. This belief simply underscores the problem with these forms: their meaning defies ready understanding.

Eliminating legalese and clarifying documents does not mean eliminating your use of forms. Re-inventing the wheel is not required. Redesigning is. Once these forms have been redrafted, you can use them repeatedly. Remember, however, to alter these forms to fit the particular facts of each case. For example, avoid filing a notice of motion that refers to a motion to dismiss and attaching to it a motion to strike irrelevant allegations from the complaint. The judge receiving these documents could not help but believe that you do not take your work seriously and that you are not precise in your document production. These assessments may lead the judge to look unfavorably on your motions.

Notices of Motion

The notice of motion informs your opponent that you are bringing a motion before the court to request particular relief. The notice

for Briefs. (Memoranda of points and authorities are the same as briefs and are actually persuasive documents despite their name.) Affidavits and declarations are sworn statements. The affidavit begins by stating "Wanda Witness, being sworn, states that . . ." Then you write out the statement, which is based on an interview with the witness. The witness signs at the bottom, swearing that the statement is true. The person witnessing the signature notarizes the statement.

indicates the time, date, place, substance of the motion, and supporting documents. Parts of the notice include the caption, the name and address of the recipient, the body of the notice, the date, and your signature.

The caption indicates the court in which the motion is being heard, the parties to the lawsuit, the case number and the name of the document. Altering the caption for each document to include the name of the document is central to the caption's usefulness and its role in increasing clarity for those reading it.

STATE OF KENTUCKY CIRCUIT COURT FAYETTE COUNTY

Branch 11

SUSAN G. BLACK and
DAVID R. BLACK,
                    Plaintiffs,
 	
             vs.
 	
STEWART PROPERTIES, INC.,
                    Defendant.
	NOTICE OF MOTION TO DISMISS AND MEMORANDUM OF POINTS AND AUTHORITIES IN SUPPORT
	
	Case No. 90 CV 10

Immediately following the caption, indicate the person to whom the notice is directed. If the opposing party does not have an attorney, then the notice should be directed to the party.

TO: Juanita P. Martinez

Williams, Fox, and Smith
110 Main Street
Lexington, KY 40501

You may want to eliminate this step altogether because most procedural rules require only that the summons needs to be directed to the party.[42] Including this information will clarify your documents, however, because it ensures that everyone reading the documents knows to whom the document is addressed.

The notice next indicates the time, date, place, and matter being brought before the court. This is the substance of your notice, so this should be where your language is as clear as possible. Yet this is the point where many attorneys resort to legalese. Rather than simply stating when the motion will be heard and the basis for the motion, they copy the archaic language from in-house forms or form books.

PLEASE TAKE NOTICE that upon the affidavit of _____, sworn to the _____ day of _____, 19__, a copy of which is hereto annexed, and upon the pleadings, papers and files herein, the affidavit of _____, sworn to on the _____ day of _____, 19__, and served herewith, the undersigned will move this Court at the courthouse at _____, on Tuesday, the _____ day of _____,

---

42. Irwin Alterman, *Plain and Accurate Style in Lawsuit Papers*, 2 Cooley L.Rev. 243, 288 (1984), citing F.R.C.P. 4(b) and M.C.R. 2.102(B).

19__, at the hour of _____ o'clock in the (fore)noon of said day or as soon thereafter as counsel can be heard for an order (requiring _____ etc.), on the ground that (state grounds upon which the motions will be made) and for such other and further relief as to the Court may seem just and proper and for costs of this motion.

Numerous problems exist with this form. First, the purpose of the motion is stated at the end of the form after the time, place, and day of the hearing and the time, place, and date of the supporting affidavits. Placing this information before the main purpose makes the motion difficult to read. Second, including the date the affidavits were made is unnecessary. The judge can easily determine those dates, if important, by looking at the affidavits.

Rather than simply copying this form, it could be rewritten to be clear and concise.

PLEASE TAKE NOTICE that plaintiff's counsel will make a motion to the Court for _____ on the ground that (state grounds with particularity) [43] **and for any other relief that the Court may find appropriate.**

The hearing will be held on (month) (day) (year) at the courthouse (judge's chambers) at (time) or as soon as the matter can be heard. The motion will be based on the pleadings, papers and files of the case and on the affidavits of _____ and _____ which are attached to this Notice.

Even the conventional "PLEASE TAKE NOTICE" language is unnecessary. The caption states that it is a notice of motion. This language is not a required part of the document. It would be just as valid, and shorter, to state "Plaintiff's counsel will make a motion to the Court" or "Plaintiff's counsel will move the Court." Either introduction helps clarify your documents and creates a form that you can use repeatedly.

It may be unnecessary to indicate where the motion will be heard, as noted above. While this is sometimes important in urban areas where more than one courthouse is used, some commentators believe that including this information is superfluous because both the judge and opposing counsel are well aware of the location of the judge's chambers.[44] It may be helpful, however, to indicate whether the motion will be heard in the judge's chambers or the courtroom, if you are given this information. It may also be useful to indicate the place where the hearing will be held if your court has a rotating law and motion calendar, in which motions are made to judges who may not have ultimate control of the case.

---

43. Fed.R.Civ.P. 7(b)(1) states that all motions shall state the grounds for them with particularity.

44. "If the other parties don't know where the courthouse is, they are in real trouble." Alterman, *supra* note 42, at 289.

It may also be unnecessary to state on which documents the motion is based. This will depend on the specificity you desire. If you want the court and opposing counsel to know that the motion is based on the pleadings and on attached or already filed affidavits, clarify that point by so stating in your notice or motion. Consider eliminating it, however, if you are simply going to use the generic language, "This motion is based on the record and files herein." Everything a court does will be based on those documents;[45] including the information does nothing more than require additional time to read.[46] In developing your forms, consider these options and decide which you prefer. You may also decide to develop different forms, some with the language and some without it, so you can simply select the appropriate form for each case.

Some notices include more legalese than clear language. For example, the following "Notice of Motion to Set for Trial" is twice as long as it needs to be.

_____, and _____, HIS ATTORNEY ARE HEREBY NOTIFIED THAT:

On _____, 19__, plaintiff will move the above-entitled court in department (division) _____ thereof, located at _____, City of _____, Michigan, at __M., to set the above-entitled action for trial on the ground(s) that said action is at issue, and (any further grounds). Said motion will be based upon the files and records of said case.

DATED: _____, 19__.

This notice could be revised to simplify its language and save time whenever it is used.

On _____, 19__, at (time), plaintiff will move the Court to set this action for trial because issues of fact exist.

As this revision shows, the motion can be clearer and easier to read if the unnecessary language in the original is eliminated.

In some jurisdictions, the notice of motion not only provides notice but also takes the place of a separate document entitled "Motion." Under the federal rules and many state rules, a specific document entitled "Motion" is not necessary.[47] Check the rules of your jurisdiction to determine whether a separate document is required or whether the motion can be part of the notice of motion.

---

45. *Id.* at 287.

46. However, some jurisdictions may require you to state the documents on which your motion is based. For example, N.Y. Civ.Proc.Law and Rules § 2214 (McKinney 1974) states that the notice of motion must specify the supporting papers upon which the motion is based. It is questionable, however, whether the language "this motion is based on the record and files herein" gives the court any information at all.

If you are in a jurisdiction that requires that the supporting documents be indicated, list them specifically, instead of using this general language.

47. Fed.R.Civ.P. 7(b)(1) states that "[t]he requirement of writing is fulfilled if the motion is stated in a written notice of the hearing of the motion." Many states also permit this practice. For example, *see* Minn.R.Civ.P. 7.02(a); Fla.R.Civ.P. 1.100(b); Colo.R.Civ.P. 7(b)(1).

We encourage you to separate the motion from the notice of motion because it streamlines both documents. Including all of necessary information in the notice of motion may force you to try to do too much at once. Besides providing notice and the date, time, and place of the hearing, you must also include the motion requested, the grounds for the request, and the relief desired. You need to be especially careful to state the grounds for your request as specifically as possible because the notice will be the only document received by the judge and opposing counsel. The next section provides more information on drafting this part of your document.

When revising your forms, consider the judge who is receiving numerous motions every day. Given the choice of using language that will be easy to read and understand or language that will be difficult to read and hard to understand, the choice is obvious. Nevertheless, you must make that choice by taking the time to review your forms and clarify the language you use. The judge has significant discretion in whether to grant your motion and, because many of these are interlocutory matters, you probably cannot appeal his or her decision.[48] When taking the time to draft the notice, motion and supporting documents, also take the time to revise the language.

Motions

The motion is the document that actually requests the particular relief from the judge. Under the federal rules, the motion should be made in writing, state the grounds with particularity, and state the relief or order requested.[49] Even if you practice in a jurisdiction that allows you to combine your notice of motion and motion and if you decide to combine these documents, you must still fulfill the requirements of the rules governing motions. Thus, within your notice of motion, you would also state the particular grounds forming the basis for the motion and the relief requested.

If you do not state the grounds for your motion, the court may deny your motion simply because no basis for its granting exists on the face of the document. Some states also require that a Memorandum of Points and Authorities accompany all motions.[50] If your jurisdiction does not require this support, you must decide whether to attach it. While doing so will increase the time necessary to pursue the motion, there is no point in pursuing the motion without the support needed to succeed.[51]

Your motion should be simple and straightforward. Remove legalese and clearly state why you are bringing the motion and what

---

48. Jack Friedenthal, Mary Kay Kane and Arthur Miller, *Civil Procedure* § 13.1 (1985).

49. Fed.R.Civ.P. 7(b)(1)

50. For example, Cal. Rules of Court 313(a) requires a memorandum of points

and authorities with all motions, and motions missing these documents may be dismissed by the court as not meritorious.

51. Chapter 10 discusses the drafting concerns for writing briefs or memoranda of points and authorities.

relief you are requesting. Do not allow your language to obscure the purpose of the motion, as the following example does.

> Defendant moves the Court to stay the taking of the deposition of (witness), by plaintiff, pursuant to the notice served on defendant by plaintiff on the _____ day of _____, 19__, until _____, on the ground that examination of the witness has already been commenced and is now proceeding in an action pending in the _____ Court of the State of _____, entitled _____ vs. _____, which action involves the same issues as are involved in this action, as more particularly appears from the affidavit of _____, attached hereto, which defendant is informed and believes will come on for trial before the trial in this action, and the judgment in which will be dispositive of the issues in this action; defendant intends to move for summary judgment on the ground of _____ which if granted will make it unnecessary to take the deposition referred to herein.

This motion would be clarified by rewriting.

> **Defendant moves the court to stay the deposition of (witness) by plaintiff because the witness has been deposed in an action pending in the _____ Court of the State of _____, entitled _____ vs. _____, which involves the same issues that are involved in this action. The attached affidavit of _____ supports this motion.**

> **Defendant believes that action will be resolved before trial in this lawsuit and that it will dispose of all issues in this action. Defendant will then move for summary judgment on the ground of _____ which, if granted will make (witness') deposition unnecessary.**

Even motions that are not full of legalese can be difficult to read or unnecessarily lengthy.

> _____ (Name), plaintiff (or defendant) in the above-entitled cause, respectfully moves that this court grant a continuance of the cause, which was originally set for trial on _____, 19__. The ground for this motion is that _____ (state specifically ground on which continuance requested).

> This motion is based on records and files in this cause, including notice of motion and appended affidavit, the latter papers dated _____, 19__.

This motion can be shortened and made more direct with some simple revisions.

> **Plaintiff (or defendant) requests this court to grant a continuance in this matter, which was set for trial on _____, 19__ because (state specifically ground for continuance).**

> **This motion is based on the documents in this case, including the affidavit of _____, which is attached.**

Taking time to rewrite these motions will clarify them for the court and will increase the chances that the judge will understand what you are requesting. Additionally, your new forms will provide this same advantage in the future.

Orders

The requirements for an order vary with each judge in every court and with the statutes on which the order is based. Most orders, however, contain the following sections: (1) the caption, (2) the preamble (what happened up to this point that justifies the order), (3) the order (the action the court will take), (4) the date of the order, and (5) the signature of the judge or clerk issuing the order. Depending on the order being made, findings of fact and conclusions of law may or may not be necessary.

The caption should clearly state that this document is the judge's order. Following the caption is the preamble, which is the first portion of most orders that sinks into the morass of legalese. Most forms recite everything that has preceded the motion in one long unintelligible sentence.

> Defendant's motion for an order setting aside the default judgment heretofore entered herein came on for hearing before me this (date), (name) appearing as attorney for plaintiff and (name) appearing as attorney for defendant, and the Court being fully advised in the premises, and good cause appearing therefor, and it satisfactorily appearing from the declarations and proposed Answer on file herein that the said default judgment was rendered against said defendant by reason of his (mistake, etc.) and it further appearing that said defendant has a valid defense to the action upon the merits;

As the semicolon indicates, this morass continues into the order portion. Most attorneys draft the preamble as though it were the introductory phrase of a sentence whose main subject and verb do not occur until the order section. Treating the preamble as a phrase leaves it with little coherence because it includes no subjects and verbs of its own. Additionally, the preamble itself refers to several different subjects, each one properly the basis for a sentence. The preamble should be rewritten for clarity.

> **Defendant moved this Court for an order setting aside the default judgment entered in this action. [Name] appeared for plaintiff and [name] appeared for defendant. Based on the arguments of the parties and the documents filed in support of the motion, this Court finds good cause to grant defendant's motion because of his [her] [mistake, etc.] and his [her] valid defense on the merits.**

This revision makes it much easier to determine what occurred in the case before the motion and states the basis for the order.

The next section of the order is the portion that actually orders the relief requested or some other action the judge deems appropriate. In addition to structural problems, the problem of legalese reoccurs.

IT IS HEREBY ORDERED that the judgment heretofore entered in this action against the said defendant (name) and in favor of the said plaintiff (name), in the sum of (amount) [or otherwise, according to the facts], said judgment having been entered in book _____ at page _____ on (date) is hereby vacated and set aside and defendant is permitted _____ days within which to plead or to file the answer accompanying his notice of motion.

This order could be improved by excluding the legalese and unnecessary information.

IT IS ORDERED that the judgment entered in this action against defendant for (state amount of judgment), which was entered in book _____ at page _____ on (date) is vacated. Defendant is given _____ days to plead or file the answer accompanying his notice of motion.

Many states require the moving party to draft the order resulting from the motion. While most judges are too burdened to spend time cleaning up your orders, you can be assured that they sign them with a certain distaste when they contain legalese and redundancies. Try to draft your motions so the judge will be comfortable signing his or her name.

CONCLUSION

Redrafting all these documents so they are simple and direct will make them seem like a fresh breeze when read by the judge. Most judges read impenetrable prose hour after hour, day after day. Add to that the fact that many motions can go either way on the law, and the advantage of clear motions becomes apparent. The judge may gain a favorable estimation of you based on your notices, motions, and orders, and may believe that anyone who attends to detail enough to rewrite forms to make them clear and effective will not be one to waste the court's time with meaningless motions. Take the time to help the judge form such an impression of you.

EXERCISE 1

Review the four following documents. Revise them to eliminate legalese and obtuse sentence structure.

Document 1

STATE OF WISCONSIN   CIRCUIT COURT   DANE COUNTY
                             Branch 9

SUSAN T. BROWN and
DAVID E. BROWN,

                    Plaintiffs,   ORDER DISMISSING ACTION

          vs.   Case No. 82 CV 423

FLAMBEAU PROPERTIES, INC.,
                Defendant.

Defendant having filed Motion to Dismiss plaintiffs' complaint, including both causes of action, on the grounds that each fails to state a claim upon which relief may be granted and having come on for oral argument, attorneys for plaintiffs and defendant participating in the same, and the parties having filed briefs, and the court having considered the same and the court rendering its ruling on Motion to Dismiss granting said Motion in decision dated August 25, 1982, made a part hereof by reference.

IT IS HEREBY ORDERED that plaintiffs' complaint and all causes of action arising thereunder being the same are hereby dismissed against defendant on the merits with cost.

Dated this 15th day of September, 1982.

BY THE COURT:

_____

ANDREA A. CONNOR, JUDGE

Document 2

STATE OF WISCONSIN   CIRCUIT COURT   DANE COUNTY
                             Branch 9

SUSAN T. BROWN and
DAVID E. BROWN,

                    Plaintiffs,   MOTION TO DISMISS

          vs.   Case No. 82 CV 423

FLAMBEAU PROPERTIES, INC.,
                Defendant.

Defendant by its attorney, Ellen C. Farrell, and pursuant to Wisconsin Rules of Civil Procedure 802.06(2) hereby moves the court to dismiss the complaint herein, including causes of action of each plaintiff, individually or derivative on the grounds that the complaint and causes of action of each plaintiff fails to state a claim upon which relief can be granted.

Dated this 17th day of February, 1982.

> Ellen C. Farrell
> Attorney for the Defendant
> 25 West Carroll Street
> Madison, Wisconsin 53701
> Phone: 608–959–2727

Document 3

STATE OF WISCONSIN CIRCUIT COURT MILWAUKEE COUNTY

STATE OF WISCONSIN,
                    Plaintiff

          v.   Case No. _____

MR. X,
                    Defendant.

NOTICE OF MOTION

TO: E. MICHAEL McCANN, Esq.

    District Attorney

    Safety Building

    Milwaukee, Wisconsin

PLEASE TAKE NOTICE that on the 7th day of November 1980, at 9:30 o'clock in the fore noon, or as soon thereafter as counsel may be heard, the undersigned will bring on for hearing before the Honorable Circuit Judge, in his courtroom, a Motion to Modify Sentence a true copy of which is annexed hereto.

Dated at Milwaukee, Wisconsin, this 29th day of October, 1980.

> Respectfully submitted,

> MR. X
> Defendant

> BY:

Document 4

STATE OF WISCONSIN CIRCUIT COURT MILWAUKEE COUNTY

STATE OF WISCONSIN,
                  Plaintiff,

       v.   Case No. _____

MR. X,
                  Defendant.

MOTION TO REDUCE AND/OR MODIFY SENTENCE

Now comes the defendant in the above-entitled action, by his attorneys, and, upon all the files, records and proceedings heretofore had herein, respectfully moves this court for the entry of an order reducing and/or modifying the sentence previously imposed in the above-entitled action.

The defendant respectfully requests that the court set this matter down for an evidentiary hearing so that he may elicit testimony and evidence in support of this motion.

Dated at Milwaukee, Wisconsin, this 23rd day of October, 1980.

                  Respectfully submitted,

                  MR. X
                  Defendant

                  BY:

                  _____
                  Attorney for Defendant

EXERCISE 2

Review the following document, which is a Motion for Production of Evidence and Suppression. As the defense attorney, write the Order you want the court to make if it decides the Motion in your favor.

STATE OF WISCONSIN   CIRCUIT COURT   DANE COUNTY

CITY OF MADISON,
                  Plaintiff,   MOTION FOR PRODUCTION OF
                            EVIDENCE AND SUPPRESSION
       v.
JOHN L. WALL,   Case No. 81–TR–4079 OMVWI
                  Defendant.

Defendant, by his attorney Thomas R. Jones, moves the Court:

1. For an order requiring the City of Madison to produce the ampoule used in the breathalyzer test of the defendant taken on

November 30, 1981. Defendant needs the ampoule so that he can have it analyzed by an expert of his choosing.

2. For an order requiring the City of Madison to produce all breathalyzer test results, readings, reports, and other documents relating to the administration of a breathalyzer test to the defendant on November 30, 1981.

3. For an order suppressing any and all statements or other activities of the defendant after the time he was stopped by the police officers on November 30, 1981, because the defendant was not properly informed of his rights and was not allowed to contact his attorney.

Dated this 31st day of December, 1981.

Thomas R. Jones
Attorney for Defendant
919 Monona Avenue, Suite 520
Madison, WI 53703
(608) 255-1111

EXERCISE 3

Review the following document, which is an Order correcting an inmate's prison sentence by making it concurrent with a previous sentence. Write the Motion and the Notice of Motion based on the Order. Below is background information, some of which you may want to include in the Motion.

You are a staff attorney for the Legal Assistance to Institutionalized Persons Program. One of your clients is Roger E. Clark. On February 18, 1986, Clark was convicted of three counts of armed robbery. Clark was sentenced to eight years in prison. On March 22, 1986, Clark was convicted of one count of battery to a peace officer. The judge imposed a sentence of eighteen months in prison and ordered that the eighteen-month sentence be served consecutively to the eight-year sentence. Between the sentencings on February 18 and March 22, Clark was confined in the Marinette County Jail. Clark was not moved to the Green Bay Correctional Institution until after the sentencing on March 22. According to Wis.Stats. sec. 973.15(1) (1987–1988), in order for a later sentence to be made consecutive to an earlier sentence, the defendant must be serving time for the earlier sentence when the later sentence is imposed. Under the statute, a defendant is not serving time for an earlier sentence until he is actually in prison. Time spent in the county jail is not counted as serving time in prison. Under the statute, the court did not have authority to make Clark's eighteen-month sentence consecutive to his eight-year sentence. The second sentence should not have been consecutive because Clark was in the county jail and not actually in prison when the second sentence was imposed. If the sentences are made concurrent, Clark will immediately be eligible for parole.

STATE OF WISCONSIN CIRCUIT COURT MARINETTE COUNTY

STATE OF WISCONSIN,
     Plaintiff,

   v.   Case No. A–6925

ROGER E. JAKES,
     Defendant.

ORDER

Upon motion of the defendant to correct his sentence by making it concurrent, and upon the stipulation that has subsequently been filed with the court, and in consideration of all of the records, files, and proceedings in this matter,

IT IS ORDERED THAT the consecutive sentence of eighteen months previously imposed on the defendant be corrected and modified to a concurrent sentence of eighteen months, retroactive to March 22, 1976, the original sentencing date.

IT IS FURTHER ORDERED that the written judgment of conviction be so amended.

IT IS FURTHER ORDERED that duplicate originals of certified copies of this Order and the Amended Judgment of Conviction be immediately forwarded by the clerk of courts to Mr. John Thomas, Registrar, Green Bay Correctional Institution, Box WR, Green Bay, Wisconsin 54305.

Dated this _____ day of _____, 1982.

          The Honorable Charles K. Morgan
          Circuit Court Judge

ASSIGNMENT 1

You are the attorney for Doug Bentley and his aunt and uncle, Catherine and Mike Kelly, who are the defendants named in Susan Ashland's complaint. The facts and law controlling her case are provided in Assignment 2 in Chapter 6. Prepare a notice of motion, motion to dismiss, and order granting the motion. Check your jurisdiction's rules for any requirements concerning the caption and organization of these documents. Using those rules, write these documents. Remember that you need to provide the basis for the motion, so read the cases and make your statement in the motion conform with them.

ASSIGNMENT 2

You are the attorneys for the defendants in the *Jones* case. The facts and law controlling the case are provided in Assignment 2 for Chapter 8, Persuasive Facts. Prepare a notice of motion, motion to dismiss, and order granting the motion. Check your jurisdiction's rules for any requirements concerning the caption and organization of these documents. Using those rules, write these documents. Remember that you need to provide the basis for the motion, so read the cases and make your statement in the motion conform with them.

Bibliography

Alterman, Irwin, *Plain and Accurate Style in Lawsuit Papers,* 2 Cooley L.Rev. 243 (1984).

Bender, Matthew, *California Forms of Pleadings and Practice.* New York: Times Mirror Books, 1990.

Bender, Matthew, *California Points and Authorities.* New York: Times Mirror Books, 1990.

California Continuing Education of the Bar, *Practice Under the New Uniform Law and Motion Rules,* 1984.

Fidel, Noel, *Some Do's and Don'ts of Motion Writing,* 19 Az.Bar J. 8 (August 1983).

Friedenthal, Jack H., Mary Kay Kane, and Arthur R. Miller, *Civil Procedure.* St. Paul: West Publishing Co., 1985.

Herr, David F., Roger S. Haydock, and Jeffrey Stempel, *Motion Practice.* Boston: Little, Brown and Co., 1985.

Lankford, Jefferson L., *How to Write and Argue Motions,* 25 Az.Atty. 24 (March 1989).

Owens, William Brownlee, *California Forms and Procedure.* Los Angeles: Parker & Son Publications, Inc., 1990.

Rombauer, Marjorie D., *Legal Problem Solving: Analysis, Research and Writing.* St. Paul: West Publishing Co., 4th ed. 1983.

Schneider, Elizabeth M. and Susan B. Jordon, *Representation of Women Who Defend Themselves in Response to Physical or Sexual Assault,* 4 Women's Rts.L.Rep. 149 (1978).

Spellman, Howard Hilton, *Motions During Trial.* Englewood Cliffs, NJ: Prentice–Hall, Inc., 1960.

Chapter 13

INTERROGATORIES

Rule 33 of the Federal Rules of Civil Procedure and corresponding state rules have added the word "interrogatory" to the daily life of practicing attorneys.[1] This word sometimes seems to describe a creature from a horror movie, complete with fangs and claws, threatening to destroy the life of the attorney who receives a huge packet of extremely broad interrogatories intended to bury him or her in a mountain of paperwork.[2] As reforms begin to control the use and number of interrogatories in lawsuits, however, attorneys are shrinking back in horror less when the package of interrogatories arrives. These reforms have begun to affect interrogatory practice by limiting the number of interrogatories that may be propounded and by altering the way interrogatories are drafted. Part of what led to the overuse, and what some would call abuse, of interrogatories is that they can be an extremely useful discovery device when used correctly and with forethought.

Rather than beating one's opponent into submission, or worse, imbuing him or her with a desire to respond in kind, a well-drafted set of interrogatories provides information needed for case development, helps the parties accurately consider the value of their case to facilitate settlement, and even helps you to learn your opponent's factual and legal basis for each cause of action or defense.

There are three steps to drafting interrogatories effectively. First, research the rules controlling this form of discovery in your jurisdiction generally and the law controlling the particular causes of actions and

---

1. For example, California Code of Civil Procedure sec. 2030(a) tracks Rule 33. In many other aspects, however, other California rules differ substantially from the federal rules. For this reason, the California rules are being used to show differences in interrogatory practice throughout this chapter. For a comparison of state rules with Rule 33, *see,* 11 *Bender's Forms of Discovery* App. B–73 to B–81. Besides California, the following states also differ substantially from the federal rule: Alaska, Connecticut, Idaho, Illinois, Iowa, Maryland, Michigan, Nevada, New Hampshire, New York, North Dakota, Pennsylvania, Rhode Island, South Carolina, and Texas. For a copy of those state rules, *see, id.* at App. C–1 to C–189.

2. Jacob A. Stein explains that the early interrogatory framers of the 1950s had three objectives: "(1) terrorize the [respondent] into dismissing the suit or settling under panic conditions; (2) request so much detail that it could never be assembled; and (3) obtain relevant information." Jacob A. Stein, *The Discovers,* 15 Litigation 46, 46 (Fall 1988).

defenses in your lawsuit. To draft interrogatories effectively, you need to understand the information required to win your case. Second, determine how interrogatories will fit into your overall discovery plan and when using depositions will allow you to obtain information more efficiently. Third, ask precise questions that clearly request the needed information. In this way, you will be doing everything possible to ensure the best use of this discovery device for your client.

RESEARCH THE RULES AND THE LAW

This step has two stages: researching the procedural rules that control interrogatory use and researching the law that controls the causes of action, counterclaims, and defenses at issue in the lawsuit. Complete this research before considering how to use interrogatories within your overall discovery plan and how to draft your questions. Once you have become familiar with the rules governing interrogatory use, you will not have to repeat this aspect of research.

Researching Procedural Rules

Start by reviewing federal, state, and local court rules controlling interrogatory practice in your jurisdiction. If you have a federal action, Rule 33 of the Federal Rules of Civil Procedure will be controlling. If you have a state action, find the corresponding rule in your state.[3] These federal and state rules specify how interrogatories are to be used and explain their function. They detail, among other things, that only parties and not witnesses can be required to answer interrogatories[4] and that the party served must answer them.[5] Additionally, the rules state that the answer to each interrogatory must be separate, written, given under oath,[6] responsive, and complete, not evasive.[7]

These rules created and defined interrogatory practice, but they do not impose any limits on the number of interrogatories propounded.[8] This lack of restrictions led many attorneys to propound huge numbers of interrogatories, which have been challenged. For example, an Illinois court held that 209 interrogatories with 432 separate questions were oppressive and burdensome.[9] Even more extreme was a Califor-

---

3. For example, in California, the corresponding rule is Cal.Civ.Pro. § 2030 and in Wisconsin, it is Wis.Stat. sec. 804.08. For a list of interrogatory rules for all the states, *see,* Bender's, *supra* note 1, at App. B–1 to B–81.

4. Fed.R.Civ.Pro. 33(b). Interrogatories may be served on third party defendants even though no issues between those parties are disclosed by the pleadings but may not be addressed to a party's attorney.

5. Fed.R.Civ.P. 33(a).

6. *Id.*

7. *Pilling v. General Motors Corp.,* 45 F.R.D. 366 (D.Utah 1968).

8. For example, Rule 33 itself does not impose restrictions on the number of interrogatories that may be used, although Rule 26(c) permits the court managing the discovery process to protect a party from "annoyance, embarrassment, oppression, or undue burden or expense." When faced with an objection that interrogatories are burdensome or oppressive, courts consider whether the information sought is relevant and frequently weigh the burden on the interrogated party against the benefit to be received by the propounding party. *Pilling v. General Motors Corp.,* 45 F.R.D. 366 (D.Utah 1968).

9. *Broyden v. Tronken,* 60 F.R.D. 625, 626 (N.D.Ill.1973) *See also, Zenith Radio*

nia case with 2,736 questions and subparts spread over 381 pages.[10] But challenging interrogatories under the federal rules requires going to court, an expense that undermines the inexpensive nature of interrogatories.[11]

Because of lawyers' tendency to burden opposing parties with numerous interrogatories and the inadequacy of Rule 26 to resolve this problem, many courts have imposed numerical restrictions on interrogatories through local court rules.[12] These rules mean attorneys no longer enjoy wide-open interrogatory practice. This change requires you to do more research before starting to draft and to modify the drafting process.

For the most part, the limits range from twenty to fifty, with thirty being the most common.[13] In drafting your interrogatories, determine how these rules affect your practice in order to obtain the fullest use of this discovery device. For example, some jurisdictions exempt certain questions from counting toward the limit [14] or state that some interrogatories will be counted as only one question.[15] More interrogatories can be used when the parties stipulate to do so or when leave of the court is obtained.[16]

When drafting your interrogatories, you will also need to determine how those limits are applied in practice. For example, one study indicated that limits are commonly exceeded and often without a

Corp. v. Radio Corp. of America, 106 F.Supp. 561 (D.Del.1952), where the court found that 166 pages of interrogatories with 419 questions containing 1185 subparts would expand the case to require an amount of oppressive detail that courts should not allow, despite the fact that propounding counsel asked them in good faith.

10. *In re U.S. Financial Securities Litigation,* 74 F.R.D. 497 (S.D.Cal.1975). The court struck the interrogatories, sua sponte, after determining that effective discovery could be accomplished with significantly less detail.

11. Fed.R.Civ.P. 26(c).

12. Over forty federal district courts have imposed limits on the number of interrogatories that may be sent to opposing counsel. *See,* 1 Bender's *supra* note 1, at Appendix B for the text of these district court local rules. About one-third of the states have also passed rules limiting the number of interrogatories used. Bender's, *supra* note 1, at § 3.03(3).

13. *See,* John Shapard & Carroll Seron, *Attorneys' Views of Local Rules Limiting Interrogatories* 5–6 (Federal Judicial Center Staff Paper 1986). In the survey conducted by the Federal Judicial Center, forty-five percent of respondents opposed a federal rule change imposing numerical limits (although they continued to support

local rule limitations) while forty percent did support a federal rule limitation and ten percent opposed both federal rule and local rule limitations. Federal Judicial Center Staff Paper at v–vi.

14. For example, Kentucky excludes interrogatories asking the name and address of the person answering or of witnesses or whether the party will voluntarily supplement responses from being counted in the total. Bender's, *supra* note 1, at § 3.03 n. 59.

15. Examples include Oklahoma and West Virginia, which count an answer on the existence, location and custody of documents and physical evidence to only count as one interrogatory. Bender's, *supra* note 1, at § 3.03 n. 58 (pg. 3–26).

16. Bender's, *supra* note 1, at § 3.03. Leave of the court is not necessarily given freely. One court required that when counsel wanted to serve more than 20 interrogatories, he or she had to draft the set of interrogatories, arrange a prefiling conference with opposing counsel to allow the counsel to review the set, explain why more than 20 interrogatories were needed, and determine whether opposing counsel agreed to the number. *Crown Center Redevelopment Corp v. Westinghouse Electric Corp.,* 82 F.R.D. 108 (W.D.Mo.1979).

request for waiver of the limitation.[17] In fact, only twenty percent of the attorneys who exceeded the limitation sought court permission to do so and only one of the districts studied prohibited waiver of the numerical limits.[18] The study concluded that "[i]f the local rules limiting interrogatories do have an effect, it may be simply that of deterring excesses without significantly affecting the use of interrogatories for proper purposes."[19] Thus, if your jurisdiction has rules limiting the number of interrogatories, you may find that, in practice, these limits are not as harsh as the rules indicate. Part of your research may include talking to other attorneys in your jurisdiction to determine how strictly these rules will be enforced. Rather than ignoring the rules, try to establish a practice of asking for, and granting in return, stipulations to exceed the limits when doing so will promote the proper use of this inexpensive discovery device.

These numerical limits have spawned many additional questions. One of these is exactly what is one interrogatory. Does each numbered interrogatory count as one, regardless of the number of separate subparts, or does each subpart count as an interrogatory even though by itself it may not ask for more than a small piece of information? The local rules often impose other restrictions, such as specifying the format for the preface or restricting how defined terms must be indicated within the interrogatories.[20] For example, one California rule limits attorneys' drafting flexibility by requiring that "[e]ach interrogatory shall be full and complete in and of itself" and "[n]o specially prepared interrogatory shall contain subparts, or a compound, conjunctive, or disjunctive question."[21]

These local rule limitations may force you to draft interrogatories that violate some of the drafting suggestions given below. For example, we encourage you to use subparts to clarify the information you are requesting, writing branching interrogatories. If, however, each branch is counted as a separate question, you may have to use longer, less precise questions. Nevertheless, consider the suggestions given below and try to draft interrogatories that are as clear as possible, given the rule limitations.[22]

---

17. Shapard and Seron, *supra* note 13, at 20 n. 9.

18. *Id.* at 20.

19. *Id.*

20. Cal.Civ.Code § 2030(c)5.

21. Cal.Civ.Code § 2030(c)(5). This requirement has not been judicially interpreted but it seems to require either that each interrogatory be only one question or that each interrogatory not contain "and" or "or". Bernard E. Le Sage & Steven E. Smith, "Summary of Statutory and Case Law Relating to the Enforcement of Discovery" in *Compelling, Opposing, and Enforcing Discovery in State Court* 5 (Cal.C.E. B. April 1988). California limits the number of specially prepared interrogatories for particular litigation to 35 but does allow unlimited use of uniform interrogatories developed by the California Judicial Conference. Bender's, *supra* note 1, at § 3.03 n. 61.

22. But many attorneys believe that these requirements impair the attorney who has carefully drafted his or her interrogatories. "The limitation on the number of interrogatories penalizes counsel who draft questions carefully and so reveal clearly each discrete subpart. The limitations thus encourage lengthy, difficult-to-answer questions." Shepard and Seron, *supra* note 13, at 21.

Researching the Substantive Law

One useful way to handle these restrictions is to pinpoint the information you need by understanding the requirements of the relevant substantive law. You must research the causes of action and defenses at issue in the lawsuit to determine what information you need to pursue the lawsuit successfully. If you are the plaintiff's attorney and propound the interrogatories with the complaint, your research for drafting the complaint will also control your interrogatories.[23] If you propound the interrogatories after you receive your opponent's answer, you must also research any defenses or counterclaims raised in the answer. This research is required because, in order to prevail in court or during settlement negotiations, you must provide the factual information establishing each element of your client's causes of action. Thus, you must know the elements of the causes of action and defenses to use interrogatories to locate gaps or inconsistencies in your information.

You can also use interrogatories to obtain your opponent's opinions and contentions, which may form an important part of the lawsuit. One common example is, "Do you contend that plaintiff was contributorily negligent regarding the accident on August 6, 1980?"[24] Asking for these contentions, which apply law to fact, is specifically allowed under Rule 33(b).[25] In contrast, interrogatories seeking purely legal conclusions are prohibited.[26] Thus, asking "Was defendant negligent regarding the accident on August 6, 1980?" would be improper. When questions arise concerning whether a particular interrogatory applies law to fact or asks for a legal conclusion, the courts resolve these questions case by case.[27]

In addition to asking contention interrogatories, you can ask for a list of all statutes, codes, and regulations that your client has allegedly breached.[28] This information will enable you to determine the basis for the complaint or counterclaim against your client without asking for your opponent's legal conclusions. Be careful to leave this question open-ended, or you may suggest another legal basis for your opponent's claims against your client.[29]

23. *See* Chapter 11, which discusses drafting complaints.

24. Roger Haydock and David Herr, *Interrogatories: Questions and Answers,* 1 Rev. of Litigation 263, 283 n. 89 (1981).

25. This rule states that "an interrogatory otherwise proper is not necessarily objectionable merely because an answer to the interrogatory involves an opinion or contention that relates to fact or the application of law to fact, but the court may order that such an interrogatory need not be answered until after designated discovery has been completed or until a pre-trial conference or other later time." Fed.R. Civ.P. 33(b).

26. Fed.R.Civ.P. 33(b).

27. Haydock and Herr, *supra* note 24, at 284, and the cases cited therein. Oftentimes, courts will postpone answers to these questions until much or all of the discovery process has been completed or until the pre-trial conference if the judge needs to resolve whether the question is objectionable. Therefore, while you may ask contention questions, you may not receive any answers until late in the discovery process.

28. Fred Setterberg, *The Artful Question,* 6 Cal.Law. 45, 46 (Feb. 1986).

29. *Id.*

Once you have completed this introductory research, consider how and when to use interrogatories. The information you need will be clearer and your questions more focused if you take time to determine their place in your overall discovery plan.

LOCATION WITHIN DISCOVERY PLAN

The interrogatories you prepare and when you propound them will depend on your overall discovery plan; your use of them will vary as their function varies. Use interrogatories instead of depositions when possible, because interrogatories are less expensive. Even if you cannot completely replace depositions, you can use interrogatories first to speed the discovery process and ultimately to save your client money.

When using interrogatories in conjunction with depositions, ask questions other than those simply intended to fill gaps in your information. Also ask questions that help you determine whom to depose. For example, you might ask:

Name the person responsible for implementing the contract with plaintiff and his or her supervisors to the level of vice-president.

Alternatively, you may want to take depositions before sending interrogatories because depositions require the party to speak directly, not through an attorney, and thus you can catch the other side unprepared for particular questions.[30] Interrogatories can then be used to clear up items not fully answered at deposition.[31] With strict restrictions on the number of interrogatories available, using them for clarification after deposition may soon become their primary purpose.

The timing of interrogatories also depends on your overall discovery plan. Use interrogatories early in the process when you want to force opposing counsel to investigate and obtain information while the information is fresh in the witnesses' minds.[32] Otherwise, wait until you have enough information to ask the precise questions that will force your opponent to answer specific factual contentions.[33]

Additionally, the usefulness of interrogatories often depends on the kind of information you need. For example, interrogatories are a useful first step in discovering whether your opponent has retained expert witnesses,[34] and most courts require that interrogatories be used to initiate the process of deposing an expert witness.[35] Although interrogatories will not be particularly helpful for exploring the details of an expert's opinion, they will enable you to obtain information on his

---

30. Lee David Thames, *Discovery Strategy,* 28 For the Defense 12, 17 (Jan. 1986).

31. *Id.*

32. Richard A. Lavine and Margaret M. Morrow, *Creating and Implementing a Successful Discovery Plan* § 1.25, at 19 (Cal. C.E.B., Sept/Oct 1985).

33. *Id.*

34. Edna R. Sussman, *Strategic Discovery,* 13 Litigation 37, 40 (Fall 1986).

35. Thames, *supra* note 30, at 15.

or her identity, professional credentials, opinions, and bases for those opinions.[36]

Each case requires a different discovery plan, and the use and timing of interrogatories will vary from case-to-case. Think through your discovery plan, the information you want, and the options you have to obtain it. Then use interrogatories to obtain the most information with the least cost for your client. Effective use depends on advanced planning.

DRAFTING THE INTERROGATORIES

You have researched both the procedural rules controlling interrogatories in your jurisdiction and the legal elements necessary to prove your case, your defenses, or your counterclaims. You have considered whether interrogatories will help obtain the information you desire and have considered when and how their use fits into your overall discovery plan. Now, before starting to draft, review the client file, pleadings, and any other documents filed in the case to focus yourself on the lawsuit and the information you want to obtain.

As when drafting contracts, complaints, and motions, most attorneys start with pattern or form interrogatories. Because of the prevalent use of form interrogatories, some states have restricted the use of specially drafted interrogatories, perhaps to make interrogatory practice more uniform. For example, California restricts the number of specially drafted interrogatories but does not restrict the use of official form interrogatories.[37] In this situation, using form interrogatories to the fullest extent possible will allow you to obtain information without expending your limited specially drafted interrogatories.

When using form interrogatories, focus on the particularities of your lawsuit. First, choose which interrogatories you will use. Sending all the form interrogatories for a given type of lawsuit, such as a personal injury case, is ineffective. For example, if you are a defendant's attorney in a personal injury case with a six-year-old plaintiff, it would be inappropriate to send this form interrogatory: "What was your occupation at the time of the incident referred to in the Complaint?" This error would indicate to your opponent that you are not giving the case careful consideration.

Having chosen your interrogatories, alter them to fit your client's position to request the information you need. Interrogatories that are too general or all-inclusive need not be answered.[38] So, while form

36. Lawrence Charfoos and David Christensen, *Interrogatories: How to Use Them Effectively in Personal Injury Cases,* 22 Trial 56, 57 (June 1986). *See,* Bender's, *supra* note 1 at § 3.10, at 3–80 for sample interrogatories to discover expert witnesses.

37. Cal.Civ.Pro. § 2030.5 restricts specially-prepared interrogatories to thirty-five. Section 2033.5 authorizes the Califor-nia Judicial Council to develop official form interrogatories and requests for admission for civil actions in state courts based on personal injury, property damages, wrongful death, unlawful detainer, breach of contract, and fraud.

38. *Stovall v. Gulf & South American Steamship Co.,* 30 F.R.D. 152 (S.D.Texas 1961).

interrogatories allow you to reduce drafting time, they also require tailoring to fit the case.[39] Now you are ready to begin drafting the preface, the definitions, and the questions.

The Preface

In drafting the preface, bear in mind that some local court rules limit the use or style of prefaces. For example, California rules allow only prefaces or instructions approved by the Judicial Council.[40] Oftentimes the preface will state the statute or rule under which the interrogatories are propounded, the required duties of the parties, and the time limit for answering. Additionally, the preface should state whether the interrogatories are continuing, which means supplemental answers must be provided if any of the answers change while the lawsuit is pending.[41] If your jurisdiction does not require supplemental answers, consider sending a final interrogatory just before the end of discovery to ask whether any of the previous answers has changed.[42]

As is true with all legal writing, avoid lapsing into legalese simply because the form you are following includes it. For example, avoid statements such as:

> Plaintiff requires Defendants to answer the following Interrogatories under oath within thirty (30) days after the date of service hereof pursuant to Rule 33 of the Federal Rules of Civil Procedure.

Instead, use statements such as:

> **These interrogatories are sent to you under Rule 33 of the Federal Rules of Civil Procedure. You must answer them under oath within thirty (30) days of receiving them.**

Although opposing counsel will usually revise the answers before sending them to you, a layperson will initially answer the questions. For this reason, your preface should be clear, concise, and simply worded so the layperson will understand his or her responsibilities in answering the interrogatories. You may also need to explain how interrogatories work, including the responding party's duties under the Rules. For example:

---

39. Fred Setterberg notes that most lawyers use form questions incorrectly, ignoring the subtleties of the particular case and requiring other attorneys to spend valuable time researching answers to irrelevant questions. Setterberg, *supra* note 28, at 46.

40. Cal.Civ.Pro. §§ 2030(c)(5) and 2033.5. This restriction prevents instructions attempting to circumvent the prohibition on using subparts by including instructions that call for answers in the form of subparts, even though the question does not contain any specific subparts. For example, the use of standard prefaces avoids the following attempt at multiple answers: "The word identify or identity, when used

in reference to a natural person means to state his or her full name, present business and home addresses, present employer and position with employer, the relationship, business, or otherwise, between such person and the person answering the interrogatory." Roger Haydock and David Herr, *Discovery Practice* 339–340 (1988).

41. Under Fed.R.Civ.P. 33, questions are deemed to be continuing and supplemental answers are required. However, under Cal.Civ.Pro. § 2030(c)(7), for example, questions are not continuing although attorneys may serve supplemental questions asking for updating.

42. Setterberg, *supra* note 28, at 46.

You are required to answer these interrogatories and to furnish any information available to you. This information includes
information that can be obtained by conducting a reasonable investigation to answer these questions.[43] These interrogatories are
continuing, and you are required to supplement your answers
whenever you obtain information that is different from the information provided in your answers.[44]

Write your preface to provide clear instructions so the person answering the interrogatories will be able to understand how to respond. Do
not assume that your opponent will provide instructions to his or her
client clarifying your interrogatories. Once you have developed a
standard preface, you can use it repeatedly, making only those minor
changes that may be necessary from case-to-case.

The Definitions

It may be necessary to identify certain terms, documents, dates, or
occurrences that you use in your interrogatories. For example, definitions can explain your use of a word that may raise different connotations for different respondents. For example:

Describe: This word means answer in detail and not just state the
reply in summary or outline fashion.[45]

You may also use definitions to ensure that the person answering the
questions uses a word in the legal context you intend. For example,
although attorneys realize that "person" also refers to corporations,
many laypeople do not. Thus you may want to define that term. Alter
the definition with each case, however, to delete any irrelevant possibilities.

Person: This word means any individual, individual association,
joint venture, partnership, public or municipal corporation, governmental entity or any other legal or business entity.[46]

Interrogatories will be easier to understand if you place long or frequently used definitions in a definition section rather than in the text
of the interrogatories. To show which terms are defined, you may want
to mark defined terms with underlining or bold face type.[47]

---

43. *Jackson v. Kroblin Refrigerated
Xpress, Inc.,* 49 F.R.D. 134 (N.D.W.Va.
1970); *National Labor Relations Board v.
Rockwell–Standard Corp.,* 410 F.2d 953
(6th Cir.1969).

44. This continuing duty to supplement
arises under Fed.R.Civ.P. 33 but does not
arise under all state rules.

45. Haydock and Herr, *supra* note 40,
at 339.

46. You would want to refine this definition further to include only those possibilities that would arise in answering
that particular set of interrogatories.

47. If you use definitions, be sure to
check in your jurisdiction for rules that
regulate their use. For example, some
states require that, if definitions are used,
the terms defined must be stated in boldface type or capitalized throughout the interrogatories. Cal.Civ.Pro. § 2030(c)(5).
Even if your state does not impose this
rule, you may want to follow this format
because it will help the reader understand
when terms used in the interrogatories are
included in the definition section.

You can also use definitions to help underscore the respondent's duty to answer the questions using all the information available to the party, not just the information available to that particular person.

You or your: This word means the Defendants, their predecessors or successors, if any, their employees, agents, attorneys and all other people acting or purporting to act on behalf of the defendants.

Avoid taking the extreme of defining words to include all possible interpretations. The following definition of "document," while probably including all possible variations, is so long and confusing that the respondent is likely to ignore the definition or not understand it.

Document shall mean the original and any copy of any written, typed, printed, recorded or graphic matter of any kind, however produced or reproduced, including, but not limited to, letters or other correspondence, telegrams, memorials of telephone conversations or of meetings, interoffice communications, memoranda, reports, summaries, tabulations, work papers, cost sheets, financial reports, photographs, advertisements, motion picture films, tape recordings, microfilms, other data compilations, including computer data, from which information can be obtained or translated into usable form.[48]

If a term is important enough to require a definition, write one that the person answering will be able to read and understand. Definitions should be as specific as possible and should clarify, not obscure, the information sought. It is possible to define document more simply and still inform the respondent that the broadest possible definition of the word is intended.

Document means the original and any copy of any writing of words or numbers, or films, recordings, or data compilations of any type from which information can be obtained or translated into usable form.

You may also want to include definitions specific to the particular litigation. For example:

Accident means the accident between the plaintiff and the defendant at the intersection of Fourth and Cedar Streets that occurred on November 13, 1989.

Employment manual means the employment manual used at Defendant's factory from April 1, 1982, through March 30, 1989.

---

48. When referring to an even longer definition of "document", Stein notes:

Such a definition does not, of course, spring up overnight. It represents a Darwinian adaption to the need for survival. When the simple definition of document—a writing—was used, it was evaded. The lawyer who was able to evade became suspicious that others would be just as unscrupulous as he, so he made additions to the definition. Thus the coral reef grew.

Stein, *supra* note 2, at 47.

Using specific definitions helps ensure that the person answering cannot avoid answering by asserting that he or she is unclear about the question asked.

The Questions

The questions fall into three categories: (1) preliminary questions, which request introductory material such as the name, address, occupation, and age of the responding party; (2) substantive questions, which elicit the specific information desired; and (3) concluding questions, which identify the people who helped answer the interrogatories, the people who may be called as witnesses, and the people who have relevant information or documents.[49]

Preliminary Questions

Preliminary questions ask for identification information about the person filling out the interrogatories. Before limitations were imposed on the number of interrogatories asked, many identification questions were asked; as a result, most form books include many preliminary questions. But with current limitations on the number of interrogatories, you can no longer include any unnecessary preliminary questions, such as some of the questions in the following example.

1. State your full name, age, and place of birth.

2. Have you ever used or been known by any other name?

     a. If so, state such name or names.

     b. State where and when you used or were known by such names.

     c. State whether your name has ever legally been changed and, if so, state when, where and through what procedure.

3. State your present address and the period during which you have resided at said address.

Including all these preliminary questions in most cases is unnecessary. These questions need to be revised to obtain the information more efficiently and to eliminate legalese. A more efficient method of drafting these questions would be as follows:

1. **State your full name, present address, age, and place of birth.**

2. **State whether you have been known by any other name and if so, when and where you were known by such names.**

You may be able to avoid drafting these questions and having them count against your supply of questions if they are contained in the pattern interrogatories included in some statutes. Also consider whether you can eliminate some of these preliminary questions. For example, it may be unnecessary to ask for the former names of the

---

49. Bender's, *supra* note 1, at § 3.08(1).

party involved. The limits on interrogatories require you to rethink constantly what questions to ask. Having chosen the questions to ask, revise them to be as clear and specific as possible.

Whether you can use branching interrogatories may depend on the rules of your jurisdiction. If branching questions are allowed and each subpart is not counted against the total, use them because they clearly indicate what information is requested. Each branch relates to the main question and simply requests a finite piece of information. Each branch is short and easy to understand. If you cannot use branch questions or if each subpart is included in your total count, you may want to avoid them. In this situation, use direct, declarative sentences and keep your subjects and verbs close together to make your questions clearer.

Substantive Questions

After drafting the introductory questions, draft the substantive questions that will provide most of your information. In drafting these questions, even if your interrogatories are unlimited in number, remember that you will have to sift through the endless pages of responses. Ask only what you need to know.

Draft questions clear and precise enough to obtain the needed information. Tailor interrogatories obtained from form books or from your office's files. If your questions are limited, each question asked prevents you from asking some other question. Choose wisely.

Revise any form questions to be precise and clear. Precision comes from asking for the specific pieces of information you need; clarity comes from asking the question in a way that makes it easy to understand. In the same way that at trial you "never ask a question to which you do not know the answer," never ask an interrogatory without being sure why you are asking it. Precisely what information do you hope to obtain from the answer? How will that information help you to reach your client's goals? Is it possible to ask the question in a way to ensure receiving the specific information you want, especially considering that another attorney will be reviewing all the answers?

A question that is general and not precise, while seemingly innocuous, can result in an answer harmful to your client. For example, one plaintiff in a personal injury case received interrogatories asking general background about her case. Her leg had been broken in a car accident and the defendant was attempting to find out whether this injury would significantly affect the way in which she lived her life. The defendant's interrogatory was general: "List all hobbies and forms of recreation in which you have participated in the past ten years."

In the past two or three years, this plaintiff had been a college student who engaged in little or no physical recreation or hobbies. While in junior high and high school, however, the plaintiff had been extremely active in sports as a member of several school teams, hiked extensively, rode horses, and also played many sports informally with friends. Because the interrogatory was phrased so generally, she was able to answer it truthfully and include a long list of recreation and hobbies in which she had participated over the past ten years. As a result, the defendant's attorney did not receive the information that would have helped limit the plaintiff's damages.

It may be more useful to ask for the specific information sought rather than to ask a general question in the hope of obtaining information without giving away your intended use for the information. Here the better choice may have been to focus on a more specific period of time. Thus, the question could have stated: "List all hobbies and forms of recreation in which you have participated in the past two years." This example also shows the dilemma that must be resolved when drafting interrogatories because, depending on the plaintiff, the defense attorney may have received just as harmful an answer with the revised question. In fact, some plaintiffs may have been significantly more active in the past two years than in the previous ten years. Nevertheless, the revised interrogatory would gain information more relevant to any damage claims than would the previous more general one. In contrast, the general question provided misleading information.

Clarity comes from drafting questions your reader can understand, so he or she is able to provide the information you are seeking. One of the best ways to make your questions clear is to make them direct and short. While imposed limits on the number of interrogatories may force you to draft questions that are more complex than you prefer, those limitations do not excuse the use of vague or cumbersome questions. Ask brief questions; they require direct answers.

> Are you claiming that you suffered any property damage as a result of the November 13, 1989, accident?

Ask clear questions; they are difficult to evade.

> Please give the dates on which you were able to do the following for the first time after your injury:
>
> (a) sit up in bed,
>
> (b) remain out of bed for an entire day, and
>
> (c) leave your house for any reason.

Always remember that, although your opponent will at some point review and revise the answers, the person who originally answers them will usually not be a lawyer. Write to communicate with that person, which increases the chance that you will receive useful answers.

The best use of interrogatories is for gathering facts. Focus your questions on who, what, when, where, and how.[50] Avoid asking "why" because you will usually receive a generalized, unsupported answer

---

50. Charfoos and Christensen, *supra* note 36, at 56; Setterberg, *supra* note 28, at 46–47; and Patricia A. Seitz, *Get More Information and Less Indigestion Out of Your Interrogatories,* 71 A.B.A.J. 74, 77 (March 1985). For other helpful examples of the types of factual questions that are most susceptible to being asked through interrogatories, *see id.* at 75–76; Charfoos and Christensen, *supra* note 36, at 56–59.

that requires follow-up questions you cannot ask.[51] Additionally, answering "why" requires subjective or interpretive responses affected by the witness's demeanor and credibility. These questions are better asked at deposition.[52]

By carefully determining your questions, you can not only determine the information your adversary possesses, but also force him or her to examine important documents and records and thereby shoulder some of your research.[53] In much the same way, your questions will also educate your opponent.

> Opposing counsel might not have thought of asking his [or her] own client the careful question you have composed. Moreover, your set of questions frequently sets out your strategy like a road map.[54]

If you want to surprise your opponent, you may save questions that could inform your opponent about your strategy for deposition.

Concluding Questions

Concluding interrogatories are somewhat similar to the introductory questions. They ask for information not specifically related to the lawsuit's substance. The concluding questions ask for identification information about other people who may have helped answer or provided information for answering the interrogatories.

> Identify all documents related to and all persons with knowledge of the subject matter of these interrogatories.

One problem with this example is that, while it asks for the identity of each document, it does not ask for its location or its custodian, which is more helpful information. One way to solve this problem would be to define the term "identify" to include the name and location of documents and the name, address, and telephone number of the custodians.

> **Identify** means include the name and address of each person and include the name and location of each document, as well as the name, address, and telephone number of the document's custodian.

That definition may also allow you to obtain a significant amount of information without depleting your limited number of interrogatories.

The next example is frequently included as a catch-all question in personal injury cases.

> State in detailed narrative form your complete version of how the accident that is the subject of your complaint occurred, including (1) your observations, (2) all sounds, conversations, exclamations or other things heard by you, and (3) all pertinent details you have obtained from other sources, including the name, address and telephone number of each such source.

51. Setterberg, *supra* note 28, at 57.

52. Seitz, *supra* note 50, at 75.

53. Setterberg, *supra* note 28, at 45.

54. *Id.*

The person asking the question hopes to find out the respondent's "big picture" view of the accident and perhaps to obtain information about the legal theories that will be raised. Additionally, this question attempts to determine the names of potential witnesses and what information they may provide.

CONCLUSION

After drafting your interrogatories, reread them to determine whether they will obtain the information you desire. There are several ways to trouble-shoot your questions. You may play devil's advocate after finishing your interrogatories by asking the following questions.

1. Consider whether each question can be redrafted in a simpler, less complex [more precise] fashion.

2. Ask yourself how the answer to each interrogatory will provide you with information helpful to the case.

3. Decide whether some questions can be eliminated or consolidated.

4. Consider ways the responses to your questions could be fudged and then attempt to redraft the questions.[55]

Or you may ask the following questions:

1. Do the questions advance my discovery plan?

2. Do they pursue the missing information I presume to be valuable?

3. What loopholes can the other side use to avoid answering my questions in a useful way?

4. Can I tighten the noose, and will the court allow it?

5. Can any questions be eliminated?[56]

Expect your opponent to try to avoid a direct answer and then frame your questions to force just the direct answer you want. Think in context of your discovery plan; think why you want the information; think about how your opponent will try to avoid your question; think about preventing that. If you ask these questions after drafting, and answer them as honestly and completely as you expect your opponent to answer yours, then you will have ensured the best use possible of this discovery device. A carefully asked question requires a responsive answer. Expect your opponent to try to avoid a direct answer and then frame your questions to force just the direct answer you want.

EXERCISES

Review the following interrogatories and revise them to make them direct and clear.

55. Haydock and Herr, *supra* note 40, at 341.   **56.** Setterberg, *supra* note 28, at 57.

1. State whether you are receiving and if you have ever received a disability pension or worker's compensation from any agency, company, person, state or government, and if so, please state full details and particulars to such compensation or pension, including but not limited to the amount thereof, why you received the compensation or pension, for what injuries or disabilities you received the compensation or pension, when and where said injuries or disabilities were sustained, and present disability as a result of such injuries or disability.

2. For the ranks of Correction Officer and Correction Sergeant only, list the educational requirements, training, experience, tests, evaluations or other criteria used as factors in the determination of suitability for appointment of promotion to each rank, the relative weight of each, and the grade, analysis or other indicia requisite to acceptability for permanent appointment to each rank.

3. Please state if a proposed expert witness employed or consulted by you or your attorney has ever given testimony by deposition or at trial in any other lawsuit; and if so, for each lawsuit give the name of the suit, the kind of each lawsuit, i.e., malpractice, traumatic injury, etc., the name of the court and its address, the date of filing of the suit, and the name and address of the party for whom the proposed expert gave testimony.

(a) List and identify, by date and brief description, all documents in the possession of or under the control of defendant, or any of its officers, agents or employees, relating to any and all contacts, conferences or discussions between officers, agents or employees of ...... relative to the subject matter of the patent in suit, including all correspondence between such persons relating to said subject matter.

(b) Will defendant supply plaintiff with true copies of all said documents so identified?

(c) If the answers to Part (b) are in the negative, will defendant permit plaintiff or its attorneys to examine and make copies thereof and, if so, where and when may such examination take place?

4. State the nature of the contact between the tractor-trailer and the plaintiff's automobile with reference to whether plaintiff's automobile was directly in front of the tractor-trailer, or to its right, or to its left. In other words, did the front end of the tractor collide with the entire rear of the plaintiff's automobile, or was the contact between the right portion of the front end of the tractor and the left rear of the automobile; if the latter, state how many feet of the front end of the tractor were in contact with how many feet of the rear end of plaintiff's automobile?

ASSIGNMENT 1

Draft interrogatories in the Susan Ashland case, from the plaintiff to the defendant. Limit yourself to twenty questions, asking for information that would indicate whether the Kellys were Ranger's keepers. Use the facts and law stated in Assignment 2 in Chapter 6, Issues.

ASSIGNMENT 2

Draft interrogatories in the Howard Jones case, for the defendants, Chevrolet plant. Focus your questions on the wife's pregnancy to help determine age of fetus. Limit yourself to twenty questions. Use the facts and law stated in Assignment 2 in Chapter 8, Persuasive Facts.

Bibliography

Bender, Matthew, *Bender's Forms of Discovery.* New York: Times Mirror Books, 1990.

Charfoos, Lawrence S. and David W. Christensen, *Interrogatories: How to Use Them Effectively in Personal Injury Cases,* 22 Trial 56 (June 1986).

Cooper, Allan B., and Mitchell L. Lathrop, *Use and Abuse of Interrogatories.* California Continuing Education of the Bar, October/November 1985.

Danner, Douglas, *Pattern Interrogatories: Premises.* New York: The Lawyers Co–Operative Publishing Co., 1970.

Haydock, Roger S. and David F. Herr, *Discovery Practice.* Boston: Little, Brown and Co., 1988.

Haydock, Roger S. and David F. Herr, *Interrogatories: Questions and Answers,* 1 Rev. of Litigation 263 (1981).

Lavine, Richard A. and Margaret M. Morrow, *Creating and Implementing a Successful Discovery Plan.* California Continuing Education of the Bar, September/October 1985.

LeSage, Bernard E. and Steven E. Smith, "Summary of Statutory and Case Law Relating to the Enforcement of Discovery" in *Compelling, Opposing, and Enforcing Discovery in State Courts.* California Continuing Education of the Bar, April 1988.

Seitz, Patricia A., *Get More Information and Less Indigestion Out of Your Interrogatories,* 71 A.B.A.J. 74 (March 1985).

Setterberg, Fred, *The Artful Question,* 6 Cal.Law. 45 (February 1986).

Shapard, John and Carroll Seron, *Attorneys' Views of Local Rules Limiting Interrogatories.* Federal Judicial Center Staff Paper, 1986.

Stein, Jacob A., *The Discovers,* 15 Litigation 46 (Fall 1988).

Sussman, Edna R., *Strategic Discovery,* 13 Litigation 37 (Fall 1986).

Thames, Lee David, *Discovery Strategy,* 28 For the Defense 12 (January 1986).

Chapter 14

GENERAL CORRESPONDENCE

Chaos is a term mathematicians and physicists use to describe physical systems that are understandable but difficult to predict. (Chaotic systems incorporate multiple understandable physical rules, but the interactions of those rules are so complex and so sensitive to initial conditions that the system's behavior seems unpredictable.) Weather is an example of chaos; correspondence may be another.[1] Although the individual factors in a piece of correspondence are understandable,[2] the interaction of those factors is so complex that the exact effect of correspondence is hard to predict.[3] Nevertheless, by manipulating those factors, the writer can significantly increase the odds of the correspondence being successful.

Correspondence is one of the main opportunities an attorney has to establish the goodwill and trust that makes for a solid working relationship. Effective correspondence has helped many lawyers maintain a successful practice without needing to write many briefs. Skillful correspondence has also helped attorneys maintain the solid relationships necessary to retain their clients over the years. Some successful attorneys even have built up their clientele through correspondence, in substantial part from people who were once an opposing attorney's clients. Often these clients were impressed with the attorney's correspondence and subsequently decided to hire that attorney.

The first section of this chapter discusses how priorities for correspondence differ from those of other legal documents. The second outlines how you choose your format and how and when you may use form letters. The third describes various readers and how your relationship to them affects your correspondence, and the fourth defines various common tasks correspondence must accomplish. The final

1. Other commenters have linked writing with the feeling of chaos. Lil Brannon, Melinda Knight, and Vara Neverow–Turk, *Writers Writing* 5 (1982).

2. For example, interpersonal communication science divides its research into the study of coherence, regulation, sequencing, preventatives, and repairs. Joseph N. Cappella, "Interpersonal Communication: Definitions and Fundamental

Questions" in *Handbook of Communication Science* 212–213 (C. Berger and S. Chaffee, eds. 1987).

3. For example, behavior and attitudes are known to be related, but that relationship is complex, and changes in either area can affect the other. Herbert Simons, *Persuasion: Understanding, Practice, and Analysis* 72 (2d ed. 1986).

section discusses elements of tone that you can vary, apart from the format or task, to help create the impression you want.

PRIORITIES IN CORRESPONDENCE

To write effective correspondence, the writer needs to maintain a dual focus. Correspondence communicates to the reader not only what the message is, but also how the writer views the reader.[4] Your success at legal correspondence depends not just on your knowledge of law, but also on your knowledge of people.[5] Accordingly, this chapter draws substantially from communication science, the psychology of persuasion, and business writing. These sources all help determine how to manage effectively the dual focus correspondence requires, a focus on simultaneously communicating your message and your attitude.

The relationship between the reader and writer becomes important in correspondence because the reader will respond to how the writer views that reader. This establishing of a relationship is why tone is important in letters. In general, business correspondence tries to get the reader to do something or learn something. To accomplish this, the writer needs a reader who is willing to cooperate.[6] This cooperation is encouraged by goodwill, which in turn is encouraged by a positive tone.

Even form letters establish this relationship. For example, the following two form letters communicate quite different relationships, although the content is similar. The first communicates some sense of personableness.

PHILIP A. HAUSMAN
ATTORNEY AT LAW
184 MAIN STREET
OLDTOWN, OHIO 12345
(513) 555–7002

March 26, 1983

Mrs. Mary Stevens Meade
1209 Hillside Avenue
Oldtown, Ohio 12339

Dear Mary,

Re: Measuring Change in Attitude Toward Writing

Here are   ( ) Original   (x) Copy

( ) Complaint   ( ) Sales Agreement
( ) Summons   ( ) Deed
( ) Acknowledgment of Service   ( ) Mortgage
( ) Answer   ( ) Last Will and Testament
( ) Notice of Motion   ( ) Agreement

---

4. *Id.* at 32.

5. "Good writing [is] writing that gets ideas across. And that's much more a matter of paying attention to your reader than of paying attention to your English." *Id.* at 5.

6. Rolf Sandell, *Linguistic Style and Persuasion* 70–103 (1977).

( ) Affidavit	( ) Judgment
( ) Brief	( ) Letter
( ) Order	( ) Document of title listed
( ) Interrogatories	( ) Stamped return envelope
( ) Proof of mailing	( ) Check in amount of $
(x) Other	

Various Attitude Scales

Please:

( ) File or record	(x) Keep for your records
( ) Return a copy	( ) Serve on _____
( ) Complete, sign & return	at _____
( ) Cancel enclosed document	( ) Prepare to attend on
( ) Other	

Adapt freely

Thank you,

Philip A. Hausman

PAH: amr
enclosures

Although a form letter is by nature rather impersonal, this version adds some touches suggesting a friendly attitude. It adds a personal salutation, "Dear Mary," and opens with simple wording free of legalese: "Here are." "Adapt freely" and "thank you" at the closing echo this relatively informal tone. Throughout, the author suggests a friendlier working relationship than does the author of the following letter.

Conrad Calhoun, Esq.
Attorney at Law
167 Amersley Way
Oldtown, Ohio 12345

Ms. Mary Stevens Meade
1209 Hillside Avenue
Oldtown, Ohio 12339

March 26, 1983

RE: Preparation of Trust for Mary Stevens Meade, file # 945–83

To facilitate the preparation of the above-mentioned document, please assure that our offices are provided with a copy of each of the documents hereinafter designated. Upon receipt of these documents, we will be able to proceed on the matter noted above.

( )   current will and testament

( )   any former wills still extant

( )   summary of assets

( )   any judgments made against the estate, if any are known by
       you

( )   location of current assets

( )   most recent estimated value of assets available, noting date
       estimate was made

( )   deeds to property and how title is held

   Please be advised that our office is available to assist you in
your understanding of these requests.

                              Very truly yours,

                              Conrad Calhoun, Esq.

   The second letter sounds unappealing. It has no personal salutation, and the body of the letter begins with nominalizations and a
bureaucratic tone that creates the impression that the writer wants
distance from the reader. The formality of the wording, from "facilitate" and "please be advised that" to "very truly yours," sounds
condescending, although the writer may have intended to sound respectful. Together this language creates a letter that leaves the reader
wanting to have nothing to do with the writer. Since the writer needs
the reader's cooperation, the letter's tone contradicts its purpose.[7] The
second letter does not communicate courtesy or friendliness, and the
relationship it establishes is not useful.

   Tone is central in even the most routine letters or memos. Precision and clarity are important, but tone takes on equal importance.
For this reason, tone is included both in a separate section of this
chapter and throughout other sections.

CHOICE OF FORMATS

   The first format choice you must make is whether the message
should be oral or written. If you do not want a message to be
discoverable by another party, avoid writing it down. Conversely, if
you do want a point established for the record, write to create a paper
trail.[8]

   The next choice is what to write: a memo or a letter. Memos are
generally used in-house and letters out-of-house, but there are exceptions.[9] Memo format is becoming more popular because it is easier to
produce. It avoids some time-consuming problems, such as what to put
after "Dear" ("Ms. Jones:" "Joan Jones," "Joan Jones:" or "Joan,") and

---

7. "[M]ost readers respond favorably to
a concerned and courteous spokesperson.
Whatever your personal character, let your
writing reflect a warm, human personality." Daniel McDonald, *The Language of
Argument* 4 (3d ed. 1980).

8. One example of this use of correspondence is detailed in Chapter 16 on Wills
and Trusts.

9. A more traditional view is that
memos are not used for official business
with clients and others outside the organization. Elizabeth Tebeaux, *Design of Business Communications: The Process and the
Product* 125 (1990). But in practice attorneys are now sometimes using memos for
out-of-house communication.

what to put above the signature: ("Sincerely," "Sincerely yours," "Yours very truly," or "Very truly yours,"). After wrestling with these questions, writers sometimes turn to the memo format in despair because it omits those elements altogether. Your choice between memo and letter is better made by considering the occasion causing you to write. To help you make this decision, the following subsections outline three formats for correspondence: letters, form letters, and memos.

Letters

Letters are appropriate when you are communicating on a topic about which the reader may have some feeling. For example, no writer would send a memo to a friend expressing regret over the death of a spouse, nor would an interviewer send a memo of rejection rather than a letter. These situations call for addressing the reader as an individual, and a letter does that well.

Applying this to subtler situations, choose the letter format when telling a client bad news or when communicating with another individual on behalf of a client. In the latter situation, a letter is useful because receiving mail from an attorney is alarming, and you may want to use the letter's tone to help the reader calm down. The letter format facilitates a personal tone, and you can use that opportunity to communicate whether your purpose is friendly or not. For example, a letter suggests this tone in the opening sentence.

Dear Mr. Abernathy:

> Your colleague, Heng Yon, has suggested you might be interested in . . . .

The word "colleague" in the first sentence suggests a cordial tone. In contrast, the following opening sends signals that bad news is coming.

Dear Mr. Abernathy:

> At the request of my client, Dr. Heng Yon, I am writing to inform you that . . . .

A memo, which opens with a subject line, communicates news quickly, leaving less room for signals of the writer's tone.

A letter is also the format of choice when you want to communicate deference to the reader. Write a letter to a hiring partner to apply for a position, to the president of a corporation, or to an elderly person. You might choose this format when writing to any reader who will be more inclined to cooperate if he or she sees you as respectful.

Finally, a letter is the usual format for writing messages of a social nature, such as thank you or congratulatory notes.

Denise,

> Congratulations on the well-deserved praise from Judge Crain!

Janis

Form Letters

In this age of word processors, form letters can be produced to look like individual letters; generally, this is the best choice if you choose to send a form letter. But for some routine correspondence, you may want a form letter that looks like a form letter.

For example, the first form letter included earlier could have been individualized. Nevertheless, the practitioner chose the form letter to communicate the impression he wanted. The rationale behind this form letter is that it communicates both a personal attitude and efficiency, which the practitioner believed would reassure his client he was not wasting his time and the client's money. He also believed it was a quiet advertisement because it showed the client the range of assistance possible. The form letter gave him an excuse to communicate those options. Similarly, you might use a form letter to communicate the steps in a long process. This letter would give the reader a sense of the progress of the case as subsequent copies of the form appear in the mail, with the check marks farther down the list.

What you want to avoid is any sense that you are using the form to avoid personal contact with your reader. Distancing yourself from the reader would erode trust,[10] which in turn would erode your credibility.[11]

Memos

Memos are useful for in-house communication, when frequent communication makes it unnecessary to signal how you view the reader. A memo's format focuses on content rather than on the reader. The salutation (Dear Joan,) is replaced by the subject line (RE: Discovery of In–House Statistical Summaries of Pons Corporation's Cash Flow). The closing is omitted, and initials next to the "From" line replace the personal signature. These changes in format also eliminate personal comments, such as the good wishes that often appear in the closing paragraph of a letter. A memo gets down to business and is the appropriate choice when conciseness and efficiency are the pre-eminent goals.[12]

There is such a torrent of words threatening to engulf us now that nobody should add to it unless it's absolutely necessary.[13]

10. Daniel J. O'Keefe, *Persuasion: Theory and Research* 133 (1990).

11. "[A]s a rule, only the conjunction of competence and trustworthiness makes for reliable communication." *Id.* Also, "In law, for example, competence and trustworthiness 'correspond to the most common legal reasons for seeking to impeach witnesses.'" *Id.* Respect and trust are more significant factors in the receiver's

response to the sender than is attraction. Simons, *supra* note 3, at 131–135.

12. "Talk of nothing but business, and dispatch that business quickly." Richard Hatch, *Business Communication: Theory and Technique* 9 (1977) (from a placard on the door of Adine Press, Venice, Italy, established in 1490).

13. Ernst Jacobi, *Writing at Work: Dos Don'ts and How Tos* 19 (1979).

Memo format is appropriate for detailing a research task to a subordinate, outlining a proposal to a superior, or transmitting routine information.[14] Memo format is also appropriate for requesting information from someone who routinely provides that information as part of his or her job. For example, write a memo to request a new dictaphone from your office manager, account information from a bank officer, or an explanation from the IRS. Finally, use memo format to document information for the files or to record information several readers must be aware of but not know thoroughly. Because of the volume of information in a law practice, readers must skim some information; the memo's subject line, headings, and subheadings facilitate this.

In summary, all three formats are useful, depending on your working relationship with the reader, the preferences of that reader, your task for this piece of correspondence, and the tone you want to convey.

ADJUSTMENTS FOR DIFFERENT READERS

Because the primary purpose of correspondence is to send information from one individual to another, the reader's response is central.[15] Therefore, a primary step when corresponding is considering what will make the reader more willing to accept information from the writer. Although you will adapt for individual readers,[16] you will generally have different priorities when writing to in-house readers (employers, colleagues, and employees) and out-of-house readers (clients and other lay people, attorneys and judges, and other business persons).[17]

In–House Readers

A common element of in-house writing is a need for efficiency. You want to be concise, whether your tone is cordial or reserved. Communicate your tone only in the briefest ways, and focus on the content. In general, use memo format and the tone settled by under-

14. Researchers have identified five types of on-the-job messages sent from supervisor to subordinate: job instructions, job rationale, policy and procedure, feedback, and indoctrination. Written communication from subordinate to supervisor was used less, and generally was concerned with either personnel information or technical feedback about progress toward an assigned goal. For a useful discussion of this information, *see,* Thomas Tortoriello, Stephen Blatt and Sue DeWine, *Communication in the Organization: An Applied Approach* 52–54 (1978).

15. For an example list of questions to consider when analyzing an audience, *see* Hatch, *supra* note 16, at 51.

16. For example, one researcher found that flattery will appeal to some people,

but not to people who have low opinions of themselves—they will react negatively. Simons, *supra* note 3, at 25. Yet other research shows that obvious flattery does not persuade. Tebeaux, *supra* note 9, at 142.

17. Business communication texts often divide readers into four categories. One of these lists these four categories as laypeople, executives, experts, and technicians. Kenneth Houp and Thomas Pearsall, *Reporting Technical Information* 67–69 (1980). For legal writing, these four categories would translate roughly into clients, judges, other attorneys, and paralegals, which does not delineate the most pronounced distinctions between readers of legal correspondence.

stood in-house rules.[18] In-house correspondence usually begins with the main point.[19] For example, a memo from a supervisor to an employee might state a request as follows.

> *Please call the Red Cross* to see if . . . .   We need to find some verification of Kelsey's claim that he was giving blood at the time of . . . .

The employee might begin the answering memo as follows.

> *The Red Cross should have the information we need, but* to obtain that information we will have to . . . .   The Red Cross does have a log of all donors, including . . . .   They will not release that information, however, unless . . . .

> With your OK, I will start the paperwork needed to get the . . . .

In each case, the first line states the point of the memo.

Despite this focus on efficiency, the ongoing relationship between the reader and writer still affects the correspondence. The "please" in the request signals politeness. The sentence explaining the why behind the request suggests that the writer values the reader's understanding of the situation; the reader is helping to accomplish a task. In response, the quick answer at the first of the employee's response suggests the employee is focused on the task, valuing the supervisor's goals and being efficient in meeting the supervisor's request. The concise explanation communicates the employee's competence and efficiency, and the ending communicates the employee's recognition of the boundaries of his or her authority to act. Thus the wording, content, and organization confirm the working relationship. Clarify in your own mind the working relationship you want with the reader so you communicate it appropriately.

Writing to someone above you on the organizational ladder can be simplified by taking some time to determine what your reader wants, using your common sense and your experience in the organization. Readers higher on the organizational ladder cannot spend much time on any one piece of correspondence. When writing for these readers, state the point in the first sentence and summarize your content in the first paragraph. These readers put a premium on their time, and they will appreciate it if you do, too.

One way to condense information is to state it in terms of its importance to that reader. For example, if you have secured a maintenance contract for office equipment, you can state that fact, the name

---

18. Language used in a group is influenced greatly by the power structure, more so than by the sex of the reader or writer, the socioeconomic class of the reader or writer, or any other factors. For a discussion of research in intergroup communication, *see,* Howard Giles and John Wiemann, "Language, Social Comparison, and Power" in *Handbook of Communication Science* 356–359 (C. Berger and S. Chaffee eds., 1987).

19. "The first step toward making a message efficient is to get right to the point." Hatch, *supra* note 12, at 11.

of the company, the overall cost, and perhaps how the cost compares with other competing bids. Do not go into the details of how you reached this contract or of what the service will include. Give the reader the information wanted, but do not burden him or her with the details of your job.

When deciding how much detail to include, consider the inclinations of the reader. As discussed in Chapter 9, memo discussion sections, include more detail for supervisors who want to be fully informed; provide a quick summary for supervisors who do not want to deal with technicalities. For many supervisors, the optimum amount of information lies between. For these readers, include a summary of routine information and somewhat more detail when describing any problems that have arisen or may arise in the future. If more support is needed, attach documents the reader might want to see, but summarize the important information in your memo.

Consider the working relationship you want to communicate through the tone of the letter. Again, the personal qualities of your reader will be a major influence. Is she impatient? If so, be concise and worry little about courtesy. Does he emphasize courtesy and respect for the client? If so, make sure your memos to him, although concise, do not omit these courtesies. Often the tone you want is a blend of several qualities. You will write in a conversational-yet-concise tone, a respectful-yet-confident tone, or an efficient-yet-personable tone. Finding the balance of qualities you want may take time, but when you have found it you can use it in all your correspondence with that reader.

When writing for employees whom you supervise or over whom you have some rank, clarity is critical. When achieving this clarity, worry less about conciseness, more about specificity. One common complaint employees have about supervisors is their directions are not clear. Yet even in the supervisory position, consider your working relationship with the reader. For example, if writing a memo instructing your secretary about handling rejection letters, focus on content but word your request politely, indicating your appreciation for the work done.

State the information from the reader's point of view. For example, if announcing the company picnic, begin with "You are invited to . . . ." rather than "The company picnic will be held . . . ." The former subtly reflects that you are thinking of your reader's interests, and this sense of inclusion helps build goodwill.

When writing to colleagues, avoid treating them like either employees or supervisors. So, for example, do not begin simply by stating the request because that would suggest that it is routine for the colleague to grant your requests. Instead you might begin with an acknowledgment that you are asking for something that is within the colleague's discretion to do.

If you have time, I could use your advice on a particularly troublesome issue in . . . .

or

> Joe, could you handle another case right now? I have a client who
> . . . .

Yet do not use an overly deferential tone, because you are an equal in this situation. For example, you would not write the following.

> I am requesting your review of the . . . because . . . .

Instead, you would speak less formally, perhaps as follows.

> **Could you review a contract I have written for** . . .?

Your tone with colleagues is more like informal conversation than corresponding with supervisors or employees.

In summary, when writing for in-house readers, focus on your point, state it quickly and clearly, and use the organizations suggested in the task section below. Also consider the particular concerns of the reader. Then you will avoid errors in content or tone that could hamper your communication.

Out-of-House Readers

Adjusting the format for the out-of-house reader will require you to change your approach somewhat in planning, choosing content, and revising your content. Out-of-house readers are more varied. The most common reader is the client, but other common readers of your correspondence include witnesses, experts, interested parties, and other business contacts, such as vendors. You will also write to other attorneys, including the opposition, the general bar, and the bench.

When planning your client correspondence, begin by considering the question in the client's mind, similar to your approach for an in-house reader. This will help you determine what content to include. Also consider whether the client will experience an emotional reaction to the message, and if so choose a letter format. If you are presenting good news, you may use a memo format, unless you want to use a letter to add a personal touch to underscore the news. If you are communicating news that may upset the client, choose the more personal letter format and begin by preparing the client for the bad news, as suggested below. Consider also whether the client is a willing receiver of this news. If so, your task will be informing. If not, the correspondence will involve some persuading.

Whatever choices you make, check during revision for any wording that makes the content difficult for the client, such as a term the client does not understand or a word with an unneeded emotional overtone. For example, you would revise the following.

> If you go bankrupt, then, this provision allows you to . . . .

> Since Wisconsin is a community property state, your will needs to state that . . . .

Instead, you would write the following.

> **This provision offers some protection in the event of financial difficulties, such as bankruptcy, by** . . . .

> **Clause 2(b) of this draft of your will is needed to clarify which property belongs to you solely, rather than belonging to you and your husband together. Wisconsin is a community property state, which means that** . . . .

When writing for other out-of-house readers, follow the same approach, with one exception. While you do not want to upset your client, you may occasionally want to upset other readers, although without appearing to do so. To do this, omit the preparatory introductions you add to soften the blow. Structure the correspondence as you would if simply informing the reader. The result will be correspondence with a tougher tone.

> March 13, 1990
>
> Dear Ms. McKinney:
>
> On behalf of my client, Geron's Department Store, I am writing to inform you that one week from today I will be presenting a motion to the Circuit Court of Dade County to instruct the Sheriff to repossess . . . . This action will be required unless you
>
> . . . .

This approach can galvanize the reader into action. Use it only as needed, however, because it seldom pays to make enemies.[20]

When writing to business readers, such as vendors or attorneys who are not representing an opposing party, standard business practice is your best guide, because this will be the tone and style with which the reader is most familiar.

When writing to attorneys, you can worry less about using legal terms of art; in fact you may use them extensively as a convenience.

> Dear Margaret,
>
> Good news! We won the 12(b)(6) motion, and it looks like plaintiffs will not be able to get it certified. We were not able to win a non-suit on the other counts, but we should be able to discourage them with a Rule 11 filing on the basis of the 12(b)(6). They told Judge Hertz they wanted expedited discovery, relying on his rocket docket, but he just took it under advisement.
>
> I think we can get summary judgment on two counts, and we ought to file on all four, before they notice any more depositions. I have filed an application to quash the subpoena duces tecum of Jones, since it is a boxcar demand, but I expect a cross application to compel production. They'll have to work quick, because we're on

---

20. The reader will treat you as you have treated the reader. Cappella, *supra* note 2, at 213.

the calendar Tuesday and I'm going to notice the application for a protective order by FAX Friday at 6 p.m.

Sincerely,

Jim

Avoid using legal terms for intimidation. Remember, the other attorney has a law dictionary and may only be irritated or amused by your attempts.

ADJUSTMENTS FOR CORRESPONDENCE TASKS

The organization, content, and tone of correspondence are affected not only by the format and the writer's relationship with the reader, but also by the particular task the writing must accomplish. In correspondence, this involves some combination of informing or persuading. These tasks lie at opposite ends of a continuum.

informing -- persuading

Informing and persuading create different reasons for the content of the letter. Informing provides the reader with information without advocating any particular use of the information. Examples of informing include the following:

a cover letter stating that you are delivering a document, such as a requested copy of some document;

a memo notifying the supervisor that some action has been taken, such as filing a document;

a letter responding to a request, such as telling a client that you have made the changes he requested in a contract you are drafting; and

a memo answering a question, such as letting a supervisor know how many hours you have spent on a project to date.

Persuasion, on the other hand, focuses on influencing the reader's use of the information. Although persuading involves presenting information, its purpose is getting the reader to do, think, or believe something. Examples of persuading include the following:

a letter asking someone to schedule a meeting with you,

a memo to a law clerk outlining a question you want researched,

a letter requesting further facts from a client, and

a letter requesting payment for services rendered.

Much correspondence combines these functions. For example, sometimes an element of persuasion is needed, but informing is still the dominant task. Examples of these combinations of informing and persuading include the following:

a letter of retainer, which both reviews what was discussed in a conversation and asks the client to sign the retaining contract;

a letter discussing the negotiation of a business deal; and

a memo answering questions and requesting some follow-up action.

The position you choose on this continuum is a major decision affecting the organization, wording, and content of your correspondence. If you place yourself further to the left, informing, you might begin with a balanced statement.

Your choice here will depend on your primary objectives.

This choice will require you to consider several factors.

In contrast, if you place yourself further to the right, you might indicate in the beginning that a recommendation is coming.

When deciding how to proceed at this time, your primary consideration should be establishing a solid record to prepare for an eventual lawsuit.

Although either action is possible, negotiation offers some additional advantages.

This beginning leads you to structure the body of your correspondence differently and to include different supporting detail. So if informing, you might write the following.

At this point, Dave, the choice is yours. I see three options for you. Let me know which way you want to proceed, and I will act accordingly.

But you might state the following if persuading.

Now that we have the basic terms of your will established, you need take only a few more steps to fulfill your objectives. First, you should . . . .

In the paragraphs framing your main message, echo the tone you have established.

The choice made here sometimes reflects your working relationship with the reader. You may find, for example, that some clients or employers prefer that you take a position while others prefer that you do not. Their tastes, however, cannot overshadow your duty to the profession and to yourself. Do not attempt to persuade when you cannot justify the action to yourself or another attorney. Do not simply inform when you have a duty to warn the reader and to recommend an action. The choice you make of your location on this continuum is a facet of your professional responsibility.

Informing the Reader

If you are informing the reader, your writing task is simpler than persuading, but not simple. You can begin with a summary of your message and then launch into details. You may modify your organization depending on whether the information you are providing is good news or bad.

Informing the Reader of Good or Neutral News

One way to communicate your message quickly is to write a heading communicating the main point. For example, you might write "Settlement of Contract for Client's Purchase of Whittier Canning." If you are writing a letter, you can insert a heading before the salutation or give the reader this information in the first sentence.

Dear Mr. Aitch:

> Here for your review is the version of the contract to purchase Whittier Canning that James Builder has agreed to accept . . . .

Do not start with a filler sentence; the reader does not want it and the situation does not require it.

In the body of the correspondence, elaborate or explain as needed. If you are explaining options to the reader, use "you may" to underscore that the reader is in charge. Also set out the options so the reader can see them easily. One useful way to do this is with a tabulated list. The following letter, for example, gives the various choices the reader could make.

> **Now that we have the signed confession of judgment for you, you have three actions you may take:**
>
> (1) **you may have us retain the confession of judgment in your files at our office, so that it will be available if you choose to take action on it in the future;**
>
> (2) **you may have us record the judgment in Bernalillo County, so that it is recorded although no further action is taken; or**
>
> (3) **you may have us both record the judgment in Bernalillo County and ask the Sheriff to act upon it.**

The signals of structure and wording here make the content much clearer than the more abstract below one would have been.

> We have the following options for developing the file documentation of this default: the confession of judgment retained in our office files, the confession of judgment recorded in the appropriate county, or the confession filed in the county and with the county sheriff for execution.

In the body of the correspondence, adjust the degree of detail to suit the reader. For example, if the reader of the letter above needed more guidance, you could include three paragraphs after the list, each one beginning as follows.

> **Choosing the first option of** . . . **would mean that** . . . .
>
> **Choosing the second option, or** . . . , **would mean that**
> . . . .
>
> **Finally, choosing the third option** . . . .

If possible, arrange questions in the order in which the reader will need to retrieve the information. For example, if you are asking a client for information for estate planning, group the questions so you ask all questions from one set of documents at once and label the group.

Life Insurance Policies

For each policy, list the following information:

> name of beneficiary
>
> name of owner
>
> face value of policy
>
> benefit value

If you think your reader will need help complying with the request, give that help in the letter, tell the reader how to find the help needed, or offer to help yourself. For example, you might add the following to the previous request.

Life Insurance Policies

For each policy, list the following information:

> —name of beneficiary (this is normally listed on the first page of the policy)
>
> —name of owner (this is also usually listed on the first page, and may be a person different from the beneficiary or the insured)
>
> —face value of policy
>
> —benefit value (this information may be stated in a table in your policy, with the benefits increasing with the years you hold the policy. If so, use the number . . . .)

Make sure the requests are no more extensive than needed and are unambiguously worded.

Consider setting out your list in fill-in-the-blank form, if that would be easier for your reader. Rather than drafting a separate document to respond, readers often prefer to write a response on the original and return it to the writer. Anything you do to make it easier for the reader to comply increases the chance of a timely and complete response and augments goodwill.

Finally, make sure that your request is unambiguous and that you have stated any deadline for fulfilling this request. If the request is for something to be done "when you have the time," say so, but realize this statement moves the request to the bottom of the priority list and the request may never be answered. Close your correspondence politely by offering assistance, telling how to obtain more information, or thanking the reader for cooperation. When thanking the reader, watch for the occasional situation when saying thank you seems somewhat sarcastic. In sum, take pains with each section to increase the chance of a successful response.

Informing the Reader of Bad News

When communicating bad news, consider calling or meeting instead of writing a letter. You probably do not want to communicate stand-offishness or rejection, and a written communication of bad news is likely to create that impression. Facing someone with bad news may be difficult, but it may be more effective for maintaining your working relationship. A need for documentation of the event might be the only reason to write a letter here, and you could do this after the meeting.

> Dear Jane Eyre:
>
> As I stated in our conversation on June 9, I regret having to release you from employment as governess for my daughter. Nevertheless, I must do so because . . . .

When you need to communicate bad news in writing, you must communicate the point clearly, no matter how much you want to soften the blow. In general, state the point in one clear sentence. This is important because readers are more likely to misunderstand bad news than good.[21]

Often, you can soften the blow by adding a sentence or two before stating the point. This preliminary text allows you to establish a relationship with your reader before the bad news appears, so you can separate the relationship from the bad news.[22] For example, if you had to tell a client you could not take a case because of a conflict of interest, you might begin as follows.

> Dear Ms. Eyre:
>
> I appreciate the confidence you expressed when you asked me to represent you in your employment discrimination case and was happy to accept your case. Regrettably, I have since discovered that my senior partner has represented Mr. Rochester in other matters. Therefore it would be inappropriate for me to represent you in this case because of the potential conflict of interest.

In your concern for softening the blow, do not neglect to deliver the information. Make sure you deliver the summary of that information at least by the beginning of the second paragraph.

> I appreciate the confidence you expressed when you asked me to represent you in your employment discrimination case and was happy to accept your case. I was happy to be of service to you when you prepared your will and established a trust fund for the . . . . With respect to those legal matters, I can still represent you as needed.
>
> In regard to the employment discrimination case, however, I am unable to represent you effectively because of a potential

---

21. "When someone doesn't want to recognize something, he or she honestly miss implications that would be entirely apparent otherwise." Hatch, *supra* note 12, at 255.

22. Richard Hatch describes this as the strategic aim of reducing the reader's anger at you, although you cannot perhaps reduce the reader's disappointment. *Id.* at 243.

> conflict of interest.　After talking with you, I discovered that my senior partner has represented . . . .

Delaying further may mislead the reader into thinking the news will be good, may make the reader impatient, or may make you seem tentative. None of these are useful effects for you.

In the body of the correspondence, elaborate as needed, as when giving good news.　Often, bad news will require more detail than good, because the reader will want to know more of the how and why.　If so, you may attach explanatory documents.　You want to avoid two extremes here: you do not want to look as if you are covering up by being too brief, nor do you want to look as if you are being defensive by going on too long.　Aim for balance, in light of what you know about your reader.　When giving bad news, always look for options.　Is there any silver lining here?　May things get better in the future?　Do not make up good news, but report any if you can.

If your news is somewhat good and somewhat bad, you can start with the good news but hint about the bad news to come so it will not jar the reader when it appears later.

> You may benefit at this point by doing nothing until the Weber situation is resolved.　Although we could proceed with the suit now, ...

If the good news is much less significant than the bad, it may be better placed at the end of the statement.

> The statutes in Wisconsin will not allow you to disinherit your spouse completely in your will.　Instead, to protect your estate you would have to . . . .

In any case, close the letter with a few sentences reiterating the tone you established in the opening paragraph.　This will unify your letter, which will make you sound more sincere.　It may also soften the blow of the bad news by leaving the reader with a touch of consolation.

> Thus, although you cannot pursue the estate plan you had originally envisioned, you may be able to achieve the same result using a different approach.　If you wish to pursue this further, please . . . .

> Although we have not been able to recover the funds lost through Mr. Gaither's mismanagement of your company, we have at least . . . .

Giving bad news requires a delicate balance between clarity and tact. To achieve the balance, let this letter sit overnight before mailing.[23]　If that is not possible, read the letter before mailing with an eye toward any word or phrase that will sting; see if you have worded the letter kindly but clearly.　Communicating bad news does not mean piling on

---

23.　Anne Eisenberg, *Effective Technical Communication* 301 (1982).

language; it means thinking about the reader's needs and addressing them.

Persuading the Reader

As you place your correspondence task further to the right on the informing-persuading continuum, you begin to incorporate persuasive techniques. The first step in using these techniques is determining when and to what degree it is appropriate to use them. For example, when you request action or information, you are always persuading the reader to some extent. When the request is routine, you may not spend much time explaining the request. But you may write a letter instead of a memo to suggest that the reader's cooperation is not being taken for granted.

If you decide more persuasion is needed, add it by stating concisely how the action requested will help the reader. For example, if a request entails a substantial commitment of money or time from the reader, take time to list the benefits to the reader.

When the challenge of the correspondence is more to motivate the reader than to explain the desired action clearly, you have passed the midpoint on the continuum and your primary task is persuasion. Persuading is a challenging task, in part because individual responses are difficult to predict.[24] Additionally, persuading is difficult because the reader has many ways to resist persuasion.[25] Finally, persuasion is difficult because it is sensitive to many complex variables. For example, readers are generally more readily persuaded when they do not perceive that the writer is trying to persuade.[26] They are more readily persuaded by someone who is somewhat like them, yet different in ways significant to the topic of the persuasion.[27] Furthermore, each time the writer tries to persuade the reader to change an opinion, that writer risks reducing his or her credibility in the reader's eyes.[28] Persuasive correspondence is complex and occurs within a larger framework.

In persuasive correspondence, the structure may or may not vary from a routine request. One thing that does vary is the weight you

24. William B. Gucykunst, "Cross–Cultural Comparisons," in *Handbook of Communication Science* 858 (C. Berger and S. Chaffee, eds., 1987).

25. For example, under cognitive dissonance theory, the reader may "(1) derogate the source; (2) decide that [the] disagreement is not very important, or rationalize it in some other way; (3) seek social support or supportive evidence for [his or her] own viewpoint (4) misperceive the source's position; (5) compartmentalize (ignore or forget that the cognitions are discrepant); (6) attempt to convince the source (if available) of his or her error; [or finally] (7) modify [his or her] own attitudes." Simons, *supra* note 3, at 61.

26. Sandell, *supra* note 6, at 297.

27. A persuader is likely to be most effective when similar to the audience in values and background, but different in ways that increase credibility (experience, etc.) so the persuader is a "super-representative" of the group. Simons, *supra* note 3, at 135.

28. One example Herbert Simons gives is that if you see Bill Cosby saying that Jello is great and you like Bill Cosby but do not like jello, you will subsequently like jello somewhat more but also like Cosby somewhat less. Simons, *supra* note 3, at 58–62.

give to each part as you are writing. The request for action itself is not likely to change, but the motivation to comply receives more attention.

In short correspondence, this motivation may require only a little more content. For example, you may add a phrase explaining the way the reader will benefit from this action, which should make your record keeping easier. You may state your understanding of the request you are making.

Although finding this information will be somewhat time-consuming, it should enable you to save time later when . . . .

Yet this small persuasion may help you gain the reader's cooperation.

Often, however, the persuasion will require fuller development. Then apply the general techniques for persuasion discussed in Chapter 8 on persuasive facts and Chapter 10 on argument sections. Apply these techniques, using one of several broader persuasive strategies, because the range of possible reader responses has broadened in correspondence. Before you were convincing a judge who had to make a decision within the context of the law. Here you may be writing to a reader who has the option to take no action, to make no decision, and to base that decision on factors having nothing to do with the law.

Deciding what persuasion strategy to use is a major part of your task when writing this correspondence. Possible strategies include persuading based on common goals, solving problems, seizing opportunities, warnings, and threats. To help you make this choice, this section discusses each of these strategies separately.

Persuading by Common Goals

Generally the most effective way to persuade a reader is to show the reader that doing what you suggest will accomplish something the reader wants to accomplish. You and your reader can cooperate rather than compete. This approach is useful in much of your out-of-house correspondence. For example, when writing to negotiate with an opposing attorney, you might explain how a particular settlement can benefit both parties. When writing to a nonlawyer, this explanation of a common goal can also add reassurance.

As you present your reasoning, be straightforward. The reader may be suspicious of a suggestion or request from an attorney not his or her own; allay those fears by helping the reader see your reasoning and its merit. Reassure the reader that the action you request will not hurt him or her, if possible. State the needed action clearly and make it as easy as possible for the reader to comply. As with other requests, enclose a self-addressed envelope, use a fill-in-the-blank form, and request only the action or information needed. In your closing, you can let the reader know you are available to help or answer questions.

Because this common goal approach is effective, sometimes the most persuasive letter may not seem at all persuasive in the usual sense, and it may be persuasive in part for that very reason. For example, the attorney who wrote the following letter represented a client who refused to sue for damages. The client felt he was partly at fault and, under his religious convictions, he could not accuse another. The attorney, knowing he could not take the case to court, wrote the following successful letter.

August 2, 1984

Mr. Alfred W. Hitchcock
Insurance Claims Service
Box 123
Prairie View, Kansas

Dear Mr. Hitchcock:

This letter follows our earlier conference with you concerning Hans Anderson. Since we met, Carol Kilkenna and I have discussed at some length the various elements that have to be considered with this case.

When we presented Mr. Anderson's demand of $75,000, we did so only after reviewing the available cases involving monetary awards for such a loss. We also did considerable reading on the subject of kidney loss and organ transplants. Because we think that this is a case that can be settled without going through costly and time-consuming court procedures, we have decided to spell out in detail why we feel that the demand of Mr. Anderson is justified.

We would like to present our position regarding the liability issues involved; the nature of the witnesses; the pain and suffering sustained by Mr. Anderson; and, finally, the various damage factors and how we feel the jury would react to these factors.

Since our meeting of July 19, 1984, we have re-examined the relevant state statutes, City of Praire View ordinances, and University rules regarding riding bicycles on sidewalks. We are persuaded that Mr. Anderson was riding legally on the sidewalk at the time of this accident.

The state law on this issue is contained in sections 346.804 and 346.94, Stats. These provisions empower local authorities to decide the legality of sidewalk bicycle riding. Section 346.94(1) prohibits riding bicycles on the sidewalk unless local authorities permit such bicycle riding.

The local authorities in Prairie View permit bicycle riding on sidewalks, except in a business district. A business district is considered any area with predominantly commercial-type uses which generate heavy pedestrian traffic during business hours. The business district must have a minimum street frontage of 100 feet. Prairie View General Ordinance Section 12.01 defines "business district" more completely as:

> the territory contiguous to and including a highway when within any 600 feet along such highway and there are buildings in use for business or industrial purposes, including but not limited to hotels,

banks, or office buildings, railroad stations and public buildings which occupy at least 300 feet of frontage on one side or 300 feet collectively on both sides of the highway.

An examination of Charter Street, revealed in the series of photographs we took of the accident scene, reveals that the buildings in the area are not public buildings of the sort which have heavy pedestrian traffic. Most of the buildings are related to Prairie University physical plant operations. The general public does not use these buildings for commercial purposes. The only people who ordinarily go in and out of the buildings are University employees on University business.

As long-time residents of Prairie View, Carol and I are aware that riding bicycles on the sidewalk is a widely accepted practice very much encouraged by bicycle safety specialists. We feel quite strongly that, in the light of the non-commercial character of the area, Mr. Anderson's riding a bicycle on the sidewalk did not constitute negligence.

From a common law standpoint, we doubt that a local jury would find any significant percentage of negligence on Hans' part. The visual perspective that the truck driver had was entirely different and far better than that of the bicycle rider. The truck driver had an intimate familiarity with the building and the potential risk that truck passage across the sidewalk entailed. We do not contend that the truck driver was necessarily one hundred percent negligent. However, we do contend that a local jury would attribute virtually all of the negligence to the truck driver.

One of the factors that has to be taken into consideration in making an evaluation of this case is the relative believability of the witnesses. Although we have not taken the deposition of the truck driver, we understand that he regretted the incident and was reasonable. We have no reason to believe that his conduct or behavior as a witness would discredit the State. We do believe, however, that the jury would tend to favor the young, straightforward bicyclist. Hans has told us his story in an objective, clear fashion, and we would expect him to do so on the stand. His appearance and attitude are refreshing. We believe that jury sympathy would be with him. All things considered, there would certainly be no disadvantage to Hans' case arising out of a comparison of the likely witnesses. He would probably have some advantage in this regard.

We described to you at our meeting some of the considerable pain, discomfort, and mental anguish that Hans felt between the time of the accident and his ultimate recovery. The accident occurred at about 10:50 in the morning. Hans sustained a significant rib injury and was taken to the University Hospital. He was conscious all of this time and in increasing pain. He was transferred to the Veteran's Hospital about eight hours later. He continued to be conscious. Each movement from litter to ambulance, to litter to bed, bed to litter, litter to CAT scan, etc. caused serious discomfort. During this time, he was bleeding internally, although he continued to be conscious. He suffered appreciable pain while the physicians sought to determine the cause of his discomfort and injuries. It was apparent that he was experiencing considerable internal hemorrhaging. The presence of his family and pastoral staff from Prairie View Lutheran Church praying at his bedside made him well aware that he was in very serious condition, although he was unable to talk to them. His body movements were restricted by pillows in an attempt to ease his rib pain. He was nauseated. He started to suffocate during the night preceding the operation because of the build-up of mucus and blood in his body. He has a very strong recollection of two hospital attendants finally forcing a tube down his gullet so that the fluids could be pumped out, and he could breathe without assistance. His description of how his breathing was impeded previous to the use of the stomach pump and how he couldn't speak to describe his condition is most vivid. Hans was in and out of pain almost from the time of the accident until the time that surgery was commenced. He doesn't purport to have been fully conscious during all of this time, but he was in major pain during the many times that he was conscious. His consciousness extended to the point where he even now has a firm recollection of receiving the anesthetic as a preliminary step to the surgery. His post-operative recovery was impeded by his rib injuries. In order to protect against deflation of his lung or lung collapse, he had to exhale strenuously several times a day, and in each instance, there was accompanying pain involving the rib area.

Hans tells us that he was in the hospital approximately two weeks. He was under medication for pain during the time that he was in the hospital, and he left the hospital to recuperate in the home of a friend whose wife was a nurse. His pain was persistent at that time, and when he was discharged from the hospital, he went to his friend's home with pain pills.

Even by the time Hans went back to school, he couldn't walk in a truly erect position, and it was difficult for him to attend classes. During this time, he had to be transported to and from his classes by automobile.

All in all, Hans went through a substantial amount of pain. He made a good post-operative recovery due to his efforts, diligence and excellent physical condition, but this does not detract from the fact that he suffered.

What about the damages? We would concede that perhaps one in one hundred people are born with one kidney. We recognize that Hans can probably get ordinary life insurance without having to pay a premium for it up to certain dollar amounts. We also recognize that Hans will, at all times, be conscious of the fact that he has lost his safety valve. Hans' mother, a relatively young woman, has a circulatory problem and has had at least one stroke. She has had vein surgery in this regard. Should Hans develop circulatory problems in the future, the fact that he has only one kidney would be a substantial disadvantage. Hans will go through life aware of the fact that he has only one kidney. Although he can physically do most of the things that a person with two kidneys can, Hans will always have to be aware of the fact that he cannot involve himself in any sports activities (such as soccer) where his kidney would be exposed. Hans should not rough-house or scuffle. Should he contract diabetes or other ailments which impose a strain upon the renal system, he will simply not have the reserve that you or I might have under similar circumstances. He tells me that he is constantly mindful as he rides his bike that a serious accident could do him in.

We also recognize that if he were to have an impairment in his sole kidney, dialysis or possibly a kidney transplant would have to be considered. Unfortunately, if the kidney needed replacement when he was in late middle age, he might not be able to obtain a replacement kidney. Although he might obtain a kidney from a family member, the psychological effects of his so doing would be stressful on both himself and the donor. Surprisingly enough, there are few available since such organs are only taken from the bodies of persons who had sustained head injuries. There probably aren't more than 10,000 such potential transplant organs of all types available nationally annually. There are surgical risks in kidney transplants. Although the success rate has risen drastically over the last 20 or 25 years, the fact is some are still unsuccessful. We can't specifically forecast the value that a jury might attribute to this loss, but it would be significant.

One of the things that impressed us most in our investigation of this matter is the fact that Hans will find it extremely difficult to obtain health and hospitalization insurance. In checking with under-writers of these types of insurance, we found that under ordinary circumstances, it would be extremely difficult for Hans to get such insurance, unless he were a part of a very large group (and even this is uncertain). Hans is intending to obtain a theological degree, and whether or not his future will make him part of a large group eligible for group coverage is problematical.

We can't specifically attribute a shorter life expectancy to Hans than to a person with two kidneys, and we doubt that statistical evidence exists on this point. On the other hand, I think it is quite clear that we can show that he will be susceptible to complications arising out of other physiological conditions to a far greater extent than a person with two kidneys. This is one of the reasons we usually would have a jury evaluation of such risks.

We feel a jury would react favorably on Hans' claim. We believe a Dale County jury will not assume that Hans is as good as new. I always insist on having the tires checked and replace them when the treadware or casingware requires change. I wouldn't think of starting out on even a local trip without a spare tire. This is the situation in which Hans finds himself. No one questions that he can't operate with a fair degree of success despite his injury. On the other hand, his position is not enviable. It can be assumed, almost to a certainty, that if liability were proved, he would get a reasonable damages award. What would be a "reasonable amount" is a judgment call.

On the basis of what we have set out in this letter, we think that this case merits the claim we have made. We welcome your serious consideration of our demand.

> Very truly yours,
>
> Allen W. Spohn
>
> Henderson, Avero, and Long

One final touch that may increase your success is to reiterate that the decision is a good one after it has been made, when the reader is most likely to have second thoughts.[29]

Persuading Through a Problem–Solution Approach

The problem-solution structure is a traditional form that many clients may easily understand. This logical pattern is well suited to memo format, lending itself to division into subsections. In this structure, begin by describing the problem; in later paragraphs describe your solution, persuading the reader to accept it.

Explain the problem as concisely and clearly as possible.

> In the past six months, several attorneys have found it difficult to get their motions, briefs, and other court documents back from word processing in time to proofread and correct them before submitting them. As a result, ...

This preliminary step is logically necessary to convince your reader that the problem requires action. If you do not succeed on this point, the reader has no reason to accept your solution.

After convincing the reader that a problem exists, explain your solution, including why it is feasible and worth its cost. At this point, think particularly about benefits the reader will see. These might be different from the benefits seen by you or your client, so focus on benefits that will persuade your reader.

> **By scheduling your deadlines so that you get your briefs to the typists one day earlier, you will be able to avoid unplanned late nights at the office** . . . .

or

> **Disciplining ourselves to get major documents to the typing pool earlier will allow us to reduce substantially our costs for overtime work, decreasing our personnel costs and ultimately improving each partner's income** . . . .

---

29. Research has shown that one of the vulnerable moments in the persuasion process is after the decision has been made. O'Keefe, *supra* note 10, at 66–67. At this point, the arguments against the position taken seem to have more force with the decider. If, however, the persuader follows up with some communication about the desirability of the decision made, this regret is reduced. *Id.* at 67–68.

rather than

> This will allow the typists to schedule their assignments more easily.

When using this approach with legal readers, do not leave unanswered questions. Yet avoid letting the memo get too lengthy or delaying too long before getting to your point. For these reasons, the problem-solution approach may not be the best choice for writing to a senior partner or lawyer out-of-house.

Persuading Readers to Seize Opportunities

An opportunity-benefit structure is useful when you are persuading the reader to take action but you do not want to label the need for action as a problem. It is well-suited to situations where you initiate the correspondence because it provides a positive framework. In this structure, explain first that an opportunity exists.

> The closing of the local branch of Carson, Carson, Englemeier, and Schneiderman makes available the seventh floor of the First Federal Building. Thus we have an opportunity at this time to expand our offices up one floor and gain space needed currently for our new computers and for record storage. It would also provide space we could use to expand . . . .

Explain that the benefit is substantial and worth pursuing, getting the reader to agree with you on this common goal.

After convincing the reader of the opportunity, explain your proposal for taking advantage of it. This part focuses on how your proposal is feasible.

> Although leasing the seventh floor would double our office space, it would only increase our costs by 60%. Thus our cost per square foot would decrease . . . .

> To cover this increase in fixed costs, we would need to increase income by only . . . .

Persuading Readers Through Warnings

The strategy of warning involves notifying the reader that some undesirable consequence will result if he or she does not take or refrain from a certain action. A warning's persuasiveness depends on the reader's motivation to avoid something. The strategy of using warnings is similar to the opportunity-benefit approach because, just as that approach creates a positive framework, the warning strategy creates a negative one. This negative tone makes warnings similar to threats, and, even though offered neutrally, they may erode the writer's working relationship with the reader. The overall negative tone leads the reader to think about avoiding the negative consequences, but not to achieve some other benefit.

To use a warning strategy, use the organization of the problem-solution approach, stating the warning as the problem in this case.

Explain the warning clearly but unemotionally, especially because you want to distinguish this warning from a threat. You may present a warning just as you would present bad news to a reader. The difference in this situation is not in the structure or content, but in the reason why you have chosen the structure and content. This makes this approach particularly useful because the reader cannot clearly accuse you of working against his or her interests.

Persuading Readers Through Threats

When persuading a reader, turn to threats as a last resort. Even though lawyers have more opportunities to threaten effectively than most other writers, do not be misled into thinking threats are your most effective persuasive strategy. Threats will not foster a working relationship with your reader and are hard to use effectively.[30] Moreover, if they are ineffective, they can be expensive to implement.

Before you decide to threaten, consider your options carefully. To help you do this, you may find it useful to ask yourself the following questions.

1. Have I tried all the cooperative approaches available?

   Once you have begun to threaten, it will be difficult to return to a cooperative relationship. Before you burn the bridge, make sure you will not want to return.

2. Is there anything I can actually do, and therefore, can threaten to do and carry out the threat?

   Idle threats have a low chance of succeeding, especially if the other side has a lawyer, and a high chance of undercutting your credibility.

3. Are the reader's options limited under the threat—are they limited to things the reader will not want, so taking the action you want is the one likely response open to the reader?

   Avoid a threat that provides an option undesirable to you or not awful for the reader, because both the cost and the likelihood of a failure then become too great.

4. Would a neutral reader see the threat as fair and appropriate?

   You do not want to create a paper trail that can support a later claim of duress or create sympathy for the other side. In this situation, there is a good chance you could end up with a court or arbitrator deciding the situation, and you want to prepare for that audience.

If cooperative persuasion has not worked, you may have no other viable strategy. You may have to "back the hearse up to the door," as advertising copywriters put it.[31]

---

30. O'Keefe, *supra* note 10, at 166.

31. Thomas Pearsall and Donald Cunningham, *How to Write for the World of Work* 20 (1982).

If you decide a threat is appropriate, then as you draft your letter ask yourself the following questions.

1. Have I presented the threat unemotionally?

2. Is the threat clear and unambiguous?

3. Have I clarified the possible options the reader has?

4. Have I stated that it is up to the reader?

5. Have I stated a time frame for making the decision?

6. Does the tone of the letter avoid irritation or outrage? Is it instead businesslike and rather impersonal?

Avoid bluffing. Remember, most people fear lawyers, but their responses are not necessarily to fold and do what the lawyer says. Instead, your threat may move them to call lawyers of their own.

The persuasive strategy you choose depends mainly on the consequences you can present to the reader. When positive consequences exist, present those first. They may persuade the reader and will not cost your goodwill. When you must resort to using negative consequences to persuade the reader, let the consequences themselves do the persuading, rather than depending on emotional writing.

ADJUSTMENTS FOR TONE

Although your tone will shift depending on your relationship with the reader and your task, that tone should remain businesslike in all correspondence. Even in a tough letter where your tone may be one of impersonal firmness, you will be more effective if you maintain a businesslike image that does not communicate loss of emotional control. Similarly, no matter how friendly your relationship with the client is, focus your correspondence on the matter at hand. The client wants to know you are getting the job done. In all your correspondence, be courteous. Treat each reader as someone whose goodwill it will be advantageous to have, if at all possible.[32]

Three things to avoid are condescension, impatience, and irritation. Although you may experience these feelings in your work, communicating them in out-of-house correspondence generally does not positively influence the reader.[33] With in-house correspondence, your feelings may influence your reader but they are often ineffective for obtaining the results you want. For example, if you complain to a supervisor about your unhappiness at work, the reader might respond emotionally.

---

32. This is not only a good ideal, but a pragmatic goal. Research by Granovetter indicates that weak ties, such as acquaintances and people with whom you have infrequent contact, are more likely sources of some useful information, such as information from new areas of knowledge. For example, Granovetter found that "people were nearly twice as likely to hear about new jobs through weak ties than strong ties." Peter Monge, "The Network Level of Analysis" in *Handbook of Communication Science* 251 (C. Berger and S. Chaffee, eds. 1987).

33. One exception here might be a vendor, because the vendor is hired by you and thus benefits from your goodwill.

But what you probably wanted was a particular action, not an emotional response, and the correspondence did not lead to that result.

Do not communicate condescension, either through sarcasm or a demanding tone,[34] because it will not inspire cooperation. Even if you do get a person to comply through such tactics, it will be resentful compliance, which can lead to that person creating obstacles or rebelling at some future request. Similarly, communicating impatience is usually not effective. If the out-of-house reader does not like you or your client and wants to frustrate your plan, communicating irritation will signal that the reader is successful and will encourage him or her to continue. If the in-house reader is moving slowly, communicating irritation may make that reader feel bad but is not likely to cause him or her to be more efficient. Finally, irritation can imply you are feeling that you may fail in your task, which could be good news for the adversarial reader. If not, it will only irritate the reader.

Effective tone results from blending several different dimensions, which together communicate the writer's style of communication and attitude toward the situation. These dimensions may be described as three continuums:

feeling about the subject: unemotional _____ emotional

involvement with reader: impersonal _____ personal

stance toward reader: formal _____ informal

As with the informing and persuading continuum, choose the appropriate position on each dimension and then blend the three to create the tone you want, just as a painter chooses and mixes colors on a palette to create the right hue.

Some of these dimensions are correlated; as a document becomes more personal, it generally becomes more emotional and more informal. For example, a congratulatory note to a colleague is often more emotional as well as more informal. Some are closely related to particular tasks. A persuasive letter on behalf of a client to another party is likely to be unemotional and impersonal. Because the interaction of these dimensions is complex, each is discussed separately.

Unemotional _____ *Emotional*

Your legal correspondence will usually lean toward the unemotional. Although the content of the correspondence may stir emotions, the delivery should not. An unemotional tone is effective, especially when the reader is frustrated.[35] For example, if you are trying to convince your employer to give you a raise, you want to sound reasoned, not emotional.

> **I base this request for a salary increase on my length of service with Carer's Insurance, the strength of my career**

---

34. Especially when trying to be clear, you must watch for the possibility of creating a demanding tone. Tebeaux, *supra* note 9, at 130.

35. Sandell, *supra* note 6, at 79.

> reviews, and my success in securing several new corporate clients.

But not the following.

> I feel that I deserve a salary increase for several reasons. First, my length of service with Carer's Insurance clearly entitles me to a salary review. Second, my career reviews have been, I believe, excellent and I am proud to provide this record for your review. Finally, ...

If you are writing a collection letter, do not distract from that message by showing that you or your client are getting emotional. You might write the following.

> **If you do not contact us within seven days to arrange payment of the balance due, we will, on behalf of our client, file** . . . .

But would not write the following.

> If you continue to avoid our attempts to contact you about this bill, we will be glad to talk to you in front of a judge.

You can reduce emotion by avoiding modifiers that express judgment. For example, the request for a salary increase was more effective without the writer's judgments of "excellent" or personal statements of "I am proud."

A somewhat more emotional tone is appropriate and desirable when you are celebrating or commiserating with the reader. For example, some emotion is needed to make a congratulatory note believable.

> **Just wanted to let you know how much I enjoyed your presentation last week at the Bar luncheon. Congratulations on a tough job well done; your remarks really stirred the crowd, even after a big meal.**

An unemotional tone would be inappropriate and might sound reluctant.

> Your speech before the Bar last Wednesday has caused several members to ask about ways to improve our referral service, and thus you communicated effectively.

Impersonal --*Personal*

This dimension is related to emotion, because more emotional text becomes more personal. But you can be personal without being too emotional. Legal correspondence at its most effective does not reach extremes on this continuum. Extremely impersonal language is ineffective because it can sound defensive and is usually hard to read.

> In response to the request for an explanation of the definitions included in the draft of the contract received by your office for review, the explanations of these definitions have been included in the attached . . . .

Very personal language is easier to read, but often sounds unprofessional.

> Well, since you were wondering what I meant by "force majeure" in the draft you got, I thought I'd send over . . . .

The middle ground is more appropriate.

> **In response to your question about the significance of Clause 12, the reason for this "act of God" clause is to prevent either party from being able to sue the other when** . . . .

> *Formal* _____*Informal*

The choices are generally subtle on this dimension. For example, avoid both of the following because they are too extreme.

> It would be appreciated if you would sign the enclosed copy and return it to me in the envelope enclosed herewithin. Your assistance in this matter is appreciated.

> Just sign it, stuff it, and send it back. See ya!

But you might use either of the following.

> **Please sign the enclosed copy of this agreement and return it in the enclosed envelope. I appreciate your assistance in this matter.**

> **Just sign the copy and return it to me in the enclosed envelope. Thank you for your help.**

Your choice here depends on your personal image. If you always wear a suit to the office, prefer speakers with more formal styles, and prefer more reserved greetings from people, you will probably choose a more formal writing style for your correspondence. If you hate dressing up and do it only for a day in court, if you like a down-to-earth speaking style, and greet your friends without reserve, you may choose a more informal style.

Whichever style you pick, watch for two common problems: inconsistency and inappropriateness. For example, if you use an informal style, write the following.

> **If you agree, please sign this form and return it to me as soon as you can.**

But not the following.

> If you agree, please sign the enclosed form and forward it to my office expeditiously.

The latter can seem insincere or unprofessional because it is inconsistent. Similarly, if you choose a formal style, write the following.

> **If you find this alternative acceptable, please sign the enclosed release form and return it to our offices so that we may proceed.**

But do not write the following.

> If you find this alternative acceptable, please sign the enclosed release form and bring it back right away.

Here inconsistency is likely to make the writer look like he or she is trying to be impressive—a pitfall that catches many formal writers.

Also avoid extremes. No matter how much you like an informal style, avoid emotion-laden slang in your legal correspondence.

> I know this whole situation has been a real bummer for you.

Instead write with conversational but standard words.

> **I know this situation has been discouraging for you.**

No matter how much you love elegant language, do not drive your reader to the dictionary unnecessarily.

> This situation, I know, leaves you discombobulated and wishing for legerdemain rather than legal processes.

Instead, write

> **This situation, I know, leaves you frustrated and wishing for some magic rather than the slow legal process.**

As with the previous continuum, almost all legal correspondence avoids the extremely formal or informal. Extremely formal language is inappropriate in correspondence generally, and informal language does not create the aura of an educated writer that most lawyers want. Express your own professional style in correspondence, but be consistent so the reader knows who you are and appropriate so you always seem professional.

CONCLUSION

Writing effective correspondence requires you to call into play your skills as a writer, your understanding of persuasion, and your common sense about people. It involves many variables whose interactions are understandable, but infinitely varied and complex. Because writing correspondence means blending many concerns into one unit, it is hard to keep all those concerns in mind when writing. Mastering the blend takes practice.

INFORMING EXERCISE

One common correspondence situation is a letter of retainer. Read the following letters of retainer and note the strengths and weaknesses of each. Then write your own version of a letter of retainer.

Example A.

This letter will confirm our discussion of [day, date].

You have requested that we represent you in the above-captioned matter. Our representation will be limited to _____

_____

_____

_____

The scope of our representation will not be expanded unless agreed in writing by our firm. We have agreed to represent you and will

[   ] begin the representation once you have returned to us the items outlined in this letter.

[   ] continue the work begun since our discussion according to the terms outlined in this letter.

[   ] My legal services will be provided to you at the rate of $_____ per hour. Any time spent by another attorney in our office will be billed at that attorney's normal hourly rate. These rates may be modified over time, although at this moment we do not anticipate changes until July 1st. We do not ordinarily notify clients of rate changes. Services may include, but need not be limited to, office conferences, phone conferences (0.2 hour minimum), court time, travel time, review of file materials, and legal research and other investigation.

[   ] My basic hourly rate for services rendered is $_____ and this will be an important factor in determining our total fee in this matter. Rates of other attorneys in our firm vary depending upon experience, years of practice, and other factors. Our rates may be modified over time, although at this moment we do not anticipate changes until July 1st. We do not ordinarily notify clients of rate changes. However, in establishing our fee, we will consider all relevant circumstances, including our experiences and ability in a particular area, the responsibility involved, the results obtained, and the nature of the employment such as unusual work hours and extraordinary time pressures, all as specified in the ABA Code of Professional Responsibility EC2–18 and DR 2–106. Services may include, but need not be limited to, office conferences, phone conferences (0.2 hour minimum), court time, travel time, review of file materials, and legal research and other investigation.

[   ] Because of the nature of this matter, currently it is not possible to provide an accurate estimate of our total fee. However, we will attempt to provide such an estimate in the future, if possible, upon your request. In any event, we will attempt to make efficient use of our resources. Further, we shall reserve the right to associate other counsel on your behalf whenever we deem it necessary or desirable upon notifying you. Such representation shall be at that attorney's normal hourly rate, if acceptable to you.

[   ] Our present estimate of total fees in this matter is

    [   ] $_____

    [   ] in the range of $_____ to $_____.

However, unanticipated complications or additional incidental services that you may request could result in a higher total fee. Consequently, this should be considered as a good faith, though non-binding, estimate. In any event, we will attempt to make efficient use of our resources. Further, we shall reserve the right to associate other counsel on your behalf whenever we deem it necessary or desirable upon notifying you.

Such representation shall be at that attorney's normal hourly rate, if acceptable to you.

In addition to our legal fees, we may incur and consequently will be reimbursed by you for various out-of-pocket costs, such as recording or filing fees, sheriff's fees, deposition costs, mileage charges, photocopies, telecopier charges, and long-distance telephone calls.

It is expressly understood that we have made no promises, assurances or guarantees as to the outcome of this matter. Payment of our bills is not contingent upon the outcome of this matter.

You shall at all times have the right to terminate our services upon written notice. If you choose to terminate our services, it is understood that we will be paid in full or that arrangements will be made for payment before the file is released. We shall at all times have the right to terminate our services upon written notice in the event that you either fail to cooperate with us in any reasonable request, to timely pay the periodic statements, if any, in full as submitted, or not replenish any retainer, or in the event we determine in our reasonable discretion that to continue our services to you would be unethical or impractical.

Until all fees and costs are paid in full, we shall retain a lien on your file. If the file is released to you, we shall have the right to make copies of any portion thereof and to withhold internal office memorandum and personal notes.

[ ] Payment of our bills, including requested retainers or prepayments, will be due within 30 days of their dates. We cannot overemphasize the importance of timely attention to these payments. If full payment cannot be made within that time period, arrangements must be made with us by the end of that 30 days for an alternative payment plan.

[ ] Although our practice is to require full payment within 30 days, in your case, we have already discussed and agreed to an alternative payment plan. This plan will take effect if your monthly bill exceeds $_____ and, despite your good faith effort to do so, you are unable to pay it in full. Given those circumstances, we will accept a $_____ payment and will carry the remaining balance forward. We reserve the right to renegotiate this alternative payment plan during the course of our representation.

[ ] All bills not paid at the end of 30 days shall have interest charged against them at 18% per annum, which shall be computed on a monthly basis. Thus, you will be charged 1–1½% per month interest on the outstanding principal balance of your bill.

[ ] Attached to this letter is credit information entitled "Credit Disclosures," the contents of which are incorporated in this letter.

[ ] By this letter, we acknowledge receipt of your payment of $_____ as a non-refundable retainer to be applied against our fees

and against out-of-pocket costs incurred by us. We reserve the right to request an additional amount in the future as this case progresses.

[ ] If this letter properly sets forth our understanding or is an acceptable arrangement for you, please sign and return the enclosed copy of this letter

>   [ ] along with a check in the amount of $_____ as a non-refundable retainer to be applied against our fees and against out-of-pocket costs incurred by us.

A self-addressed, stamped envelope is enclosed for your convenience. If we do not receive this within 10 days from the date of this letter, we will assume that you have obtained other counsel and will mark our file "closed" and do nothing further. We will furnish a bill for services rendered to the day we closed our file.

[ ] If this does not properly set forth our understanding or is not an acceptable arrangement for you, please contact me within 5 days from the date of this letter. At such time, we will stop working on this matter and will incur no additional legal expense for you until the misunderstanding has been resolved or until an acceptable arrangement has been established.

If you have any questions concerning the items covered in this letter, please do not hesitate to contact me.

Sincerely yours,

_____

[Attorney]

Enclosure

[ ] The above is understood and agreed to.

Date:
                          _____
                          [Client]

Approved as to Form by: _____
Date:

Example B.

[Date]

Re: _____

Dear _____:

This letter confirms our meeting on _____, _____, 1990, during which we agreed to represent you regarding _____. Because I have found that it is important for there to be a clear understanding of our financial arrangements, it has become my practice to send my clients a letter confirming those arrangements shortly after I begin representation.

My fees for legal services will be based on an hourly rate of $_____ per hour. This rate may vary over time, although I do not anticipate any changes until July 1. When I, or any other member of our firm, perform services on your matter, we will record the time spent, the nature of the services performed, and our hourly rate. Services may include, but need not be limited to, office conferences, phone conferences, court time, travel time, review of documents, and legal research. If you ever have any questions about the services we are providing or the charges for those services, feel free to contact me.

You will also be charged for out-of-pocket expenses, including such items as long distance telephone calls, photocopies, faxes, computer aided research and document drafting, court costs, and fees for filings, recordings, court reporters, witnesses, or service of process. When appropriate, we will forward invoices for expenses which exceed $50.00 to you for direct payment. Any expenses paid by us and charged to you will be itemized on our monthly statements.

Our complete itemized statements will be sent to you each month. The full balance due should be paid within 30 days of receipt. If you ever have any questions about the charges for services we are providing or the services themselves, feel free to contact me.

When we are initially retained by a client who does not have an established relationship with our firm, we generally require an advance of $_____. Please forward this advance payment to us. It will be applied against your final statement for services and disbursements or against any delinquencies in your account. We may require additional advances, if necessary, to cover anticipated fees or expenses.

When our representation ends, we will, at your request, make available any papers, property, and file materials to which you are entitled. We may retain our internal notes and memoranda, our work product, and any duplicate materials.

Please confirm that this is an acceptable arrangement by signing both copies of the letter and returning one copy to me along with the requested advance. If we do not receive a signed copy of this letter and the advance within ten days, we will conclude that you are no longer interested in having us represent you and will close your file. You will remain responsible for any charges incurred up to that date. A return envelope is enclosed for your convenience in forwarding the requested advance and the signed letter to us.

We hope that our relationship will be founded on mutual confidence and respect. Therefore, we encourage you to discuss with us the progress of work performed for you, our billing policies, and the details of our statements.

We are pleased to represent you and look forward to working with you.

Sincerely,

[Attorney]

Enclosures

The fee arrangements described in this letter are agreed to:

Dated: _____   _____

PERSUADING EXERCISE

The following series of letters is a realistic exchange of correspondence regarding a dispute over a bill. The appraiser is asking to be paid the final portion of his fee, but the City refuses because of errors in the appraiser's work, errors which resulted in a loss of revenue for the City. Read each letter and discuss how it is effectively or ineffectively written. In each example, you will find many things that need to be improved, but you may also find some good ideas that could be implemented more effectively.

WILLIAM WILSON REAL ESTATE APPRAISAL CONSULTANTS, INC.

EXECUTIVE OFFICES . P.O. BOX 2, Othertown, Mass.

August 4, 1989

Ann Burns, Clerk
City of Goodville
Goodville, Massachusetts

I am sorry that it has taken me so long to respond to your June 23, 1989 letter, which was a reply to our request for payment for services rendered.

Since the law clearly states that the Clerk and the Board of Review, as part of their duties, are to review the roll for errors, omissions and duplications of assessments, it would seem inappropriate for us to assume the responsibility.

Also, if you remember, prior to the values being put on the roll, you reviewed with Arlene Haunschild a list of all the Personal Property Assessments, prior to their being entered.

We would appreciate a prompt and reasonable settlement of this account.

Respectfully yours,

William Wilson
President

CC: City Attorney Mary Wright

CITY OF GOODVILLE
Goodville, Massachusetts

August 10, 1989

WILLIAM WILSON Real Estate Appraisal Consultants
WILLIAM WILSON, President
1111 W. Main St.
P.O. Box 2
Othertown, Mass.

Dear Mr. Wilson:

Bill Willing, City Clerk for the City of Goodville, has given me a copy of your dunning letter of August 4, 1989, and I've re-read the City's letter of June 23, 1989, that was addressed to you. That caused me to take more notice of your letter, and that in turn raised a question only you can answer.

Specifically, your letter appears to say that your firm takes no responsibility for errors in the assessments your firm undertakes, and that when errors occur through faulty mathematics and substandard investigations done by your firm that it's the City clerk's fault for not having done an independent assessment of his own with which to check your work. Is this the position you're taking when you say "it would seem inappropriate for us to assume the responsibility" for errors, omissions and duplications of assessments?

I would appreciate a reply at your earliest convenience. The assessment you did resulted in a $5,749.08 expense for the City, and as you know the City Council has refused to pay the last $500.00 of the $7,200.00 bill for your services, at least partially, because of the lack of an explanation of why your firm should be paid for a late and erroneous assessment. I'm sure you would be welcome at a meeting of the City Council to answer the Aldermen's questions and speak in favor of reversing the resolution denying your payment of your bill. The Council meets on the first and third Tuesdays of each month at 7:30 P.M. in the City Hall. Please give us some advance notice if you intend to come to a meeting so that a line can be placed on the agenda that must be delivered to the media to comply with the Massachusetts Open Meeting Law.

Sincerely yours,

City of Goodville
Mary Wright
City Attorney

WILLIAM WILSON REAL ESTATE APPRAISAL
CONSULTANTS, INC.

EXECUTIVE OFFICES . P.O. BOX 2, Othertown, Mass.

August 21, 1989

Mary Wright
City Attorney
City of Goodville
Goodville, Mass.

Dear Ms. Wright:

I am replying to your letter of August 10, 1989 which was in response to my earlier communications. I suppose that we could continue exchanging self-serving letters forever but it would not solve the problem of your owing me $500.00 which is your contractual obligation.

There are of course, many statutes in Massachusetts which allow any community the ability to recap its money regarding errors, omissions and duplications.

If a reasonable settlement could be reached, I would be more than happy to discuss it with you, for litigation would only result in a fee for yourself and our legal counsel.

I would appreciate a prompt response.

Respectfully yours,

President

CC: Dudley Domore, Mayor

CITY OF GOODVILLE

Goodville, Massachusetts

August 25, 1989

William Wilson
P.O. Box 2
Othertown, Massachusetts

Dear Mr. Wilson:

I am afraid I didn't explain the constraints on my powers to you clearly enough in my previous letter to you, as you apparently see a lawsuit as the only response open to you if I don't send you a check. This is not the situation. I think a thumbnail sketch will do it.

The City Council got a copy of your bill, and in the course of dealing with the general claims brought it up for action. There was a consensus of opinion that the City had been substantially damaged by what appears to have been negligence on the part of your firm, that the bill was adding insult to injury, and that there was no reason to pay for work that was for practical purposes not done because it was done so negligently. The Council determined that you would not be paid, but neither would you be asked to reimburse the City for damages caused by your faulty assessment. Considering that you had already been paid the greatest portion of your demands, the City Council felt that you would see the reasonableness and justice of the City's position.

It is becoming swiftly apparent that you do not see the reason in not paying you the last portion of your demands and in effect using the money to defray approximately 10% of the damage the City suffered by your firm. This is most unfortunate for both of us—for you because you apparently feel put upon, and for me because I must respond to your letters without being able to do anything to salve your indignation. As I tried to point out in my last letter, the bills must be paid by the City Council. I cannot bind the City to any disbursements.

Therefore, you have three options: you can come before the Council and present your side, being prepared to answer why you should be paid for doing damage to your client, or you can sue and prepare to tell a jury why you should be paid your demands in full and not be asked to pay for even 10% of the damage your negligence caused, or you can forget it and be glad that you had been paid so much before your negligence was brought to your client's attention.

Sincerely,

CITY OF GOODVILLE

Mary Wright
City Attorney

PERSUADING EXERCISE

In light of the discussion you have just had, revise the attorney's original letter, writing to avoid the pitfalls that caught the writers of the previous series of letters.

ASSIGNMENT 1

Write a letter of retainer to Ms. Timm, using the facts in the sample opinion letter at the end of Chapter 15.

ASSIGNMENT 2

Write a cover letter to accompany the interrogatories you are sending to the Kellys on behalf of Susan Ashland, based on Assignment 1 at the end of Chapter 13.

Bibliography

Andrews, Deborah C. and Margaret B. Blickle. *Teaching Writing Principles and Forms.* New York: MacMillan Publishing Co., Inc., 2nd ed. 1978.

Berger, Charles R., and Steven H. Chaffee, eds., *Handbook of Communication Science.* Newbury Park, CA: Sage Publications, 1987.

Brannon, Lil, Melinda Knight, and Vara Neverow–Turk, *Writers Writing.* Montclair, NJ: Boynton/Cook Publishers, Inc., 1982.

Eisenberg, Anne, *Effective Technical Communication.* New York: McGraw-Hill Co., 1982.

Fowler, Roger, ed., *Essays on Style and Language: Linguistic and Critical Approaches to Literary Style.* London: Routledge and Kegan Paul, 1966.

Hatch, Richard, *Business Communication: Theory and Technique.* Chicago: Science Research Associates, Inc., 1977.

Houp, Kenneth W. and Thomas E. Pearsall, *Reporting Technical Information.* New York: MacMillan Publishing Co., Inc., 1980.

Jacobi, Ernst, *Writing at Work: Dos Don'ts and How Tos.* Rochelle Park, NJ: Hayden Book Co., 1979.

Mansfield, Carmella E. and Margaret Hilton Bahnick, *Writing Business Letters and Reports.* Indianapolis: Bobbs–Merril Educational Publishing, 1981.

McDonald, Daniel, *The Language of Argument.* New York: Harper and Row, 3d ed. 1989.

Novello, Don, *The Lazlo Letters.* New York: Workman Publishing Co., 1977.

O'Keefe, Daniel J., *Persuasion: Theory and Research.* Newbury Park, CA: Sage Publications, 1990.

Pearsall, Thomas E., and Donald H. Cunningham, *How to Write for the World of Work.* New York: CBS College Publishing, 2d ed. 1982.

Sandell, Rolf, *Linguistic Style and Persuasion.* San Francisco: Academic Press, 1977.

Simons, Herbert G., *Persuasion: Understanding, Practice, and Analysis.* New York: Random House, 2d ed. 1986.

Tebeaux, Elizabeth, *Design of Business Communications: The Process and the Product.* New York: MacMillan Publishing Co., Inc., 1990.

Tortoriello, Thomas R., Stephen J. Blatt, and Sue DeWine, *Communication in the Organization: An Applied Approach.* New York: McGraw–Hill Book Co., 1978.

Chapter 15

OPINION LETTERS

Opinion letters do not involve the wide range of variables present in general correspondence; their primary readers are clients and their primary task is to answer clients' questions. They do, however, blend the writer's concerns with those of a legal researcher. Writing opinion letters allows you to synthesize much of what you have learned while working on writing tasks discussed in earlier chapters.

The purpose of the opinion letter is to give the client the answer to a legal question and to give legal advice. An opinion letter attempts to state how the law will apply to a particular set of facts, based on the expectation that "the courts will proceed in an orderly manner in the direction indicated by prior decisions."[1] You write this correspondence to inform, rather than to persuade. So you will use the general tone and focus discussed for informing clients in the correspondence chapter. Even though the client may use the letter to help persuade others (to obtain a loan commitment, purchase property, or negotiate a deal), your purpose as you write the letter is to answer the reader's question.

When you have to give bad news, the techniques in the correspondence chapter will be helpful. Although you may need to say no, be sensitive to your client's hopes, wishes, and fears.[2] For example, instead of saying "Claims like yours have been flatly rejected by the Nebraska courts," rephrase your statement to be less harsh: "This claim has been unsuccessful in other cases" or "is unlikely to prevail." But your client needs to understand your answer, including when your answer is not the one he or she had wanted. You can be sensitive to your client's wishes and still honestly state your opinion on the likelihood of their success.

Unlike general correspondence but like research memos, opinion letters contain more complex content and provide the reasoning behind a point. The depth of this research depends on the needs of your reader. To handle this complexity, opinion letters need a more elaborate structure than general correspondence. Opinion letters commonly have the following sections: (1) the date and addressee of the letter, (2)

---

1. Mortimer Levitan, *Dissertation on Writing Legal Opinions,* 1960 Wis.L.Rev. 22, 23.

2. Raymond Ocampo, Jr., *The Opinion Letter,* 3 Cal.L.Rev. 28, 28 (Jan.1983).

an opening, which includes a reference to the question and the client's request for an opinion, among other things; (3) a fact section, which recounts the facts upon which your opinion is based; (4) an answer to the question, which is often labelled the conclusion; (5) an explanation of the reasoning behind that conclusion, which may be called a discussion; and (6) a concluding section, which includes a polite closing and may include advice about how to proceed. This chapter discusses these sections and provides guidance for drafting each.

Before addressing the specific sections of opinion letters, you should recognize that, within this structure, there is still quite a bit of latitude. For example, the tone may be formal or conversational, the reasoning may be technical and in-depth or may only summarize the information, and the opinion may or may not include citations. The major factors you should consider when making these choices are your reader's needs and your professional obligations to your client. These considerations are the subject of the next section.

GENERAL CONSIDERATIONS

Your opinion letter, no matter how formal or complex, should: (1) answer the client's question, (2) be understandable by the client, and (3) clarify the opinion's limitations, including that the letter itself does not create legal rights and does not give an answer that will remain unchanged over time, facts, or jurisdiction.

Answering the Client's Question

In your opinion letter, address the specific question asked rather than discussing the law in general. There are several ways to do this. You can begin the letter with a reference to your conversation with the client and the client's question.

> At our meeting on January 15, 1989, you asked for my opinion as to the possibility of successfully suing Dr. G.W. Haverford for malpractice based on the following facts.

You can also refer to the question in a subject line.

> RE: Possibility of suing Dr. G.W. Haverford for failure to warn of risks associated with transplants

When you state your conclusion later in your opinion letter, you can state it using the terms of the reader's question.

> You can sue Dr. Haverford with a reasonable probability of success.

If the client worded the question more informally and you need to introduce the client to the more specific legal question, you can accomplish that in your opening sentences.

> When we met in my office on January 15, 1989, you asked me to determine whether you could legally require Dr. Haverford to pay for the medical costs you have incurred as a result of the complications you suffered after he performed surgery. To do this,

as we discussed, you would need to bring a lawsuit against Dr. Haverford for medical malpractice. Accordingly, I have researched this question for you.

The purpose of each of these techniques is to keep the letter focused on the specific question you are answering. This is necessary because you are indeed answering a specific question. You want to ensure that your client does not attempt to broaden the answer to apply to other questions because, without additional facts and research, you cannot provide advice on those questions.

Making the Answer Understandable to the Client

Since you are writing for one particular reader, you can tailor your explanation to that person. For example, if the reader is a business-woman with extensive experience in the area, you may use more technical business terms and may state the pros and cons of the alternatives in specific, no-nonsense terms. If, in contrast, your client is a retired, elderly woman who has trouble remembering details, you may want to state your point simply and without technical words. You may also focus on explicitly stating the potential outcomes rather than the complicated reasons behind those outcomes and summarize these outcomes, so your reader can see how it all fits together. If your reader is a person with no experience in the area your opinion addresses, you may introduce needed technical language but include definitions.

Additionally, you may adjust the formality, technicality, and amount of explanation in your letter based on your reader's preferences. Some readers, just like some supervisors, want quick, concise answers, unencumbered with legalese or extra words. Others may want more formal documentation with legal citations and explanations of the law behind the answers. For example, if you are writing to a corporate executive who values time highly and does not like to bother with details, your opinion may include a separate summary of the reasoning. Then the executive can read that portion and file the letter without reading the full support, even though that support must be included. If you are addressing a particularly uncertain issue, one whose ramifications could be profound for your client, you may need to write a longer letter. Subdivide your explanation section to detail your reasoning systematically, stating each main point the reader should note in a subheading. Within the text under each heading, you can state each reservation in a matter-of-fact tone, but state it specifically so the record is clear.

Clarifying the Opinion's Limits

One of the most important portions of an opinion letter that you must communicate to the reader is the opinion letter's limitations. These limitations include ones based on time, jurisdiction, and facts. Your opinion will be limited by time because the law is constantly changing. Thus, your opinion should clearly state that it is limited to the legal consequences of the stated facts for this particular moment in time. You must indicate to your client that he or she cannot simply file the opinion, pull it out six months later, and expect it to be as valid as on the day you wrote it.

> This opinion is based on the facts you gave me, the current Montana statute regarding restrictive covenants in employment contracts, and pertinent Montana case law. If the law changes, then this opinion is also subject to change.

> In addition, the law may change over time and affect the validity of this opinion. Thus it is limited to the law as it currently stands.

Additionally, you must indicate that your opinion is limited to the jurisdiction in which you practice.[3] As an attorney licensed in one state, you are not qualified to practice in other jurisdictions, and your client needs to understand that he or she cannot use your opinion rendered in one state to resolve a problem that occurs in another state.

> As you know, we are not admitted to practice law in any state other than the State of New York and are not experts in the law of any state other than the State of New York.

> This opinion is limited to the application of the facts stated below to the law of Minnesota and should not be used for any other purpose.

You must also indicate that your opinion is based on the facts you have included in your letter and any change in the facts noted may result in a change in the opinion reached.

> The facts you provided me are set out below. Because a change in the facts might alter my opinion, please contact me if any facts are incorrect or omitted.

> Please review the facts I have included and contact me if any facts are misstated or if you have any additional information.

The following sections on interviewing the client and drafting the facts section provide suggestions for helping you obtain the facts and write them.

> Finally, be sure your client realizes your opinion letter does not create any legal rights. In order to convey this to your client, you must realize it for yourself.[4] You must also indicate this limitation to your client.

---

3. Most lawyers also are comfortable giving an opinion based on federal law. If your client needs an opinion based on state law outside your jurisdiction or if your client needs the opinion of a specialist, you have many options. You can hire local counsel to research the matter and provide an opinion letter which you will incorporate into your own letter. Or you can have local counsel provide a separate opinion letter directly to the client. You should discuss this matter with your client. Remember, if you incorporate the local counsel's or specialist's opinion into your own, you will become liable for that opinion.

4. Some attorneys mislead others into believing that their opinions have the force of law, when, in fact, they confer no genuine protection at all. Levitan, *supra* note 1, at 32.

My opinion is based on the following facts and does not create any legal rights.

Please understand that this opinion does not create any legal rights.

These limitations will be present in virtually all opinion letters although different opinion letters have different limitations. Clean opinion letters are those in which the lawyer, after applying the law to the facts, reaches a conclusion substantially free of doubt.[5] For example, "The shares have been authorized and validly issued, and are fully paid and nonassessable" is a clean opinion.[6] You are able to apply a given legal rule to particular facts and determine the legal conclusion.

More frequently, the lawyer needs to write what is known as a reasoned opinion letter, where the reasoning is explained.[7] Reasoned opinions are needed when the law is unclear, when the facts are not straightforward, or when reasonable arguments might lead to differing legal interpretations.[8] These letters resemble the office memorandum because they often contain citations to relevant case law or statutes and present different sides of the issues when these are needed by the reader.

Even though you must qualify your answer in a reasoned opinion letter, remember your client does want an answer. Do not include so many reservations that your client has not obtained an answer to the question asked. If there are alternatives, discuss them and their relative merits. Do not hedge with general terms like "probably" or "likely," but instead state the qualifications of your opinion as specifically as you can. You may need to indicate these reservations with phrases such as

although similar cases have reached different results, so that the law is not settled here,

although courts have differed on this issue, the most recent case,

while no controlling authority exists on this matter,

Thus, your answer can be clear and unambiguous, even though your answer may not be simple or definite.

Additional limitations may arise in some situations. For example, business transactions are often based on one side's attorney providing an opinion letter either on matters at issue between the parties or on problems that must be resolved before the transaction can be completed.

The rendition of legal opinions has been called, accurately, "the quintessence of a business lawyer's practice." Legal opinions play a pivotal role in our economy: "No major corporate or commercial transaction is complete unless as a condition of the

---

5. John Sterba, Jr., *Drafting Legal Opinion Letters* § 1.4, at 7 (1988).

6. *Id.*

7. *Id.*

8. *Id.*

closing, the participating lawyers deliver opinions on relevant legal matters." [9]

These opinions are frequently subject to negotiations about the limitations or qualifications placed on the letter. When negotiating with another attorney to receive an opinion letter, do not ask your opponent to give an unqualified opinion letter when you know you would be unable to provide such a letter.[10] Recognize the qualifications that must exist, and then attempt to obtain a letter with no more than those necessary qualifications.

Rendering opinion letters is one of the riskiest aspects of law practice. You can open yourself to many possible malpractice allegations if the opinion you present does not meet established standards.

> Depending on the circumstances, an improvidently rendered opinion may lead to disciplinary action by state or federal authorities, a negligent malpractice or negligent misrepresentation action, a common law fraud action, claims under the federal and state securities laws, penalties under the Internal Revenue Code, prosecution and civil actions under the RICO statute, an action alleging an unfair trade practice, a demand for punitive damages and criminal prosecution under the securities laws and the mail fraud, wire fraud, and false statement statutes . . . . In truth, the analysis of lawyers' opinion letter liability is really a particularized study of the body of legal malpractice law, itself a large and growing field.[11]

The standard of care that attorneys are held to in rendering opinion letters is "to use such skill, prudence, and diligence as lawyers of ordinary skill and capacity commonly possess and exercise in the performance of the tasks which they undertake." [12] Nonspecialists will be held to the specialist's higher standard of care if they hold themselves out as specialists and then they fail to exercise a specialist's skill and knowledge.[13] When presented with a matter outside your area of specialty: "(1) be competent, (2) become competent, (3) get help, or (4) get out." [14]

Malpractice, however, does not usually result simply from the failure to prognosticate correctly. It is difficult to criticize a lawyer's performance in anticipating the actual outcome of any single case.[15]

---

9. John P. Freeman, "Legal Opinion Liability" in *Drafting Legal Opinion–Letters* § 10.1, at 400 (1988).

10. Sterba, *supra* note 5, at § 1.5, at 10.

11. Freeman, *supra* note 9, at § 10.1, at 400–402. (citations omitted.)

12. *Id.* at § 10.2, at 404. The source of these standards, which is the duty to provide competent representation to a client, comes from the ABA Model Code of Professional Responsibility and its Model Rules of Professional Conduct. *Id.* at § 10.4, at 407. Disciplinary rule 6–101 indicates that

actionable malpractice may be punished as ethical misconduct when it is based on inadequate preparation, neglect, or practice in an area in which the lawyer lacks skill. Model Rule 1.1 requires competent representation of a client which requires "the legal knowledge, skill, thoroughness and preparation reasonably necessary for the representation." *Id.*

13. *Id.* at § 10.9, at 414.

14. *Id.*

15. Detlev Vagts, *Legal Opinions in Quantitative Terms: The Lawyer as Har-*

While malpractice liability exists, it usually flows from not providing competent representation rather than from making an incorrect statement of the probable results of a case. Your reputation as a lawyer will be tied to your opinions, and you must exercise competence, care, and skill in drafting your opinion letters.

PREPARING THE OPINION

When a client requests your opinion, begin by meeting with him or her. This client often will have expert knowledge, experience, and understanding of his or her particular field, which will give you essential background knowledge before you research the legal implications of the question.[16] After you obtain this background information, ask your client questions about the facts. As with pleadings, make sure to ask the hard questions now, because your answer to the client's question will be based on these facts. Clients often want to present a situation in the light most favorable to themselves, so you will probably need to probe to get a more realistic picture of the situation. Verify as many facts as possible, when doing so will not cause unnecessary expense or too much effort.[17] This is especially true when you are uneasy about the accuracy of the facts.

If the facts you uncovered are not thorough or are not yet clear to you, consider drafting the facts section of the opinion and submitting those facts separately for the client's approval before you complete the rest of the opinion. Be sure to include a statement that your opinion will be based on these facts and that your client should inform you of any additional facts because they would probably alter the answer. Making sure your client realizes the impact of withholding any legally significant facts may prompt the client to provide them to you. Submitting the facts section before completing the rest of the letter prevents having to redraft the letter to respond to new facts.

Another point to clarify in your meeting with the client is the particular question the client wants answered. A client may not yet quite know what he or she wants; you may provide a significant service to that client just by helping define the question. Additionally, you will be helping yourself focus the statement of the problem so that your framing of the question and subsequent research can be more efficient. When you have completed your research and determined your answer, your first drafting question will be whether to put your opinion on paper, where it may be discoverable.[18] Also consider whether your opinion would best be presented orally. Then you can alter your presentation to the client's response, which helps assure that the client understands your opinion and does not have an inappropriate response to the answer. Opinion letters require diligent preparation. Because

supex or Bookie?, 34 Bus.Law. 421, 428 (1979).

16. Levitan, *supra* note 1, at 28.

17. Harold Segall and Jeffrey Arouh, *How to Prepare Legal Opinions: Boldness*

and Caution, 25 Prac.Law 29, 32 (June 1979).

18. See the discussion of this concern in the format section of the correspondence chapter.

malpractice liability and professional embarassment can attach to an incorrect opinion, many attorneys prefer to provide oral advice instead of written opinion letters.[19]

Assuming you do need a written opinion, your next step will probably be to organize the information within each section. Here the principles discussed in the chapters on objective issues, objective facts, and memorandum discussion sections should help you.[20]

Date and Addressee

The first considerations are the date of the letter and the addressee of the letter. The date on the letter indicates when the legal conclusions contained in the letter take effect. Sometimes you provide an opinion letter in connection with a business transaction and date it for the day the transaction closes. If your opinion requires you to update public records after the letter is provided, you may want to indicate that reservation in the letter.

An opinion letter is usually intended to be received by the addressee, who is the client. Sometimes the letter is addressed to a third party or the third party's attorney. When drafting these letters, be sure to consider whether you are waiving the attorney-client privilege between you and your client by providing your opinion to third parties.[21] Because you may be liable to third parties, you should also consider who may foreseeably rely on the opinion and whether you should not issue the opinion at all or qualify it in some way.[22] The basic rule has been that a lawyer has no duty to persons beyond those addressed, in the absence of fraud, collusion, or recklessness from which fraud can be inferred, or special circumstances indicating that a duty to a third party has been accepted.[23] But the lawyer owes a duty of care to specific persons or limited classes whom the lawyer knows will receive the letter and rely on it. Given the potential liability that attaches when drafting opinion letters, you may want to include language to prevent reliance on the opinion by third parties.

> This opinion is provided by us as counsel for XYZ Corporation and is solely for its benefit.

> This letter is not to be used, quoted, or circulated for any other purpose.

While this language may not completely preclude third party reliance, it does indicate that you did not intend for anyone other than the addressee to rely on the opinion.

---

19. Sterba, *supra* note 5, at § 1.3, at 6.

20. See Chapter 6, Objective and Persuasive Issues; Chapter 7, Objective Facts, and Chapter 9, Discussion Sections.

21. Sterba, *supra* note 5, at § 2.4, at 17.

22. *Id.* at 17.

23. Fuld, *Lawyers' Standards and Responsibilities in Rendering Opinions*, 33 Bus.Law. 1295, 1309 (March 1978). *See also, National Savings Bank v. Ward*, 100 U.S. 195 (1879); *Ultramares Corp. v. Touche*, 255 N.Y. 170 (1931).

The Opening

The opening provides the context for the opinion letter and states the question you will be answering. Often the opening will refer to the meeting or phone conversation in which your client first requested the opinion.

> On April 12, 1990, we met in my office to discuss your concerns about the offer to purchase you submitted for the house at 2010 Main Street.

> In response to our conversation on April 12, 1990, I am enclosing my opinion regarding the validity of your offer to purchase the property at 2010 Main Street.

Starting your letter by reminding your client of the letter's context helps to clarify the letter's focus. This organization allows the client to determine immediately whether you understood the question asked or the nature of the advice sought.[24] It also sets the tone and establishes the working relationship in this letter.

This opening sentence can also indicate the question presented. As the examples above show, the client wanted to know whether the offer to purchase was valid and the opening sentence provided both the context and the question asked. If the matter is somewhat more complex and you need to state the question asked more explicitly, then follow the opening with a statement of the question.

> You have requested my opinion regarding the likelihood that the Federal Trade Commission or the Justice Department's Antitrust Division would attack an acquisition of Center Corporation's stock by First Corporation as a violation of Section 7 of the Clayton Act.

The Facts

When writing the facts, use the techniques discussed in the chapter on writing objective facts. State the facts as objectively as possible. Make sure you have included all the legally significant facts, the ones that will alter the result of your opinion. Consider including notations indicating the source of the facts, such as who supplied them or how they were otherwise obtained.[25] Many facts are based on documents that you should review before stating your opinion. As stated above, be sure to note in this section that your opinion is based on the facts.

The Conclusion

When writing your conclusion, begin with your answer to the question in your first sentence.

> Based on the facts stated above, you can sue Dr. Haverford with a reasonable probability of success. The most likely theory

. . . .

---

24. Segall and Arouh, *supra* note 17, at 31.

25. *Id.* at 32.

Then add any needed specifics.

> The most likely theory to sue under would be negligence, claiming that Dr. Haverford was negligent in not informing you of the risks involved in the course of treatment she recommended.

Also you may refer here to major limitations you will discuss later.

> Success in this case, however, will depend on whether we can convince the jury that these risks are not common knowledge, so you could not reasonably have known of and assumed those risks without the doctor's specific discussion of those risks.

Although you want to keep this section short, you do want to state your answer fully enough to be accurate. Note major points here but do not go into the supporting reasons. State your answer firmly. Do not provide your client with a nebulous or tentative conclusion but do indicate any qualifications that limit your opinion.

Explanation Section

Remind the reader throughout this section that you are explaining the answer to his or her question. The value of the opinion letter is based on its accuracy in predicting what the legal consequences of the relevant facts are within a given question. Thus, "the cardinal rule in writing opinions is that the reasoning must dictate the result, [but] the result must not dictate the reasoning."[26] Careful reasoning is imperative. Lead your reader step-by-step through your reasoning, if necessary, to ensure that he or she understands the limitations inherent in your reasoning.

The organization of the explanation section should follow the same organization of the issues. Develop your letter sufficiently to show the client that you understand the problem and you have provided the information necessary to answer the question.[27] It should include "references to the major legal principles, the trend of decisions in the jurisdiction, the application of legal rules to the present facts, possible arguments which may be raised by both sides, and the probable result if the legal problem is litigated."[28] Limit your letter to resolving two or three issues. More than that may be difficult for the reader to remember and may be impossible for you to address thoroughly in a letter.

It is particularly important to discuss those arguments helpful for your client's position. Although your letter should be a neutral assessment of the issues, your client wants and will appreciate your special attention to his or her side of the case.[29] The client will be most interested in how the law resolves his or her problem, rather than in the law itself. Therefore, avoid abstract explanations of the law. Where explanations are needed, let the reader know why this information is necessary to understanding your answer.

26. Levitan, *supra* note 1, at 34.

27. Ocampo, *supra* note 2, at 28.

28. *Id.* at 57.

29. *Id.*

The jury's decision on whether the risk is common knowledge is critical here because Dr. Haverford will be excused from liability for your injury if . . . .

Depending on your client's needs, you may need to provide a more in-depth analysis of the law controlling the situation. If you include summaries of the cases controlling the outcome and present each court's reasoning, be sure to include citations. If your opinion is based on interpreting statutes, you may want to include the relevant portions of the statute either in the text or as attachments.[30] Do not skimp on support simply because this document is a letter, not a brief or an office memo. While you will not include the kind of support and full-blown analysis that you might include in a brief or a memo, your letter will include the highlights of that information, depending on the complexity of the question(s) you are answering and the needs of your client.

When you can explain the law without teaching the reader new terms, do so. If you must use a legal term with which your reader will not be familiar, define it. You can do this gracefully by adding an explanatory note to inform the reader without insulting his or her intelligence. To avoid overemphasizing the definition, put it in a dependent phrase. For example, you may insert a parenthetical.

> This assumption of risk (a plaintiff may not recover for an injury when she voluntarily exposes herself to a known danger) can be
>
> . . . .

You may add the explanation as a phrase at the end of the sentence.

> This is called an assumption of risk, or . . . .

Or, if the explanation is long, you may add it in a sentence following the sentence in which the term was introduced.

> This is called an assumption of risk. In the law of Wisconsin, assumption of risk means . . . .

The Closing

In the closing to your letter, summarize any action that your client needs to take. Also communicate that you stand ready to be of service. Try to avoid having your closing sound like an attempt to generate more legal fees.

> Please do not hesitate to call if you have any questions about this opinion or any other matter.

> I hope this letter answers your question fully. I'm glad that this issue can be resolved so easily for you. If you have any questions in the future, feel free to call.

---

30. There are two advantages to including the relevant statutory sections: "(1) the writer of the opinion can't quote the pertinent portions of the statute without reading the statute very carefully to ascertain which portions are really pertinent; (2) the reader of the opinion can read the opinion with understanding without referring to unavailable statute books." Levitan, *supra* note 1, at 34.

Due to the high standards you must meet when providing an opinion letter, many firms restrict the signing of these letters to certain people. These people review all opinion letters leaving the office to consider the impact that expressing a particular legal opinion in one case will have on other cases within the firm or whether one opinion will preclude taking other possible clients or cases.[31] Firms may also establish internal peer review procedures in order to obtain an independent review of the opinion letter before it leaves the office.[32] Peer review often helps the attorney negotiate the limitations placed on the letter so as to avoid providing an unreasonably broad opinion.[33]

Once you have the content and organization in place, revise your opinion for readability, using the techniques discussed in the chapter on jury instructions as a general guide. Then revise with an eye for tone, especially remembering to maintain clarity while being tactful. Finally, reread for polish; you want to avoid any grammatical, spelling, or other errors that could detract from your professional credibility with your reader. This will increase the reader's confidence in your work.

CONCLUSION

In summary, an opinion letter begins and ends with the form of any other business correspondence, but the middle takes on the form of a research memo. The letter should demonstrate your objectivity. You should not distort the answer for your client and you should make sure that you do not appear to be judging or condemning your client's conduct.[34] You are providing an opinion on a legal matter, not a guarantee, and your letter must reflect this inherent limitation.

EXERCISE

Read the following sample of an effective opinion letter and determine how it applies the techniques discussed in this chapter. Rewrite those sections of the letter that do not follow these techniques.

Law Offices
SMITH AND JONES
Boise, Idaho

February 4, 1978

Mrs. Jean Timm
80 Lakewood Gardens Lane
Mayville, Idaho

RE: Deductibility of live-in attendant's wages

Dear Mrs. Timm:

On January 17, 1978, we met in my office to discuss your 1977 federal income tax return. At that time you asked whether the wages

---

31. Sterba, *supra* note 5, at § 1.6, at 13.   33. *Id.* at 14.

32. *Id.*   34. Ocampo, *supra* note 2, at 57.

of the live-in attendant you employed during 1977 would be deductible. My opinion is based on the following facts. Please review these facts and contact me if any facts are misstated or if you have any additional information.

FACTS

On October 2, 1976, you received a serious back injury in a car accident. You were hospitalized from October 2, 1976, to January 3, 1977. Your doctor wanted you to stay in the hospital longer, but you wanted to go home. Because your injury would require you to be bedridden indefinitely, your doctor required you to hire a live-in attendant before she would allow you to leave the hospital.

On January 4, 1977, you hired Joseph Crosby as your live-in attendant. Crosby had received his nursing training in a five-week course. Crosby's duties included assisting you in doing your prescribed bed exercises, administering your medicine, preparing all of your meals, running errands (such as buying medicine, groceries, or knitting yarn), and mowing your lawn every two weeks during the summer. Crosby did a few daily cleaning tasks, but a cleaning service came in once a week to do the general cleaning. Crosby had one day off a week. He worked for you until December 18, 1977, when your condition had improved to the point that you could get in and out of bed by yourself. After December 18, 1977, you hired part-time help to assist you.

During 1977 you paid Crosby $8,000 and provided his room and board. Your question is whether Crosby's $8,000 in wages could be a deduction on your 1977 federal income tax return.

CONCLUSION

Part of Crosby's wages is a deductible medical expense. If you have adequate records to estimate the amount you paid for Crosby's food, a portion of his board is also deductible. The amount of the deduction will depend on the amount of time Crosby spent performing nursing services. This opinion is based on the current version of the Internal Revenue Code.

EXPLANATION

One of the basic rules of the Internal Revenue Code is that personal, living, and family expenses are not deductible. The medical expense deduction is an exception to this general rule. The exception allows the deduction of amounts paid for the diagnosis, cure, mitigation, treatment, or prevention of disease, or for the purpose of affecting any structure or function of the body. The Internal Revenue Service's principal concern when it reviews medical expense deductions is to prevent taxpayers from deducting expenses of a personal, living, or family nature. Taxpayers have the burden of proving that the deductions they claim fall within the medical expense exception.

Among the expenditures that qualify for the medical expense deduction are taxpayer payments for nursing services and nurses' board. Crosby's wages are deductible to the extent they were payments for nursing services. Many of Crosby's duties, such as helping you with your bed exercises, administering your medicine, and preparing your meals, were the type of nursing services you would have received in a hospital or convalescent home. Some of his duties, such as running errands, mowing the lawn, and doing daily cleaning chores, however, were services of a personal, living, or family nature. We should discuss Crosby's duties in greater detail to determine the percentage of his wages that you can reasonably deduct as a medical expense.

Crosby's board will be deductible in the same proportion as his wages if we can reasonably estimate the amount you spent on his food. We need receipts, cancelled checks, or personal records of your expenses to help us determine how much you spent for food while Crosby was living with you. We need the same information for the period after he left to estimate how much of your total food bill was for his board. The more information you have, the more accurate we can be, but do not be concerned if you have not kept exhaustive records. As long as the amount of your deduction is reasonable, the I.R.S. probably would not require full documentation of your expenditures if it audited your tax return.

I hope this letter adequately answers your question. Please make an appointment to see me sometime in the next two weeks. Bring all the records that I requested at our first meeting and the information about your food expenses. After this second meeting, I should be able to complete your tax return within two weeks.

Please call me if you have any questions.

Sincerely,

Roger Smith
Smith & Jones

RS:jr

ASSIGNMENT 1

You are an associate in a Madison law firm. This afternoon, you met with Dr. Christine Beck, who is a dentist employed by the M & M Dental Clinic, S.C.

Seven years ago, right after she completed dental school, Dr. Beck was hired by the dental clinic. At that time, she signed an employment contract that includes a restrictive covenant. The covenant states that if Dr. Beck leaves the clinic, she agrees not to practice dentistry within a 100–mile radius of Madison for five years. The contract does not specify what damages Dr. Beck would owe the clinic if she were to breach the restrictive covenant. The contract also covers more routine aspects of Dr. Beck's employment, including sick leave, vacations, salary, and general duties.

Because she is tired of city living, Dr. Beck now wants to leave the M & M Dental Clinic and open her own practice in Cross Plains, which is in Dane County, just fifteen miles west of Madison. She wants to know whether the dental clinic can enforce the restrictive covenant against her.

When you questioned Dr. Beck further about her work for the clinic, she gave you the following information. Two years after she joined the clinic, Dr. Beck approached many of the health maintenance organizations and employers in Madison about affiliating or contracting with the clinic for dental care. As a result of her efforts, the clinic is now affiliated with one Dane County HMO and four large Madison employers. Dr. Beck has strong connections with each of these groups and handles most of the business interactions for the clinic. Most of her time, however, is directly devoted to patient care.

The shareholders of the clinic do not yet know about Dr. Beck's plans to set up a practice of her own. She expects the clinic shareholders to object when she leaves the clinic and to sue her for breaching the restrictive covenant. The shareholders will probably fear that Dr. Beck's withdrawal from the clinic may cost it the affiliation with the HMO and the contracts with the large employers.

Dr. Beck believes, however, that most of the clinic's patients will stay with the clinic and the affiliation and contracts will not be affected if she opens her office in Cross Plains. On the contrary, she is the one who will probably lose business because almost 60% of the clinic's patients are Madison residents who would find it inconvenient to travel to Cross Plains. Most of the remaining patients live in various parts of Dane County. Dr. Beck believes that her new practice in Cross Plains would not affect the clinic's business, even though she is very popular with the patients. Therefore, she hopes that the restrictive covenant is invalid. She is also concerned about the large area and length of time of the restriction.

You have researched Wisconsin law about restrictive covenants and have found the following statute and three cases. When you read the cases, it may be helpful to (1) quickly skim them to get a general understanding of the law and its historical development, (2) carefully read them to determine what parts of the opinions are applicable to Dr. Beck's situation, and (3) carefully reread the applicable parts of the opinions to determine how the law applies to Dr. Beck's situation. Then write an opinion letter to Dr. Beck, laying out the answers to her questions.

The relevant statute is the following Wisconsin statute.

Restrictive covenants in employment contracts. A covenant by an assistant, servant or agent not to complete with his employer or principal during the term of the employment or agency, or thereafter, within a specified territory and during a specified time is lawful and enforceable only if the restrictions imposed are reasonably necessary for the protection of the employer or principal. Any such restrictive covenant imposing an unreasonable restraint is illegal, void and unenforceable even as to so much of the covenant or performance as would be a reasonable restraint.

Relevant cases for this assignment are *Lakeside Oil Co. v. Slutsky,* 8 Wis.2d 157, 98 N.W.2d 415 (1959); *Behnke v. Hertz Corp.,* 70 Wis.2d 818, 235 N.W.2d 690 (1975); *Chuck Wagon Catering, Inc. v. Raduege,* 88 Wis.2d 740, 277 N.W.2d 787 (1979); and *Geocaris v. Surgical Consultants, Ltd.,* 100 Wis.2d 387, 302 N.W.2d 76 (App.1981) (see footnote 1).

ASSIGNMENT 2

Draft an opinion letter based on the Howard Jones problem included in Assignment 2 in Chapter 8. You are the attorney for the defendants. You have received the plaintiff's complaint and you read the applicable cases and statute. You have decided that the best option is to respond to the complaint with a motion to dismiss for failure to state a claim, rather than answering. Write an opinion letter explaining to the defendants what you will be doing and why you have decided on that option. Provide a detailed explanation of your decision because your clients want to participate in the decision of what to do during the law suit.

Bibliography

Fuld, James J., *Lawyers' Standards and Responsibilities in Rendering Opinions,* 33 Bus.Law. 1295 (March 1978).

Levitan, Mortimer, *Dissertation on Writing Legal Opinions,* 1960 Wis.L. Rev. 22.

Ocampo, Raymond L., Jr., *The Opinion Letter,* 3 Cal.Law. 28 (January 1983).

Segall, Harold A., and Jeffrey A. Arouh, *How to Prepare Legal Opinions: Boldness and Caution,* 25 Prac.Law. 29 (June 1979).

Sterba, John M. Jr., *Drafting Legal Opinion Letters.* New York: Wiley Law Publications, 1988.

Vagts, Detlev F., *Legal Opinions in Quantitative Terms: The Lawyer as Harsupex or Bookie?,* 34 Bus.Law. 421 (1979).

Chapter 16

WILLS AND TRUSTS

This chapter reviews the drafting principles associated with writing a contract but applies them to the task of writing wills and trusts. As with contracts, with these documents you must determine the clauses you need, find examples of those clauses, and revise them to fit your client's needs. Unlike contracts, wills and trusts do not require you to work out compromises between the parties. The testator's desires are supreme.[1] Your job is to ensure that they are effectuated after his or her death.

Wills are the central instruments in most people's estate plans, and at the heart of many wills is the testamentary trust.[2] The essential feature of a testamentary trust is that property is held by an individual or corporation for the benefit of another person or persons.[3] The trustee has a legal obligation to hold and manage the property for the beneficiaries, and the beneficiaries have legal rights enforceable against the trustee.

Drafting a will, with or without a trust, involves three stages. The first is holding an interview with your client to determine his or her desires. The second is determining the substantive and procedural law

1. A person who leaves a will directing disposition of his or her property upon death dies testate and is known as the testator; a person who does not leave a will dies intestate and the statutes of his or her state control disposition of the property. William McGovern Jr., Sheldon Kurtz, and Jan Rein, *Wills, Trusts, and Estates including Taxation and Future Interests* § 1.1, at 1 (1988). When a person dies testate, the will must be admitted to probate, through the probate courts, before it has any legal effect. Hoops, *Family Estate Planning Guide* § 14.1, at 575 (1982). When the will is admitted to probate, the court appoints an executor to administer the testator's estate and to oversee disposition of the property. *Id.* at § 14.2, at 591.

2. *Id.* at § 31, at 58. An inter vivos trust can take effect during the settlor's lifetime, can also be used to control disposition of property, and can be either revocable or irrevocable. Our discussion of trusts in this chapter is limited to testamentary trusts that are part of a will.

3. Trusts often provide professional management of property for the beneficiary who has never managed property or when age or other factors impair the beneficiary's ability to do so. *Id.* at § 32, at 58. Trusts can also be used to give lifetime use of property to a person or persons while ensuring that eventually other persons will receive the property, such as when the grantor provides the surviving spouse with a lifetime interest in a trust, with the remainder passing to the grantor's children.

that controls probating the will.[4] The third is drafting and redrafting the will so it accurately portrays your client's desires and is readable by those who will turn to it for guidance during probate. Accuracy and readability are the two most important concerns when drafting these documents.

INTERVIEWING YOUR CLIENT

The possibility of strong emotions pervades this interview. Some clients may be facing imminent death. Other clients, even those not imminently facing death, may nevertheless be feeling intense emotion as they prepare their wills. Still other clients' emotions may be related to the deaths of others close to them. By recognizing that your clients may have these emotions, you will be better able to fulfill your role as counselor and to obtain the information needed to draft these testamentary documents.

You may also need to address your own feelings about death. For example, if you are uncomfortable talking about death, you may be distracted or unresponsive when your client has trouble discussing how to structure his or her will. Although drafting wills does not require extensive reflection on your own attitude toward death, you do want to ensure that your feelings and thoughts are not adversely affecting your client.[5]

To reduce the problems that may occur in this emotionally charged atmosphere, structure your interview to proceed step by step so you can obtain all the information you need. This structure is not intended to force your client to answer questions when he or she is caught up in emotional feelings. Instead, it allows you to pause when these emotions may arise, to note where you stopped, and to return to that point without skipping any aspects of the interview.

You can provide this structure by preparing an in-depth interview questionnaire and then proceeding through the questionnaire in every interview. This questionnaire will also help you remember to ask all the questions needed to obtain the details for drafting documents that fulfill each client's wishes. The questionnaire will contain at least four categories of information: (1) domicile, (2) property, (3) beneficiaries, and (4) the individual's objectives.[6] Be specific when composing the questionnaire. It is better to have a long interview that will elicit most, if not all, of the information you need to begin drafting than to have to schedule follow-up interviews or place numerous phone calls to close gaps that you left during the initial interview.[7]

---

4. Actually, you will need to have a significant understanding of the substantive and procedural law controlling probate before you hold the interview with your client.

5. Thomas L. Shaffer, *The Planning and Drafting of Wills and Trusts* 12–19 (1979). This section on "Feelings about Death" incorporates numerous exercises on addressing these feelings in the classroom, the law office, and the courts.

6. Hoops, *supra* note 1, at § 19, at 24.

7. For sample will questionnaires, *see* Michael J. Weinberger, "Will Questionnaire" in *Practical Will Drafting* 19 (1976); Hoops, *supra* note 1, at § 310; John Price,

Be sure to give your client specific instructions concerning the documents to bring to the interview. Better yet, consider sending your questionnaire or portions of it to your client when scheduling the interview. This allows the client to prepare beforehand by gathering the documents and information needed at the interview. It also allows your client to prepare at home where the information is more readily available and where the client does not have to pay for your time. Then the client can come to the interview prepared to provide the specific information you need.

In the interview, question your client closely to determine how he or she wants to dispose of property. Even after gathering documents or answering the questionnaire, your client may be unclear about this decision. Your questions, based on the substantive and procedural requirements of your jurisdiction, may lead the client to decide on an estate plan that varies from the one originally envisioned.

Try to puzzle out exactly what your client wants. For example, if a client wants to leave his stamp collection to Uncle Jack, has he considered what he wants to happen if Uncle Jack dies before him? Does he want Uncle Jack's heirs to receive the collection or does he want it to revert to the residuary of the estate? You may have to help your client consider the likelihood that Uncle Jack will die before he does. Some other questions that your client may not have considered but that you should raise include avoiding tax consequences when possible, planning so that the documents will survive any challenges to them, and anticipating problems that arise when the document is drafted in one state and probated in another.

Also question your client closely about assets. This may be somewhat touchy, because most people are not comfortable sharing the specific details of how much property they own, how they hold title to that property, and other private information. Take time to establish rapport with your client so he or she will become comfortable enough to share this information. Stress to your client that you will be unable to make intelligent recommendations without all the facts. Additionally, many clients tend to estimate incorrectly the value of their assets and often do not understand the consequences that can result depending on the manner in which title to property is held.[8] For example, many married couples own property as joint tenants with right of survivorship, which is not subject to the terms of the will.[9] The location of the property is important as well. While all personal property and in-state real property will be distributed during the local probate, out-of-state

Contemporary Estate Planning § 1.20 (1983).

8. California Continuing Education of the Bar, *How to Draft Wills* 7 (June 1985) (hereafter C.E.B.). The best way to verify this information is to examine the documents involved. *Id.*

9. The property doctrines section of this chapter discusses these and other issues concerning title to property. Other contracts, such as life insurance policies, retirement plans, and multiple-party bank accounts, may also pass to named beneficiaries outside the control of the testamentary documents.

probate will require an ancillary probate in the state where the property is located.[10]

You should also consider holding separate interviews with each spouse. An attorney representing both spouses must address the potential conflicts of interest that can arise in this situation.[11] For example, whether property is characterized as community property or separate property can have conflicting results for each spouse. You should inform each client of the potential conflicts of interest so he or she can decide whether to allow you to continue to represent them both. If you do continue to represent both spouses, consider having them sign letters to indicate that they understand the conflicts of interest that may arise from the potential adversarial nature of estate planning and that they agree to have you represent them both.[12]

The client interview and the analysis of the information obtained during it are both time-consuming and vital to accurate estate planning. Unfortunately, many attorneys handling estate work view it as an opportunity to obtain business in the future. Because of this, they frequently do not bill sufficiently to cover the time necessary to prepare a will or trust carefully.[13] This practice forces them to rush through the job. The best way to avoid this problem is to impose realistic time demands on yourself and bill for estate planning just as for other work.

Having completed the interview, recognize that procrastination can also be a serious problem in doing estate planning work. Unlike litigation, where outside factors impose deadlines on you, estate planning, like other transactional work, does not have similar external deadlines. You must impose them on yourself to avoid the unhappy circumstance that results when several months pass following the client interview and the client suddenly dies before executing the testamentary documents. The beneficiaries-apparent would have a valid malpractice claim against you if you unreasonably delayed execution of the documents.[14] After finishing the client interview, set deadlines for yourself to draft the documents and have them executed.

DETERMINING THE SUBSTANTIVE AND PROCEDURAL LAW

After gathering the estate planning information and documents, go to the library. The transfer of property at death is complicated by statutory requirements for probating the will, tax consequences, and property doctrines. Researching these areas of law will allow you to understand the impact that these and other considerations play in developing an estate plan. While this chapter cannot touch on all the

---

10. McGovern, *supra* note 1, at § 14.1, at 588. These ancillary probates can be costly and often require retaining local counsel.

11. C.E.B., *supra* note 8, at 9.

12. M. Bradley, G. Dionisopoulos, T. Drought, J. Frank, M. Hogue, J. Kussmaul, R. Langer, J. McMullen, S. Merrell, R.

Nelson, J. Perlson, C. Rasmussen, L. Roberson, R. Severson, and P. Tilleman, *Eckhardt's Workbook for Wisconsin Estate Planners* § 2.2b, at 2–7 (1990).

13. Johnston, *Legal Malpractice in Estate Planning and General Practice*, 17 Memp.S.U.L.Rev. 521, 528 (1987).

14. *Id.* at 534.

factors that you must research and consider before drafting, it will review several of these statutory requirements, tax consequences, and property doctrines.

Statutory Requirements

The law controlling wills and trusts is essentially statutory, although countless cases exist interpreting those statutes. These statutory requisites are quite specific in each state, and you must strictly adhere to them. For example, one court held that a will was not executed correctly because it had not been attested to by two or more witnesses "in the presence of the testator" as the statute required.[15] One of the witnesses was not in the room with the testator when he signed the will. Although the witness checked with the testator over the phone to verify that the document was his will and that he had signed it, the court ruled that the statutory requirement of presence meant "physical presence" when the will was signed.[16]

Some of the statutory details that you must know and understand to probate a valid will can be seen by reviewing malpractice cases. For example, these cases have been won for not using the required number of witnesses, using a person named in the will as a witness, omitting an essential clause from the will, or inaccurately drafting an essential provision.[17] The great weight of authority remains opposed to reforming a will's terms to correct inadvertent mistakes, regardless of the testator's intent.[18] Knowing these details will allow you to effectuate your client's wishes and prevent malpractice claims against you by unhappy beneficiaries.[19]

You must also consider the problem of drafting a will in one jurisdiction and having it probated in another. You can resolve some of these problems by looking beyond the law of your jurisdiction when drafting your documents so the will can meet the requirements of those states too.[20] For example, your jurisdiction may require only two witnesses to the will, but some others require three. Using three witnesses will protect your client better by ensuring that all states will recognize the will as valid.[21]

---

15. *Matter of Jefferson's Will*, 349 So.2d 1032, 1032 (Miss.1977).

16. *Id.*

17. Johnston, *supra* note 13, at 522.

18. *Id.* at 523.

19. Although lack of privity of contract historically precluded beneficiaries from bringing malpractice suits against attorneys, this is no longer true today. Most states today have either overturned the strict privity barrier to malpractice suits or have used a third-party beneficiary theory to provide standing to beneficiaries. *Id.* at 523–524. Some states, such as Nebraska,

New York, and Minnesota, have not followed this majority trend. *Id.* at 524–525.

20. Commonly, each law firm or attorney will develop a will execution form that satisfies all possible jurisdictional requirements for probating the will.

21. Schwartz, *Sins of Omission and Commission in the Drafting of Wills and Trusts*, 11 Inst. on Est.Plan. § 1101.2, at 11–4. Two witnesses suffice in all but two states. Vt.Stat.Ann. tit. 14, § 5 requires three witnesses; La.Rev.Stat.Ann. § 9.2442 requires two witnesses plus a notary public.

If the testator owns property in more than one state, there may be questions about which state is entitled to tax the property upon the testator's death, whether the property will be considered to be community or individual property, which state's rule against perpetuities controls when inter vivos trusts are established, or what powers of appointment the executor or trustee may exercise.[22] Consider retaining local counsel to handle probating out-of-state assets, at least in those states where you are not licensed to practice.[23]

Tax Consequences

One of the most significant aspects of estate planning practice is understanding the tax consequences of the transfer of property at death. These tax consequences often lead general practitioners to shy away from preparing any but the simplest testamentary documents. And with good cause. The tax laws change frequently and the decisions interpreting tax regulations must be continuously updated.

Do not proceed in this area of law unless you have or can obtain the training to become qualified in this complex area. The tax consequences surrounding your client's death require an awareness of estate, inheritance, gift, and income tax ramifications of the estate plan and how federal and state tax laws interrelate. A simplified example shows how knowledge of the tax laws, how they coordinate, and how they can be used in establishing your client's estate plan is vital to protect your client's interests. For example, current federal law allows each individual to transfer up to $600,000 free from transfer tax and, additionally, allows each spouse a marital deduction to transfer any amount of property at any time from one spouse to another tax-free.[24] When the spouses' total estate exceeds $600,000, you can use the unified credit, in combination with the marital deduction, to obtain substantial tax savings in the surviving spouse's estate.[25] This is accomplished by transferring property exceeding $600,000 to the surviving spouse in those forms qualifying for the marital deduction, thus avoiding tax on that property.[26] The details of these tax consequences are beyond the

22. *See*, Hoops, *supra* note 1, at §§ 361–378, for a further discussion of these and other conflict of laws issues that arise with multi-state estates.

23. This practice coincides with the limitation noted in opinion letters that restricts their validity to the state in which the opining lawyer practices. See Chapter 15, Opinion Letters.

24. *Workbook for Estate Planners, supra* note 12, at § 1.17a. Federal gift tax allows individuals to make lifetime transfers of $10,000 per year, per donee, tax-free. Federal estate and gift taxes are coordinated to allow a unified credit of $600,000 against transfer taxes so that when the credit is applied against estates

of $600,000 or less, no tax liability exists. *Id.*

25. *Id.* The marital deduction was established in 1948 to equalize the tax treatment of persons living in community property and common law states. In simplest terms, the marital deduction allows a deduction from the decedent's gross estate equal in value to any interest in deductible property passing to his or her surviving spouse. Hoops, *supra* note 1, at § 190, at 450–451.

26. *Workbook, supra* note 11, at § 6.8b. To determine what property qualifies for the marital deduction, *see* § 6.13. To prevent the surviving spouse's estate from having large taxes assessed, you can estab-

scope of this chapter, but consider them when drafting testamentary documents.

Property Doctrines

In addition to the statutory requirements and the tax consequences, also consider the applicable property doctrines. These come into play because the will or trust you are drafting is intended to change the ownership of the testator's property from the testator to those people or organizations named as beneficiaries. How title to property is held for each of your client's assets will control whether your client can dispose of the property under his or her will or trust and also will control whether the will or trust is needed to transfer title. For example, if your client owns property in joint tenancy, it will not be controlled by your client's will or trust.[27] In contrast, if the property is owned as tenancy in common, a right of survivorship does not exist for the other tenant(s) in common, and your client may transfer his or her interest through the will or trust.[28] Concurrent estates can also exist in personal property such as cars, bank accounts, and securities. You must determine how title is held and then discuss with your client whether he or she is content with the title controlling the disposition or wants to change the way title is held to reach a different result.

If your client is married, you must also consider whether the state in which your client is domiciled is a community property or common law property state because this will affect what property the testator may dispose of in the will. Your client can dispose of all of his or her separate property under the will or trust, but can only dispose of his or her share of community property.[29] Whether a property is separate or community may also affect other areas, such as the tax consequences at the time of death.

Equally important to knowing the law before drafting these documents is knowing when you should refer the matter to a specialist.[30] Estate planning is a complicated area that requires extensive knowledge in tax and future interests law for drafting anything more than

lish a trust to place the decedent's $600,000 in a trust for the surviving spouse's lifetime benefit. This allows the spouse to receive income and principal from the trust, while not "owning" it for tax purposes upon his or her death. *Id.* at § 6.8a.

27. Joint tenancy's outstanding feature is the right of survivorship inherent in it, which means that each joint tenant owns the whole property, subject to the equal rights of the other joint tenant(s). Thus, your client's title to the property does not "pass" to the survivor as in testate or intestate succession. John E. Cribbett and Corwin W. Johnson, *Principles on the Law of Property* 106 (3d ed. 1989).

28. *Id.* at 111.

29. Additional questions arise when couples move from a separate property state to a community property state, or vice-versa, and how their property will be treated at death. These problems of choice of law between jurisdictions can have significant impact on what property is included in the decedent's estate and to what property his or her spouse is entitled. McGovern, *supra* note 1, at § 3.10, at 147–150.

30. As noted in the chapter on drafting opinion letters, be competent, become competent, get help, or get out.

the most basic will. Failure to make the referral can result in a malpractice action being pursued against you.[31] For example, if you usually do not handle estates substantial enough to warrant considering a marital deduction, you may want to refer that client to a specialist. Otherwise, if you incorrectly draft the will for a client entitled to this deduction, you could lose that important benefit for your client.

DRAFTING CONSIDERATIONS

This section discusses the drafting considerations for wills and trusts. The first section discusses the primary drafting principles for these documents: accuracy and readability. The second discusses organization. The third section discusses how to draft standard will clauses, and the fourth covers ways to prevent challenges to the will. By reviewing these sections after having interviewed your client and researched the procedural and substantive law, you will be prepared to draft testamentary documents that accurately portray your clients' desires while remaining readable for all who use them.

Accuracy and Readability

The primary principle when drafting wills and trusts is accuracy. The document must portray the client's wishes accurately because your client will be unavailable to explain any clauses that are ambiguous. Inaccuracies or ambiguities in these documents may require judicial interpretation. This interpretation can frustrate the client's wishes because the court's reconstruction of the client's intention may not coincide with his or her desires and will cause delay, expense, and inconvenience.[32]

A secondary need is for readability. Readability is important so the client can review the documents and determine whether they actually say what he or she wants. While your client may not be able to understand some of the technical language required to effectuate the estate plan, he or she should be able to understand why it has been inserted and what its purpose is. For example, you may decide to use the phrase "descendants per stirpes" to specify how the residuary estate will be divided. While you may have to explain to your client that this means that the descendants of a named beneficiary take that beneficiary's share in equal parts,[33] your client will understand the reason for the clause once you explain it.

31. *See, Horne v. Peckham,* 97 Cal.App. 3d 404, 158 Cal.Rptr. 714 (1979), where the court held that a general practitioner was liable for malpractice for not referring a complicated estate matter to a specialist in the area. The court used the standard that a general practitioner has a duty to refer to a specialist if a reasonable generalist would have referred the case under similar circumstances. *Id.* at 414, 158 Cal. Rptr. at 720. The court also held that if

general practitioner does work usually performed by a specialist, the generalist will be held to the higher standard of care imposed on the specialist if errors occur. *Id.*

32. Schwartz, *supra* note 21, at § 1100, at 11–13.

33. Hoops, *supra* note 1, at § 32, at 48. *See, Lombardi v. Blois,* 230 Cal.App.2d 191, 40 Cal.Rptr. 899 (1964).

Always be prepared to explain any clause, phrase, or word that you use to your client.[34] One attorney told us of including a clause in a will that she took from an in-house form will because all the form wills contained that clause. She did not take the time to understand it exactly, but included it in case it was important. It was important because it was the one clause about which her client questioned her. She found herself in the unfortunate situation of having to inform her client that she did not understand the clause either. Avoid putting yourself in this situation.

Also consider readability for the additional people who will use the testamentary document. For example, the beneficiaries will scan it to determine what they will be receiving, the executor or personal representative will read it carefully to determine what powers have been granted by the testator, the trustee will read it to determine what his or her role is, and the court will read it to determine the client's intent if the will is challenged. For all of these audiences, you must draft a will that remains readable while resolving complex and often competing considerations. One easy way to increase readability is not to capitalize words needlessly such as will, codicil, guardian, and executor. In everyday language, those words would be in lower case.[35] Using traditional capitalization will enhance the readability of these documents.

Some attorneys worry that revising will language to make it more readable will make it impossible to retain the information necessary to probate a will successfully.[36] But readability can be achieved without sacrificing accuracy. The success of plain English in such complicated situations as insurance contracts shows that this concern is unfounded. Second, some attorneys believe that clients who expect legalese might be uneasy about a will drafted in plain language. Or they might think that the streamlined will deprives the will of the solemnity and dignity found in traditional wills.[37] Whether the clients do actually feel this way, however, is not documented.

Even if your client feels uneasy, you could try explaining your purpose to them: the will is drafted to be more readable for everyone and be more accurate in stating the client's desires. You may also find that using some graphic techniques, such as bold, italics, and different size type faces for headings, may help your clients find that the will

---

34. H.M. Grether, *The Little Horribles of a Scrivener*, 39 Neb.L.R. 296, 301 (1960).

35. Leon Feldman, *"Simple Will" can be simplified further to produce a more concise but effective document*, 10 Est.Plan. 290, 293 (September 1983).

36. Lawrence Cusack described his experience with this problem when, after reviewing several form books, he pulled together a will that used "plain English" throughout. Lawrence Cusack, *The Blue–Pencilled Will: What's wrong with a will*

in plain English?, 118 Trusts & Estates 33 (August 1979). He provided the will to six reviewers and five of them agreed that the edited version was more readable and might please a client for those reasons. The sixth reviewer felt that nothing would be gained by "word-plucking" through standard testamentary language, because most clients did not care about the language and the time saved in typing would be insignificant. *Id.*

37. *Id.*

looks sufficiently official. You could try including some resonating language in the opening and closing of the will to set the tone your client wants, leaving the substance of it clearly stated.

Organization of Wills and Trusts

Having considered the drafting principles inherent in will and trust drafting, next consider the organization of these documents. Many lawyers simply follow the organization included in form books when drafting, even though it may not enhance accuracy or readability. The document will be more readable for your client if you organize it to proceed from what is most important to the client to what is least important or least understandable. For example, rather than starting your wills with a clause calling for payment of "just debts" as do most form wills, begin with those clauses that most interest the client, the disposition of his or her estate to the named beneficiaries.[38] Place technical provisions and definitions at the end, where they do not distract from the document's readability.[39]

One way to simplify both the organization and the language of your documents is to use everyday language in the clauses and then include a definition section that explains the use of any terms with a particular meaning. This allows you to state the information that is most important to the client in the document's body and relegate technical language that may be confusing to the definition section. For example, you could draft the following clause.

> **Tangible Personal Property.** I give all my tangible personal property:
>
> (a) to my wife, Jane Smith ("my wife"),
>
> (b) if my wife does not survive me, to my descendants,
>
> (c) if none of these persons survive me, to my heirs.

Then you can use the definition section to define tangible personal property,[40] survival (usually requiring thirty to ninety days' survival after the testator's death), descendants, heirs, and how distributions are to be made between them. This format allows the will to be straightforward and readable without excluding the details necessary to effectuate the testator's wishes.

Some people may object to this format because they find it inconvenient to have to turn to the definition section while reading the

---

38. S. Johanson, *The Orphan's Deduction: How to Handle a Troublesome Drafting Problem*, 14 Inst. on Est.Plan. 26 (1980).

39. *Id.*

40. Trying to write a definition of tangible personal property so that it covers all possible items creates the risk that you will omit something. One will left "all of my personal property, consisting of furniture, carpets, curtains, china, linen, miscellaneous prints and pictures, antique chandeliers, Louis XVI mantel, mirror and fireback installed in drawing room in my residence, and miscellaneous bric-a-brac . . . ." The court held that the bequest did not dispose of the testator's rare book collection. The court also held that if the phrase "consisting of" had been replaced with "including", it could have construed the clause to include the collection. *Matter of Jones' Estate*, 38 N.Y.2d 189, 379 N.Y.S.2d 55, 341 N.E.2d 565 (1975).

document. If you or your client object to this format, develop another that allows for clear organization and readable clauses. One alternative is to reserve definitions for particularly complex terms, thus reducing the amount of cross-referencing necessary. Another option is to put the most important, and usually least confusing, clauses on distribution of property at the beginning of the document and place the more complex, confusing clauses at the end. If you use a definition section, do not use it to reinsert your anxieties about drafting a will in plain English. For example, most lawyers agree that it is unnecessary to have the client "hereby give, devise, leave and bequeath" his or her property.[41] Either "give" or "leave" would be sufficient. Having eliminated these unnecessary words from the body of the document, do not reinsert them in the definition section.

> Whenever the term "give" is used in this will it shall include the terms "devise", "bequeath", "leave", or "devise and bequeath".

When deciding what terms to define, remember that overusing definitions will make the document difficult to read. Virtually every term in a will can be defined to clarify its meaning. But poorly defined terms have led to much litigation. For example, when defining a term as seemingly straightforward as "children" or "issue," you must consider the questions that may arise when using these terms. Some of these include the following.

1. Is the term "children" to be limited to immediate offspring?

2. Is the term "issue" intended to include remote descendants beyond the immediate offspring?

3. Are the offspring of several different marriages to be included?

4. Are adopted children to be included?

5. Are adopted children to be considered the children of their natural parents so as to be included in a gift to the children of the natural parent?

6. Are children born outside marriage to be included?

7. Are stepchildren to be included? [42]

Thus, even when using everyday terms, you must be careful to have discussed these questions with your client and make sure that your definition of the term fits his or her desires.

One way to ensure that you ask your client about how to define these important terms is to prepare a section of your interview questionnaire or checklist to include definitions that will be used in most wills. In this way, you can be sure to ask your client how to define

---

41. An historical reason is at the base for many of these ingrained redundancies. At various times, English common law had two languages to choose from—between Celtic and Anglo Saxon, between English and Latin, between English and French. Given these choices, lawyers began to pick one word from each language. Once these were all translated to English, the usage remained. Thomas Word, Jr., *A Brief for Plain English Wills and Trusts*, 14 U.Rich. L.Rev. 471, 473 (1980).

42. Schwartz, *supra* note 21, at § 1110.5.

these standard terms and then ask the questions needed to implement that definition.

Another way to clarify organization is to use headings and number clauses.[43] Headings can enhance readability when they serve as signposts telling each section's contents and clarifying the document's organization. Because their value will be lost if they add confusion, the language of these headings should be as clear and simple as possible. For example, do not use "Article First, Article Second, Article Third . . . ." because this uncommon phrasing would jar most people. Instead, use headings such as these for easy understanding.

Article I.   Distribution of My Estate.

Article II.   Payment of Charges Against My Estate.

Article III.   Directions for Division of My Residuary Estate into the Marital Trust and the Residuary Trust.

Article IV.   Miscellaneous and Technical Provisions.

Article V.   Executors and Trustees and Their Authority.

Numbering clauses is useful because it allows easy cross-reference from one point to another. When numbering clauses, use either letters or whole numbers, rather than decimals. While decimals may be useful in a long contract or particularly complex will or trust, the simple will with few subparagraphs will be more understandable if you use traditional outline format with whole numbers.[44] Thus, your sections would be A, B, C, and D and the clauses under each would be 1, 2, 3, and 4, instead of 1.1, 1.2, 1.3, and 1.4.

Making your organization clear and straightforward will enhance both the accuracy and readability of your documents. Accuracy is enhanced because your client will be able to check whether the document expresses his or her wishes more easily. Readability is enhanced because the organization combines with clear language in each clause to allow the client to understand the document. Now you must draft your clauses.

Drafting Standard Will Clauses

Because the subject matter of most wills is similar, they often include standard clauses. Many attorneys simply repeat these clauses from sample wills or form books for each client. Whenever using standard clauses, however, make sure that you revise them in two ways. First, revise for accuracy, making sure that the clause is appropriate to your client's situation. Second, revise for readability, making sure that you are not using language that is difficult to read or unnecessary to achieve the purpose of the clause. For example, the following clause is an example of one that adds nothing but verbosity and confusion to the will.

---

43. See Chapter 5, Contracts.   **44.** Schwartz, *supra* note 21, at § 1110.5.

In the name of God, Amen: Know all men by these presents: That I, _____, of the City of _____, County of _____, and State of _____, being in good bodily health and of sound and disposing mind and memory and not acting under duress, menace, fraud or undue influence of any person whomsoever, calling to mind the frailty of human life, and being desirous of disposing of my worldly estate with which it has pleased God to bless me, while I have strength and capacity so to do, do make, publish and declare this my Last Will and Testament, hereby revoking all other wills, legacies, bequests, or codicils by me heretofore made, in the manner and form following: [45]

This clause could be easily revised.

I, _____, make this will.

The simpler clause achieves the same result as the one above while indicating from the start that the will is straightforward and understandable. Continue this trend of revising standard clauses to increase accuracy and readability throughout the will and the trust.

Payments of Debts and Funeral Expenses

Most wills move from the opening paragraph to a clause ordering the payment of "just debts" and funeral expenses. Many attorneys include a "just debts" clause because they believe that the client expects to find this clause in his or her will and will be content only if it is included.[46] But the clause is not needed legally because all jurisdictions require the testator's fiduciary to pay all debts and funeral expenses.[47] Eliminate it because it often causes more problems than it solves. For example, it may not be desirable to pay off all debts immediately upon the testator's death. Does your client want to force his or her spouse to pay off a mortgage with a favorable interest rate just because of his or her death? [48] Additionally, although the form books often use the language "just debts," this clause is not clear and may require the client's estate to pay bills it may not be required to pay. For example, does this clause require payment of debts even though the creditor has filed for bankruptcy or missed the publication date for filing debts with the estate?

If you must include this clause, be sure to clarify which debts are to be paid and who is to bear the burden of paying these debts. For example, suppose the testator borrowed $25,000 from a bank and assigned his life insurance policy as collateral for the loan. The policy's beneficiary was the testator's daughter. The will directs all debts to be paid and the bank collects the insurance proceeds to satisfy the debt. Must the estate reimburse the daughter for payment of the

---

45. Frank E. Cooper, *Writing in Law Practice* 338 (1963).

46. *Id.* at 339.

47. Hoops, *supra* note 1, at § 313, at 10.

48. *Id.*

debt? [49] What would the testator have intended? Make sure that you know what your client wants when revising this clause.

Additionally, your client may be willing to use a clause directing the payment of funeral expenses, which excludes language on the payment of other debts. You could include the following clause, which may satisfy your client's concerns without causing the problems noted above.

> I direct my executor to pay the expenses of my last illness, funeral expenses, and expenses of administration from the residue of my estate, whether or not those expenses are attributable to property included in my probate estate.

Bequests

If you organize the will around the main concerns of your client, the next clauses will probably cover your client's distribution of his or her property to named beneficiaries. These clauses usually include special bequests of particular property to certain individuals or organizations and a residuary clause that disposes of the remaining portion of the estate. When your client wants to make special bequests, draft them as specifically as possible when naming both the recipient and the bequest. For example, write

> **I bequeath to Sylvia Smith, Route # 1, Box 470, Ashland, Missouri, my wedding rings, my inlaid turquoise ring, my turquoise pendant, and any artwork or handmade items created by me and in my possession at the time of my death.**

rather than

> I bequeath to Sylvia Smith all my jewelry and artwork or handmade items in my possession at the time of my death.

Providing an address assists the executor of the will in contacting the beneficiaries. Additionally, the first example specifies the exact items that Sylvia Smith is to receive upon the testator's death. The second example does not specify which jewelry is bequeathed and does not specify that the artwork and handmade items bequeathed are only those that were made by the testator. This lack of specificity may cause problems for the executor when distributing the client's property.

The bequest would be even clearer if the testator specified the artwork and handmade items that were bequeathed. However, this specificity is often impossible because the testator may acquire or lose certain items between the time the will is made and his or her death. In this example, the testator felt certain that the specific pieces of jewelry would be in her possession at the time of her death but was uncertain what artwork would be in her possession. Another way to increase flexibility is to refer in the will to a list extrinsic to the will that includes bequests that may change over time. If you include

---

49. Schwartz, *supra* note 21, at § 1102.

specific items in the will, consider taking pictures of the items and incorporating them into the will to clarify their identification.

When making specific bequests, it is often helpful to state an alternative recipient in case the intended recipient does not survive the testator. When a recipient dies before the testator, the bequest will lapse, meaning that it becomes part of the residue unless the testator indicates a contrary intent or a controlling statute produces a different result.[50] Because these statutes may lead to results that conflict with your client's choices, you should always ask your client what his or her wishes are and carefully draft the appropriate clauses to effectuate those desires.

> I leave my Van Gogh painting to my niece Louise Howard if she survives me; if my niece Louise Howard does not survive me, I leave my Van Gogh painting to my nephew Bill Howard if he survives me. If both my niece Louise Howard and my nephew Bill Howard do not survive me, I leave my Van Gogh painting to my residuary estate.

If your client makes several special bequests, you may want to include a general lapse clause in the will so that you would not need to repeat the last sentence in the example above for every bequest. The following clause handles all bequests and ensures that a beneficiary's heirs will not receive property that your client would prefer to have included in his or her residuary estate.

> If all the beneficiaries of any special bequest do not survive me, that bequest will become part of my residuary estate and be disposed of as stated in that clause.

Similarly, you must clarify how to distribute property to beneficiaries in a named class. For example, suppose your client wants to leave a piece of property to his brother Adam and his sister Betty's three children. Do Adam and Betty's children take the property on a per capita basis, where each receives one-fourth of the property, or on a per stirpes basis, where Adam receives half and Betty's children receive the other half in equal shares?[51] Be sure to recognize these questions and ambiguities when they arise and then resolve them when drafting.

Residuary clauses distribute the residue of the testator's estate, which is everything remaining in the estate after payment of all

---

50. Shaffer, *supra* note 5, at 84–85. Most anti-lapse statutes limit the alternate takers to the issue of the deceased beneficiary, although some are broader. Robert L. Mennell, *Wills and Trusts in a Nutshell* 129 (1979). For example, Maryland's statute substitutes the testate or intestate takers of the deceased beneficiary. These anti-lapse statutes come into play only if the testator does not specify his or her intention on what should happen if any bequest should lapse. *Id.*

51. Always check within your jurisdiction for how these terms of art are defined. Different states may define the terms differently and even within one state, the definition may change depending on certain factual circumstances. Robert J. Lynn, *Introduction to Estate Planning in a Nutshell* § 2.17, at 42 (1983).

bequests, debts, expenses, and taxes.[52] Most residuary clauses contain a large amount of legalese and unnecessary language.

> All the rest, residue and remainder of my estate, of whatsoever kind and nature, and wheresoever situate, of which I may be seized or possessed or to which I may be entitled at the time of my death, not hereby otherwise effectually disposed of, I give, devise, and bequeath absolutely and in fee simple, to my wife, _____. If my said wife _____ shall predecease me or if we shall die simultaneously, then and in that event, all the rest, residue, and remainder of my property, real and personal, and wheresoever situated, including all property over which I shall have a power of appointment, I give, devise, and bequeath absolutely and in fee simple, to my son, _____.

This clause could be rewritten to be more concise and clear while achieving the same result.

> **I give the rest of my estate to my wife, _____. If she dies first or simultaneously, I give the rest of my estate to my son, _____.**

It is unnecessary to list the property left in the estate, especially when the description is as broad as the one above. If your client wants to leave everything remaining in his or her estate to one or two people, that clause can be simple and straightforward, which will make it less susceptible to questions about its interpretation.

Disinheritance

If your client decides to disinherit an expected beneficiary, draft the disinheritance clause with special care. Disinheritance is an emotional issue and frequently results in challenges to the will. These challenges are often based on the belief that disinheritance is ineffective unless the person disinherited receives $1 or other nominal consideration.[53] Except for the rights given to a surviving spouse, however, a testator may dispose of his or her property in any manner chosen.[54] The best practice is to disinherit the person specifically by naming him or her in the will, rather than simply leaving the person out of the will completely. Otherwise, the person excluded may challenge the will, not believing that the testator would have intentionally excluded him or her. A specific clause clarifies the testator's intention which can

---

52. Hoops, *supra* note 1, at § 327, at 49–50.

53. *Id.* at § 318, at 22.

54. Most states impose restrictions on a spouse's ability to dispose of his or her property, and many require a statutory minimum to be granted to the surviving spouse. Shaffer, *supra* note 5, at 64–69. Community property states treat community property as a substitute for an elective share by providing half of the community property of the couple to the surviving spouse, which is often more generous than most states' elective shares. McGovern, *supra* note 1, at § 3.10, at 133. You must examine these statutes carefully to determine whether and to what extent your client may disinherit his or her spouse.

prevent the courts from resolving any ambiguity by including the individual due to judicial reluctance to uphold the disinheritance.[55]

Many testators also prefer to state the reasons for the disinheritance, perhaps hoping to soften the emotional feelings that may result. Rather than saying "I leave nothing to my sister Anne," the testator may want to say

> Having made several gifts to my sister Anne during my lifetime, I make no provision for her in my will.

When stating the reason for disinheriting, be careful not to include reasons that may no longer exist at the time of the testator's death and may open the door for a challenge to the will.

> I have made no provision under this Will for my husband, _____, because he is adequately provided for financially and is a joint tenant with me on our home and other assets.

What happens if the husband loses his financial well-being between the time the will is executed and his wife dies? What if the property that the spouses held in joint tenancy no longer exists? The husband would have reason to challenge the will and may be successful. He could easily argue that his wife's intent was to disinherit him only if those conditions remained true and because they were no longer true, his wife could not have meant to disinherit him. In drafting these clauses, try to clarify what should happen if any of the conditions change.

Be careful not to copy these clauses straight from form books, because they will undoubtedly contain the legalese you are attempting to remove from your documents.

> I have in mind, but make no provision for my son, James, not because of any lack of affection for my said son, but because it is my belief that his welfare will be best served by the disposition herein made of my estate.[56]

Rewrite this clause as follows before including it in the will.

> **I have made no provision for my son James, not because of any lack of affection for him, but because his welfare is best served by this distribution of my estate.**

Some attorneys prefer to place the reasons for disinheritance in a collateral document outside the will in the testator's own language and handwriting so that no question arises about whether the intent and reasons for the disinheritance were the testator's, not the attorney's. This can be especially useful depending on the reason for the disinheritance, because a probated will is a matter of public record.

Guardianship

For clients with minor children, selecting guardians for their children in case both parents die is often the most important aspect of estate planning. Be sure to determine what your clients want to do

55. Hoops, *supra* note 1, at § 318, at 23.   **56.** *Id.* at § 318, at 24.

with this important clause. While it may be fairly obvious to everyone that the surviving parent will be appointed guardian upon the testator's death, it is important that the client name a successor guardian. Many clients may want to name the children's grandparents as successor guardians, but this may not be a wise choice. If the grandparents do not survive the testator, then the choice of successor will be fruitless. If they do survive but are elderly, it is likely that they may die before the children reach maturity, which would force the children to cope with loss of their caretakers once again.[57] Other questions about guardianship that you must resolve include how the guardianship should work, whether the guardian must post a bond, whether the guardian is also a trustee of funds for the children, and whether compensation should be provided.

Once again, avoid copying clauses appointing guardians directly from form books because they will rarely be worded as clearly as they could be.

> I hereby appoint my beloved wife, _____, guardian of the person and estate of my infant son, _____. In the event that my wife shall predecease me, or shall fail to qualify, shall resign or be removed, I appoint my friend, _____, guardian of the person and estate of my infant son, _____. It is my will and I direct that neither my said wife nor the aforesaid _____ shall be required to furnish any bond for the faithful performance of their offices as such guardian, any provision of law to contrary notwithstanding.[58]

Instead, rewrite this clause to make it more readable by eliminating the legalese.

> **I appoint my wife, _____, as guardian of my son, _____. If she predeceases me or cannot serve, I appoint _____ as guardian. I direct that the guardian not be required to furnish any bond as guardian.**

It would also be wise to rewrite the clause to exclude naming the child needing guardianship. Adding the names simply raises problems if other children also survive the testator or if other children survive but the named child does not. It would be better practice to name the guardian of all surviving minor children and include a definition of children in the will. Some testators choose to handle guardianship matters in a separate letter incorporated into the will so they can change the letter without having to revise the will.

Wills With Trusts

Many clients want to establish a testamentary trust as part of their will and may also request that you establish an inter vivos trust while they are still alive. Theoretically, trust documents are rather straightforward. They have two main purposes: they state the duties of the trustee, who is the person managing and controlling the trust's assets,

---

57. *Id.* at § 330, at 55. **58.** *Id.* at § 330, at 56.

and they state how the trustee is to distribute the assets or income from the assets to the named beneficiaries.

A trust is created when the owner of property separates the title of the property from the benefits of the property. Trusts are often developed to avoid the tax consequences of the testator's death or to allow for someone to control the assets when the testator considers the beneficiaries incapable of doing so. The trustee holds legal title to the assets in the trust but has a fiduciary duty to control those assets and distribute them for the benefit of the beneficiaries.

When writing a trust, first determine what property will be held in trust, then name the trustee and state the trustee's powers, and finally explain the distribution of the trust. All trusts must have a "res" or property that is placed in the trust, and you should describe this property specifically. Usually any interest in property that is real or personal, legal or equitable, can be held in trust.[59] For pour-over trusts, which are created when testamentary transfers are made to an existing inter vivos trust, using the language "the residuary of my estate" to indicate the property is sufficiently specific to define the res.[60]

Additionally, besides a res, all trusts require a trustee to be named, although failure to name a trustee will not usually result in the trust failing if a trustee can be appointed equitably.[61] Besides naming the trustee, the trust should also name alternate and successor trustees. It is usually wise to have one of these alternates or successors be an institution so you can be sure that a trustee will be named, according to the client's wishes, in case the individual trustees cannot or refuse to serve.

Having focused on accuracy and readability when drafting your client's will, continue that focus when drafting the trust document. One way to make trust documents easier to understand is to write them in the first person, rather than in the traditional third person. When written in third person, the client often becomes confused over who is the grantor and who is the trustee.[62] You can increase both accuracy and readability by drafting the trust in the first person. For example, the agreement would begin as follows.

> I, Rita Black, desire to create a trust and agree with the First National Bank of Homeville (my trustee) to the following:

Then write the remainder of the trust agreement with the client speaking her directions directly to the trustee. Not only does this

---

59. *Id.* at § 330, at 37. A simple expectancy, however, cannot be held in trust and property sometimes cannot be transferred by the testator due to the manner in which title is held in the property. For example, property held in joint tenancy passes to the survivor and cannot be transferred by one joint tenant to a trust. *Id.*

60. *Id.* at § 330, at 37.

61. *Id.* at § 330, at 39.

62. Word Jr., *supra* note 41, at 480.

increase readability and accuracy for the client, it also provides consistency between the form of the will and that of the trust.[63]

Appointing the Executor and Trustee

In addition to appointing guardians, most wills also nominate executors and all trusts appoint trustees. This appointment is as important as the appointment of a guardian for minor children. The executor's duties are administering the estate and distributing the assets to the beneficiaries. The trustee's duties are more extensive and require significant discretion. Two different clauses or sets of clauses are involved in appointing both executors and trustees: the first nominates the individuals or corporations to serve in those capacities, the second describes the fiduciary powers they have.

In naming the executor, many people name a family member or friend without considering the person's ability to fulfill the fiduciary duties required of the position. If your client is concerned about an individual's ability to perform but is also concerned that failure to name the individual will cause hard feelings, you may want to suggest naming co-executors or co-trustees, with a corporation nominated as the other fiduciary. This allows the individual, usually the surviving spouse or child(ren) to serve, while ensuring that someone with experience will be available to assist.[64]

It is wise to name alternate executors or trustees as well, in case one or more of those named is unable or unwilling to serve. Appointing a corporation (such as a bank or trust company) as alternate executor or trustee is done frequently. This usually ensures that one of those named in the will or trust will, in fact, survive the testator. When appointing a corporation, the testator should realize that the individuals whom he or she believes will handle the estate or trust may no longer be working in that capacity when the will or trust come into effect. The testator should focus on the qualifications of the institution in making the choice, not on the individual who may currently be serving that function. Whenever choosing trustees, you need to make sure that your jurisdiction allows them to serve. Many states restrict executors or trustees to persons domiciled or corporations doing business in that state.[65]

Clauses appointing executors and trustees are usually filled with legalese, so form clauses need to be redrafted to increase readability.

> I hereby nominate, constitute and appoint as Executors and Trustees of this, my last Will, my beloved husband _____. In the event that my husband shall decline to act, or shall predecease me, or for any cause whatever shall cease or fail to act, then I nominate, constitute and appoint the Fiduciary Trust Company, New York, New York, as Executor and Trustee of my said will, in the

63. *Id.*

64. Hoops, *supra*, note 1, at § 336, at 67–68.

65. *Id.* at § 336, at 68.

place and stead of any one of the persons first named herein. It is my will and I direct that my Executors and Trustees, and their successors, shall not be required to furnish a bond for the faithful performance of their duties in any jurisdiction, any provision of law to the contrary notwithstanding.

The following clause is shorter and much easier to understand than the first, while providing the same direction to those probating the will and trust.

> **I nominate my husband, _____, to serve as my executor and trustee, if living; if he does not so serve, I nominate the Fiduciary Trust Company, New York, New York, as executor and trustee of my will. I request that a bond, as set by law, not be required for any Executor or Trustee named in this will.**

The second set of clauses that concern executors and trustees delineates the executor's or trustee's duties under the will or trust. Start by conferring with your client to determine how expansively to grant the powers. Oftentimes, the testator recognizes that the executor or trustee needs flexibility and discretion to make decisions that are most favorable for the estate. The purpose of the extensive powers frequently granted in wills and trusts is to allow for this flexibility. Explicit grants of power will override statutory restrictions, unless the statute or court rule expressly prohibits the specific power granted.[66]

In deciding which powers to grant to the executor or trustee, you should determine which powers are granted under a fiduciaries' powers act in your jurisdiction. In states with statutes delineating the executor's or trustee's powers, you can incorporate the statutory language by reference, thereby giving the executor or trustee all the powers permissible by law. When considering which powers to include, review the testator's assets and determine what decisions and actions will likely need to be made in administering the will or trust. Simple wills may not require an extensive listing of the fiduciaries' powers. In those cases, you will not need to include all the boiler-plate clauses that are found in form or practice books.[67]

When revising to eliminate legalese, also revise these clauses so they accurately describe the powers that are applicable in your client's situation. If your client desires to grant his or her executor or trustee the fullest range of powers, it is possible to eliminate pages of descriptions of powers and to include a clause providing expansive powers.

> I confer upon my trustee the authority to do and perform any act that she determines is in the best interest of my trust, with no limitations.

66. *Id.*

67. For example, Hoops lists 5 pages of clauses describing fiduciaries' duties. *Id.* at § 338, at 81–86. He also provides a checklist that delineates the powers con- tained in each clause so that you can easily check which clauses to use depending on the powers to be granted. *Id.* at § 338, at 88–89.

While many clients may be uncomfortable with granting these unlimited powers, especially in terms of a trustee's duties, many clients are content to grant fairly extensive powers.[68] Take care not to limit the fiduciary unduly because he or she was selected due to the testator's trust in his or her judgment.

Testimonium Clause

The testimonium clause threatens to pull legalese and ponderous language back into wills.

> IN WITNESS WHEREOF, I the undersigned testator, have on this 20th day of January 1990, signed and sealed, published, and declared the foregoing instrument as and for, my Last Will.

Even the short "In witness whereof, I have hereunto set my hand this 20th day of January 1990" is unnecessary. Wills are not set aside because the signature is not preceded by this "fairy dust." [69] It is useful to include the date at the end of the will to help ensure which will is the most recent version. Use either "Dated this 20th day of January 1990" or "I sign my name to this will on January 20, 1990" instead of the clause above. Just as you began the will without the legalese usually found in the opening clause, end it in the same way.

Attestation Clause

Following the testimonium clause comes the attestation clause. The attestation clause is not part of the will and is not technically required for its validity, unless required by statute.[70] Once the testator's and witnesses' handwriting are established, most jurisdictions presume that the will was executed in the manner required.[71] However, the attestation clause states that all the formalities required to admit the will to probate were performed. Thus, it prevents the will's rejection if the witnesses cannot remember whether each formality was performed and has become standard in virtually all wills.[72]

Eliminate legalese from this clause as well.

> The foregoing instrument, consisting of twenty (20) pages, was on the 20th day of January 1990, signed and sealed at the end thereof and at the same time published and declared by Herbert Johnson, the above named testator, as and for his Last Will in the

---

68. Additionally, some attorneys have concerns that a clause this simple may receive objections from institutions with which the executor or trustee must work that are used to finding an explicit listing of powers.

69. Cooper, *supra* note 45, at 344 (quoting Arensberg, *The Language of Wills*, 21 Pa.B.A.Q. 116 (1950)).

70. Hoops, *supra* note 1, at § 341, at 93. No state's statute requires the use of an attestation clause. The requirement of due execution can be satisfied by having the witnesses sign below the testator's signature as "witness." An attestation clause is very important, however, in that it states a prima facie case that the will was duly executed and may thus be admitted to probate even though the witnesses predecease the testator or cannot recall the events of execution. Dukeminier and Johnson, *Wills, Trusts, and Estates* 205 n. 20 (4th ed. 1990).

71. Hoops, *supra* note 1, at § 341, at 93.

72. McGovern, *supra* note 1, at § 4.3, at 169.

presence of each of us, who, this attestation clause having been first read to us, did at the request of the said testator, in his presence and in the presence of each other, sign our names as witnesses thereto.

Consider this revision.

> **This will was signed by Herbert Johnson who stated it was his last will in our presence, and having read this attestation clause, we sign as witnesses, at his request, in his presence and the presence of each other.**

The witnesses should then sign and print their names and provide their addresses so that they may be easily contacted if needed. When choosing witnesses, it is useful to choose those who are younger than the testator. Additionally, the witnesses should not be beneficiaries under the will, so that no question of undue influence or duress arises. You should consider serving as a witness in most cases, because you can provide valuable testimony concerning the execution of the will. Always include three witnesses because some states require that number.[73]

Many attorneys add a self-proving affidavit at the end of the will. These affidavits allow the will to be admitted to probate on the basis of the affidavit without needing to bring the witnesses into court to testify that the requirements for the will to be admitted to probate were met.[74] Some confusion has resulted, however, on whether the witnesses must sign both the attestation clause and the self-proving affidavit. The technically correct form is for the testator to sign the will, the witnesses to sign the attestation clause, and then for all of them to sign the self-proving affidavit, which is then notarized.[75] Some courts require that both be signed or they find that the will cannot be admitted to probate.[76] An example of a self-proving affidavit follows.

> I, _____, the testator, being duly sworn, signed this instrument willingly, executed it voluntarily, and am over eighteen years of age, of sound mind, and under no constraint or undue influence.

_____

Testator

> We, _____, _____, and _____, the witnesses, being duly sworn, declare that the testator signed this instrument willingly. Each of us, in the presence and hearing of the testator, signed this will as witnesses, and to the best of our knowledge, the testator is

---

73. Shaffer, *supra* note 5, at 71–72.

74. McGovern, *supra* note 1, at § 4.3, at 170. As of 1985, thirty states permit self-proved wills. Mann, *Self–Proving Affidavits and Formalism in Wills and Affidavits,* 63 Wash.U.L.Q. 39, 41 n. 9 (1985).

75. *Id.* at 41.

76. *Wich v. Fleming,* 652 S.W.2d 353 (Tex.1983); *In re Sample's Estate,* 175 Mont. 93, 572 P.2d 1232 (1977).

over eighteen years of age, of sound mind, and under no constraint
or undue influence.

Witness

Witness

Witness

When executing wills, it is a good idea to develop a procedure and
follow it exactly. This may require you to develop a checklist to ensure
that you take each necessary step.[77] Doing this will allow you to testify
in court that you performed all the steps on your checklist, even though
you may not recall that particular execution.

This chapter has outlined many of the standard clauses that are
included in most wills. However, other clauses are frequently necessary to address the client's needs and the complexity of his or her estate
plan. When drafting those clauses, keep in mind the goals of accuracy
and readability. Doing so will ensure that you provide the best possible
assistance to your client.

Challenges to the Will

When drafting, you must anticipate the possibility of challenges to
the will. For example, suppose your client has a new wife and family
and wants to disinherit his children from an earlier marriage. Those
children may try to challenge whether your client was incompetent or
under duress when making the will. Suppose your client is a single
person who wants to leave her property to her unmarried partner and
wants to avoid challenges by her family. In these situations, you need
to create a paper trail that will show that the testator was competent
and not under duress when making the will.

One way to create this paper trail is to ask the client to write to
you before the initial interview, setting out his or her desires and
specifying the beneficiaries under the will. Then you can send a letter
to the client repeating those desires and setting up the initial interview.
After drafting the document, mail it to the client asking whether it
states his or her desires. The client can respond by mail. Then when
the will is signed, you can ask these questions again. A few weeks or
months after the execution, ask the client to write you, thanking you
for drafting the will to conform to his or her desires. This will give you
a paper trail over several months that establishes that the will does
state the desires of your client. This paper trail, when shown to the
plaintiffs upon receipt of their initial complaint, will often result in
them voluntarily dismissing the complaint. Although this may seem to

---

77. For an example of a checklist, *see*
Hoops, *supra* note 1, at § 342, at 95–96.

be considerable work, attorneys in this area realize that litigation means drafting failure and that avoiding litigation is one of the most important of your roles in will drafting.

CONCLUSION

Drafting a will, with or without a trust, calls for your understanding of the interrelation of statutory law, tax law, and property doctrines. It also requires carefully interviewing your clients and determining their wishes. Having determined those wishes, your job is to draft testamentary documents that accurately reflect your clients' wishes while remaining readable to them and others who must use the documents. By focusing on accuracy and readability, you can transform these documents from ones that are confusing and even frightening for your clients into ones that allow them to feel comfortable with the steps they have taken to protect their property's disposition upon their deaths.

EXERCISE

Revise the clauses of the following will with an eye toward accuracy and readability as discussed in this chapter. Revise the following will to increase its clarity and readability. The clauses are substantially correct but difficult to read and understand.

LAST WILL AND TESTAMENT

OF

STATE OF UTAH

CITY OF PROVO

I, _____, of said State and City, being of sound and disposing mind and memory, do make, publish and declare this my Last Will and Testament, hereby revoking and annulling all others by me heretofore made.

I

I direct that all my just debts and funeral expenses be paid out of the proceeds of my estate by my Executrix, hereinafter named, as soon as the same may be conveniently done after my death, except that any debt or expense secured by mortgage, pledge or similar encumbrance on property owned by me at my death shall not be paid by my estate, and such property shall pass subject to such encumbrance.

II

If any beneficiary dies prior to the entry of an order, decree or judgment in my estate distributing the property in question, or within five months after the date of my death, whichever is earlier, any interests which would have passed to said beneficiary under other provisions of this will are to be disposed of according to the plan of distribution which would have been effective under this will if such beneficiary had predeceased me. It is my intention that my property or interest which is distributed from my estate as a result of any court order, decree or judgment will not be revoked or otherwise affected by the subsequent death of the distributee.

III

I give, devise and bequeath all of the property of all kinds, wherever situated, belonging to me at the time of my death, absolutely and forever, to my wife.

IV

If my wife does not survive me, I give all of the property of all kinds, owned by me at my death, to my issue, *per stirpes*.

V

If at the time of my death neither my wife, nor any child of mine, nor any descendants of a deceased child of mine shall survive me, then in that event I give all of the property of all kinds owned by me at the time of my death, as follows:

(A) One-half (½) thereof to those persons who at the time of my death would be entitled to receive my personal estate if I had died intestate, according to the laws of the state of my domiciliary then in force.

(b) One (½) thereof to those persons who at the time of my death would be entitled to receive the personal estate of my wife if she had died intestate at that time, according to the laws of the state of my domiciliary then in force.

VI

For all purposes under this will, adopted children, whether of mine or of any other person, shall have the same status and interests as natural-born children. The reference in this will to my issue and to my children shall include children of mine born or adopted after the execution hereof and all of my children shall receive only such rights and interests as are granted herein.

VII

I nominate my wife, _____ to be the Executrix, without bond, hereunder. If she does not so act, for any reason, I nominate my father, _____ to be the Executor, without bond, hereunder. I empower the personal representative of my estate, without order of court and without notice to anyone: to sell, convey, option, lease or mortgage any property, real or personal, publicly or privately, upon such terms and conditions as shall seem best to such personal representative; to settle, compromise or pay any claim, including taxes, asserted in favor of or against me or my estate; to permit any of the beneficiaries hereunder to enjoy the use in kind, during the administration of my estate, of any tangible personal property without liability on the part of the personal representative for injury, consumption or loss of the property so used, and without liability on the part of the beneficiary for unintentional, non-negligent injury, consumption or loss of the property so used; upon any division or partial or final distribution of the estate, to partition, allot and distribute the estate in undivided interests or in kind, or partly in money and partly in kind, at valuations determined by the personal representative, and to sell such property as the personal representative may deem necessary to make division or distribution. I desire and direct that the personal representative of my estate consult with the Personal Affairs Officer at the nearest military installation and the Veterans' Administration to ascertain if there are any benefits to which my dependents might be entitled.

IN WITNESS WHEREOF, I have hereunto set my hand and seal to this, my Last Will and Testament, consisting of three typewritten pages, on all pages of which I have attached my signature, this _____ day of _____, A.D. 19__.

_____ (SEAL)

The foregoing instrument was signed, sealed, declared and published by _____ as his Last Will and Testament, in the presence of us, the undersigned, who, at his special instance and request, do attest as witnesses after said Testator has signed his name thereto, and in his presence of each other, this _____ day of _____, 19__.

_____

_____

_____

_____

_____

_____

STATE OF UTAH
CITY OF PROVO

We

_____, _____, _____, and _____, the Testator and the witnesses, respectively, whose names are signed to the attached or foregoing instrument, being first duly sworn, do hereby declare to the undersigned authority that the Testator signed and executed the instrument as his Last Will and that he signed willingly, and that he executed it as his free and voluntary act for the purposes therein expressed; and that each of the witnesses, in the presence and hearing of the Testator, signed the Will as witness and that to the best of his knowledge the

Testator was at that time eighteen years of age or older, of sound mind, and under no constraint or undue influence.

TESTATOR   _____,

WITNESS   _____,

WITNESS   _____,

WITNESS   _____,

Subscribed, sworn to and acknowledged before me by the Testator, and subscribed and sworn to before me by _____, _____, and _____, witness, this _____ day of _____, 19__.

(SEAL)

_____

Notary Public

ASSIGNMENT 1

Draft your will without a trust. You may give yourself any amount of property that you desire and can dispose of it in any way that you desire. Make sure to include the following clauses: at least three specific bequests, a residuary clause, one clause disinheriting someone, a clause naming an executor, a testmonium clause, and an attestation clause. When drafting your will, focus on making your will as accurate and readable as possible.

ASSIGNMENT 2

The excerpt from the following will is substantively correct but difficult to read and understand. Using the techniques discussed in the chapter, revise these clauses to increase their clarity and readability.

LAST WILL AND TESTAMENT

OF

PEG HARRIS

I, Peg Harris, a resident of and domiciled in Westen County, Georgia, make, publish and declare this to be my Last Will and Testament, revoking all Wills and codicils at any time heretofore made to me.

FIRST: I direct that all my legally enforceable debts, the expenses of my last illness and funeral, the expenses of the administration of my estate, and all estate, inheritance and similar taxes payable with respect to property included in my estate, whether or not passing under this Will, and any interest or penalties thereon, shall be paid as soon after my death as may be practicable out of my residuary estate, without apportionment. If there is any indebtedness owing by me, whether secured or unsecured, which has not matured at the time of my death, I authorize my Personal Representative to pay such indebtedness either in full or in accordance with the terms of the instrument evidencing such indebtedness as my Personal Representative may deem advisable under the circumstances. Notwithstanding the foregoing, all charges to principal not deducted in computing the Federal estate tax shall be paid first out of the property passing to the Unified Credit Trust hereinafter provided for, and then out of my residuary estate. Notwithstanding the foregoing, if any estate, inheritance or similar taxes may be imposed because I shall have had, exercised or released a power of appointment given to me by some other person, the same shall be apportioned, to the extent provided or permitted by applicable law, among the beneficiaries of the property which is the subject to said power of appointment. If at the time of my death I am the beneficiary of a qualified terminable interest property (QTIP) trust, and the principal of that trust is includable in my estate for tax purposes, I direct, pursuant to the provisions of Section 2207A of the Internal Revenue Code, that my Personal Representative or the trustee of the trust withhold from the share of the remaindermen of the trust the amount by which the estate tax in my estate exceeds the amount of the estate tax which would have been payable had the trust property not been included in my estate for tax purposes. The provisions of the Article FIRST shall not apply to the extent that contrary provisions concerning the payment or apportionment of any such taxes have been or shall be made in any *inter vivos* instrument executed by me relating to any insurance, trusts, gifts or other transfers, jointly owned property or accounts, or property subject to power of appointment.

SECOND: I give all tangible personal property owned by me at the time of my death (except cash), including without limitation personal effects, clothing, jewelry, furniture, furnishings, household goods, automobiles and other vehicles, together with all insurance policies relating thereto, to my husband Kevin Harris, if he survives me, or if he does not survive me, to my then living children Kathryn and Mark, in substantially equal shares, to be divided between them as they shall agree, or if they cannot agree, or if either of them shall be under the age of eighteen (18) years, as my Personal Representative shall determine. If any of said children shall be under the age of eighteen (18) years at my death, my Personal Representative may sell any property bequeathed to said child under this Article Two, as my Personal Representative may deem appropriate, or my Personal Representative may hold such property or any proceeds thereof, without bond, until said child attains said age or such earlier time as my Personal Representative may deem proper to deliver any such property or proceeds to said child, or to said child's guardian or any person with whom said child resides for the use of said child, or, if there is a separate trust for the benefit of said child, to my Trustee to be administered as a part of said trust. All costs of obtaining possession, appraising, safeguarding, delivering or selling such property shall be paid as expenses of administering my estate.

THIRD: I hereby confirm my intention that the beneficial interest in all property, real, personal or mixed, tangible or intangible (including joint checking or savings accounts) which is registered or held, at the time of my death, jointly in the names of myself and any other person or persons (excluding any tenancy in common), shall pass by right of survivorship or operation of law and outside of the terms of this Will to such person or persons, if he, she or they shall survive me. To the extent that my intention may be defeated by any law or rule of court, I hereby give, devise and bequeath all such beneficial interest in all such jointly held property to such other person or persons who shall survive me.

FOURTH: I give the sum of One Thousand and $^{00}/_{100}$ths ($1,000.00) Dollars to Jean Ehrlich, if she survives me. I give the sum of Five Hundred and $^{00}/_{100}$ths ($500.00) Dollars to Douglas Brown, if he survives me.

FIFTH: Reference is made to the power of appointment given to me by my mother, Winifred Smith in her Last Will and Testament dated July 23, 1983. I hereby exercise said power of appointment, and direct that all property which is the subject of said power of appointment shall be given and disposed of as hereinafter provided with regard to my residuary estate.

SIXTH: If my husband Kevin Harris survives me, I direct my Personal Representative to allocate to the disposition provided for in the next following paragraph of this Article SIX (the "Unified Credit Trust") a sum equal to the maximum amount by which my Federal taxable estate (determined without regard to this Article Six) may be increased without causing an increase in the Federal estate tax payable by reason of my death after taking into account all credits available against such tax; provided, however, that the credit for state death taxes shall be taken into account only to the extent that it does not result in an increase in the state death taxes which otherwise would be payable. For the purposes of determining the sum disposed of by this Article Six, the values finally fixed in the Federal estate tax proceeding relating to my estate shall be used. I recognize that the amount of any sum allocated may be affected by the action of my Personal Representative in exercising certain tax elections, and that no sum may be allocated.

I give the sum determined as aforesaid to my Trustee, IN TRUST, to hold the same in accordance with the following provisions:

(a) My Trustee shall manage, invest and reinvest said sum and shall pay the entire net income therefrom to or for the benefit of my husband or my children, in such proportions as my Trustee may determine, from and after my death and for so long as my husband lives, in quarter-annual or more frequent intervals as determined in the absolute discretion of my Trustee.

(b) My husband shall have the right to withdraw from the principal of this trust, in each calendar year, an amount not exceeding the greater of $5,000 or five percent of the principal of this trust valued as of the date the request to withdraw is made by written notice to my Trustee. Such right to withdraw shall not be cumulative from year to year. In addition, my Trustee may pay to or for the benefit of my husband or my children, for their care, support, maintenance, health, education and general welfare, from the principal of this trust, such amounts, including the whole thereof, and in such proportions, as determined in the absolute discretion of my Trustee; provided, however, that my Trustee shall make no such payment to my husband until the principal of the trust established under the first paragraph of Article SEVENTH below is first exhausted.

(c) Upon the death of my husband, I direct that the principal of this trust then remaining shall be paid and distributed to my then living issue, in equal shares, *per stirpes*. If, however, any child of mine then shall be under the age of thirty (30) years (each such child being hereinafter referred to as a "Beneficiary"), the share of such Beneficiary shall not be paid or distributed to such Beneficiary but instead shall be held by my Trustee, IN TRUST, pursuant to the following provisions:

    (i) My Trustee shall hold, manage, invest and reinvest each share set aside for each Beneficiary in a separate trust for the benefit of each Beneficiary and shall pay so much or all of the net income from each such trust to or for the benefit of the Beneficiary thereof, in quarter-annual or more frequent intervals, as determined in the absolute discretion of my Trustee. Any net income not so paid shall be accumulated and added to principal at least annually.

    (ii) In addition, my Trustee may pay to or for the benefit of each Beneficiary from the principal of each Beneficiary's trust, such amounts, including the whole thereof, as determined in the absolute discretion of my Trustee.

    (iii) When any Beneficiary shall attain the age of twenty-one (21) years, one third of the principal of such Beneficiary's trust then remaining shall be paid and distributed to such Beneficiary. When any Beneficiary shall attain the age of twenty-five (25) years, one half of the principal of such Beneficiary's trust then remaining shall be paid and distributed to such Beneficiary. If any Beneficiary is twenty-one (21) years of age, but under twenty-five (25), upon the creation of such Beneficiary's trust, one third of the principal of such Beneficiary's trust then remaining shall be paid and distributed to such Beneficiary, discharged of trust. If any Beneficiary is twenty-five (25) years of age upon the creation of such trust, two thirds of the principal of such Beneficiary's trust then remaining shall be paid and distributed to such Beneficiary, discharged of trust.

(iv) When any Beneficiary shall attain the age of thirty (30) years, the trust for such Beneficiary shall terminate and any remaining principal and income shall be paid and distributed to such Beneficiary, discharged of trust. If such Beneficiary dies before said age, such principal and income shall be paid and distributed to such persons or entities (other than such Beneficiary, creditors of such Beneficiary, the estate of such Beneficiary, or creditors of the estate of such Beneficiary), in such proportions and in such manner, outright or in trust, as such Beneficiary may appoint by a Will, executed after attaining majority and admitted to probate, specifically referring to this power of appointment, or absent such appointment (or absent my Trustee receiving notice of the existence of such a Will within 3 months after the death of such Beneficiary) to any then living issue of such Beneficiary, in equal shares, *per stripes*, or if such Beneficiary has no issue to the spouse of such Beneficiary, or if such Beneficiary has no spouse, to my then living issue. If any such issue is a beneficiary of a trust under this Will, the same may be held in accordance with such trust. If there are no then living issue, the same shall be paid and distributed to those who would take from me as if I were then to die without a Will, unmarried and the absolute owner of the same, and a resident of the State of Georgia.

SEVENTH: If my husband Kevin Harris survives me, I give all the rest, residue and remainder of my property and estate, both real and personal, of every kind and wherever located, to which I shall be in any manner entitled at the time of my death, including any property over which I may have any power of appointment or testamentary disposition (collectively referred to as my "residuary estate"), to my Trustee, to hold the same in a separate trust (referred to as the "Marital Deduction Trust"), to manage, invest and reinvest the same, and to dispose of the net income therefrom and principal thereof, as follows:

(a) My Trustee shall pay the entire net income therefrom to my husband Kevin Harris for so long as he lives, in quarter-annual or more frequent intervals as determined in the absolute discretion of my Trustee.

(b) My husband shall have the right to withdraw from the principal of this trust, in each calendar year, an amount not exceeding the greater of $5,000 or five percent of the principal of this trust valued as of the date the request to withdraw is made by written notice to my Trustee. Such right to withdraw shall not be cumulative from year to year. In addition, my Trustee may pay to or for the benefit of my husband, for his care, support, maintenance, health, education and general welfare, from the principal of this trust, such amounts, including the whole thereof, as determined in the absolute discretion of my Trustee.

(c) Upon my husband's death, any accrued income shall be paid to the estate of my husband and the principal of this trust at that time remaining shall be paid and distributed to or for the benefit of such person or persons among a class composed of the then living issue of mine of whatever degree and whenever born, and in such estates, interests and proportions as my husband may appoint by specific reference to this power of appointment in his Last Will and Testament, admitted to probate.

Bibliography

Bradley, M., G. Dionisopoulos, T. Drought, J. Frank, M. Hogue, J. Kussmaul, R. Langer, J. McMullen, S. Merrell, R. Nelson, J. Perlson, C. Rasmussen, L. Roberson, R. Severson, and P. Tilleman, *Eckhardt's Workbook for Wisconsin Estate Planners.* Madison, WI: State Bar of Wisconsin, 1990.

California Continuing Education of the Bar, *How to Draft Wills.* 1985.

Cooper, Frank E., *Writing in Law Practice.* Indianapolis: Bobbs–Merrill Co., 1963.

Cribbet, John E. and Corwin W. Johnson, *Principles of the Law of Property.* New York: The Foundation Press, Inc., 3rd ed. 1989.

Cusack, Lawrence X., *The Blue–Pencilled Will: What's Wrong With a Will in Plain English?*, 118 Trusts & Estates 33 (August 1979).

Dukeminier, Jesse and Stanley M. Johanson, *Wills, Trusts, and Estates.* Boston: Little, Brown and Co., 4th ed. 1990.

Feldman, Leon, *"Simple Will" Can Be Simplified Further to Produce a More Concise But Effective Document,* 10 Est.Plan. 290 (Sept. 1983).

Grether, Henry M., *The Little Horribles of a Scrivener,* 39 Neb.L.R. 296 (1960).

Henry, J. Gordon, *How Not to Draft Wills and Trusts—Common Drafting Errors to Avoid,* 5 Notre Dame Est.Plan. 841 (1980).

Hoops, Frederick K., *Family Estate Planning Guide.* New York: The Lawyers Co–Operative Publishing Co., 3rd ed. 1982.

Johanson, Stanley M., *The Orphan's Deduction: How to Handle a Troublesome Drafting Problem,* 14 Inst. on Est.Plan. 1505 (1980).

Johnston, Gerald P., *Legal Malpractice in Estate Planning and General Practice,* 17 Memp.S.U.L.Rev. 521 (Summer 1987).

Joslyn, Robert B., *Use of Plain English in Drafting Wills and Trusts,* 63 Mich.Bar J. 612 (July 1984).

Laurino, Louis D., *Avoiding Will Construction Problems,* 11 A.L.I.–A.B.A. Course Materials J. 83 (1987).

Lynn, Robert J., *Introduction to Estate Planning in a Nutshell.* St. Paul: West Publishing Co., 3rd ed. 1983.

Mann, Bruce H., *Self–Proving Affidavits and Formalism in Wills Adjudication,* 63 Wash.U.L.Q. 39 (1985).

McGovern, William M., Jr., Sheldon F. Kurtz, and Jan Ellen Rein, *Wills, Trusts, and Estates Including Taxation and Future Interests.* St. Paul: West Publishing Co., 1988.

Mennell, Robert L., *Wills and Trusts in a Nutshell.* St. Paul: West Publishing Co., 1979.

Note, *Avoiding Inadvertent Syntactic Ambiguity in Legal Draftsmanship,* 20 Drake L.Rev. 137 (Sept. 1970).

Page, William Herbert, *Page on the Law of Wills.* Cincinnati: W.H. Anderson, 1960.

Practising Law Institute, *Practical Will Drafting 1976.*

Practising Law Institute, *Basic Will Drafting 1989.*

Rubenstein, Neil J., *Attorney Malpractice in California: The Liability of a Lawyer Who Drafts an Imprecise Contract or Will,* 24 U.C. L.A.L.Rev. 422 (1976).

Schlesinger, Edward S., *English as a Second Language for Lawyers,* 12 Inst. on Est.Plan. 700 (1978).

Schwartz, William, *Sins of Omission and Commission in the Drafting of Wills and Trusts,* 11 Inst. on Est.Plan. 1100 (1979).

Shaffer, Thomas L., *The Planning and Drafting of Wills and Trusts.* New York: The Foundation Press, Inc., 1979.

Squires, Lynn B. and Robert S. Mucklestone Inc., *A Simple "Simple" Will,* 57 Wash.L.Rev. 461 (1982).

Word, Thomas S., Jr., *A Brief for Plain English Wills and Trusts,* 14 U.Rich.L.Rev. 471 (1980).

Chapter 17

RESEARCH PAPERS

The previous chapters of this book have led you from discovering your writing process through refining that process by altering and strengthening it, as you have learned to draft the various documents discussed in each chapter. This chapter now turns to applying your writing process to a major research paper or document. In many respects, drafting research papers is similar to the other drafting tasks you have already learned. What is different about writing the research paper is that you will be applying not just some but all of the writing techniques you have learned.

Research papers take numerous forms. For example, you may write a research paper for a seminar, a note or comment for the law review, a research memorandum for a trial practice course, or brief for an appellate advocacy course. Once in practice, you may write similar documents, such as an interoffice memorandum deciding whether your firm should pursue a client's case, a memorandum of points and authorities urging a trial court to grant the preliminary motions you made, or an appellate brief urging a court to affirm or reverse the lower court's decision.

This chapter takes you through the writing tasks required to draft an excellent research paper. It addresses these tasks as they arise within the six steps that we have students complete when drafting their project papers for our advanced legal writing seminar.[1] While you may not write out each step in your own process, you must address all of the tasks if you are going to succeed in your goal. These six steps are (1) the initial proposal, (2) the progress report, (3) the outline or rough draft, (4) the complete draft, (5) the good draft, and (6) the final draft.

THE INITIAL PROPOSAL

The initial proposal should state your precise issue, the type of document you plan to draft, and any questions you may have in proceeding. Even if only for your own use, this last element is helpful. Specificity and clarity in this proposal provides an opportunity for your

---

1. For a fuller description of this seminar, *see*, Barbara J. Cox and Mary Barnard Ray, *Getting Dorothy Out of Kansas: The* *Importance of an Advanced Component to Legal Writing Programs*, 40 J.Legal Ed. 351 (1990).

professor or supervisor to steer you in a specific direction or to identify problems with the proposal, so you may address them now.

In a proposal, you must determine the topic and complete the background research. Many times, a professor may assign you a topic when writing in an upper-division seminar. A senior partner may provide you with a memo to the file made after a client interview, stating the relevant facts and presenting issues for you to research. In these cases, you will not be given a choice in selecting your topic but you may need to clarify the topic or narrow its focus.

In other situations, you may be given a list of topics from which to choose or may be told to select any topic corresponding to the relevant course. You may be choosing a topic on which to write a law review article, competition paper, or conference paper. In these cases, your initial proposal encompasses choosing and developing a topic.

Topic selection itself often requires some background research before undertaking any substantive research. At this stage, you are simply doing the preliminary work necessary to decide whether your ideas are feasible. For example, if you are writing a law review article or a competition or conference paper, you want to write a paper that is different from those already published. In these situations, survey the literature to make sure your topic has not been pre-empted. Often you must narrow the issues to find a niche between previous papers. If you are writing an office memo or a brief in support of your client, complete preliminary research to determine how others have handled this issue previously. In either situation, this preliminary research allows you to determine your initial focus for researching and drafting and to become confident in your choice of topics.

If you are writing your initial proposal for another's review, describe your topic explicitly. Obtaining this focus permits you to spend less time doing irrelevant research. If you have a choice, next determine the type of document you will be writing. Having the type of document in mind allows you to be more selective in your research tools. For example, if you are writing an appellate brief to the Montana Supreme Court, you will focus your research on Montana law and, perhaps, law from neighboring states. But if you were writing about the same issues in a law review article, you would have to expand your research to consider how all courts have handled those issues.

Part of selecting the document will be recognizing your audience. Different readers have different needs, and one of the jobs of the initial proposal is to determine those needs and alter your focus to meet them.[2] Using the example above, if you were drafting an appellate brief to the Montana Supreme Court, you would focus on presenting the relevant facts and prior precedent, making an argument in support of your client, and addressing policy concerns the court may need to

___

2. For more on determining your reader's needs, see Chapter 9 on Discussion Sections of Memos.

resolve when making its decision. If you were drafting a law review article, you would focus on presenting the issue you are addressing, providing the legal context for the issue, raising the problem you are addressing, and resolving that problem.

THE PROGRESS REPORT

After making your initial proposal, you focus the issue further, complete the research, and resolve any problems that arise.[3] The progress report summarizes this process. Whether you write a progress report for your reader, you may find it helpful to monitor your progress so you remain focused. Monitoring helps you set and meet interim deadlines so you can meet the final deadline without cutting short the last steps in the process.

A progress report facilitates conversation with your professor or supervisor after you have completed your research and before you begin drafting. When drafting a progress report for another reader, explain your progress specifically enough so the reader can help you. State your issue, summarize your research to date, and explain what you plan to do next. Mention any concerns that you have, so the reader can advise you. Even if you do not draft a progress report, you can confer with your supervisor. Discussing your ideas with someone after having completed your research and before beginning to draft allows you to obtain help in deciding how to proceed. You may discover that the result you had originally intended is not feasible, and you can alter your plans before you become resistant to changing them.

As part of this report, revise your issue. You will have completed the majority of your research by this point, and it is likely that the issue you stated in the initial proposal will have changed. Oftentimes, when you draft the initial proposal, you cannot anticipate the direction your research will lead. While doing your research, remain flexible enough to vary your ideas and make alterations, or you may find you are forcing your research to fulfill your initial ideas, which may limit your objectivity.

Even if you plan to write a persuasive paper, conduct your research as objectively as possible. Many attorneys find it useful to research as though they were trying to reach the result opposite the one planned. This pushes you to consider all the possibilities and challenges your thesis to its fullest extent. Researching objectively also allows you to

---

3. We will not be discussing the various research tools in the law library and how to use them. There are numerous excellent books available that provide this information. *See,* Christopher Wren and Jill Wren, *The Legal Research Manual: A Game Plan for Legal Research And Analysis* (2d ed. 1986); J. Myron Jacobstein and Roy Mersky, *Fundamentals of Legal Research* (1987); Christina Kunz, Deborah Schmedemann, C. Peter Erlinder, Matthew Downs, and Ann Bateson, *The Process of Legal Research: Successful Strategies* (1989). Additionally, these books, as well as others, also provide assistance in developing your research strategies. Two helpful sources are Mary Ray and Jill Ramsfield, *Getting It Right and Getting It Written* 179–183 (West 1989) and Helene Shapo, Marilyn Walter, and Elizabeth Fajans, *Writing and Analysis in the Law* 131–143 (1989).

anticipate the other side's arguments and find its weaknesses, which you can then exploit when you draft your paper.

Once you have identified your topic and before starting your research, develop a working list of the major points that you think you will make. In essence, this list of your major points functions as a road map for your research. Thoroughness is needed in developing search words to use when researching, in consulting the sources that may provide information, and in recording the information you obtain.

Developing search words is required in virtually all types of research and for virtually all research sources. Even computerized systems require you to develop queries based on words you think will be found in the needed documents.[4] Thus, your skill at choosing these words is central to your skill as a researcher. Do not simply develop a few search words and be content when they provide some documents. Developing search words is an attempt to determine how the editors of the research tool you are using have organized the documents. For example, if looking for cases discussing the implied warranty of habitability in rental units, anticipate all the possible places the editors may have located documents pertaining to that issue. Do not stop after looking up "landlord/tenant" or "the implied warranty of habitability." Also look under "rental units," "landlord's duties," "unlawful detainer actions," "defenses" to those actions, "implied covenants," "leases," "public policy," "repair and offset," and so forth. Only by checking as many locations as possible can you be assured that you have completely mapped out the issue you are researching and found as many relevant documents as possible.

As you change research tools, continue to use all your search words with each tool and change them, if necessary. Editors organize material in different ways. Avoid overlooking information simply because you did not take the time to develop new search words when the ones you had did not achieve the results you desired. Instead, keep altering and refining your search words as you work through your research.

Consult as many sources as you can within your time constraints. These constraints may include deadlines and your client's ability or willingness to pay for extensive research. If you have a brief to write in one week on a state law issue, you may not be able to consult sources across the country to determine how all jurisdictions have handled the issue. But you can thoroughly consult the sources for your jurisdiction to find how your state's courts have answered the question.[5]

---

4. If you are starting from a known case or statute, it is possible to Shepardize that case or statute and begin your research that way. If you have a known case, it is possible to obtain the key number from that case, consult the digest, and locate additional cases that way. But if you do not have such a starting point, begin in the indexes of the research tools you consult, which requires developing search words to enter those indexes.

5. This is one of the times that doing computer-assisted legal research may help you. For example, once you find the important cases in your state, you can take the most relevant digest key numbers and complete a national search using Westlaw's key number system. This

Be creative in considering possible sources for documents. Remember to use tools such as A.L.R. and law review articles. If you can find an A.L.R. annotation or a law review article on the topic you are researching, you will find that much preliminary research has already been completed. This will save you time and your client money. But never rely on these annotations or articles alone. Different factual scenarios or different jurisdictions may lead to different results. Also consider using loose-leafs, bar bulletins, legal history sources, non-legal sources, and other possibilities. Despite time constraints, use your time creatively to obtain information that will help your client. For example, when researching a personal injury case involving the question of whether an avalanche was an obvious and inherent danger in the sport of skiing, one student contacted the U.S. Department of Agriculture, which has regulations on determining when an avalanche is likely. This student was able to use this non-traditional source to make the argument that his client, the ski resort, had not been negligent.

Another aspect of being thorough is updating the documents you find. Because the law is constantly changing, you cannot assume that even recently decided cases are the latest word on a particular issue. Thoroughness here means Shepardizing your information, using computer-assisted research for up-to-the-minute information, and consulting loose-leafs, advance sheets, and pamphlets to ensure that the law you found is current.

Making a decision based on out-dated information is embarrassing. One attorney told us of drafting a decision for a state court of appeals and focusing on the main cases she had learned in law school. After two judges had signed it for release, the chief judge asked her why she had not discussed the U.S. Supreme Court case released the previous week. She discovered that the Court had completely changed the analysis to resolve the issue. Both she and the court had to start from scratch.

Update your information periodically throughout the research project so you can alter your paper if anything changes during the process. As you locate useful sources, update them so you can determine whether they are still current. When you have completed the final draft and just before turning in your paper, update one final time to ensure that what you have written is still correct.

Finally, be thorough when taking notes. It is quite frustrating to have to redo research because you did not record all the information needed to use the points you discovered. Make sure to note all the information needed for your citations. Take notes as precisely as possible so you do not find yourself running back to the source repeatedly. At the same time, avoid copying reams of material straight from

search would take you quite some time to complete if you did it by hand searching through the American Digest system and thus you might eliminate it if time or money is a concern. But that same search would be much less time-consuming if performed through computer-assisted research.

the documents. Read the source before taking notes or photocopying so you only include those points important to your issue. Many people photocopy much, if not all, of their research so they have ready access to the actual documents and do not need to spend as much time taking detailed notes. If you proceed this way, mark relevant portions to avoid having to reread the whole document.

You should provide pinpoint cites for cases and articles whenever possible so your reader can go directly to the relevant point and decide whether he or she agrees with your assessment of the document. Omit them only when a specific page reference is unnecessary because the whole document supports the point. A lack of specific page cites frustrates your reader, who does not want to leaf through a sixty-page case to find the language you noted.

Whether you photocopy your documents or take notes, develop a system for organizing the information. Most research papers require extensive research; keeping track of it is daunting. One option is to make a list of the issues and note every document related to each. Another is to keep a running list of all the documents you consulted and rearrange them into coherent groups when your research is complete. If you photocopy your documents, you may also find it helpful to keep a running list of relevant points with page numbers on the document's first page, so you can scan the first page and remember the document's value to your research. Or you may keep track of the different research tools you consult and list all the documents you found in each tool. Even if a source proved fruitless, note that you checked it and that it was not helpful because, when doing complex research, you can forget why or even whether you considered and rejected a source. Whatever system you use, remember to be thorough and efficient.

Like your writing process, your research process is personal to you. There is no one way to do research correctly or efficiently, no one way that works for all people. Your goal is to develop a process that works for you and to use it effectively. Whether you use index cards, copies of documents, yellow pads filled with notes, or a computer data base is not important. What is important is that you obtain all the information you need and organize it so you can retrieve it. Depending on your deadlines, you may do your research days or weeks before you sit down to write the paper. Your process must allow you to pick up your notes and use them even when you may have forgotten what you found when you did the research.

THE OUTLINE OR ROUGH DRAFT

Having completed the bulk of your research, you are ready to begin writing. As they begin to write, some people find that they go back and forth from writing to researching to fill in gaps and explore areas that only become clear during the writing process. This movement between writing and research and back again is usual. While you may need to do more research, do not let your desire to research prevent you from writing.

Writing an outline or rough draft involves discerning the points you need to make and providing the large-scale organization for your research paper. Many people choose to outline at this point rather than to write a rough draft because outlining allows them to focus on organization, rather than wording. Outlining requires choosing the ideas that will be the focus of your main sections and grouping them into a large-scale organization. Group and regroup your main points until you find the organization that most clearly leads the reader through your paper. As you do this, keep the wording of your thoughts on each point abbreviated. Save the development and refinement of your ideas for the drafts to come later.

This is the time to determine what points to make and how to organize them. If you catch yourself agonizing about some particular word choice or sentence structure, push yourself to move along, focusing on the big picture. One of the major benefits of doing several drafts of a research paper is knowing that you will return to your paper and can safely ignore small-scale concerns during this step.

This is not to say that if you are struck with ideas for developing some points and feel an urge to write some passages that you should not do so. To avoid losing valuable insights or helpful language, include them in your notes. But once the flash of brilliance has passed, and it will pass, return to developing your major points and sub-points. Resist shifting from organizing to writing in mid-stream. Otherwise, you will not achieve your goal for the outline, which is to develop logical, clear large-scale organization.

Some people find they are unable to organize material effectively using an outline. They simply are not comfortable with the less verbal, skeletal process that outlining requires. These people find it more useful to organize their thoughts as they write them. For example, they may write out a specific issue or sub-issue in detail, concentrating on all the concerns that come with writing. In this situation, there is nothing wrong with starting with a rough draft instead of an outline. In fact, if this process works best for you, you will only cause yourself frustration by trying to outline first. But do make sure to check your large-scale organization at some point in the overall process.

If you want to organize before drafting, you may want to try some of the following ideas first before resorting to writing a rough draft to see if they work better for you than traditional outlining.

ORGANIZATION FOR THOSE WHO CAN'T OUTLINE

The following steps can help you organize successfully, even if you have never been able to master the more traditional method of organization, outlines.

1. Brainstorm.

   Try listing all the points you want to make or might want to make, or just list everything you can think of. Do not worry about order, quality, or anything else at this stage except coming up with ideas. Allow enough time for this stage, so you do not cut it short.

2. Group your ideas.

   Read through all your listed points and see if they fall into any logical groups. Try grouping the points several different ways before you settle on one way that makes the most sense to you. Often the organization that occurs to you first will be adequate, but not optimal. Alternatively, if your list of points includes six or fewer items, you may already have your logical groups. If so, fill in more supporting points on those items and then check to see if you are still satisfied with those groups.

3. Organize the groups.

   Look at each group and decide which point is the major one and which are subordinate, or supporting, points. At this stage you may still find some errors in your grouping, but you can revise those groups as needed. You may also find that you have stated the same thing in two different ways, so that you can strike out redundant points.

4. Subdivide further, if needed.

   Divide your arguments, and divide the subpoints made in those arguments. Check each item to make sure that it should not be subdivided further. Remember that you need to make only one point at a time. Even though all your points are inextricably interrelated, you must divide them into manageable portions, or paragraphs, for the reader.

5. Order the groups, points, and subpoints.

   After the points are divided, decide how to order them. To determine this order, think about what will be logical to your reader, rather than what seems important to you. To help determine what is logical to the reader, ask yourself the following three questions.

   (a) Is there some point that logically comes first? For example, if your case involved a jurisdiction question, that question would logically come first because the court will not look to any other issues until they have determined that it is the court's job to decide those issues.

   (b) Is one point more significant than the others? For example, if your case involves clear-cut violations of freedom of speech and also involves some technical violations of proper notice, you may want to start with the violation of the freedom of speech. This point may convince your reader that justice favors your side, and will probably make more compelling reading. The technical point may then provide a convenient peg upon which to hang the hat of justice.

(c) Is one point stronger than the others? For example, if your case involves a clear-cut violation of proper notice but also involves a potential-but-debatable violation of freedom of speech, you may start with the violation of proper notice. This way you can establish some justification for your client's position before you present more questionable justifications.

6. Write.

At this point, you will have all the information provided by a traditional outline, and you can rewrite it in outline format, if you wish, or go directly to writing your rough draft. If you had started trying to outline by writing a Roman numeral at the top of the page, you would have been expecting yourself to do all of these previous steps in your head, which is why trying to write a traditional outline is futile for many people.

7. Check the organization.

Once you have written your rough draft, recheck your organization. In fact, many successful writers write a rough draft first and then outline or go through the organization steps listed above. One way to check your organization is to read the first sentence of each paragraph throughout the document. This should give you a summary of the points of the paper, although it will not document the proof of those points.[6]

We suggest trying these ideas before turning to a rough draft, not because outlining is inherently preferable to writing a rough draft, because it is not. But you need to generate ideas and determine large-scale organization at this step. This involves thrashing through what you are saying at the large-scale level. You cannot work at this level if you are continuously drawn to small-scale concerns. If you try to write without adequately organizing your points, "you find yourself trying to do three things at once: with every detail that presents itself to your mind, you must decide (1) whether or not to include it, (2) if so, how and where to fit it in, and (3) how fully to develop it."[7]

You should organize your paper for your reader's ease, not for your own. Will your reader need a background section in order to understand your paper or does he or she already know the background and want you to proceed to the focus of the paper? Will your reader be able to understand why you are organizing the paper the way you are or will he or she need to be told the importance of the organization? Will your reader need a thorough overview before you get into the details of the

---

6. Ray and Ramsfield, *supra* note 3, at 127–129.

7. Weihofen, *Legal Writing Style* 139 (1980).

paper or does he or she know where your paper is headed so that a detailed overview is less important?[8] Answer these questions before writing a complete draft of your paper.

THE COMPLETE DRAFT

When writing the complete draft, add in the content that supports your organization. This step focuses on letting your creativity flow. Do not rein yourself in or rewrite. Separate this step from the rewriting, revising, and polishing steps that come later. Many people find that writing footnotes or even correcting their spelling interrupts the creative flow and deflects their energy away from the task at hand. "The most common mistake most writers make, one that costs them hours and hours, is to rewrite and write simultaneously. This forces the id of creative thought to work simultaneously with the super-ego of correction, an impossible and insufferable pairing." [9]

Try to write out an entire draft of your paper. What you are attempting to do in this step is to get the thoughts in your head onto paper or into the computer. You have done the research, the brainstorm, and the organizing that are essential preliminary steps to writing. Now write.

Writing a complete draft does not require starting at the first point on your outline and going in linear fashion through each and every sub-point all the way to the end. Many writers find that creative thought does not progress in such a nicely structured manner. Do not force your creativity into straight lines or rigid boxes. Instead, allow yourself to write whatever portion of your paper will come at any given point. Do not worry that you will lose your organization and find yourself with a confused mess of ideas. You can always retrieve your organization after you have written the draft.

Otherwise, you may find yourself faced with writer's block. This occurs when you find your creative energy dissipated and you cannot make yourself continue to write. Few things are more frustrating, especially when you have deadlines to meet. One effective way to avoid writer's block is to allow yourself to write what seems easiest. If you are clear about a paragraph or sub-section that will come in the middle of your paper, start your draft with that paragraph or sub-section. Writing often helps you continue to write. You can then move either to the points that logically precede it or follow from it.

Keep writing until all of your thoughts are written out. This is a rough draft; it does not need full documentation or even coherent language but does need to be completed. Complete this step before starting to rewrite. Finishing the rough draft allows you to see how your thoughts play out. Your draft may be a fraction of the size of the

---

8. We believe, however, that an overview improves most long papers. Remember, you are not writing a mystery or suspense novel; leaving your reader in the dark is not part of your job.

9. Ray and Ramsfield, *supra* note 3, at 185.

finished paper, but that is not important. You will fill in the documentation, work on the small-scale organization, and add the footnotes later. Or your draft may be much longer than the finished paper, but that is not important either. You will shorten it later as you tighten organization, revise for conciseness, and omit redundancy. What is important is working through all your ideas as completely as possible before going back and rewriting them.

THE GOOD DRAFT

This draft involves moving your energies from the creative forces you just employed to the critical forces you now need. You are moving from being satisfied with getting your thoughts on paper to being concerned with how effectively you communicate your thoughts.

The best way to make this shift from the creative to the critical is to allow the paper to sit for a while before starting this step. Allowing it to sit gives you some perspective on the ideas you have developed and expressed so you are better able to critique them. Always be aware of your ability and willingness to critique your own work. If critiquing comes easily, you will find that you can begin this next step after a short period of time. If critiquing is difficult, you will need more time to distance yourself from the initial draft. Distance allows you to be less impressed with what you already have completed and more concerned with taking what often amounts to a rambling, disorganized mess and moving it towards a concise, organized research paper.

Many lawyers believe they do not have the time to gain distance from their drafts due to short deadlines. But often they can do something else between drafts, to clear the head and regain focus. For example, do one or two other tasks between drafts. Complete some pressing correspondence, make a phone call, discuss a different matter with your staff or colleagues, or eat lunch. Try to leave the computer or set aside the writing pad to walk around the block or around the office.

The steps that need to be taken in rewriting will tax your brain and your humor. At this step, revise the draft, concentrating on organization and thoroughness. Take your completed draft, and fit it into your initial organization. Then change the organization if it no longer seems to be the most appropriate; it is too early in the process to be overly attached to your original organization. Rearrange your sections so they logically lead the reader from your introduction to your conclusion and build on the preceding section to reach a clearly understandable conclusion. In addition, write introductory and conclusory paragraphs for your major sections and add clear transitions from point to point and from paragraph to paragraph.

Now focus on thoroughness, filling any gaps. Determine whether any material that would help your reader has been excluded. Oftentimes, you may find that you understand where you are headed because you have done all the research, but your reader will probably not have this same understanding. At this stage, you should be nearing the point when all the substance is included.

Concentrate on content, ideas, and organization, making sure that all the components of your paper are included and logically placed.[10] To determine whether you have completed this rewriting stage or need to spend more time here, review the following questions.

CHECKLIST FOR REWRITING

1. Content and ideas

   a. Is the law right?

   b. Have I included all the relevant issues?

   c. Have I included all the relevant research?

   d. Have I updated all the research?

   e. Have I included all the necessary background information?

   f. Have I eliminated those points that I found while doing my research but do not add to the document?

2. Large-scale organization

   a. Do I have a logical organization?

   b. Have I provided an overview so that the reader can understand how my paper progresses from introduction to conclusion?

   c. Have I put threshold issues first?

   d. Have I given the answer first and then the explanation?

   e. If writing persuasively, have I organized the issues in the most persuasive order, putting the strongest first, the second strongest last, and the weakest in the middle, unless logical organization precludes doing this?

   f. Can any legal reader follow my logic?

   g. Can the intended reader follow my logic?

   h. Have I used positions of emphasis well? [11]

Once you are satisfied with your answers to these questions, move to the small-scale steps of revising your paper. Making this shift can be difficult. You may find it helpful at this point to step away from your draft again. Many attorneys believe they are finished with the project once their organization is logical and their content is complete. However, this is a major reason why the documents seen most often in

---

10. Ray and Ramsfield, *supra* note 3, at 185.

11. Many of these steps were presented in Ray and Ramsfield. Some additions have been made to expand the list beyond questions needed for briefs, memos and opinion letters, the focus of the list in that entry. *Id.* at 185–186.

the legal arena tend to be poorly written. To attain excellence, you cannot stop here.

What you may find helpful at this stage is doing across-the-board checks, similar to those you did while drafting contracts.[12] These checks allow you to focus on correcting one or two things at a time, rather than trying to do too much in one reading. This also allows you to decide which concerns are most important to your research paper and to focus on these first. Then, if time runs short, you can sacrifice those steps that can be eliminated with less cost to the quality of your paper.

The following list is an example of things to consider when revising.

CHECKLIST FOR REVISING

1. ACCURACY

No amount of readability will replace accuracy, so make sure you check first for the content of each legal point. Ask yourself the following questions.

(a) Is the content accurately stated? Could any points be misinterpreted because of ambiguity?

(b) Are irrelevant facts or other irrelevant information excluded?

(c) Are terms of art used correctly?

(d) Are key terms used correctly?

(e) Are paraphrases accurate?

(f) Are names of parties and their status correct?

(g) Are the citations accurate? Are pinpoint cites used for specific propositions, rules, holdings, quotes? Are case names spelled accurately? Are page numbers and years accurate?

2. SMALL–SCALE ORGANIZATION

(a) Are paragraphs internally logical?

(b) Are there topic sentences that give the overall message of each of the paragraphs, usually at the beginning of the paragraphs?

(c) Are there clear and precise transitions between paragraphs?

(d) Are there strong transitions between sentences?

3. READABILITY

(a) Are subjects and verbs close together?

(b) Is there more active voice than passive voice?

---

12. See Chapter Five on Contracts.

(c) Are sentences free of nominalizations?

(d) Are unnecessary modifiers eliminated, such as clearly and obviously?

(e) Are sentences not overly long?

(f) Are lists clearly structured?

(g) Are unnecessary prepositional phrases eliminated?

(h) Is the text generally concise?

4. STYLE

(a) Is style consistently objective or persuasive, depending upon the purpose of the text?

(b) Is the tone and level of formality appropriate and consistent?[13]

Now show your paper to someone else for review. At this point, you will have taken it about as far as you can without outside assistance. Asking for outside assistance can be scary because the reviewer may think you still have significant work to do before reaching the excellence you desire. Nevertheless, you are trying to reach a goal and this assistance will help you proceed to that goal. Excellent writing does not come easy. But it does come to those who persist and have some understanding of the process. You have the choice to reject the criticism at any point. If you believe your reviewer's suggestions will cause problems, do not feel compelled to incorporate them. Feel free to ask for, consider, and then reject some of the criticism you receive. Considering the criticism, whether or not you accept it, allows you to see the paper anew.

THE FINAL DRAFT

Having completely reviewed your paper, revised it, and received outside assistance to improve it, now do the final draft. Unless you have unrelenting time pressures, do not skip this step, even though many of your classmates or colleagues will do so. At this point, your paper is probably quite good. You have taken it through successive steps and worked toward making it excellent. Do not stop just short of excellence, even though you may believe that your paper is as good or better than anything you have written before. Take it through the final step to achieve the excellence that is possible.

This polishing involves removing errors, unclear phrases, and awkward passages. Correct the details that differentiate a good paper from an excellent one. Focus on what you know about yourself as a writer. Develop a checklist to guide you. If spelling is a problem for you, check

13. Ray and Ramsfield, *supra* note 3, at 183–84. Ray and Ramsfield have additional sections on most of the elements contained in this checklist so that you can refer to those sections to find out more about each step of the checklist.

your spelling throughout. If you overuse passive voice, read through the draft checking each verb and change it as needed.

You do not need to spend a great deal of time doing this. Even an hour or two will make a difference. Remember that the legal reader is focused on details. As a result, when the details of your paper help your reader rather than distract that reader, you will communicate much more effectively.

Having taken your paper through each of these steps, you will now be as sure as possible that you have written your best paper. You can be comfortable in knowing that you have strived for excellence and that you have achieved it.

Bibliography

Bereiter, Carl, and Marlene Scardamalia, *The Psychology of Written Composition*. Hillsdale, NJ: Lawrence Erlbaum Associates, 1987.

Cox, Barbara J., and Mary Barnard Ray, *Getting Dorothy Out of Kansas: The Importance of an Advanced Component to Legal Writing Programs*, 40 J.Legal Ed. 351 (1990).

Kunz, Christina L., Deborah A. Schmedemann, C. Peter Erlinder, Matthew P. Downs, and Ann L. Bateson, *The Process of Legal Research: Successful Strategies*. Boston: Little, Brown and Co., 2nd ed. 1989.

Jacobstein, J. Myron and Ray M. Mersky, *Fundamentals of Legal Research*. Mineola, NY: The Foundation Press, Inc., 1987.

Ray, Mary Barnard, and Jill J. Ramsfield, *Getting It Right and Getting It Written*. St. Paul: West Publishing Co., 1989.

Shapo, Helene S., Marilyn R. Walter and Elizabeth Fajans, *Writing and Analysis in the Law*. Westbury, NY: The Foundation Press, Inc., 1989.

Statsky, William P., *Legal Research and Writing: Some Starting Points*. St. Paul: West Publishing Co., 3rd ed. 1986.

Statsky, William P., and R. John Wernet, Jr., *Case Analysis and Fundamentals of Legal Writing*. St. Paul: West Publishing Co., 3rd ed. 1989.

Weihoffen, Henry, *Legal Writing Style*. St. Paul: West Publishing Co., 2nd ed. 1980.

Wren, Christopher G., and Jill Robinson Wren, *The Legal Research Manual*. Madison, WI: A–R Editions, 2nd ed. 1986.

*

Index

References are to Pages

†